NED A. FLANDERS

ANALYZING TEACHING BEHAVIOR

ADDISON-WESLEY PUBLISHING COMPANY
Reading, Massachusetts · Menlo Park, California · London · Don Mills, Ontario

This book is in the
Addison-Wesley Series in Education

This book is dedicated to those thoughtful social scientists whose accomplishments will someday make what is written here obsolete

- by pushing far beyond this progress report to create new understanding of the teaching-learning process,

- by helping teachers reduce inconsistencies between intentions and actions,

- by persisting in these efforts, in spite of the difficulties, because of their deep concern for education.

PREFACE

For a number of years my friends kept asking me, "When are you going to write a book on interaction analysis?" My answers depended on the priorities of the moment, but the gist would usually be, "When we know more about it." The situation hasn't really changed; we still need to know much more about how the interaction between a teacher and his pupils can be abstracted and recorded, and how the data can be used most effectively. The prospects for obtaining more information are very good, since more researchers are at work than ever before. The point at which a book is written is apparently determined more by sabbaticals and leaves of absence than by the presumed state of our knowledge. So let's call this book a progress report, written with the anticipation that other researchers will soon follow.

This book is written for those who believe that the interaction between a teacher and his pupils can be improved. This is a curious conviction because it can have a wide range of consequences for those, like myself, who choose to hold it. It can lead to many years of research with varying degrees of success and failure. It can push a researcher out of his office and into direct contact with teachers. Sometimes he can share excitement when one teacher exclaims, "I tried asking different questions and it worked!" and the followup data reinforce his enthusiastic perception. There are moments of humility when a sincere teacher tries, but can't quite overcome his rigid habits of adult behavior as he ventures to explore new ways of interacting. Perhaps most rewarding are the contacts with college students who are preparing to enter teaching. Their vitality is contagious when they work to master skills that can be used to analyze teaching behavior. On the other hand, a belief in the possibility of improvement can stimulate anger when the educational system, in a perverse kind of way, places demands on teachers that actually inhibit the very improvement we are seeking. In short, those who hold this conviction with passion can swing from hope to despair, from reality to fantasy, and from subjective to objective reactions.

For me the most direct consequence of this conviction is a drive to develop more objective techniques for analyzing interaction, techniques which not only provide evidence of change, but also become stepping stones to a systematic inquiry into one's own teaching behavior. Here we are concerned with the fascination of self-study, with intrigue—in the sense of capturing curiosity—and with showing a person how to start. Simply presenting a chance to learn interaction analysis techniques is a first step in preparing to answer three deceptively simple questions: What kind of interaction is now taking place? Can some change be planned and then realized? Is this change an improvement? These questions are deceptive because they are very difficult if not impossible to answer. We cannot describe all of the characteristics of the existing interaction. We cannot specify in sufficient detail how one pattern of interaction differs from another. And we cannot be certain how an innovation will affect the growth and development of pupils. Without appropriate tools and techniques teachers and college students are likely to be immobilized by these questions. Given appropriate tools and techniques one may obtain partial answers and thereby establish a more objective approach to what otherwise would be exclusively a subjective problem.

It is a pity that this book does not review and summarize the many outstanding contributions made by researchers who use a different approach to understanding teacher-pupil interaction. As I suggest in Chapter 8, more than one approach is probably needed; in fact, the original outline for this book allocated several chapters to the description of systems which are different from those in this book and to a discussion of the conclusions of these other researchers. Unfortunately, such intentions exceed my resources. The title of the book is therefore a bit presumptuous, because it is based on only one approach.

This book does include a description of the ten-category system which has been associated with my name and makes suggestions about how this system can be used by college students and experienced teachers who have never tried to code verbal behavior. There is much to commend a simple, fixed, ten-category system, but a more flexible technique is required when more subtle distinctions are necessary. Thus, several chapters are devoted to exploring more flexible category clusters, multiple coding of single events, and arrangements for displaying data that are more efficient than the 10 × 10 matrix. These more flexible innovations have been tried out, but only in a preliminary and superficial way. Their inclusion in the book is an invitation for others to try them, modify them, improve them, and explore appropriate applications.

Some will say that this book is about nurturing independence and self-direction among learners rather than about analyzing classroom communication. From the standpoint of curriculum, this emphasis might even be called a bias. So be it. I gladly plead guilty. It seems almost impossible to study classroom interaction without developing value judgments about what is going on and beginning to imagine alternatives. Encouraging more independence and self-direction for pupils in the classroom and for adults who are preparing to teach certainly is an alternative, since it can be distinguished from the predominant interaction patterns that permeate classrooms today. The difficult task is to arrange for others to analyze interaction, to study its characteristics, and to arrive at their own conclusions. The bias, if it exists, is to make sure that the issue of independence is not overlooked.

There is inadequate discussion, in this book, of the problems of sampling, research design, and the statistical analysis of interaction data. The first parts of Chapters 11 and 12 introduce some of the issues, but more questions are raised than answers are given. It is difficult to make progress in this area which is of most interest to those who conduct research. We need more definitive statements about observer reliability, about suspected shortcomings of the Darwin Chi-Square Test, and about the kinds of generalizations that can be made from different sampling procedures. Such statements will require more work and more time.

There are certain trends in education which may prove to be related to improving teacher-pupil interaction. We expect advances in the field of educational technology which may alter some current teaching functions. The progress most likely to occur may be that programed instructional materials and computer assisted instruction could help to individualize procedures, let pupils proceed at their own pace, and reduce the teacher's concern with presenting information, review, and drill. As these teaching functions decrease, the teacher should be able to devote more time to problems of motivation, diagnosis of difficulties, discussions in which different points of view are compared, and individual consultations with pupils. A basic change in the role of the teacher, should these predictions become true, will be less emphasis on teacher initiation combined with pupil response and more emphasis on interaction patterns in which teachers respond to pupil initiations. Another way to say this is that educational technology may free a teacher to develop that more human responsiveness which is so often a feature of our ideal teaching models. This change in emphasis appears in many parts of this book. It involves the skills of working with ideas expressed by others, it involves asking questions in a sequence, and it involves a more purposeful variation of teaching behavior from one situation to the next.

On pages ix and x there are some suggestions about how to read this particular book. Even though each of us reads a book in his own way, you may find some of the suggestions useful.

ACKNOWLEDGMENTS

The assistance of many individuals made this book possible. I am deeply grateful to the hundreds of teachers and pupils who participated in the research activities, to my research colleagues whose suggestions, hard work, and dedication were essential and to those who reacted to early drafts of the manuscript.

Research activities take time and cost money, in this case, almost twenty years and nearly one-half million dollars. In retrospect, the product 'seems modest in terms of the investment. The University of Minnesota and the University of Michigan helped by creating appointments which included half time for research, starting in 1949. Research projects covering seven years were supported by funds from the U.S. Office of Education, supplemented by funds from the host institutions. Professional stimulation began with our team at the University of Chicago lead by Prof. Herbert A. Thelen, and continued at the Laboratory for Research in Social Relations, University of Minnesota; the New Zealand Council for Educational Research; the Offices of Research Service, University of Michigan, and with contacts at the Michigan-Ohio Regional Educational Laboratory.

Many individuals should be given special mention, but those who contributed directly to the preparation of the book manuscript have been unusually generous. Dr. Norma Furst and Dr. Barak Rosenshine at Temple University, along with Dr. William Ward, formerly with the Northwest Regional Laboratory, provided encouragement and thoughtful criticism. Mrs. William Farrell typed the original manuscript, but this was a minor contribution compared with the extra professional years that became available to me because she was a top-notch office secretary. My family, especially my wife Mary, have shown confidence and patience without reservation.

Palo Alto, California   N.A.F.
December 1969

A GUIDE TO READING THIS BOOK

Some parts of this book are quite complicated and difficult to understand; other sections are elementary and quite easy to understand. All sections of this book require work. The complex sections require work just to achieve understanding. The easy sections describe simple coding skills, but the skills of coding require persistent work during the early stages of development. Given the range of material and the inescapable individual differences among readers, I have presumed to make some suggestions about how this book might be read.

The first chapter is intended for all to read, but it is not prerequisite to subsequent material. If you are the kind who tends to skip, don't miss "The Crux of the Matter," starting on page 16, since it is intended to be just that.

For classroom teachers who seek to improve their classroom interaction and have had no previous experience with coding verbal communication, let me commend Chapters 1, 2, 3, 10, and 8, in that order. Next turn to the short section on "Single Event Time Line Displays" in Chapter 6, before reading and working with Chapter 9. It is the work outlined in Chapter 9 that should help you improve your classroom interaction. Later on, you may wish to read Chapters 4, 11, and 12.

College students and those with some experience in coding can probably profit from reading the chapters in a sequence that is closer to their numerical order. I suggest reading Chapters 1 through 5 and the first part of Chapter 6. This will provide inquiry tools, assuming that time is spent on practice as well as on reading. How to use these tools is a topic that is developed in Chapters 8, 10, and 9, in that order. Chapters 11 and 12 are there waiting to be read, but they are more meaningful after some experience in self-development and field training.

Researchers and those who help others study interaction belong to a more sophisticated group. No doubt you can find your own way through the book without a road map of presumptuous suggestions. I commend the challenge of Chapters 6 and 7. They are written for those who would push onward to further innovations and new insights based on the encoding and decoding procedures. One word of warning to those of higher rank in the hierarchy of education. Just as commissioned officers in the army seldom assign themselves to K.P. in order to understand the tasks involved, those who supervise and guide the development of teachers and college students have a tendency to depend on reading the written word as a basis for understanding, eschewing work assignments, and consistent practice. With interaction analysis, this approach is likely to be less than satisfactory.

CONTENTS

xi

Chapter One

ANALYZING TEACHING BEHAVIOR

THE CHAIN OF CLASSROOM EVENTS

Teaching behavior, by its very nature, exists in a context of social interaction. The acts of teaching lead to reciprocal contacts between the teacher and the pupils, and the interchange itself is called teaching. Techniques for analyzing classroom interaction are based on the notion that these reciprocal contacts can be perceived as a series of events which occur one after another. Each event occupies a small segment of time, and the chain of events can be spaced along a time dimension. It is clear that the event of the moment influences what is to follow and, in turn, was influenced by what preceded.

Teachers can analyze their classroom interaction in order to obtain information about the chain of events and especially their own acts of teaching behavior. Experienced teachers who wish to improve classroom instruction, and especially college students who seek to become teachers, can use this information to identify patterns of teaching and then proceed to develop and to control their teaching behavior in a continuing program of self-development. Those who assist in preservice and inservice education can learn the skills of interaction analysis to improve their own teaching behavior as well as to help others learn the same skills.

In research, systematic analysis may help to discover laws that explain the variations that exist within the chain of classroom events, giving special attention to the actions of the teacher. Such laws would express relationships between the teacher's behavior and the nature of classroom interaction. In the long run, such knowledge should help to explain differences in educational outcomes that are associated with teaching.

Each person who analyzes classroom interaction has his own reasons, but those who think deeply about teacher-pupil contacts are challenged by the task and often disturbed by what they find. Herbert A. Thelen (100)* de-

---

*References follow Chapter 12.

1

scribed our desire to understand experience as a quest of life. His metaphor was not intended to refer to a chain of small events that occurred in a classroom; nevertheless, it is an appropriate analogy:

The most fascinating question in the world is, How does one thing lead to another? Here we are, standing in the present but this is merely one tiny event in a long series that began with time and will end in the unforeseeable future. Time is a mountain whose peak is the present. The past slopes off one side and the future off the other. Looking in one direction we make explanations; looking in the other, predictions. People then, now, and in time to come will always be on the peak, midway between explanations and predictions; caught in both, both overlapping and each giving its unique flavor to the quest that is life. In looking backward we start with facts and then build an image; in looking forward we build an image and then, through action, make the facts. To the extent that we do both we are able to be wise. (p. 188)

Perhaps a teacher can commit himself to teaching only at a present moment, but he can think about teaching by considering the past, present, and future. In order to match purposes with strategies, he senses the present, reflects on the past, and plans the future. As he pauses to look forward and backward, a chain of small events stretches in both directions.

PURPOSES AND CONCEPTS FOR ANALYZING TEACHING BEHAVIOR

Recognizing that teaching exists at the present moment as part of a chain of events is only a start. *How* does one think about teaching? To what source shall we go in order *to select a set of concepts* which will help in analyzing interactive behavior? And given the range of activities, what rationale is used in deciding how *to describe what goes on in the classroom?* When these italicized words are strung together, they describe the central issue: *how to select a set of concepts to describe what goes on in the classroom.*

Concepts for thinking depend on our purpose and our predispositions to think in certain ways. The clinical psychologist talks about classroom events quite differently than a principal, supervisor, or pupil. Yet a common purpose, like deciding to help a particular child make a better classroom adjustment, would at least focus the observations and comments. The same can be said about classroom interaction.

What purposes guide the analysis of classroom interaction? Two purposes have already been mentioned: the first was to help a teacher develop and control his teaching behavior, and the second was to investigate relationships between classroom interaction and teaching acts so as to explain some of the variability in the chain of events. Please note what is not included in our purposes. There is no intention of analyzing all that goes on in the classroom or making an inventory of factors affecting the classroom. So far, at least, there has been no mention of good and bad teaching, making ratings of teaching performance, or suggesting a particular way to teach. We can anticipate, however, that neutrality with regard to teaching behavior is not likely to last. This is a book about effective teaching. Preferences about teaching behavior should arise as rapidly as our understanding of its consequences improves.

By way of summary, there are three purposes which guide what is written in this book:

1) The purpose of interaction analysis is to study teaching behavior by keeping track of selected events that occur during classroom interaction. Other events are taken into consideration only when this would assist the observation.

2) One application of these activities is to help an individual develop and control his teaching behavior. In a practical engineering sense, this can be accomplished most effectively by using the fewest number of concepts that the task requires. When thinking is parsimonious, fewer ideas are considered by those who seek insights. We are forced toward parsimonious thinking because at any moment in teaching there are more variables which could be considered than the mind can comprehend.*

3) A second application is discovering through research how to explain the variations which occur in the chain of classroom events. These explanations are meant to focus on teaching behavior and its relationships to classroom interaction and educational outcomes.

There are consequences to these purposes and we might as well be frank with each other as we face them. First, the heart of the matter lies in what the teacher does that influences the educational development of his pupils. Second, of all teacher activities, the most salient are the direct person-to-person contacts and the more indirect teacher-to-class contacts. Third, we start by accounting for events that do, in fact, occur, not what the teacher thinks is happening or what teachers "ought" to be doing. Fourth, the most important concepts are those which are descriptive of the interactive contacts. Other concepts in a field of education simply become less important; these are set aside to be learned and used only after the higher priorities have been satisfied. Fifth, the search is for the *fewest* number of ideas necessary to help a person develop and control his teaching behavior.

With these purposes in mind, concepts appropriate to the study of interaction are introduced throughout this book. So far, the concept of *classroom interaction* refers to the chain of events which occur one after the other, each

---

*As a rule, preservice and inservice education for teachers involves introducing as many new concepts as possible without regard to the present supply or future needs. This is foolish, of course, when a more urgent problem is to help teachers use effectively the concepts they already have.

occupying only a small segment of time. *Teaching behavior* has been defined as acts by the teacher which occur in the context of classroom interaction. We now define an *event* as the shortest possible act that a trained observer can identify and record. Often, during classroom interaction, the same sequence of events occurs again and again; such a sequence can be called a pattern. A *pattern* is a short chain of events that can be identified, occurs frequently enough to be of interest, and can be given a label (or name) since this often facilitates thinking.

Even these few concepts provide us with the tools for thinking about a number of significant questions. Are there certain patterns which all teachers should be able to create in the classroom? (Not in the sense of forcing all teaching into one mold, but in the sense of selecting patterns from an extensive repertoire.) Can teaching be improved by identifying and practicing behavior patterns? Are there certain patterns which can be associated with more positive pupil attitudes? Positive teacher attitudes? More extensive content achievement? More independent and self-directed pupil behavior? In what sequence and at what incidence do such patterns occur? Can patterns be used to describe models of teaching behavior? And so on.

Inferring intent from behavior

Must a teacher have intentions before he can act? Does a teacher prove his intentions by his actions? While the answer to both questions is usually "yes," the asking of one question, rather than the other, suggests a difference in point of view. One question speaks of intentions; the other speaks of actions.

It is not unusual to talk about teaching by prescribing altruistic intentions—"try to be sensitive to the needs of children" or "consider a pupil's interests and abilities before assigning a learning task." Sometimes words like "ought" or "should" are used or implied to form conditional admonitions—"teachers ought to consider the feelings of boys and girls," or "genuine acceptance must (ought to) be communicated by overt behavior," or "a teacher who is excited about his subject and competent within his field is more likely to gain respect and cooperation." Prescriptive intentions and conditional admonitions about teaching describe an end point of self-development and too often fail to suggest ways of reaching this desirable state of affairs.

The accounting of small behavioral events is a sharp departure from admonitions and prescriptions about intent. Any discussion of teaching patterns involves a different language and frequently a different way of thinking about teaching. Consider the problem of motivation as it might be discussed in terms of teacher-pupil planning. It is one thing to say that "the teacher should find ways to motivate pupils so that the learning tasks have real meaning in terms of the life experiences of the pupils." A different vocabulary is involved when you say that "a teacher can connect the interests of boys and girls to a learning task by asking open questions, by clarifying and developing selected responses which link interests to tasks, and then asking questions which become more and more specific so that the tasks and the methods of work incorporate the suggestions of pupils." The first statement is a conditional admonition and speaks to a set of intentions. The second statement literally suggests a pattern of teaching acts, communicates meaning in terms of teaching behavior, and implies a model or strategy.

Another interesting distinction here is that reasoning from a statement of intent is primarily deductive, while reasoning from a set of behaviors is more often inductive. Given a statement of intent, such as the one about motivation in the preceding paragraph, the next steps usually attempt to clarify the meaning of the initial generalization, then to give examples, and finally to suggest specific ways to start. This reasoning process is essentially deductive. On the other hand, the objective analysis of behavior identifies a series of acts, these can then be grouped into patterns of behavior, and finally the patterns can be strung together into strategies of classroom teaching and learning. This latter reasoning process is essentially inductive. We will understand teaching more completely when these two reasoning processes are combined and brought into balance. Our intentions help to set goals for teaching performance, and an analysis of behavior helps to explain what actually occurs.

It may be that our understanding of teaching is inadequate because there is too much emphasis on conditional admonitions and too little attention to an analysis of the behavior associated with these intentions. For all except the most gifted teachers, there is a gap between fairly good intentions and the teaching behavior which occurs in the classroom. Perhaps teachers know what they ought to do, but they don't reach their aspirations as consistently as they would prefer. It is this observation which suggests that the study of classroom interaction may improve the quality of teaching simply because it would reduce the gap between intent and action—with a built-in safeguard that causes the shift to be in the direction of more effective teaching.

TECHNIQUES OF INTERACTION ANALYSIS

Interaction analysis is a label that refers to any technique for studying the chain of classroom events in such a fashion that each event is taken into consideration. An observer sits in the classroom, or views a video-sound playback, or just listens to a voice recording and keeps a record of the flow of events on an observation form. He might punch the keys of some mechanical device if it is available. He is trained to use a set of categories. He decides which category best represents each event and then writes down the code symbol of that category. His speed of recording depends on the category system, the skill of the observer, and the difficulty of the interaction, but an average speed of 10 to 30 symbols per minute can be expected. The product of his observation is a long list of code symbols, one symbol to one event. An analysis can be made of the frequency of events in each category, a profile of the distribution can be drawn, or a simple display can be created which shows how each event is a part of the chain. Inferences about the chain of events can then be made, keeping in mind the limitations of the overall process.

The development of these systematic recording techniques has been going on for at least 30 years.* The first efforts were isolated projects, but interest in the technology has increased until now many researchers are developing their own systems.

Ever since 1900 researchers have attempted to evaluate teaching performance without too much success. It is rather remarkable that Morsh and Wilder (70) could conclude their review of these research efforts during the period 1900 to 1952 with the statement:

No single, specific, observable teacher act has yet been found whose frequency or percent of occurrence is invariably (and) significantly correlated with student achievement. There seems to be some suggestion, however, that (a) questions based on student interest and experience rather than assigned subject matter, (b) the extent to which the instructor challenges the students to support ideas, and (c) the amount of spontaneous student discussion, may be related to student gains. (p. 4; parenthetical letters not in the original.)

Since 1952 the search to find teaching acts which are significantly and consistently correlated with positive pupil attitudes and content achievement adjusted for initial ability has been much more successful (see Chapter 12). The progress in this area was possible, for the most part, because of the development of systems for analyzing classroom events.

Although many find interaction analysis procedures complicated at first, the techniques have also been criticized because they are too simple minded. Nevertheless, these techniques have achieved whatever success they now enjoy primarily because most of what goes on in the classroom is ignored while selected features of the *verbal communication* have been retained. The categories used in most systems refer only to statements which are made by the teacher and the pupils. Not only are other features of the classroom ignored, but many features of the verbal communication itself are simply beyond the scope of the classification procedures. The nature of these techniques and the compromises involved are topics to which most of this book is devoted. Techniques of interaction analysis capture selected elements of classroom verbal communication

---

*In Medley and Mitzel's review (67, p. 254) E. Horn (1914) is cited as the earliest reference.

which have proven to be helpful in the analysis of teaching behavior; first, for the improvement of instruction; second, for the preparation of future teachers; and third, for the prediction of educational outcomes.

Someone might object, at this point, by saying that modesty in claiming a narrow base for interaction analysis is all well and good, but on previous pages there were statements about "analyzing the chain of events in the classroom." What kind of inferences *can* be made from interaction analysis data?

Given some of the more advanced systems, a good deal can be inferred about classroom events even though only a small proportion of the verbal communication is recorded. It is possible, for example, to reach conclusions about the reinforcement and support that a teacher provides during classroom instruction, to decide whether the teacher or the pupils suggested the ideas that are discussed, to estimate the balance of initiation and response on the part of the teacher as well as on the part of the pupils, and a number of other interesting features of teacher-pupil relationships. Furthermore, this can be done for one teacher during a short teaching episode or a 1-hour lesson, as well as for many teachers grouped to provide interesting comparisons according to a research design—each observed for 6 to 10 hours.

Systems of interaction analysis have not yet distinguished themselves by progress in analyzing the logic of classroom discourse. However, the first steps have been taken in this area and more can be expected. The inferences involving more detailed discriminations about logical processes are more difficult to achieve and will require intensive research and development.

The major contribution of interaction analysis may well be that the inferences reached are based on events which can be said to have occurred with a greater degree of certainty than is usually true of classroom observations. In addition, the data are already organized in terms of useful concepts before there is an attempt to make interpretations. The following might serve to summarize what has been said so far and to anticipate what is to come:

1) Observers are trained to assign very small bits of interaction into a limited number of categories.
2) Procedures for processing these bits of interaction by statistical reduction or combining the data into displays have improved.
3) Both the quantified data and the display facilitate reaching inferences about larger, more complex features of the interaction.
4) This overall procedure is more objective and contains less error than would otherwise occur when *direct* judgments or ratings are made about the same large and complex features.
5) Some interaction analysis procedures preserve and display the sequence of the original acts which the observer recorded so that inferences about sequences in the chain of events can be reached.

PROSPECTS AND PROBLEMS FOR
IMPROVING CLASSROOM INSTRUCTION THROUGH
THE USE OF INTERACTION ANALYSIS

It is relatively easy to learn the skills of interaction analysis. Like any other assessment technique it only requires some practice, a little guidance, and some time to think about what you are doing. The more difficult problem is how to use these skills wisely. In the short history of interaction analysis, pages could be written about its misuse as well as its proper use. There are many difficult human relations problems to be solved with any technique that shows promise of providing useful information about professional behavior. In this section, some of the problems and prospects are introduced. The assumption behind the discussion is that the long range goal is to improve the classroom instruction in our schools.

INTERACTION ANALYSIS AND TEACHER EDUCATION

Someday teacher education will focus more sharply on the care and nurture of teaching behavior. When this happens, systems of interaction analysis could become the foundation of a program to prepare teachers. This prospect, by the way, is being investigated vigorously at a few institutions.

In teacher education the ultimate criterion of success or failure can be found in the classroom performance of the beginning teacher. By assuming that classroom interaction is a series of events and that teaching behavior consists of acts, or patterns of acts, embedded in the chain of classroom events, then a first step is to break down the patterns of teaching behavior into teachable skills. These patterns could be arranged into a series of learning experiences which start with the simple and move on to the more complex. The purpose would be to link knowledge about teaching to the student's overt behavior *at each step along the way* so that regular reinforcement or criticism can come from personal, sequential experiences in skill development. The goal of such a program is to help students explore, investigate, and in some cases discover for themselves relationships between teaching behavior and classroom interaction. Because of the learning experiences, this kind of pedagogical knowledge would automatically be incorporated in the students' repertoire of behavior patterns, and this is the only kind of knowledge that has utility during a moment of teaching.

Traditionally, professors of education have been responsible for exposing students to knowledge about teaching through lectures, demonstrations, field observations, readings, assignments, and then testing the students' knowledge. The inconsistency between college teaching methods and what is being taught is shrugged off as inconsequential or defended weakly by citing the college students' maturity. The argument that educational theory will be appreciated as soon as a person has had some teaching experience is at best a rationalization, and at its worst shortsighted indifference. The issue is whether those who teach future teachers do or do not have a responsibility to help the student incorporate this knowledge into his own behavior at each step along the way through an organized sequence of learnings. Is it desirable? Is this possible?

Education faculties are often divided into departments such as theory, methods, and practice teaching. Each department is further subdivided into compartments [sic] such as educational history, philosophy, psychology, curriculum, fields of specialization, elementary, secondary, and so on. Such an organization can have a long history and a rich tradition, which is to say that no one can quite remember how such divisions were originally created, but there is a strong tendency to maintain them. Indeed, this is how the history of any organization is extended and how its traditions become rich. One consequence is that too often an innovation is first screened to see if it is compatible with the organization. Should it pass this test, it is subsequently evaluated in terms of its potential merit. This procedure works quite well for any proposed innovation which can be preempted by a single subdivision. Yet the study of teaching behavior and classroom interaction involves theory, is basic to teaching methods, and can facilitate practice teaching so that its application involves nearly all subdivisions. Whenever an innovation touches an organizational structure at many points, the results are at least confusion and often resistance to change which can reach remarkable intensities. The net result is that curriculum innovations are most often restricted to single subdivisions. It is most difficult to obtain the approval of the entire faculty on any issue, even for deference toward motherhood, partly because it might be seen as a small loss in the academic freedom for the individual professor or an erosion of departmental authority.

Genuine progress toward an improved teacher education program may involve more than a small loss of academic freedom; education professors may need new insights and the time to develop new skills. Helping college professors embrace inservice education may take considerable tact and thoughtful planning. Nevertheless, it is exciting to think of faculty members working with college students to improve teacher education by analyzing each others teaching behavior, seeking concepts and models of teaching, and developing theories to account for their shared experiences. Surely such adult inquiry is a worthwhile goal for college or university instructors.

In Chapter 11 suggestions about teacher education are considered in more detail. No matter how difficult improving collegiate teacher education programs may be, this approach to effective classroom instruction seems more efficient than expending the same resources on the inservice education of teachers on the job. The preference is illustrated by the story of two lifeguards who became exhausted after rescuing a succession of persons who were barely afloat as they were swept downstream. Finally one lifeguard went upstream and stopped the man who was shoving people off the bridge—until they could be taught to swim in the swift current.

INTERACTION ANALYSIS AND INSERVICE EDUCATION

It is a rare teacher who approaches teaching as if it were a process similar to learning and therefore continues to inquire into alternative methods in such a way that his own behavior becomes an object of inquiry. Just as it is a radical idea to ask professors of education to accept the responsibility for helping their students translate knowledge into action, it is equally radical to ask a fully certified, employed teacher to give up the sanctuary which we call the "privacy of the classroom" and expose the interaction to assessment procedures. Yet the assessment of teaching behavior is at least a two-headed task and does not flourish with objectivity when the only feedback mechanism is a self-controlled mirror. Surely there is some way to escape the personal illusions which often confound improvement.

Many teachers would like to improve their own effectiveness. This involves making a change and then deciding whether the change was or was not an improvement. Both steps, verifying change and judging improvement, cannot be easily accomplished by a teacher alone in his classroom. He needs help in circumventing private perceptions. Yet inquiry into a matter that is so personal requires a special kind of partnership if it is to avoid becoming an intellectual, emotional, and spiritual striptease. Personal illusions need not be peeled off, one by one; instead a constructive inquiry into existing behavior and alternatives for change can be planned and carried out.

Interaction analysis, in combination with other inquiry techniques, can provide information about the communication that now exists, can help to identify alternatives that the teacher would like to try, can provide data to indicate whether a change has occurred, and can become a reference point for deciding whether a change was or was not an improvement. This systematic approach to self-development is more likely to flourish within the mutual support of a partnership or small action team with work scheduled throughout the year on a regular basis.

One of the least understood problems of inservice education is how to create an environment for the teacher which not only encourages change, but makes it reasonably probable. Assuming that a teacher's present performance is the product of his current resources and incentives, a substantial change in performance must surely require a substantial change in the "change environment." It is quite possible that the "density" of a change environment has been grossly underestimated. Too often inservice activities are merely in-door spectator sports which attempt to provide new knowledge and inspi-ration. Different speakers and indifferent audiences join for one-shot affairs before the semester starts and a few booster shots during the academic year on the assumption that something will be said and heard that will cause the teacher to act differently. What the teacher may actually need are new incentives, space, time, and resources which permit him to translate knowledge he already has into more effective patterns of teaching behavior in a continuing program of self-development. The former increases the gap between intent and practice; the latter decreases the gap.

Not enough is known about how to help a teacher change his behavior so that a different chain of events takes place in the classroom. Surely a prom-ising place to start is with an analysis of present classroom interaction that emphasizes patterns of teaching behavior.

The problems and prospects of using interaction analysis for the inservice education of teachers are considered in Chapter 11.

INTERACTION ANALYSIS AND RESEARCH ON TEACHING EFFECTIVENESS

Research on teaching effectiveness attempts to discover relationships between teaching behavior and measures of pupil growth. The most common research design (which leaves much to be desired) compares an "experimental treat-ment" group of classes with a control group. The teachers in the experimental group may have attended an inservice training program, or they may be teaching the "new math," or they may simply have completed the M.A. degree. Pretests and posttests of pupil achievement and attitude are administered to all classes and an analysis of the scores shows that there were, or were not, significant differences between the two groups of classes that are being compared. In most research on teaching effectiveness, no assessment of classroom interaction takes place and the investigator finds himself in the rather awkward position of trying to explain his results. It is a little ridiculous to spend the time and energy to assess pupil growth only to conclude that the pupils in the classrooms taught by the experimental teachers learned more, or did not, but fail to collect data which helps to explain why the results turned out the way they did. Perhaps the experimental teachers asked questions differently, or they may have reacted to the ideas expressed by pupils differently. Interaction analysis provides information about the verbal communication which occurred, and this often helps to explain the results.

The use of some form of interaction analysis to clarify differences between the experimental and control classes depends on a logical relationship which presumably exists between "the treatment" and teacher-pupil interaction.

For example, the new mathematics curricula are supposed to stimulate more pupil initiative, especially in proposing solutions to problems and in identifying the relevant features of a problem. Since this kind of pupil behavior is a part of verbal communication, it can be assessed by interaction analysis. Such a procedure would help to evaluate the mathematics teaching in two important ways: first, the data are used to show the extent to which this feature of communication was present in the experimental classes; and second, the data can show to what extent this feature was absent in the control classes. It is in this sense that interaction analysis can explain why the results of research on teaching effectiveness turned out one way or another.

THE CHALLENGE AND TRAGEDY OF CURRENT TEACHING PRACTICES

The challenge of current teaching practices is that they can be improved, but only by creating environments for change that are much more powerful than those which have thus far been made available to teachers. The tragedy of current teaching practices is that ways to improve them have been available but not implemented and the incidence of less effective teaching patterns is unknown and probably more extensive than we would like to believe. This may be an extravagant indictment, but in this section some of its features will be outlined with more detailed information.

THE CURRENT NATIONAL SCENE

What may well be the greatest system of education in man's history now suffers on a national scale from inequalities of educational opportunity. This contradiction to our national aspirations produced a crisis, in the late 1960's, which consumes our attention and requires emergency measures. For example, the range of annual payment for educating one child both between states and within states is much too wide and does not provide equal opportunity; sharp conflict over desegregation and *de facto* segregation creates confusion; our response to the deterioration of schools in depressed rural and urban areas has been so slow that interventions into school districts come from national agencies and local citizens; and the first installment costs for educational rehabilitation in our ghetto areas have been enormous, with second and third installments soon to fall due. The tragedy is that public debate is concerned with symptoms and the harried political decisions are shaped by expiations. The "times are out of joint" for a thoughtful consideration of the more difficult and fundamental problems. So children can be bussed, federal aid can be withheld, the college bound can be accelerated, and those who need terminal education in high school can follow special curricula financed by crash programs, but what about improving the chain of events which occurs during classroom interaction?

Teachers are in contact with pupils constantly during the twelve years of public education. To whatever extent these contacts are influential, it is in the classroom that patterns of thinking should be set, attitudes should be shaped, and participation can influence the growth of independence and self-direction. Teaching behavior is the most potent, single, controllable factor that can alter learning opportunities in the classroom. Equalizing educational opportunities depends, in the last analysis, on: How often does the teacher ask questions? What kinds of questions are asked? What happens to ideas that are expressed by children? To what extent and under what conditions are pupils encouraged to express their own initiative? We need to know what actually takes place in our classrooms.

SOME EARLY RETURNS FROM STUDYING
CLASSROOM INTERACTION

During the past 10 years scattered and uncoordinated glimpses of classroom interaction have been recorded by researchers who were not trying to survey existing conditions; they were merely trying to develop systems of observation. The early returns are not very encouraging. While it is true that teachers talk more than all the pupils combined, from kindergarten to graduate school, the major problem appears to lie not in quantity, but in quality.

Item.   The percent of all talk that appears as questions asked by the teacher can be estimated at: 13 to 16 percent in grades one through six (46), 10 to 12 percent in junior high school (38), and 6 to 8 percent in senior high school (74). These figures tell us little, but on the average, more than two-thirds of all teacher questions* are concerned with narrow lines of interrogation which stimulate an expected response.

Item.   The percent of all talk that appears as a teacher statement which reacts to or makes use of an idea previously expressed by a pupil can be estimated as 3 to 5 percent in grades one through six (46), 4 to 9 percent in junior high school (38), and $3\frac{1}{2}$ to 8 percent in senior high school (74). This means that very little teacher talk is devoted to a consideration of ideas or opinions expressed by the pupils; their ideas are not dealt with adequately.

Item.   The percent of all talk that appears as questions asked by the pupils varies with grade level, subject being studied, and so on, but the range is from

---

*See Figs. 5−5 and 5−6, p. 142; look at column total 41 compared with 42.

about 1 percent to about 3 or 4 percent.* It is shocking, however, to discover that less than 20 percent of these infrequently asked questions are thought-provoking questions; most pupil questions ask for clarification of directions or ask for statements to be repeated, etc.

Item.   When teaching cycles are analyzed as a pattern of pedagogical moves in high school social studies classes, the median of teacher-initiated cycles is 88 percent (9, p. 219). This means that most "structure" in learning activities is established by the teacher.

Item.   When classroom interaction shifts toward more consideration of pupil ideas, more pupil initiation, and more flexible behavior on the part of the teacher, the present trend of research results† would suggest that the pupils will have more positive attitudes toward the teacher and the schoolwork, and measures of subject-matter learning adjusted for initial ability will be higher. A relatively small percentage increase in attending to pupil ideas, for example from 6 to 12 percent, has a constructive influence on educational outcomes.

By way of summarizing the current state of affairs in our classrooms, it does not seem very far out of line to suggest that teachers usually tell pupils what to do, how to do it, when to start, when to stop, and how well they did whatever they did. It is true that at national professional conventions, in schools of education, and as a conversation topic in the teachers' lounge, better teaching intentions are discussed, but very little is said about the conditions described in this indictment. Surely our good intentions are met and classroom inter-action is more pupil oriented in some unknown proportion of our classrooms. My conservative guess, however, is that at least one-half of all the pupils in the country, if not the world, experience chains of events that are inconsistent with our educational aspirations and contrary to what we would like to believe. This is a tragedy in terms of social science knowledge.

HARBINGERS OF OUR PRESENT PROBLEMS

Critics of education are a dime a dozen in any generation, but some are more thought provoking than others. Most critics are forced to tease out their insights without the benefit of supporting data. Only a few of our generation have anticipated the present quality of classroom interaction which current re-searchers are only beginning to describe. Consider, for example, what Nathaniel Cantor (23, Chap. 3) was saying in 1953 when he stated his nine assumptions

---

*Figures of this magnitude have been separately reported by Dodl (27), Parakh (75), and Johns (57).
†Evidence to support this assertion is developed in greater detail in Chapters 10, 11, and 12.

to orthodox teaching. He believed that teachers acted as if they assumed:

1) That the teacher's responsibility is to set out what is to be learned and that the student's job is to learn it. (p. 59)
2) That knowledge taken on authority is education in itself. (p. 59)
3) That education can be obtained through disconnected subjects. (p. 61)
4) That the subject matter is the same to the learner as to the teacher. (p. 64)
5) That education prepares the student for later life rather than that it is a living experience. (p. 65)
6) That the teacher is responsible for the pupil's acquiring of knowledge. (p. 67)
7) That pupils must be coerced into working on some tasks. (p. 68)
8) That knowledge is more important than learning. (p. 70)
9) That education is primarily an intellectual process. (p. 71)

The little data on classroom interaction that are available tend more to support than to deny Cantor's opinions. He was correctly concerned about the way teachers use their authority arbitrarily, that independence is often considered to be an evil that is punished, and that dependence on others and conformity to outside pressures become the accustomed response to a new experience. Cantor distinguished himself by being one of the first to suggest a primitive theory about how teachers should alter their behavior in a predictable sequence during a cycle in teaching. He describes "challenge" as a function of the teacher in creating a "difference" which pupils can then resolve as a problem in learning. He criticized teaching behavior when a challenge is introduced too early. First it is necessary to build rapport and trust with individual children *vis-a-vis* particular problems; then challenge will stimulate objective curiosity rather than defensive compliance. The sequence suggests a definite shift in the role of the teacher as problems become more clearly identified, hopefully by methods that avoid creating excessive dependence on the teacher's authority.

In writing about conformity and creativity in the classroom, the ASCD 1962 Yearbook Committee (6), reacting to the ideas of Earl C. Kelley, Carl R. Rogers, A. H. Maslow, and Arthur W. Combs, wrote:

Experiences which inhibit the individual's freedom to be and to express his deeper self reduce his ability to be creative. Creativity is not learned from restraint. It is a product of the lowering or removal of barriers. It is a matter of being different, of daring to change, of venturing forth. . . . Conformity and creativity are essentially antithetical— what produces one tends to destroy the other. (p. 144)

The early glimpses of current classroom interaction which have been described appear to be more conducive to conformity than to creativity. If these early returns are confirmed by more broadly based and representative surveys, then serious questions can be raised about the ability of our schools to provide youthful citizens with the kind of cool judgment and independent thinking that our social unrest demands. Yet we must remind ourselves that current classroom interaction is guided by professionals who subscribe earnestly to helping each individual reach the fullest educational development of which he is capable. Teachers, for the most part, want to create a chain of classroom events which approach the highest standards of thoughtful inquiry. To find a way in which well intentioned teachers can achieve their own worthwhile goals by controlling classroom interaction may be the most significant challenge that professional educators face!

In the context of this discussion, it does not seem unusual for Herbert A. Thelen (100) to start an entire book about education with the following words:

> As judged by our hopes for mental health, social stability, or scientific competition with Russia, our schools are good, indifferent, or bad, depending on how you define your terms. As judged by what could be done if we were to understand and apply modern knowledge to educational problems, all our schools are obsolescent. . . . We know a great deal about the nature of man, knowledge, and society; about the dynamics of learning by individuals; . . . . But most of this knowledge has so far made almost no dent at all on educational practices, and, with the present tendency to think that educational problems can be solved with money and organizational changes, the likelihood of any significant improvement is discouragingly slight. This state of affairs is downright maddening. (p. 1)

THE CRUX OF THE MATTER

A number of things have been said, up to this point. It is possible to think of teaching behavior as a part of the chain of events that occurs in the classroom. This kind of thinking creates an orientation toward behavior and the concepts involved lend themselves to an analysis of teaching acts. Techniques for analyzing current, average classroom interaction reveal a high degree of teacher domination in setting learning tasks and in thinking through problems so that pupils' ideas and initiative are underdeveloped. As a result, teachers and pupils rarely experience thoughtful, shared inquiry. In classrooms that are above average in positive pupil attitudes and content achievement, the teacher-pupil interaction exhibits a somewhat greater orientation toward pupil ideas and pupil initiative. In spite of these differences in contrasting classrooms, most teachers say that they want to be more attentive to the pupils and their ideas. Given these considerations, it would be quite natural to get on with the job of dissemination, practice, and innovation. Why wait? The teachers are ready and tentative programs can be designed.

There is an unresolved crucial issue that can be seen most clearly by accepting, for the moment, the complete validity of all statements made in the preceding paragraph. Suppose, for purposes of discussion, that our knowledge about teaching behavior and its consequences was "the truth" beyond a shadow of doubt. The teachers who most need to change their behavior and to improve classroom instruction may be the most likely to adopt certain teaching patterns because "experts or research showed" that these patterns were most effective. This very *readiness to accept knowledge on someone else's authority* may be one cornerstone of the difficulties that below average teachers have while working with pupils in the classroom and accepting help from supervisors. Such readiness is inconsistent with the nature of more effective teaching-learning processes and the optimum self-development of the teacher. Perhaps the *experience* of seeking knowledge about teaching through behavior analysis is just as important as the kind of knowledge that is acquired, and both should be of the highest quality. This position is not incompatible, for example, with the curious fact that data about *how* the teacher and pupils interact can be used successfully to predict subject matter achievement between classes. Since pupils learn more and like learning better when their own ideas are taken into consideration and when the situation provides an opportunity for them to show initiative, then perhaps the same conditions would help a teacher who wants to improve classroom instruction. Yet how can we help teachers to succeed in achieving this goal if we make use of strategies which are logically inconsistent with our objective? We cannot disseminate research results as our only approach to improving instruction.

The crucial issue, then, is *to decide how teachers and college students can explore various patterns of interaction and discover for themselves which patterns they can use in order to improve instruction.*

One answer might be to start by helping teachers learn to use procedures of interaction analysis in combination with any other techniques that provide teachers with information about their own behavior. If these skills are used wisely, teachers will find out what they need to know in order to improve classroom instruction. This might work well for the more resourceful teachers and for college students with an insatiable curiosity and plenty of drive. Yet this proposal seems inefficient because no generation of learners starts from scratch to build knowledge, but instead incorporates proven procedures and existing knowledge in order to take advantage of previous accomplishments. Nearly everyone can benefit from a kind of road map that helps to keep a goal in mind and presents alternate routes for reaching it.

We seek the most effective training strategies, that is, ways to combine the skills of analyzing classroom interaction with knowledge that researchers have already found by using these techniques. By clever design, training experiences to learn the skills of interaction analysis can be preplanned to lead the trainee toward particular discoveries. These, in turn, accelerate the growth of insights into teaching behavior. By exercising the utmost care, a series of such experiences might be efficient, but still protect the opportunities of teachers to introduce their own ideas and to take the initiative in planning their own projects of self-development. The training experiences might be similar to laboratory experiments in a really creative freshman chemistry course whereby a student rediscovers and proves to his own satisfaction that the electrolysis of pure water produces two volumes of hydrogen and one volume of oxygen. Thus, in about 2 hours, a student demonstrates to his own satisfaction what several scientists took a lifetime to find out.

Now let us return to our provisional assumption about the validity of what we know about teaching behavior. Suppose our present knowledge is not valid; then surely the dissemination of incorrect information might do more harm than good. Further, given the brief period during which systematic investigations of teaching behavior have occurred, it is practically certain that we will learn much more during the next few decades. The incompleteness of our knowledge and the lack of certainty about its validity are less likely to cause harm so long as the elements of exploration and inquiry are a continuing part of professional development.

There is an additional consideration which encourages modest optimism in helping teachers analyze their own behavior in an effort to improve classroom instruction. There is a possibility that additional research on teaching behavior will continue to confirm that as teaching becomes less and less effective, it involves fewer unique patterns, becomes more rigid, and more repetitive. On the other hand, as teaching becomes more and more effective, the repertoire of behavior patterns expands, variations in sequence seem almost endless, and the entire process is more flexible, creative, and difficult to describe. Now, you may ask, why does this provide reason for optimism?

Level One.   Suppose there were a limited number of behavior patterns and only a few sequences necessary to describe interaction in the least effective classrooms. These patterns might be a part of lecturing, asking narrow questions, giving restrictive directions, and so on. Such patterns are the most common, easiest to learn, and involve straightforward applications.

Level Two.   Now suppose that in order to move up to average teaching effectiveness, only a few new patterns are involved. Certain critical skills such as making primitive distinctions among questions, alternative ways of clarifying and making use of pupil ideas, and providing more effective explanations with praise, directions, and criticism need only be understood and added to the repertoire. A few additional patterns greatly increase the possible sequences so that these few new skills permit a large increase in teaching flexibility.

Level Three.   The most artistic and effective teaching would not only involve all that was mentioned above, but it would become more purposeful. Models of teaching strategies, more subtle discriminations in teaching behavior, and ways to organize events around the logic of the subject matter would now be introduced. One might hope, however, that the same strategies of training that helped to lift teaching from level one to level two could now serve equally to reach level three. Teachers would continue to explore, assess, and analyze their own behavior, and attempt to relate their results to educational outcomes, but the problems being investigated would simply be more advanced. For example, teachers might explore the effects of purposely lifting the level of abstraction of discourse when seeking to make generalizations or to place learning problems in a broader context. At other times, they might try to lower the level of abstraction as individual learning tasks were being specified for pupils. To accomplish these shifts by accident is a lower level of teaching performance; to plan and then carry out such shifts is a higher level of performance.

Systematic levels of teaching performance would facilitate teacher training, rather than impede it, because it could lead to a logical curriculum in the self-development of a teacher. Teaching behavior patterns and the procedures for analyzing these patterns could be taught, simultaneously practiced, and then tried out in the classroom. As the patterns themselves became more complicated and required more subtle distinctions, the analytical skills of the trainees would also be improving. The essential philosophy and strategy of self-development would remain the same throughout. Teachers would learn to identify patterns of teaching behavior, learn to act out these patterns, and then explore their utility through applications in their own classrooms.

THE SEARCH FOR CONVICTIONS

Interaction analysis is a tool of action and its use requires a substantial commitment of time and energy. It is not likely to remain long in the hands of any person who is without convictions. In fact, its use develops convictions about teaching and alters those we already possess. Convictions are rarely products of thinking only; the heart, hands, and head are all involved in a blend of both the objective and the subjective. Interaction analysis can help to develop the value systems about teaching, which we call convictions, by contributing information which is primarily objective. There are, however, subjective problems in using the technique that need to be understood.

THE INQUIRY PROCESS WHEN BEHAVIOR IS
AN OBJECT OF INQUIRY

It seems quite simple to state the steps of scientific inquiry. A problem is identified; ways to describe it come from thoughtful consideration; a plan of investigation is developed; the plan is carried out, which often requires collecting information or simply trying something out; the results of this activity are then analyzed; and new problems appear so that the same cycle can be repeated. Attention to concepts, care in logic, and creative hunches all play an important part in the success of the endeavor. This kind of outline is so simple to state, but it is quite difficult to apply these steps with imagination in classroom teaching and especially difficult in the analysis of teaching behavior.

One reason that the scientific method is difficult to apply to teaching and the improvement of teaching is that a simple statement of the steps involved ignores the subjective feelings, emotions, and attitudes which any investigation generates. The subjective elements of the process cannot be denied, and to take them into consideration provides a more complete understanding.

Teachers can often recognize the subjective aspects of classroom teaching. Educators know that when the cognitive elements of learning are taught in a negative emotional context, the process is like a stone that enters the stomach, cannot be assimilated, and therefore is quickly excreted. There is universal dissatisfaction when geography and geology are taught in such a way that what the pupil sees or recognizes as he travels across the country remains unchanged. We can agree that all knowledge is confronted and then learned in a social and emotional context. Yet we have great difficulty in recognizing the implications of these observations when adults are introduced to pedagogical knowledge and when they are confronted with learning the skills of teaching. The end product sought is continuous self-development; there is no particular stopping point; *ends* are never fully achieved. We fail to understand that the *means* of achieving these ends shape behavior, influence feelings and attitudes, and most directly determine success and failure. While these features are recognized in classroom teaching, it is quite possible that they are both unrecognized and much more pervasive when one's own behavior is an object of study.

Interaction analysis as a technique involves a great deal of cognitively oriented busywork. Categories are to be memorized, their use requires practice, tabulation and clerical duties demand attention, and the analysis procedures, while interesting, tend to predominate—pushing aside the consideration of how one feels about what he is doing. The skills can actually create an intellectual, semiobjective haven into which we can retreat in order to avoid facing the subjective elements of studying behavior and trying to help create changes in behavior. This is a weakness of interaction analysis when the purpose is to help a person study his own behavior in order to control it more effectively.

It is an interesting task to try rewriting the steps of scientific procedure in such a way that a more adequate emphasis is given to the subjective elements of the process. The effort seems especially worthwhile when one's own behavior is being studied and when the procedures used, like interaction analysis, often turn attention away from feelings, emotions, and attitudes. The interplay between the cognitive and the effective elements of inquiry are illustrated by the proposed steps described below.*

Step One. A teacher manages the classroom in response to priorities as he sees them. At any moment he considers youngsters, curriculum, resources, his self-concept, past experiences, relations with peers and superiors, and so on. The features of the present setting are ordered into a list of priorities and the potency of each priority has an objective and subjective impact; the teacher both thinks and feels.

Step Two. Risking a change results from a disequilibrium in the setting, a jolting or rocking of the self-concept, a difficulty, a change in perceived priorities, peer or superior pressure, an outside interaction, or any of a number of things including a slowly growing conviction that finally reaches the ignition point. Aside from changing simple acts, more extensive changes in teaching patterns are conceived by a teacher when he *experiences* subjective dissatisfactions, reinforced by cognitive dissonance. These *feelings* create the tension system that is resolved, ultimately, by exploring alternatives.

Step Three. Tensions can create restlessness in mind and body. Plans are imagined; alternatives are considered in terms of time, space, and materials; and feelings of optimism or despair can color all of these considerations. During a flash of insight or, more likely, after continuing appraisal, a possible plan appears in the foreground, separated from a background of discarded alternatives.

Step Four. According to the teacher's cognitions and feelings (fear, optimism, confidence, etc.) that involve the self-concept, resources versus demands, and a sense of pressure, some kind of challenge is perceived. As it takes shape, feelings are reorganized and energy is activated to a standby status. There is a readiness to venture; first steps seem clear; it is the moment before a move.

Step Five. The teacher moves with some degree of independence, committing himself to some degree of risk, clinging to certain anticipations. He leaps, falls, or is pushed into a nonreversible action which may be tentative or it may be bold. During this time the teacher's very existence is itself a change process, he lives through a change and experiences the associated sensations.

---

*You might try writing your own outline of the steps of inquiry when a teacher studies his own classroom interaction. The author found the following two references helpful: C. M. Hampden-Turner (49) and H. A. Thelen (100, pp. 89–91 and Chapter 6).

Step Six.   During the initial action and later, when the tempo slows, he will constantly compare his investment with real and expected returns. Through training, his orientation might be toward the more objective data from interaction analysis or some other kind of evidence, but the satisfactions most urgently sought are affective sensations—the thrill of risk taking, the curiosity of new perceptions, the reinforcement of coordinated team effort, the release of tensions, and the concentrated absorption of self-discovery. Emotionality and cognitive effort are in phase, rising and falling together (96).

Step Seven.   He returns to step one, two, or three to recycle, either grudgingly or occasionally with enthusiastic alacrity, depending on the resolutions that have occurred. Under the best of conditions, when his communication is most open and free, he explains his insights to professional colleagues and seeks their reactions and the reactions of his pupils. He wants to share his satisfactions and is driven to act out his insights. With increased confidence, he begins to fashion his own change environment with greater independence. He continues to integrate his concepts for thinking and the behaviors associated with each concept.

These steps are not likely to occur richly and fully amid the routines of professional service and the pressures of daily survival. The seeds of self-development are not likely to flourish when sown at the beginning of the semester or in a college lecture and then left to survive unattended. Helping a teacher change his behavior or starting a college student down this road of self-inquiry are not simple tasks.

THE COMMITMENT TO INQUIRY

We must inquire into the chain of events in the classroom because it is a moral responsibility. This kind of morality is based on the notion that experience, the things that actually occur in the classroom, must be admitted as evidence in advocating or defending, in distinguishing one moral position from another, and in creating our own value systems.

Even though how we act is clearly a moral issue, it is not very often that teachers think of morality in terms of their own everyday teaching pattern. The notion, for example, that current teaching methods might be immoral is a topic that would stimulate much conversation among teachers. Recently, a group of researchers met to discuss their results. Most, if not all of those present at this international meeting accomplished their research by accounting for events that occur during classroom interaction. The researchers did their best to present their findings in terms of cold, objective facts. A philosopher, with a humanistic bent, who was familiar with the research results, chose to interpret the data in terms of moral standards and expressed his position in words that shocked some of us, to say nothing about the potential reactions of teachers who labor diligently with good faith in the classroom. He said (63):

> ... *About the act of saying* (he was referring to speaking in the classroom) *we may ask, typically, questions of morals and manners. . . . Does the teacher talk too much? Does he respect the feelings and opinions of his students? Does he listen carefully to what students say? Does he encourage students to bring up matters of interest to them? Etc. These questions are quite the same as one would ask about a dinner partner. It's a revealing feature of moral progress that we have to make such a big deal over simple, decent* civility *for students in the classroom. . . . Since students lack political and economic power to force teachers to treat them with good manners, it is of positive social value that many teachers come to want to behave more decently toward students: interaction analysis often serves as a kind of conversion experience to bring about that new desire and, perhaps, even more important, to provide a new convert with the skills and techniques of good classroom manners.*

A commitment to inquiry goes much further than a concern for manners during classroom interaction. The steps of inquiry described in the preceding section, properly carried out, may well be consistent with the steps of natural learning as they occur with adults and children alike. Interaction analysis is merely a data collecting tool for teachers; its use is similar to data collecting by pupils during learning. How such tools are used in learning engenders feelings and a teacher could experience the same feelings in his learning that pupils experience in theirs. Given this similarity, we might prefer to make the commitment that *the procedures which are followed to help a teacher change his behavior should be consistent with those that the teacher will carry out to help his pupils learn.*

Most knowledge is the product of comparisons which occurred when alternatives were recognized, carried out, and then appraised. Each person has a right to create and to relive such experiences as he acquires knowledge. Conclusions can be reached on the basis of initial personal experience, then reformulated and generalized on the basis of further reading, consulting, and group discussion. Knowledge and skills obtained in this fashion are personal in that there is an element of self-directed discovery. We might wish to commit ourselves to *increase the opportunities for independent action during learning to the fullest possible extent that is compatible with developing self-control.* This may be especially desirable when we help teachers analyze their own behavior.

Finally, we might note in a commitment to inquiry, that our present knowledge about teaching is incomplete and, in some cases, of questionable validity. The safeguard against institutionalizing misconceptions lies in preparing future teachers and helping experienced teachers in such a way that self-development involves a continuing exploration. It is the living through a change of behavior that helps a person establish the habit of continuing growth, that is, living through the feelings of uncertainty and meeting the challenge of analyzing a dissonance. It is a helpful coincidence that these same experiences place a teacher in a better position to understand what pupils go through when they learn. The commitment to inquiry, therefore, includes *promoting convictions developed from personal experience, values that are open to subsequent reformulation, and habits of self-direction that are deeply rooted in skepticism and curiosity.*

THE SENSE OF URGENCY

It is difficult to live in these times without feeling a sense of urgency about achieving what might be called "authentic behavior." The discrepancy between intention and action may be a result of social incompetence that we can no longer tolerate in our human relations. As each individual's social space becomes more and more compacted, behavior itself may comprise and define our perceptions of what people are like and what exists. Contradictions which are downright dangerous already abound: the way we think about human beings and the way we treat each other; what government professes and the way its army and its police act; and what we think education is all about compared with the events that take place in the classroom. No one has yet found the key to these mysteries, but in the field of education there are certain questions to which answers cannot be delayed much longer. In a very small and modest way, this book speaks to two questions which do seem urgent.

Can objective data provide insights into subjective problems? Some writers who are called existentialists are quick to say "no" to this question, while insisting that existence precedes essence. By this they mean that a man must first exist before we can tell what kind of a man he is, but this determination is essentially subjective. They might also say that a teacher must first teach before we can decide what kind of a teacher he is. This book is dedicated to the proposition that teaching behavior indeed determines what a teacher is, but sharp exception is taken with those who would deny the utility of assessing behavior. It *is* the tiny bits of behavior that constitute teaching. To *know* what teaching is impels us to take the little bits into account and use them to display a conception of the teaching that is taking place. To know what teaching *is* plunges us into a subjective problem; to know what teaching acts occur is by definition an objective problem. It may take years of research and development before we can synthesize the subjective and objective elements, but there can be no escape from confronting the question.

Can objective data about behavior help in changing behavior? Perhaps the corrolary question is: Can we be stringently objective in our assessment of behavior and then be compassionate, sensitive, yet still be realistic in the way we make use of the information? There seems to be some truth behind Roubiczek's assertion (81):

> *Actions will produce the right kind of subjective insight, however, only if they are based on the right attitude. Kierkegaard demands this attitude when he observes: "The majority of men are subjective towards themselves, while being objective against all others, terribly objective sometimes—but the real task is exactly the opposite; to be objective towards oneself and subjective towards all others." We should not give in to our natural tendency to be severe towards others and lenient to ourselves, for we shall understand others only if we try to understand them from within, by attempting to make their experiences our own.* (p. 103)*

A teacher can be more objective toward himself when he can accept an assessment of his behavior and assimilate its meaning in terms of his innermost thoughts. Yet the success of this acceptance will depend on his attitude and his perceptions of the circumstances. Being open and objectively curious about one's own teaching behavior is not a natural state of affairs in our culture. The necessary attitudes have to be nourished and the permissive circumstances have to be patiently arranged and, if necessary, creatively rearranged. Success may result most often from a partnership with another teacher that is devoted to inquiry and exploration.

Now look at the demands on the partner who may have helped to assemble the objective assessment! Will he *force* his objective data *against* another and excuse his own behavior because of his own subjectivity? Can he be objective in his assessment of his own helping function? Success may depend on how well he can blend integrity and objectivity with compassion and empathy. Such a blend may be more likely when both partners openly explore the essence of existing behavior, become entranced by curiosity, and consumed by the search for insight. No one knows exactly how all this can be brought about, but the skills of interaction analysis—however long one may labor to learn them—will be of little use until this question is answered.

Sensing urgency

A sense of urgency about understanding teaching behavior will come, if it is to come at all, from seeing the problems of improving classroom instruction in bold relief and broad perspective. Today most college students are prepared for teaching and teachers in our schools are provided with inservice education without specific assistance in learning to identify, to practice producing, and

---

*From P. Roubiczek, *Existentialism for and against*. Cambridge, England: Cambridge University Press, 1966. Quoted by permission of the publisher.

to analyze teaching behavior. Concepts for thinking about teaching are frequently used even though they cannot be defined in terms of specific actions that a teacher can perform. Perhaps the most serious problem is the almost universally accepted notion that "one year of teaching experience" is a standard unit for setting salaries, granting privileges, and achieving status. This, along with the twin concept of "one unit of graduate education credit," provides little incentive for creating a program of self-development in which more than "one year of experience" can occur in one year. To improve the quality of classroom instruction, the chain of interaction events must first be altered and then judgments made about quality. Not very many teachers have the skills and resources to explore such possibilities even though many are willing to try.

To decide that this state of affairs needs to be improved and to expend time and energy on the task reflects a sense of urgency. Just how a sense of urgency develops is likely to be different for each person. Aside from devoting 15 years of research to the problem, let me confess that one incident increased my own sense of urgency. What follows is a single anecdote from which no generalization is possible and none is intended. It is simply a case study of a critical incident, critical only in the sense that I never forgot it and it strengthened my convictions about the urgent need to analyze and, if possible, improve classroom instruction.

A pupil attitude inventory was administered to a sample of more than 100 classes. The higher class averages occur in rooms in which more pupils like their teacher and enjoy their schoolwork; such scores, incidently, are positively correlated with content achievement adjusted for initial ability. The teachers of those classes which scored in the top and bottom 15 percent were interviewed for reasons that need not be discussed here. One teacher, whose class scored in the lowest 5 percent on attitude but was average in initial ability, said this during the interview:

> Now I don't want to brag, but it so happens that my graduate credits beyond the master's degree and my sixteen years of teaching experience make me the highest paid and the most qualified teacher in this school system. I think it is a shame that the administration sees fit to assign students to my class who don't want to learn. It is a waste of my training.

We can be certain that this point of view is not typical of classroom teachers. The remark indicates only that one teacher expressed perceptions that are desperately inconsistent with what our society asks of a teacher. Even though it is a single instance, what I can never forget is that this teacher who was the highest paid and the highest qualified in the school district, expressed the above perception seriously, and taught in a classroom in which the pupils were below average in positive attitudes and below average in content achievement adjusted for initial ability. This single experience, rightly or wrongly, increased my sense of urgency about work that had already been underway for a number of years.

THE TASK AHEAD

The first part of this chapter introduced the notion that classroom interaction can be viewed as a chain of events, and then briefly sketched the consequences of this kind of thinking in relation to a variety of topics. Optimism about progress in the improvement of classroom instruction was expressed in several sections. Criticism of current, average classroom interaction, teacher preparation programs, and the inservice education of teachers was also expressed. In the most recent section, discussing a search for convictions, additional negative statements were made about teaching and the present performance of teachers. It would be unfortunate if the total chapter led to the inference that there is little that can be done to improve classroom instruction or that present teachers are not doing their very best, as they see it, in order to provide education for our youth. The total impact of this book is meant to be optimistic. By actually studying what goes on during classroom interaction with new concepts, hard work, and self-development, teachers can indeed reach the objectives which they now hold for effective classroom instruction.

Subsequent chapters will introduce you to techniques for analyzing classroom interaction. Six chapters focus on procedures for coding communication events. There is more information in these chapters than you will need in order to start your own study of classroom interaction. There are also ways that our present knowledge can be improved and extended by inventing more effective methods of helping teachers improve classroom instruction. Perhaps these chapters will present ideas which you can use to make your own unique contribution to education.

Chapter Two

AN INTRODUCTION TO CODING PROCEDURES

THE PAUSE BEFORE YOU LEAP...

Systematic coding during classroom observation is a skill that takes practice to acquire. This chapter provides an orientation which is purposely brief so that you can start practicing as soon as possible. The first section describes what is meant by interaction analysis. The second section describes some of the reasons for using interaction analysis by illustrating the most common applications. The third section, and major portion of the chapter, introduces a category system which was widely used during the period 1960 to 1967. Learning the categories, procedures, and ground rules for this system will prepare you to use it for your first observation. This system will also serve as a background for learning more sophisticated coding skills which will be considered in Chapters 4 and 5.

A person without any coding experience should expect to devote about 4 hours to practice exercises, tape recordings, and live classroom observation before the various skills involved start to come under control. These initial efforts may seem confusing and are not always rewarding. Some persons require up to 12 hours to reach the point at which their individual style emerges and they feel confident to make professionally important discriminations. Crossing a "sound barrier" into productive and rewarding coding should occur sometime between the fourth and the twelfth hour.

WHAT IS CLASSROOM INTERACTION ANALYSIS?

Classroom interaction analysis refers not to one system, but to many systems for coding spontaneous verbal communication, arranging the data into a useful display, and then analyzing the results in order to study patterns of teaching and learning. Each system is essentially a process of encoding and decoding, i.e., categories for classifying statements are established, a code symbol is assigned to each category, and a trained observer records data by jotting down code symbols. Decoding is the reverse process: a trained analyst interprets the display of coded data in order to make appropriate statements about the original events which were encoded, even though he may not have been present when the data were collected. A particular system for interaction analysis will usually include (a) a set of categories, each defined clearly, (b) a procedure for observation and a set of ground rules which governs the coding process, (c) steps for tabulating the data in order to arrange a display which aids in describing the original events, and (d) suggestions which can be followed in some of the more common applications.

Most of the category systems which have been developed thus far have been restricted to verbal communication, but any kind of spontaneous behavior could presumably be encoded, provided a practical procedure was available.

Coding systems of all sorts are used constantly in our daily affairs. We use ZIP codes for addressing our letters, area codes to facilitate a telephone call, and we distinguish ourselves from other animals by our use of language, which is the most elaborate and flexible encoding-decoding system used by man. Language permits man to abstract phenomena and classify them within category systems, thus providing the foundation upon which modern science has been built.

Knowing language and how it is used provides a firm basis for understanding interaction analysis systems. Speakers and writers encode. Listeners and readers decode. The words used are code symbols which stand for ideas, and the purpose of language is to communicate these ideas accurately, excluding ideas which are not relevant. So it is with interaction analysis. The code symbol stands for a category which defines a particular type of statement. All statements judged to be of this type are assigned the same code symbol, regardless of certain differences which may be obvious, but are considered to be not relevant. The tabulated code symbols represent the statements which were made, and a display of these data can be interpreted to recreate some aspects of the original flow of communication within the relatively severe limitations of the category system.

Classroom interaction analysis systems seek to abstract communication by ignoring most of its characteristics. For example, a category such as "teacher asks a question" is used to code many different statements, provided they are all questions. Once the same code symbol is used for all of these statements, the differences among them are ignored and lost forever. Yet this loss is offset by keeping an accurate record of the number of times that a teacher attempts to solicit verbal expression from the pupils, which is the characteristic common to all statements with this code symbol. This process is sensible only when keeping an accurate record of teacher questions is crucial to some investigation. This procedure makes no sense at all when what is lost by the process is more important than what is gained.

Poor logical relationships between what is being investigated and the nature of the observation system employed has been the basis of much criticism regarding the use of interaction analysis. To cite an example, suppose a supervisor becomes interested in a particular system in order "to evaluate" a teacher. Here the required logical relationship is impossible until the supervisor specifies those aspects of the teacher's behavior which are central to the evaluation. In addition, a value model or criterion of what is "good" and what is "bad" must be described *in terms of the categories* in order to make direct comparisons between what is observed and what is desired. The most serious problem, however, may be a conflict between the purposes of the supervisor compared with those of the teacher. The supervisor seeks a valid comparison between a representative sample of teaching performance and a preferred model. Yet a teacher may "put on" a nonrepresentative act in order to obtain the best possible evaluation. Suppose the teacher is a good actor and the observation system is very accurate. The net result would then be unsatisfactory. Even though it may be possible to develop elaborate plans whereby any deception can be identified, ordinary observation systems are not designed to evaluate teachers in the sense of giving the teacher a rating. These systems are also not designed to detect deception.

WHAT ARE SOME COMMON APPLICATIONS?

Classroom interaction analysis can be useful whenever it is necessary to record the presence or absence of particular behavior patterns* during a period of observation. This need arises during the preservice preparation of future teachers, the inservice training of experienced teachers, and the conduct of research on classroom teaching. To accomplish this kind of observation, it is necessary to select behavior patterns which can be identified, to use an observation procedure which is practical, to record in a fashion which preserves the original sequence of events if this is necessary, and to tabulate and analyze the data in ways that are consistent with the design of the investigation.

The problems of using interaction analysis are different when immediate feedback of coded information is necessary, compared with applications in which immediate feedback is not necessary.

---

*Speaking is a behavior and speech forms are a pattern, so that "behavior patterns" in the above sentence is appropriate. Most teacher influence is exerted by the spoken word.

IMMEDIATE FEEDBACK APPLICATIONS

Inservice and preservice teacher education helps teachers to act differently as a result of their participation. Not only is a change in behavior sought, but often the learning activities are supposed to increase the use of specified behavior patterns which presumably improve the quality of classroom instruction. Interaction analysis can be helpful in several phases of such a program. For example, it can be used as a pretraining and post-training measure in order to decide whether the participants are learning how to perform particular behavior patterns while teaching their regular classes.

Classroom interaction analysis also lends itself to training exercises. For example, some trainees can practice performing certain behavior patterns while others practice observing these patterns. The observers and actors then discuss the completed performance in terms of personal growth toward professional goals. Later, they may discuss how these ideas apply to classroom instruction. Since assessing changes in behavior as well as deciding whether such changes are or are not improvements both require technical observation skills, it is possible to use interaction analysis as the major theme of inservice or preservice education. In such programs all trainees learn interaction analysis and then use the technique to pursue individual self-improvement goals which can be selected by each participant and are unique to the preferences of each participant.

Whenever observation information is fed back to a teacher, it is usually desirable to do so while the impressions of the situation are still fresh in the minds of both the observer and the actor. The ideal feedback instrument might be described in the following way. Behaviors of interest are coded accurately, and the code symbols are tabulated into a display which highlights desired comparisons. The entire process must keep up with the tempo of the spontaneous behavior so that at the moment the observation ceases, we have a display of summarized data which could provide instant feedback if this is desired.

Systems of interaction analysis can be combined with voice or video recording. However, any recording requires at least as much time for playback as the elapsed time of the original recording. During this playback, further delays may be caused by deciding what behaviors should be studied, what concepts would be most useful, and stopping, from time to time, to be sure that events are understood.

Perhaps the most intensive feedback would occur when both recording and observer coding were combined. The concepts and more objective information of interaction analysis can be used to anticipate crucial interaction points and to interpret what was heard (and/or seen) during the playback.

Helping a person change his behavior in ways that improve the quality of classroom instruction is not easy, and much remains to be learned about the process. Classroom interaction analysis can provide reasonably objective information which helps the trainee who is trying to change his own behavior, as well as the trainers who are in charge and who may wish to evaluate their own performance by assessing the effectiveness of the program.

APPLICATIONS WHICH DO NOT INVOLVE IMMEDIATE FEEDBACK

In research that is designed to study patterns of teacher-pupil interaction, feedback to a teacher is often undesirable. In fact, in some research designs, everything possible is done to avoid influencing the observational setting. In such studies, interaction analysis data from successive observations can be allowed to accumulate and tabulation is delayed until it is most convenient. Great efficiencies can be realized by punching all the data at once and using a computer to tabulate and analyze the data.

Perhaps the most important research application of interaction analysis is to study teaching behavior and classroom interaction in an effort to develop theories of instruction. Given certain classroom settings and learning objectives, it would be reasonable to expect lawful relationships between what the teacher does and the effects of his behavior on the learning of pupils. It seems quite likely that an ideal, most effective teacher would adjust his own behavior to the learning situation of the moment. As the situation changes, we would expect changes in the teacher's behavior. Interaction analysis can be used to quantify the degree of flexible adaptation which is characteristic of a teacher's behavior and the nature of such adaptations. From information of this sort, theories of instruction may someday be generated.

Interaction analysis has much to commend it as an independent or control measure whenever two methods of teaching or two different curricula are being compared. A common design is to expose experimental classes to the new curriculum and compare the learning of these classes to a control group or to previous levels of achievement established before any curriculum change occurred. Too often little or no evidence is provided which documents the differences in teaching patterns which presumably distinguish one curriculum from another. An analysis of the teachers' behavior can indicate whether new content material is being taught with or without expected changes in the classroom interaction. It can also provide data which may help to explain why differences in learning outcomes appeared or failed to appear. To explain why is to develop theory.

Perhaps the simplest of all research designs involving interaction analysis is to locate classrooms in which positive pupil attitudes and content achievement are above average in order to compare them with similar classrooms in which these same measures are below average. Paper-and-pencil tests, machine scored, are efficient tools for selecting such classrooms from a large population of classrooms. Once identified, the contrasting classrooms can be visited by trained observers who collect interaction analysis data. Depending on the category systems used and other aspects of the research design, a wide variety of hypotheses can be investigated to see if they account for the differences in pupil attitude and achievement.

SUMMARY

Classroom interaction analysis can be used for inservice and preservice education in order to help teachers improve classroom instruction. Usually such training requires some kind of objective feedback to the person who is trying to change his behavior. More efficient procedures and equipment which make this application more practical are described in subsequent chapters. Interaction analysis is also used for research on the teaching-learning process. The technique provides a method of quantifying concepts which refer to spontaneous behavior and which heretofore could be measured only indirectly. When measures of teaching behavior are associated with pupil attitudes and achievement, it is possible to start building primitive theories of instruction.

A TEN-CATEGORY SYSTEM

The system you will study in this section was developed by Flanders (35) and others* at the University of Minnesota between 1955 and 1960. The category system still has many useful applications, although efforts to increase the number of categories and modify the procedures have already been successfully completed.

Table 2–1 lists ten categories: seven are used when the teacher is talking, two are used when any pupil is talking, and the last category is used to indicate silence or confusion. So far as communication is concerned, these three conditions, (a) teacher talk, (b) pupil talk, and (c) silence or confusion, are said to exhaust all the possibilities. Category systems which exhaust all possibilities are *totally inclusive* of all possible events, and since any event can be classified, a totally inclusive system permits coding at a constant rate throughout the observation. This is essential whenever you wish to reach conclusions about the proportion of time spent in one or more categories.

Suppose we decided to code in only two teacher talk categories, giving directions (Category 6) and asking questions (Category 4). Given valid data,

---

*Individuals at Minnesota who influenced the early development include: Sulo Havumaki, Thomas Filson, Edmund Amidon, Theodore Storlie, and J. Paul Anderson. Earlier work at the University of Chicago also influenced the shape of the ten categories. These individuals include: Herbert Thelen, John Withall, and John Glidewell. In fact, the work of John Withall provided the first experiences of the author in the field of interaction analysis.

TABLE 2—1

Flanders' Interaction Analysis Categories* (FIAC)

Teacher Talk	Response	1. *Accepts feeling.* Accepts and clarifies an attitude or the feeling tone of a pupil in a nonthreatening manner. Feelings may be positive or negative. Predicting and recalling feelings are included.
		2. *Praises or encourages.* Praises or encourages pupil action or behavior. Jokes that release tension, but not at the expense of another individual; nodding head, or saying "Um hm?" or "go on" are included.
		3. *Accepts or uses ideas of pupils.* Clarifying, building, or developing ideas suggested by a pupil. Teacher extensions of pupil ideas are included but as the teacher brings more of his own ideas into play, shift to category five.
		4. *Asks questions.* Asking a question about content or procedure, based on teacher ideas, with the intent that a pupil will answer.
	Initiation	5. *Lecturing.* Giving facts or opinions about content or procedures; expressing *his own* ideas, giving *his own* explanation, or citing an authority other than a pupil.
		6. *Giving directions.* Directions, commands, or orders to which a pupil is expected to comply.
		7. *Criticizing or justifying authority.* Statements intended to change pupil behavior from nonacceptable to acceptable pattern; bawling someone out; stating why the teacher is doing what he is doing; extreme self-reference.
Pupil Talk	Response	8. *Pupil-talk—response.* Talk by pupils in response to teacher. Teacher initiates the contact or solicits pupil statement or structures the situation. Freedom to express own ideas is limited.
	Initiation	9. *Pupil-talk—initiation.* Talk by pupils which they initiate. Expressing own ideas; initiating a new topic; freedom to develop opinions and a line of thought, like asking thoughtful questions; going beyond the existing structure.
Silence		10. *Silence or confusion.* Pauses, short periods of silence and periods of confusion in which communication cannot be understood by the observer.

*There is *no* scale implied by these numbers. Each number is classificatory; it designates a particular kind of communication event. To write these numbers down during observation is to enumerate, not to judge a position on a scale.

we can compare the incidence of these two events, such as, "this teacher asked twice as many questions as he gave directions," or given two different observation periods, we might conclude that twice as many questions were asked in the first observation, compared with the second. However, since the two-category system used is not totally inclusive, there is no way to reach conclusions about the proportion of time spent in one or both of these two categories in terms of total teacher talk, all verbal communication, or total time spent during the observation. These latter comparisons are often important and therefore totally inclusive category systems are usually preferred, especially since more information is obtained without additional time spent in the classroom. We could make this two-category system totally inclusive by adding a category called "none of the above," and then tally at regular time intervals using this last category whenever there are no teacher questions or no teacher directions.

A first step in preparation for observation is to memorize the code numbers in relation to a key phrase or word which are indicated by italics in Table 2–1. An observer who enters a classroom without having committed the code numbers to memory is in about the same position as an individual who decides to learn the touch system of typewriting the day before a 150-page manuscript is due. The hunt-and-peck system of typing is not fast enough, just as looking up the category code number before you tally it will be too slow to keep up with classroom communication. The trained observer acts like an automatic device, albeit highly discriminating, and codes without hesitation at the instant an event is recognized.

PURPOSE AND THE NATURE OF THE CATEGORY SYSTEM

The major feature of this category system lies in the analysis of *initiative* and *response* which is a characteristic of interaction between two or more individuals. To initiate, in this context, means to make the first move, to lead, to begin, to introduce an idea or concept for the first time, to express one's own will. To respond means to take action after an initiation, to counter, to amplify or react to ideas which have already been expressed, to conform or even to comply to the will expressed by others. We expect the teacher, in most situations, to show more initiative than the pupils.

With this ten-category system, an estimate of the balance between initiative and response can be inferred from the percent time of teacher talk, pupil talk, and silence or confusion. These percents alone are not very good predictors of pupil learning and attitudes because the *quality* of the statements is associated with educational outcomes just as much, if not more, than the *quantity*. Since the teacher has more authority than any pupil, it is not surprising to discover that the teacher's communication, which is a sample of his total behavior, will be the most potent single factor in establishing a balance of initiation and response. It is for this reason that seven of the ten categories are devoted to discriminations among teacher statements.

A more accurate estimate of the initiative-response balance of classroom interaction can be reached by comparing the teacher tallies in Categories 1, 2, and 3 with those in 5, 6, and 7. The teacher is responding to pupil behavior in a supportive manner when he uses ideas expressed by pupils, praises or encourages their behavior, and makes constructive reactions to their attitudes or feelings. He is initiating his own will and making use of his authority whenever he expresses his own ideas, gives directions with the expectation of compliance, or becomes critical of pupil behavior.

We usually find, but not always, a complementary and logical relationship between the initiative-response balance of teacher statements and the same balance expressed by the pupils. An above average use of Categories 5, 6, and 7 is more likely to be associated with a higher incidence of Category 8. The above average use of 1, 2, and 3 is more likely to be associated with Category 9. What is meant by "above average" will become clear in subsequent chapters, but a relatively small shift in the tallies located in 1, 2, and 3 versus 5, 6, and 7—say 10 percent—appears to have a consistent and logical effect on the behavior and perceptions of the pupils. The importance of this balance will be supported in subsequent chapters by showing that it can be used to predict how much subject matter pupils learn and their general attitudes— toward the teacher and the class activities—at levels which are higher than would be expected by chance. Such evidence indicates that the teacher's verbal communication pattern is associated with pupil learning and pupil attitudes toward learning.

As you might expect, the balance of initiation and response for the teacher, as well as the pupils, will vary from one learning activity to the next, even with the same class. It will also vary according to the teacher's preferred style of instruction, the subject matter being taught, the age and maturity of the pupils, and various other characteristics of the classroom learning situation. Tracing this variation provides us with knowledge about teaching behavior and about relationships between what a teacher does and how pupils react.

By way of summary, then, every category system has a purpose, and this category system can be used to study the balance between initiation and response. With seven categories of teacher talk, and only two for pupil talk, more information is provided about the teacher, and therefore how teacher statements influence this balance can be studied with this particular set of categories. A different category system would be needed in order to investigate other problems of teaching and learning, for example, how different pupil reactions affect class learning.

In order to refer efficiently to these ten categories and the associated procedures, described in the next section, the acronym FIAC (Flanders Interaction Analysis Categories) is used on subsequent pages.

THE PROCEDURE OF OBSERVATION

An observer sits in the classroom in the best position to hear and see the participants. Almost as often as possible, he decides which category best represents the communication events just completed. He then writes down this category number while he simultaneously assesses the continuing communication. Observation continues at a rate of 20 to 25 tallies per minute, *keeping the tempo as steady as possible*. This usually works out to about one tally every 3 seconds. There is nothing magical about a 3-second period. An experienced observer, after considerable practice, tends to classify at this rate with this particular category system. A gifted observer might settle down to a faster rate, after considerable experience, and another category system might force a slower rate, even for a gifted observer. Having a regular tempo is much more important than achieving a particular rate because most conclusions depend on rate consistency, not on speed. For example, a comparison between two categories in one observation or the same category in two different observations is possible only when the tempo of coding is the same for both categories and for both observations, whether or not that tempo is one tally every 2, $2\frac{1}{2}$, 3, or $3\frac{1}{2}$ seconds. There is a tendency to increase the rate of coding during rapid interchanges, especially if rare events are occurring. Apparently, experienced observers hate to miss rare events, like Categories 1, 2, 7, and 9. On the other hand, during a long period of lecture, the observer may relax and inadvertently slow his tempo compared to periods of more rapid exchanges. No observer is a perfect metronome, but with experience two observers can train themselves to code at quite similar and regular rates.

Don't worry about tempo too soon. Accuracy in tempo should be emphasized only during the latter stages of training, sometime after the first 4 hours. A constant tempo usually will appear after several live classroom observations, and to be concerned about it prematurely is a waste of time.

During practice on the initial exercises in this book, the arabic numbers which represent code symbols are each written down, one after the other, in a sequence which follows the statements that are being coded. This has the advantage of permitting a check of your work and deciding how your code symbol corresponds to the suggestions in the text. Record the practice exercises on an ordinary sheet of paper so that each answer space is numbered chronologically.

Recording procedures for live classroom observation, video or sound recordings, will require various printed forms, depending on what is to be done with the data. During practice observations designed to check your reliability with another observer, a histogram, on its side, such as the form shown in Table 2–2, may be most convenient. In other applications, an ordinary sheet of paper may be used. If you draw $\frac{1}{2}$-inch columns on yellow legal pads, there is often enough room for about 400 coded symbols to be written down in their original sequence, top to bottom, left to right. A zero is used for Category 10. It is also possible to use I.B.M. mark-sense cards in the classroom by marking with a soft pencil. These can be punched automatically in later processing. Forms which preserve the original sequence permit the tabulation of a matrix display which is described in Chapter 3. A form that can be used in microteaching, which usually consists of short 4- to 6-minute teaching segments, might be best recorded on a time line display; this is another form which is explained in Chapter 6. In automatic recording, which makes use of electronic equipment or the remote terminal of a shared-time computer, the observer uses a pushbutton device, similar to the base of a pushbutton telephone. This is by far the most convenient. In short, there are many different ways to record code symbols. Choose the best procedure for the task at hand.

TABLE 2–2
Tallying Hash Marks by Categories

Category Number		Completed Tally Marks Made by an Observer	Total Tallies	Percent
Teacher	1	|||	3	0.8
	2	|||||		6	2.5
	3	||||| ||||| ||	12	5.0
	4	||||| ||||| ||||| ||||| ||	22	9.2
	5	||||| ||||| ||||| ||||| ||||| ||||| ||||| ||||| ||||| ||||| ||||| ||||| ||||| ||||| ||||| ||||| ||||| ||||| ||||| ||||| ||||| ||||| ||||| ||||| ||||| |||||	130	54.2
	6	||||| ||||| |||||		16	6.7
	7	||||	4	1.6
Pupils	8	||||| ||||| ||||| ||||| ||	22	9.2
	9	||||| ||||| ||	12	5.0
Silence	10	||||| ||||| ||||	14	5.8
		Total	240	100.0

PRACTICE IN DISTINGUISHING CATEGORIES

Now it is time to go to work. If you have not already done so, memorize the code symbols which are associated with the key words of the categories.

Assignment One: Turn to Table 2–1 and memorize the 10 code symbols associated with each category. Don't ask yourself, what is 7?, then give the key word "criticism." Memorize in the reverse direction by covering the numbers. In observation the event occurs first, is then coded, and then recorded.

What follows is designed to elicit your participation. There will be questions which you are to answer. Since all questions are answered immediately, in the sentences which follow, you will have to discipline yourself to look elsewhere as you formulate your answers; try looking at the ceiling or close your eyes as if lost in thought, but don't fall asleep! Should you find the questions too easy at first, take heart, they will become more difficult as you proceed. Perhaps your learning is helped by writing things down. If so, get some paper and a pencil now, so you can make notes and respond to questions in written form.

Assignment Two: Read the rest of this section, stopping to answer questions as you proceed.

In order to code verbal interaction you must be in a situation in which it is likely to occur. This may sound silly, but in a classroom time periods of considerable length often occur during which the 10 categories would not be useful and therefore should not be used. For example, there may be very little talk as the pupils work on assignments at their desks. The 10 categories are also of very little use during long periods of sustained teacher lecturing. Given an appropriate setting, the first assumption is that only three conditions can exist, either the teacher is talking, the pupils are talking, or there is silence or confusion. There are certain code numbers, which you have already learned, which apply to each of these three conditions.

1) When the teacher is talking, you select a code number from —— to ——.
2) When a pupil is talking, you select either —— or ——.
3) Silence or confusion requires the code number ——.

Whenever the teacher is talking, use a number from 1 to 7, for pupils 8 or 9, and for silence or confusion is coded the number 10, or just write zero.

In assessing the balance of initiation and response, when the teacher is talking, certain code numbers refer to response and others to initiation.

4) When the teacher statements respond to feelings or attitudes, encourage or make use of pupil ideas, the three code numbers are ——.

5) *When teacher statements initiate, the three code numbers used are* ——.

6) *Pupil statements in response to the teacher are coded by the number* ——.

7) *Pupil statements showing initiation are coded with the number* ——.

When the teacher is talking, the response categories are numbers 1, 2, and 3, and the initiation categories are 5, 6, and 7. Pupil responses are coded with an 8, and pupil initiation with a 9.

The observer's perception of the initiation-response balance between the teacher and the pupils can and should enter into his judgment while coding. The most common state of affairs occurs when the teacher initiates and the pupils respond. Thus, we expect more 5's, 6's, 7's, and 8's, compared with 1's, 2's, 3's, and 9's. When these latter numbers are used with discretion, decoding seems to be more valid.

In order for the reader to become more familiar with the category meanings, each is discussed in the material that follows. Keep in mind that the context of the class discussion is missing and this will make your task more difficult. The happy thought, of course, is that when you code in a classroom, it will be easier because of the context.

CATEGORY 1

Category 1 consists of teacher statements which accept and clarify an attitude or the feeling tone of a pupil in a nonthreatening manner. The feelings may be positive or negative. Predicting or recalling feelings are included. These are relatively rare and infrequent teacher statements. Perhaps this is because most persons in our culture, both teachers and pupils, tend to suppress both positive and negative emotional reactions in the classroom. The cliche, "let's not get emotional about this!," illustrates the point. Another reason for the low incidence of Category 1 is the use of a special rule. The rule requires that the teacher literally names or otherwise identifies the emotion or feeling before the observer can code using "1." How would you classify these teacher statements?

8) *"My! But this class seems excited! Tell me what happened on the playground during recess."*

9) *(The teacher sees the class is excited after recess.) "This would be a good time, I think, for us all to put our heads down on the desks and be very, very quiet for about one minute."*

10) *"My! But this class seems excited! I'm going to ask you all to put your heads down on your desks for about one minute."*

The statement in item (8) can be coded with a 1 because the emotion or attitude is cited, the teacher offers no value judgment, and responds to excitement by making a constructive response. With this neutral approach, the teacher may be able to help the class discuss excitement more objectively. Is it appropriate and fun on the playground? Should it be completely absent in the classroom? How is it expressed in the classroom? On the playground? And so on. In statement (9) the teacher is responding to the same symptoms, but does not name the emotion in her speech, and merely gives a direction; this would be coded 6. By using this initiation, the teacher seems to be saying: "This class is too excited to work as a group. It is my job to take some appropriate action without taking time to explain it." In item (10) the two statements are combined, the teacher acknowledges the emotion by naming it and takes the initiative of giving a direction. One alternative is to code both phrases, i.e., first write down a 1 which is then followed by a 6. This is probably the preferred way since a rare event, like 1, is recorded whenever possible.

CATEGORY 2

Praise and encouragement are statements which carry the value judgment of approval. To look directly at a boy or girl and nod your head while saying, "Um hm"—with the proper inflection—is to communicate to the pupil that he is on the right track and the teacher would like him to produce more of the same. A distinction between Categories 2 and 1 is that in the latter there is an element of objective diagnosis which is missing in Category 2. Both categories are used for statements which have overtones of warmth and friendliness, but Category 2 adds teacher approval as well.

Teachers have internalized so thoroughly the notion that giving approval is a reward and that it is a much better method of control than punishment, that they have many related superficial verbal habits. Exclamations such as "Right!," "Good!," "OK!," and similar expressions are often expressed automatically as soon as most pupil statements terminate. Genuine praise can usually be separated from superficial verbal habits. Pupils probably ignore the latter as a result of excessive use. Genuine praise often takes longer than 3 seconds to express so that the observer records more than one code symbol. Be sure and record more than one 2 when extended praise is given by a teacher. Here are some examples which you can code that are somewhat longer; each will require three or four code symbols. How would you record these statements?

11) T: "George, have you the answer to problem eight?"
    S: "Yes. It is 5286 yards."
    T: "Right. Mary, will you take number nine?"
12) T: "George, have you the answer to problem eight?"
    S: "Yes. It is 5286 yards."

> T: "Good for you! You remembered to convert feet to yards didn't you? Mary, will you . . ."

Both of these sequences begin with a teacher question and pupil response. Thus your first two code symbols will be 4 and then 8. In (11) you have to decide whether to insert a 2, so that it is coded 4, 8, 2, 4, or whether to ignore the very short praise word and record 4, 8, 4. You can resolve this issue by asking this question, "After observing several teachers on several occasions, do I want to distinguish situations in which single praise words were used from situations in which they were not used?" If the answer is yes, then you have to decide how this is to be done. One way is to insert a single 2 in order to represent single praise words. However, tempo also enters in and you may not have time to record a single 2 every time a teacher uses such words. Letting these short words slip by uncoded part of the time may be a good idea when such words are merely verbal habits. In the second sequence, the teacher not only gives praise, but he suggests one reason for praising George's answer. The teacher is saying, in effect, "George, that is a good job *because* you had to be careful to convert feet into yards." Short praise expressions ignore the "because" extensions. You can code this difference by recording a 4, 8, 2, 2 in the case of (12).

CATEGORY 3

A teacher can respond to the ideas pupils express by (a) acknowledging the pupil's idea by repeating the nouns and logical connectives just expressed; (b) modifying the idea, rephrasing it, or conceptualizing it in the teacher's own words; (c) applying the idea, using it to reach an inference or taking the next step in a logical analysis of a problem; (d) comparing the ideas, drawing a relationship between the pupil's idea and one expressed earlier by either pupil or teacher; and (e) summarizing what was said by a pupil or a group of pupils. In the FIAC system all of these different teacher responses are included in Category 3. However, as one proceeds from responses (a) to (e) above, it is highly probable that more elapsed time would be required, the farther down the list one goes. Thus, the same issues arise with Category 3 that were just discussed in the Category 2 section. Because more time is involved, two or more coded 3's are often used with teacher responses like (b) through (e) which distinguishes them from the more superficial (a) response.

You will discover, when you have a chance to read the results of research using interaction analysis, that the incidence of Category 3 appears to be associated with above average classroom measures of both content achievement and positive pupil attitudes towards schoolwork and the teacher. Conservative and restrained use of this category by an observer should enhance its diagnostic utility. Category 3 is used, most frequently, when the cognitive orientation of the teacher incorporates the ideas expressed by the pupils. When there are many more 3's in the profile of one observation, compared with another, the appropriate inference is that the higher incidence of 3's indicates that the teacher attended to pupil ideas and integrated them into the classroom discourse through his own active response statements. In this way the pupils are encouraged to take the initiative so there can be more teacher response.

Here are some illustrations of Category 3 statements set in the context of class discussion. Try your hand at coding them.

13) S: *"The rain on the desert would make many plants grow."*

 T: *"Mary thinks plants would grow because of the rain. Would you agree or disagree, Jerry?"*

14) S: *"The rain on the desert would make many plants grow."*

 T: *"OK, that's one suggestion, who has another?"*

15) S: *"People would come to live on the desert and there would be cities and everything."*

 T: *"Jane thinks that fertility of the soil is necessary to support a high concentration of people."*

In Item (13) the teacher acknowledges Mary's statement and refers it to another pupil to support, modify, or refute. This would be coded 3, since the teacher is attending to pupil ideas and asking questions based on pupil ideas. Notice that a *teacher question based on pupil ideas is not coded 4.* Item (14) is much more difficult to code, since it comes very close to rejecting rather than using a pupil idea. For example, should a teacher continue to use this response, it seems quite probable that after about the third or fourth time the pupils would talk less enthusiastically. On the other hand, if it was agreed that many ideas were to be suggested in a kind of brainstorming pattern, and if each idea were being written on the blackboard, then the teacher's response in (14) might be seen by most of the pupils as acceptance and utilization of their ideas. As it stands this statement should probably be classified with a 4.*

Item (15) raises a whole host of problems concerned with synonyms, paraphrase, abstracting, and subtle changes of meaning. In (15) Jane did not say what the teacher said Jane said. Jane's ideas were translated by the teacher into his own terms, presumably in order to push toward certain

---

*This is a good example to show how paraphrasing sometimes helps in coding statements. If you think that the proper paraphrase of the teacher statement in item (14) is, "Mary talks too much; I'll ignore her statement and ask somebody else," then you might code it 7. If it sounds like, "Somebody else, give me a suggestion," then you might code it 6. If it was more like, "Now that we have one, who has another suggestion," then you might code it 4. And so on.

preferred concepts which the teacher has in mind. The issue is whether the teacher is introducing a new idea, which would be coded 5, or whether the teacher is building on Jane's idea, which would be coded 3. Based only on the evidence at hand, it looks like too big a leap in abstraction and the teacher statement could be coded as a 5. To give another example, suppose a teacher asks about the causes of World War II. A list of events is given by one student, and the teacher refers to these events by using the word "provocations," a word that the pupil did not use. How this is to be coded will depend on the circumstances, but the discussion does suggest a criterion. When a teacher makes use of an idea in such a way that you think the pupil would no longer recognize it as the one he suggested, do not use Category 3. It may well be that one of the more important functions of teaching is *to help* youngsters so that they cluster their own ideas into a set, define the characteristics of that set, and then give it a label, thereby learning the power and efficiency of abstracting by actual practice. When the teacher takes over this function, a most teachable moment may have been lost, even though useful new concepts have been introduced.

CATEGORY 4

Questions asked by a teacher which serve to move the conversation to a next step, to introduce a new problem element, and involve ideas which the teacher thinks are important, are coded 4. A second requirement is that the teacher acts as if he expects an answer.

Questions are usually fairly easy to recognize, even when they are open. For example, "Who has another idea he would like to add?" Not all questions are classified in Category 4, however. See item (13), and then consider the following questions.

16) *"Jack, would you please close the window?"*
17) *(Holding up John's paper) "Has anyone ever seen an essay so well written and so well organized?"*
18) *"Didn't you hear me say, 'stop talking!' Are you deaf?"*
19) *"If you become very excited, how do you think it will affect your performance?"*

In statement (16) the teacher expects compliance to a command, and this would be coded 6. The intent of the teacher in (17) is to give praise, and this would be coded 2. You probably had no trouble coding (18) as criticism, Category 7. And as you could guess from earlier discussions, (19) is coded as 1.

One of the most common problems discussed during observer training is whether Category 4 is used in the following situation. The pupils are eagerly expressing their own ideas, coded in Category 9, and the teacher decides who can talk next by either pointing his finger, or nodding his head, or simply calling out names, such as "John," "Jennifer," "Jackie," and so on. How are these teacher actions or statements to be coded? We might begin by noting that there is no right or wrong answer in an absolute sense. Consistency in observation procedure, however, is essential to systematic decoding, so some agreement must be reached concerning the coding of these teacher actions. Whatever convention is finally adopted, it should help an observer record the main features of the interaction with minimum distortion. In the situation we are discussing, the major pattern consists of pupil initiation, which will be recorded by the high incidence of Category 9. The use of Categories 5 and 6 for relatively inconsequential teacher behavior is rejected as inconsistent with the main pattern of the interaction. We are left to choose from 1, 2, 3, 4, or 10. Ten is not a good choice, since the teacher is acting or talking, and 10 denotes the opposite. One is not a good choice, since the affective aspects of interaction are not involved. A logical argument in favor of each of the three remaining alternatives can be advanced, but not one of these is clearly compelling. Aside from inventing a new category, there is really no good solution. One of the better ground rules we have used is to ignore the teacher and record the series of 9's which indicated pupil initiated talk. The possibility of inserting a 10 between one pupil speaker and the next may be satisfactory for special projects, but can hardly be recommended as a general policy, since this would confuse the interpretation of Category 10. This discussion illustrates, in brief outline, the sequence which a team of observers might follow in order to establish and maintain higher reliability. Various alternatives are considered, and one is chosen as a ground rule for that team on that particular project.

Teacher questions can be coded in any one of the seven teacher categories: in Category 1 if they are objective, nonthreatening inquiries involving attitudes or emotions and designate the feeling or emotion; in Category 2 if they are intended to praise; in 3 if they are based on ideas previously expressed by pupils; in 5 if they are categorical and no answer is expected; in 6 if they are directions; and in 7 if they are critical, or designed to catch pupils who are daydreaming. Usually the questions which are coded 4 are genuine invitations to participate. Closed and narrow questions curtail the freedom of pupil participation, while the open and broad questions expand this freedom. There is quite a difference between (a) "What is the name of the man I'm thinking of?" and (b) "Would anyone care to add anything to what has been said?" In the FIAC system both broad and narrow questions are coded with a 4. For this reason, it is difficult to assign Category 4 to a pattern of teacher response or to a pattern of teacher initiation.

CATEGORY 5

Lecturing, expressing opinions, giving facts, interjecting thoughts, and off-hand comments are all classified in this category. In a way, it is sort of a catchall for teacher statements, primarily because it usually has the highest frequency, and an incorrect tally, more or less, would be least likely to distort the teacher's profile, compared to some other teacher category.

Among experienced observers, there seem to be three issues that arise in connection with Category 5. First, the teacher responds to and makes use of an idea expressed by a pupil (coded 3) and then in clever and ingenious ways interjects his own ideas as he builds on those expressed by the pupil (when do you change to Category 5?). Second, the teacher starts to ask a long and involved question (coded 4) but explains the question for a while before returning to finish it (when do you shift in and out of 5?). Third, the teacher is giving directions (coded 6) and seeks to explain the assignment, how it is to be done, opinions about it, and so on (when do you shift to 5 and back to 6?). Each of these will be discussed in turn, but it might be well to point out that there is no sure way to handle these problems, and they cause a residual lack of reliability among observers.

What usually happens in the 3 to 5 shift is that such clever teachers are often quite skillful in maintaining a teacher response pattern. Thus, as the teacher begins to shift to his own ideas, a short period of doubt occurs during which the observer continues to code in Category 3. After a few Category 3 tallies, he then shifts to 5. If the teacher then returns to Category 3, a period of doubt again occurs, as before, only this adds additional coded 5's and tends to compensate for the earlier extra 3's. Thus, when the observer makes his shift, following those of the teacher, the errors tend to cancel in the long run. Real skill in making the 3 to 5 shift is possible only with experience, when most of the procedures are automatic, and the observer can really listen to pupil statements. Unless you know what a pupil said, you cannot code the 3 to 5 shift accurately.

In general, observers report less trouble in distinguishing questions from lecture, compared with detecting a clever 3 to 5 shift. When a teacher asks an involved question, it is desirable to code this consistently with 4's if this can be done with reasonable confidence. For example, "Now if it is true that Minnesota iron ore reserves are becoming depleted, and if they fail to pass a sales tax, and if . . . , then how will the state government maintain its income?" The observer should avoid shifting to 5 for statements about the logical conditions or premises on which a question is based. When you discover that what you thought was going to be a question is now a lecture, make the shift. Often a teacher will give you clues, such as interrupting his own question.

The shift from 6 to 5 and back again would be equally difficult if content and grammar were the only clues available. However, long, extended directions are often symptoms of teacher domination and the extended use of Category 6 helps to record this. Excessive initiation is a teaching behavior which is relatively easy to recognize and it is also a relatively persistent pattern which teachers repeat. It is important, in such circumstances, to code such explanation with a 6 in order to reflect this aspect of teaching behavior. Shift to 5 only when there is evidence that the statements are unrelated to the expected overt compliance that is a part of giving directions.

CATEGORIES 6 AND 7

Both of these categories are used for statements which are intended to produce compliance. Such statements tend to enhance the authority of the teacher, and the *excessive* use of this kind of initiation will slowly, but surely, create such high dependence on the teacher that pupils become unable to do their schoolwork except under direct teacher supervision. How would you code these examples?

20) *"Today we are going to begin our unit on Argentina."*
21) *"Please take out your geography books and turn to page 67."*
22) *"Perhaps you would find it easier if you placed all these sentences (pointing to pupil's paper) in an 'Introduction.'"*
23) *"One of your troubles is that you forgot to follow directions."*
24) *"The only papers I'll accept are those written neatly and in ink."*
25) *"I want you to think about that for a little while."*

The observer's problem with statement (20) is to determine whether or not compliance will occur as a result of the statement. If it is merely an announcement, code it 5; if there is compliance, code it 6. Statement (21) is a straightforward Category 6. Statement (22), as it stands, could be considered to have an element of doubt. For example, suppose it was preceded by a pupil statement, "I'm having trouble with the beginning and I can't figure out what to do with these sentences; they seem important, but they don't fit." Now the teacher statement could be coded Category 3. As it stands, it sounds like an opinion and could be coded 5. There would have to be special circumstances present before (22) would be classified as 6 or 7. Statement (23) in most instances is a straightforward 7, since the implication is that the pupil should have been doing something, but isn't. Incidently, it is not a very helpful statement, since it gives only a vague clue about what the pupil should do next. Item (24) could be either 6 or 7, depending on what took place earlier. When recrimination seems to be present, use Category 7. Statement (25) presents the observer with the problem of deciding whether a teacher direction should be coded 6 when it is impossible for the observer to determine whether or not compliance occurred. About the only judgment to be made is to code it 6 when you think the teacher thinks he is telling a pupil to do something.

Categories 6 and 7 are used to indicate close supervision and direction by the teacher. Both categories help to establish a true teacher initiation-pupil response pattern. Even questions, especially during restricted, teacher directed drill can be coded 6. Here is another instance in which the paraphrase test is helpful. When a teacher says, "Marie, three threes?" and you can paraphrase this to mean, "Marie, I now want you to multiply 3 × 3 and tell me your answer," then you are justified in using Category 6.

CATEGORIES 8 AND 9

Pupil talk is coded with these two categories. There are several dimensions which help to separate response from initiation. Consider predictability of the answer, for example:

26) T: *"What is meant by 'county seat'?"*
   S: *"It is the place where the county government exists."*
27) T: *"What did you find most interesting about this unit on governmental systems?"*
   S: *"I thought the way the lobbyists operate was very interesting."*

Just from knowing the question in (26), you can predict that a correct answer will be a definition which should refer to "county seat." Question (27) is more open and even though it calls for an opinion, so many different answers could be given that the pupil has the opportunity to take some initiative. Thus in (26) you would code the answer 8, and in (27) 9. It is helpful to think of teacher questions along a continuum of narrow to broad and use these impressions as cues for *anticipating* subsequent pupil statements.

Another dimension which enters into separating 8's from 9's is the voluntary embellishment or enlargement of a topic. Here, the pupil's answer provides more information than was required by the question. How would you code this response?

28) T: *"Bill, did your family go camping this summer too?"*
   S: *"Yes, we went camping up in the northern part of the state, and you should have seen what happened the night a bear came prowling around the garbage cans!"*

The sequence of code symbols to record all statements in (28) would be 4, 8, and then 9. A shift from 8 to 9 is more common when pupils feel free to express their ideas. First the teacher's question is answered, then the pupil embellishes the answer with additional information.

Another aspect of identifying 8's and 9's is the contrast of indifference or conformity versus the expression of will through independent judgment.

Consider the following:

29) T: *"Do you think we should plan a picnic?"*
   S: *"Oh, I dunno. It's OK with me, I guess."*
   (on the other hand, another pupil might say)
30) S: *"Well, we've had several picnics and the weather is beginning to get worse. I think we should plan something interesting that we can do inside."*

The code sequence in (29) would be 4, 8, but in (30) the pupil statement reflects an independent judgment and can be coded 9.

Another dimension which separates 8's from 9's is the element of creativity and higher mental processes compared with noncreative and lower mental processes. However, a pupil statement can sound creative when it is merely repeated from memory. This is equally true of generalizations, theorizing, the interpretation of data, and synthesizing. Consider these statements.

   T: *"What makes you think that our population has more than doubled during this period?"*
31) S: *"It shows it on that graph in our book, ah, here on page 67."*
   T: *"What about the chart? What part supports your argument?"*
32) S: *"Well, it says in the book that the chart shows that the population has more than doubled."*
   T: *"OK, thank you, Jim. Jane, what do you think?"*
33) S: *"Well, the bars in the chart show that the population is doubled. You can tell by the height. But it isn't clear where the author got his figures, so we really don't know whether to believe the graph or not."*

The pupil responses in (31) and (32) reflect dependence on the teacher's questions and on the authority of the book, in spite of the efforts of the teacher to solicit the pupil's own opinion and interpretation. Only in the last part of (33) is there evidence to support the coding of pupil initiation.

Distinguishing between 8's and 9's depends, somewhat, on the purposes of the observation. Usually, teachers and observers would like to infer, from the proportion of 9's compared to all pupil talk something about the freedom of pupils to express their own ideas, to suggest their own approach to a problem, and to develop their own explanations or theories. This may be accomplished more effectively when the observer is conservative in his use of 9. For example, not only will he use 8's when the evidence is clear, but he will also use 8 for all cases in which there is some reasonable doubt about 9. In this way, he reserves 9 for those cases in which he is confident.

High reliability between observers in the use of 8 and 9 requires additional training, fairly constant communication among observers, and usually live observation settings. Distinguishing between 8's and 9's from a voice tape recording is often very difficult, if not impossible.

One of the weaknesses of the FIAC system is that Category 9 is the only code symbol which can be used for off-target remarks by pupils, counter-dependent statements, and resistance to compliance. That is, both cooperative as well as uncooperative initiation falls into the same category. The consequences of this difficulty will be discussed in greater detail in those sections which deal with the interpretation of data.

CATEGORY 10

When there is a pause in classroom communication or when there is noise and confusion, Category 10 is used. There is very little point in recording a series of 10's for longer than 1 or 2 minutes. This category system of interaction analysis is intended for situations in which a verbal interchange exists between the teacher and pupils or in which such an exchange is imminent. The observer can note the time that this exchange starts and usually can tell when it ends, at which time he also jots down the time. When an interchange no longer is expected, the observer simply stops coding.

Another shortcoming of Category 10 is that nonproductive confusion is not distinguished from thoughtful analysis and other productive pauses. Should this aspect of classroom interaction be of interest in a particular project, an eleventh category should be added, defined, and then used in order to make distinctions about silence that are of interest to the teacher and observer. Just as in the case of resistance in Category 9, it is possible to make fairly good guesses about silence which is nonproductive compared with more productive silence.

It may help to remind ourselves that the FIAC system was not designed to answer detailed questions about pupil talk and different kinds of silences. Newer systems to be described in later chapters can make more distinctions in this kind of classroom communication by providing the necessary categories. By devoting only two of 10 categories to pupil talk, and one to silence, the inferences about pupil talk and silence are limited.

SUMMARY AND GROUND RULES

Having concerned ourselves with the 10 categories, it is now time to summarize some of the concepts which were most important and to establish certain ground rules which become conventions for coding.

The notion of *reasonable doubt* was used at several points in the discussion of difficult classifications. We can establish the ground rule that when doubt exists, *an observer will classify doubtful statements into categories which are consistent with the prevailing balance of teacher initiation or teacher response.*

The experienced observer is sensitive to the balance of teacher initiation and response that develops from the beginning of an observation. He purposely lets the existing balance influence his doubtful classifications according to the above ground rule. This rule is followed if, and only if, there is an element of doubt. Whenever there is clear evidence, the statement is always coded according to the category definitions.

34) *A teacher has been lecturing about New Zealand geography, and then says, "Some of you have been asking about the South Island alps. . . ."*

Would you code this 3 or 5? There are several elements of doubt. The teacher is making an assertion which the observer in most instances cannot verify. Notice, also, that no pupil was named and the particular aspect of the South Island alps which was questioned is not clear. Yet the teacher is making a reference to an element of the classroom discourse which was introduced earlier by pupils. Because this statement occurs within a pattern of teacher initiation and pupil response, the experienced observer would tend to classify the statement 5.

To illustrate how the teacher statement in (34) might be a signal that the teacher is shifting the initiation-response balance, it is conceivable that his total statement might have been, "Some of you have been asking about the South Island alps. Mary, I believe you wanted to know how high this ridge of mountains was. Can anyone answer Mary's question?" At this point in the conversation, there is clear evidence for Category 3, and the ground rule does not apply since there is no longer any doubt.

Suppose, for example, a teacher has been reacting to Jim's proposed solution to a problem during math, namely, that he was certain that a steamship had travelled 100 miles because it was going 20 miles per hour for a period of 5 hours. How would you code the following teacher statements?

35) *"Let me show you an interesting way to multiply by five. Just divide by two and add a zero to the quotient."*

36) *"Jim must have remembered that distance equals rate of speed times the elapsed time, keeping the units straight, of course."*

37) *"Well, if Jim is right and it only took 5 hours, then what would happen if the ship was forced to travel at half speed?"*

In statement (35) the teacher chose to introduce a new method of multiplication at a moment which he thought was appropriate because of Jim's answer. Since this is a new element, introduced by the teacher, an experienced observer would probably code it 5. In statement (36) the teacher asserts that Jim probably thought about the problem in a particular way. If this assertion is valid, then the teacher is indeed responding, but if the assertion is false, then the teacher is introducing the idea. Coding statement (36) with a 3 would be justified primarily on the basis of the teacher's previous response pattern. There would be clear evidence for a 3 if the teacher was repeating what Jim said in order to explain how he arrived at an answer. Statement (37) cannot be coded properly out of context. The first part shows clear evidence of 3. The second part looks as if it is a clear 4. An experienced observer would probably write down first a 3 and then a 4.

A second ground rule involves maximizing information by making a special effort to record events which occur infrequently. Normally Categories 4, 5, and 8 are the most frequently occurring categories. The rule might be stated, *be sure and record events which are numerically most distant from Category 5, except Category 10.* Stated another way, 1 is preferred to 2, which is preferred to 3, which is preferred to 4, which is preferred to 5; and 7 is preferred to 6, which is preferred to 5; and 9 is preferred to 8, although only when the evidence is clear that two or more code symbols could be used.

For teacher statements this second ground rule comes into effect after the first ground rule. In cases of doubt, the first ground rule helps in selecting a category when the choice is among 1, 2, and 3 versus 5, 6, and 7. The second ground rule helps in making a choice among the three response categories *or* among the three initiation categories. The first ground rule applies to teacher statements in which there is a reasonable element of doubt. The second ground rule is helpful when the observer wonders whether to add a second tally during a 3-second period by speeding up the tempo of tallying in order to record rare events. When speeding the tempo is undesirable, the second ground rule suggests which of two categories to record.

This second ground rule must be applied with care when dealing with pupil statements. You will recall that in the discussion of Categories 8 and 9, you were admonished to use 9 only when the evidence was clear and to use 8 in cases of doubt. This policy still holds, and so the second ground rule applies to pupil statements only when additional tallies are under consideration and not when the issue is one of doubt.

The notion that statements are classified into their regular categories when the evidence is clear means that ground rules do not apply under such circumstances.

Since classroom interaction is so complex and involves many nuances, category definitions, ground rules, and their explanations can never completely cover all the classification problems that will arise. Training can anticipate problems and suggest guidelines, but with experience the observer will confront problems which become legitimate exceptions. There is a rationale or model of reasoning which can be used when confronted with difficult categorization problems. This line of reasoning takes into consideration the entire encoding and decoding process. After some experience in observation has been obtained, you are urged to ask yourself, when confronted with a difficult classification, "What will be the consequences of one or another alternative on the *decoding process*?" In effect this question suggests that difficult classification problems can be solved by working backwards. First, ask yourself what kind of decoding interpretations you intend to make when one category is higher in frequency than another. For example, when 6 is higher than average, you may wish to infer that the teacher gave many directions and gave the observer the impression of closely supervising all aspects of classroom learning. Now, if you have a classification problem which involves a possible 6, think of the inferences you will make and that may help in a specific coding problem. Such analyses often lead to creating special categories for one particular discussion, a topic which is discussed in Chapter 6.

After you are in your third or fourth hour of coding training, including live observations, it may be helpful to read, once again, the material about discriminating among the categories which started on page 39.

SUMMARY

Now that you have completed your introduction to the nature of the categories, the time has come for more practice in coding classroom interaction. Chapter 3 contains some typescripts of classroom recordings which is one way you can start, but alone it is not the best way. Practice in coding is best carried out in a classroom during those periods when the pupils have an opportunity to talk with the teacher. A magnetic voice recording which is very clear is probably the next best during the initial efforts to use this 10-category system. Video recording, even when it has a good sound track, may be too distracting when you are first starting, but more helpful in the later stages when more subtle discriminations can be made. Certain problems, like shifting between Categories 3 and 5 or making distinctions between Categories 8 and 9, are best resolved in live classroom observation. Chapter 3 can give you a start, but skill in coding depends much more on your own initiative and your desire to persist until you have achieved a sense of confidence through experience.

Keep in mind that there are other chapters in the book which will introduce you to decoding, to procedures for displaying data, to more complicated and flexible category systems. In short, much work lies ahead.

Chapter Three

RECORDING AND ELEMENTARY
TABULATING PROCEDURES

OVERVIEW

Ready to work? The first section contains three practice exercises to gain experience in coding; the second section includes a discussion of forms and materials for live classroom observation; and the third section is concerned with elementary tabulating procedures.

THREE EPISODES

Episode A provides practice in the use of Categories 4, 5, 6, 8, and 10. Episode B adds Categories 3 and 9. Episode C provides practice for Categories 1, 2, and 7. These three typescripts are fiction, although they are based on voice recordings of class interaction. They have been rewritten in order to meet the requirements of progressive practice in coding and to make them much more concise than unabridged verbal interaction.

Before you start coding a typescript, locate a sheet of paper and provide numbered answer spaces for a total of 100 code responses. An example is shown in Table 3–1. A number in parentheses has been used to indicate points at which code judgments are to be made. The statement which *precedes* such a number is to be coded, not the statement which follows. Perhaps the material shown below will help as an example.

T:	Now what I'd like to have you do next is to take (28) the	6
	paper and write your name along the top edge. (29) ### (30)	6, 0
P:	Is this the way you want us to do it? # (31)	8
T:	Yes. We're going to use these papers for our new/ (32)	5
P:	I bet I know. We're going to use them for our art! (33)	9

The above excerpt makes use of "T" for teacher and "P" for pupil. It begins at the twenty-eighth code response and ends with the thirty-third. A 1-second silence is indicated by a # mark; ### indicates a continuous 3-second pause. The slash mark / is used to indicate that the speaker has been interrupted.

TABLE 3–1
Sample Answer Sheet

Number	Episode A B C	Number	Episode A B C	Number	Episode A B C	Number	Episode A B C
(1)	— — —	(26)	— — —	(51)	— — —	(76)	— — —
(2)	— — —	(27)	— — —	(52)	— — —	(77)	— — —
(3)	— — —	(28)	— — —	(53)	— — —	(78)	— — —
(4)	— — —	(29)	— — —	(54)	— — —	(79)	— — —
(5)	— — —	(30)	— — —	(55)	— — —	(80)	— — —
(6)	— — —	(31)	— — —	(56)	— — —	(81)	— — —
(7)	— — —	(32)	— — —	(57)	— — —	(82)	— — —
(8)	— — —	(33)	— — —	(58)	— — —	(83)	— — —
(9)	— — —	(34)	— — —	(59)	— — —	(84)	— — —
(10)	— — —	(35)	— — —	(60)	— — —	(85)	— — —
(11)	— — —	(36)	— — —	(61)	— — —	(86)	— — —
(12)	— — —	(37)	— — —	(62)	— — —	(87)	— — —
(13)	— — —	(38)	— — —	(63)	— — —	(88)	— — —
(14)	— — —	(39)	— — —	(64)	— — —	(89)	— — —
(15)	— — —	(40)	— — —	(65)	— — —	(90)	— — —
(16)	— — —	(41)	— — —	(66)	— — —	(91)	— — —
(17)	— — —	(42)	— — —	(67)	— — —	(92)	— — —
(18)	— — —	(43)	— — —	(68)	— — —	(93)	— — —
(19)	— — —	(44)	— — —	(69)	— — —	(94)	— — —
(20)	— — —	(45)	— — —	(70)	— — —	(95)	— — —
(21)	— — —	(46)	— — —	(71)	— — —	(96)	— — —
(22)	— — —	(47)	— — —	(72)	— — —	(97)	— — —
(23)	— — —	(48)	— — —	(73)	— — —	(98)	— — —
(24)	— — —	(49)	— — —	(74)	— — —	(99)	— — —
(25)	— — —	(50)		(75)		(100)	

The arabic numbers which designate code response points are in the text in parentheses. The written material in front of a number is to be judged in choosing a code symbol. The teacher statement, "Now what I'd like to have you do next ..." precedes number (28) and is coded with Category 6. Your method of response is to write down your code symbol answer as an arabic number beside the appropriate number on your answer sheet. Use 0 for 10 to save time. Be sure and keep these answer sheets because they will be used in some of the elementary tabulation and display problems to be found later in this chapter.

The correct response—or more accurately, the coding that I would recommend—is shown to the right of the statements. For example, 6 is on the line which contains serial number (28); 6 and 0 are the code responses for (29) and (30), respectively. You can cut a strip of paper so that it will just cover these suggested code symbols. You can then write down your own answers without copying. You can uncover the suggested code symbols by moving the strip of paper down the page in order to check your answers. Perhaps you would like to experiment with the rate of reinforcement by uncovering the answers after each line is completed, after five lines, ten, or wait until you finish the page. Perhaps the best plan is to check more often at first and then gradually increase the number of code symbols you record before checking.

After you are adjusted to the procedure, perhaps after you have finished Episode A, you should try to approach the live conditions of coding. In live conditions, interaction is continuous and leaves no time for pondering a particular code symbol. You can approach these conditions by forcing yourself into a rhythm: read the phrase before a serial number just once, pause only long enough to write down the first code symbol which comes to mind, then move on immediately to the next phrase. You are not interested in the errors that occur when you have as much time as you need; instead you want to study errors which result from making rapid judgments.

Let me emphasize, once again, that voice recordings and live classroom visits should comprise at least half of your practice time, during the first 4 hours of practice coding. Therefore, the three typescripts in this chapter are at best introductory. To break through the "sound barrier" into smooth, consistent coding, practice in live classrooms is essential.

Assignment One: Using your answer sheet and the procedures already described, proceed to code Episodes A, B, and C. Keep a copy of your code symbols for later use in this chapter.

EPISODE A

The setting of the first two episodes is in a junior high school mathematics class. The lesson, which occurs early in the school year, attempts to show pupils that letter symbols can be used to represent different things. A cluster of letters, even the letters in one's own name, can be used to order food and drink in a restaurant. The children have a picture of a short order soda fountain and a legend or list in which letters of the alphabet are used to designate particular dishes and drinks. This kind of lesson was used in an experimental mathematics book associated with one branch of "the new math."

The only code symbols used in Episode A are Categories 4, 5, 6, 8, and 10. The one exception is Category 3, which is used briefly after number (85).

T:	Today we are starting our new math books, (1) and I'd	5
	like to say just a few things about these books (2)	5
	before I pass them out. # You all know, (3) we're a	5
	lucky class because we'll have a chance to use (4)	5
	these books before anyone else does. You can see (5)	5

	this one I'm holding does not have a hard cover (6) and	5
	is lithographed or mimeographed, or something like	
	that. (7) It is not printed like most of the books that	5
	we use. (8) The people who wrote this book have some	5
	new ideas (9) about how to study math and we are one of	5
	several (10) classes that have been asked to try out this	5
	book and (11) see if it is any good. # (12) Here, take	5, 5
	these books, Jim, and pass them out (13) to these two	6
	rows. Jerry, please pass out the books for (14) these	6
	two rows, and Bill, please pass out the rest. (15)	6
	### (16) ### (17) Now, do you all have a book? (18)	0, 0, 4
P:	I need one. # (19)	8
T:	Please open your books and scan through them. (20)	6
	### (21) ### (22) Now turn to page 18 where you will	0, 0
	find a picture. (23) Bill, will you please read the	6
	description below the picture? (24) #	6
P:	(reading) "This is a short order restaurant with a	
	new system for (25) ordering what you wish to eat and	8
	drink. (26) Each item on the menu is designated by a	8
	letter. (27) For example, the letter "A" stands for an	8
	apple. On the last (28) day of school the students from	8
	high school (29) come in and order by using the letters	8
	in their name. (30) So if/	8
T:	Hold it there, just a minute. (31) Let's see if we all	6
	understand this. You order by asking for a letter. (32)	5
	What letter stands for a chocolate malt, Peter? (33)	4
P:	# It must be letter "L," I think. (34)	8
T:	How much do you have to pay for "L," Mary? (35)	4
P:	It says on the list that a chocolate malt costs 35¢. (36)	8
T:	OK. Now, Bill, what would you like to order (37) if you	4
	were in this store, say, something to drink? (38)	4
P:	I dunno, I guess maybe a coke. # (39)	8
T:	OK. How would you ask the waitress for it? (40)	4
P:	You'd have to ask for "P." (41)	8
T:	Bill, when you were reading earlier, it said you would	
	order (42) according to the letters in your name. # (43)	5, 5
	So what would you be ordering? # (44) ### (45)	4, 0

P:	You mean I should order B − I − L − L? (46)	8
T:	Sure, like the book said. What food goes with those	
	letters (47) #	4
P:	Bananas. # (48) And a hamburger. ## (49) And two	8, 8
	chocolate malts. # (50)	8
T:	Notice, class, when you have two letters in your name (51)	5
	which are the same, you double your order of that item. (52)	5
	Now I think we are beginning to understand how to order	
	in this restaurant. (53) What would you be able to order,	5
	Tom? (54)	4
P:	I get a hot fudge sundae, for "T"; # (55)* and a hot dog	8
	in a bun, for "O"; # (56)* and a raspberry milkshake for	8
	"M." # (57)*	8
T:	Now Bill and Tom, come up to the blackboard and show us	
	(58) how you would figure out how much it would cost. (59)	6, 6
	### (60) ### (61) Now while these two are up here, who	0, 0
	in the class has a really long name? (62)	4
P:	I do. I'm Jeanette; there are eight letters in my name. (63)	8
T:	Anyone have more than eight letters? ## (64) You think	4
	so, Marilyn, let's see, your name has only seven letters.	
	(65) What would Jeanette get, Marilyn, if she ordered her	5
	name? (66)	4
P:	For "J" she gets a hamburger with onions; (67) # and "E"	8
	is for a strawberry ice cream; (68) # and, ### (69) "A"	8, 0
	is for apple, and "N" is for french fries. (70) Then	8
	she still has two "E's" and two "T's," ah, (71) so that's	8
	two more strawberry ice creams and two hot fudge sundaes.	
	(72)	8
T:	Now we must learn to figure the cost. #(73) Let's see	5
	how Tom and Bill made out. (74) Tom please show us how	5
	to work out the cost of an order. (75)	6
P:	Well, 30¢ for the sundae, 20¢ for (76) the hot	8
	dog, and the raspberry milkshake costs 35¢. That's 85¢	
	altogether. (77)	8

---

*This is 8 and not 9 because Tom is using the legend in the book.

T:	You are next, Bill. #(78)	6
P:	Mine cost 10¢ for the bananas, 25¢ for the (79) hamburger	8
	without onions, and 35¢ each for two chocolate malts,	
	that's $1.05. (80)	8
T:	Now, suppose Bill had placed his figures in a different	
	order. (81) Suppose, for example, it was 35 + 35 + 10 + 25.	5
	(82) Would that be a different order than you used, Bill?	5
	(83)	4
P:	Yes. I had it 10 + 25 + 35 + 35. (84)	8
T:	What happens when we move these items around? Do we	
	get (85) the same answer or do we get a different answer?	4
	Mary? (86)	4
P:	You get the same answer. The sequence doesn't make any	
	difference. (87)	8
T:	Are you sure? Jerry what do you think? (88)	4
P:	I agree, the order doesn't make any difference. (89)	8
T:	Apparently Mary and Jerry think that the numbers could be	
	(90) in any order and you would still get the same answer.	3
	(91) You should remember that we were adding these num-	3
	bers (92) and not dividing, multiplying, or subtracting,	5
	just (93) adding. So far, in our study of this book,	5
	when numbers are added (94) it doesn't make any difference	5
	what the order is (95), which number we start with,	5
	which number we end with, (96) we will get the same	5
	answer. This book will have some (97) more to say about	5
	the order of adding numbers. (98) Please turn to page	5
	19, where there are some problems about the restaurant. (99)	6
	Start at the top and see how many you can do. (100)	6

Remember to save your answer sheet of coded statements which will be used later.

EPISODE B

This second episode is based on the same mathematics lesson. However, the addition of Categories 3 and 9 makes the pattern of interaction quite different. There is no intended implication that the pattern in either episode is superior or inferior. In fact, if you found yourself either criticizing or "second guessing" the teacher during your practice in Episode A, you are missing the point of this early practice. Instead of thinking about teaching strategies, you should be trying to speed up your coding and establish a steady rhythm.

If you have space on the old answer sheet, use it. Otherwise, find a new sheet of paper and number it to 100 so that you have space for the code symbols of Episode B. You may find it difficult to distinguish between Categories 3 and 5, as well as between 8 and 9. This is to be expected. Usually consistency in making these distinctions occurs nearer the 4-hour point of your practice and often requires your presence in a live classroom setting. Even with experienced observers, these two distinctions account for a high proportion of the "residual error" during observation. In short, you will always be making an error in at least one out of 10 code symbols, and when these two distinctions are involved, even more often.

T:	Today we start with some new math books. (1) Jerry, will	5
	you and Bill and Don please pass these books out (2) so	6
	that everyone has one? This is your own book so put your	
	name on it. (3) As soon as you have a copy, you can scan	6
	through it (4) because I'm going to ask you some questions	6
	about it in a moment. (5) ### (6) ### (7) Is this	6, 0, 0
	any different than the math books we usually have? (8)	4
	### (9)	0
P:	The printing is hard to read; it looks kinda crummy. (10)*	8
T:	Yes, that's true. It is harder to read, especially at	
	some spots. (11)	3
P:	It doesn't have stiff covers like most of our books. (12)*	8
	It just has a heavier piece of red paper at the front and	
	back. (13)*	8
T:	That's right, no hard covers. #(14)	3
P:	It looks like it was made out of regular size typing	
	paper. (15)*	8
T:	Yes. The type of print, the soft covers, and the size,	
	these (16) are all differences that you've noticed. (17)	3, 3
	This book is for us to try out, before it is printed like	

---

*Whether these pupil comments are 8 or 9 is a good question. The teacher's questions tend to be open, thus giving the pupils some degree of freedom, but the pupil responses could be predicted from previous teacher statements. That is, the pupils would comment about the book. When in doubt, use 8.

	a regular book. (18) We have to help find any mistakes or	5
	parts of the book (19) that are hard to understand. (20)	5, 5
	How do you think we can best get this job done? (21)	4
P:	Can we write in these books? (22) Because if we could, then	9
	we could make notes where it is hard to understand. (23)	9
T:	Yes, you can write in these books and mark points you don't	
	understand. (24)	3
P:	Well, maybe besides doing the assignments, we can talk (25)	9
	about how well the assignments are explained. (26) I mean	9
	the whole class can take the time, every now and then, (27)	9
	to talk about it and maybe have just one book marked up	
	(28) to show where more than one person agrees that some-	9
	thing is wrong. (29)	9
T:	In other words, Mary, you think the whole class (30) can	3
	discuss an assignment on the basis of their own marks, (31)	3
	but keep one class book to indicate spots where several	
	students found it difficult. (32) Maybe we could test your	3
	suggestion right now if we tried one exercise. (33) Turn to	3
	page 18, look at the picture of the restaurant, and read the	
	explanation below. (34) ### (35) ### (36) ### (37)	6, 0, 0, 0
	### (38) Jerry, what do you think this assignment is all	0
	about? (39)	4
P:	It is some kind of restaurant where you can get things to	
	eat and drink. (40) But I've been in restaurants before, and	8
	I never heard about these letters (41) for different things	9
	or this business of ordering by your own name. (42)	9
T:	Can anyone explain to Jerry how letters and names work? (43)	3
P:	Everything they have for sale is ordered by a letter. (44)	8
	Like "A" stands for apples. So if you order something, (45)	8
	you use a letter. I guess it is some special game (46) to	9
	order by using your name, just to see what you get. (47)	9
T:	Does anyone want to add something to this explanation? (48)	4
P:	Well, the examples all show the first name, but it isn't	
	(49) clear whether there is a rule about this. # (50)	9, 9
T:	That's true, it doesn't say you must use your first or your	
	(51) second name. I suggest we use our first names, and	3

	follow the examples. (52) But how would you use your first	5
	name to order? (53) Mary, how would you order if you	4
	played the game? (54)	4
P:	Well, with M—A—R—Y, for "M" I would order a raspberry (55)	8
	milkshake. For "A," I only get an apple. For "R," I get	
	a raspberry (56) sundae. And for "Y," I get a club	8
	sandwich. (57)	8
T:	Then to order M—A—R—Y, you think about each letter in (58)	3
	your name and for Mary you'll get what she just described. (59)	3
	Bob, with two 'B's" what would you order? (60)	4
P:	Can't I use Robert, that is my real first name, you know. (61)	9:
T:	Sure, I guess it depends on how hungry you are. (62)*	3
P:	Well, with Robert, I get a raspberry sundae, a hot dog, a	
	banana, (63) strawberry ice cream, #(64) another raspberry	8, 8
	sundae, and a hot fudge sundae. (65)	8
T:	Let's see who has the longest name, and then figure out	
	the cost. (66)†	4
P:	My name is Jeanette, which is eight letters. (67)	8
T:	Anyone with a longer name? (68) # No? Ok. Jack, please	4
	come to the blackboard and add the prices. (69) Jeanette,	6
	you read the order and the cost of each item for Jack. (70)	6
P:	OK. The "J" is for a hamburger with onions; that's 30¢.	
	(71) The "E" is for a strawberry ice cream; that's 20¢.	8
	(72) But I have three "E's," so I get three strawberry (73)	8, 8
	ice creams. The "A" is for an apple at 10¢. (74) The	8
	"N" is for french fries at 15¢. Now what's left? (75)	8
	Oh, yes. Two "T's," that's two hot fudge sundaes at 30¢	
	each. (76)	8
T:	How much would all that cost, Jack? (77)	4
P:	It comes to $1.75. #(78)	8
T:	Before you sit down, Jack, the prices Jeanette read and that	
	you wrote down (79) were in an order which was different than	5

---

*Could be a 2 for humor, or a 1 if real hunger was involved. Without additional information, 3 is about as good as any other code.
†The intent is to ask a question. Use paraphrase: Who has the longest name? How do you figure cost?

	(80) the way Jeanette spells her name. (81) Will this make any difference in the total cost? (82) ### (83)	5, 5 4, 0
P:	You mean the three "E's" in a row, each 20¢? (84)* It would add up the same, in any order. (85)	8 8
T:	Jack says that you can put these numbers in any order and get the same answer. (86) Can anyone figure out how to prove or disprove what Jack said? (87) Jerry?	3 3
P:	It has to be the same because the same numbers are involved. (88) I think you could even mix up the numbers (89) themselves and get the same answer. (90) For example, 30 + 15 is 45, but shift the 5 and 35 + 10 is still 45. (91)	9, 9 9 9
T:	Now, Jerry's theory is that not only can you rearrange (92) the numbers which you are adding, but you can (93) interchange numbers within the prices. (94) Are there any rules about changing numbers, or can you do it any old way? (95)	3 3 3 4
P:	Keep the dimes and cents separate when you change. (96) That way, the final list will have all the numbers (97) that the first list had and it has to add up the same. (98)	9 9 9
T:	Does a zero make any difference? ## (99)	4
P:	I'll have to think about that. (100)	9

Remember to save your answer sheet of coded statements for later use.

EPISODE C

The third episode is set in an elementary classroom at the fifth or sixth grade level. This self-contained classroom is currently the scene of a city planning project. A model of a city is being constructed on a large table. Pupils build models of buildings, streets, and rivers. The typescript will appear a bit unrealistic because it was intended to provide practice in using Categories 1, 2, and 7. The above average incidence of these categories tends to make the syntax awkward.

You will find more footnotes. One suggestion is to ignore them until you have finished the entire episode. Again, you will need a recording sheet that has room for 100 code symbols in serial order. Save your answer sheet for later use.

---

*True, the pupil is asking a question, but not all pupil questions need to be coded 9. Requesting clarification of the teacher's question keeps pupil response within the structure given by the teacher.

T:	Boys and girls! May I have your attention please! (1)	6
	### (2) (crossly) Billy and James! We are all waiting for	0
	you! (3) Everyone come over to the model city. We are (4)	7, 6
	going to have a report from the Traffic Committee. (5)	6
	### (6) Now we are all so nice and quiet that we are	0
	ready for the meeting. (7) Can anyone remember the	2
	problem we had about automobile (8) traffic and what	4
	Bobby's Traffic Committee was going to decide? (9)	4
P:	They had to decide which streets were to be big streets	
	(10) and which streets were to be little streets. (11)	8, 8
T:	Good for you, Marie, that is exactly what they were going	
	to do. (12) And who remembers why we need to make some	2
	streets big? (13) George?	4
P:	More cars can travel on big streets that have more lanes. (14)	8
P:	It started when we put in all the factories and we had to	
	(15) decide how the factory workers could get across the	9
	river (16) to where we put most of the houses. #(17)	9, 9
T:	That's right. The men have to get from their homes to	
	where they work (18) don't they? And we found out that the	5
	streets were too small for the many, many cars (19)* when the	5
	factories closed and when they started in the morning. (20)*	5
	There is already a six-lane street that we call Main St.	
	(21), which carries a lot of traffic, and why won't that	5
	work? (22)	4
P:	It isn't even in the right place. It doesn't go (23)	8
	between the factory and the houses. And besides (24) the lanes	9
	on Main Street will be for both city cars and cars going	
	(25) right through on the main highway. ## (26)	9, 9
T:	Robert! *That* is a very clear statement! Good for you! (27)	2
	Show us with this pointer how your idea works when cars come	
	in and leave the city. (28)†	2

---

*Numbers (19) and (20) could be coded 3 when the observer knows that the teacher is summarizing previously expressed pupil ideas.

†(28) could also be coded 3 or 6, but to code it 2 presumes that the teacher intended to help the class understand why Robert's ideas were useful.

P: Well, cars can come in from this side and go right out

this side (29),* or they can be going in the other direc-   9

tion. (30)*   9

T: So Robert has shown us that Main Street will already be

busy (31) with city shoppers and highway traffic. (32)   3, 3

Now Bobby, will you tell us what your Traffic Committee

has decided? (33)   4

P: Our Committee has two plans, really. Sarah, Joan, (34) and   9

I, have one plan which we will talk about first. (35)   9

Harold and Willy have their own plan which is different (36)   9

and they will talk second. The factories are up here (37)   9

north of Main Street. Most of the new houses are

here (pointing) (38) south of Main Street and south of   9

the river. (39) We need two large streets going north and   9

south, one here and the other there. (40) Harold, it's your   9

turn.

P: We think it would cost less (41) if you made only one new   9

large street, going north and south. (42) Then we plan to build   9

some new houses north of the factories (43) so that the cars   9

won't cross either the river or Main Street. (44)   9

T: Bobby, Sarah, and Joan have one plan to build two new (45)   3

streets between the present houses and the factories. (46)   3

Harold and Willy think it would cost less to build new houses

(47) north of the factories for the workers. Did your   3

Committee talk about which plan would cost more? (48)   3

P: That's why Harold and I made the second plan. (49) It cost   9

a lot of money to build two bridges (50) over the river and   9

to move traffic across Main Street. (51)   9

T: Show us what you mean, Willy, with the pointer. (52)†   3

(Willy points) ### (53) Now Bobby, apparently you and Joan,   0

and Sarah thought your plan would be better. Why? (54)   3

---

*The choice of 9 instead of 8 is based on the further enlargement of Robert's ideas in (24) and (25).

†(52) is difficult to code: 6 means direction, 3 makes use of a pupil's idea. If the teacher statement sounded more like, "You're unclear, get the pointer," then code 6; but if it was more like, "Show us what YOU mean," then use 3.

P:	Well, houses cost a lot and new houses need new streets and (55) everything. Willy kept arguing with us. (56)	9, 9
P:	You argued just as much as we did, I betcha. (57)	9
T:	I think Bobby and his group and Willy and Harold are both so interested and enthusiastic (58) about their two plans, that	1
	they just naturally want to argue about which plan (59) is	1
	better. It may help the class when a committee has two re-	
	ports, (60) especially when there are two points of view and	1
	each side wants to show how its plan would work. (61) How	1
	can our class decide which is the better plan? (62)* Mary?	3
P:	The city doesn't have to pay for houses, just for the streets.	
	(63) I think/	9
P:	If the city doesn't build the houses, who will? (64)	9
T:	It looks to me as if the whole class is going to get just as	
	excited as the committee. (65) Let me ask my question	1
	another way. How can we find out how much bridges, (66)	3
	new houses, and streets cost? (67)	3
P:	Well, our committee on Housing is supposed to be finding out	
	how (68) much it would cost to build houses. We plan to ask	9
	about it (69) next week when we visit the City Hall. (70)	9, 9
P:	Couldn't we ask about streets, and water and sewer at the	
	same time? (71) (several pupils begin to talk, argue, etc.)	9
T:	Boys and girls! Quiet down. (72) ### (73) Remember our	7, 0
	rule about too many talking at once. (74) James, I notice	7
	you haven't been paying much attention. (75)† Would you and	7
	Billy like to go back to building model houses? (76)†	4
P:	Yeah. We'd rather build houses than talk about the streets.	
	(77) Besides, we're way behind and need more houses. (78)	8, 9
T:	Well, if you are behind, it would be better for you (79) to	3
	go back to work on the houses, while the rest of us talk. (80)	3
	Does anyone else want to work on his own project? (81)	4

---

*Notice the teacher turned thought away from feeling and toward ideas.

†Deciding to code statements (75) and (76) with a 1, 3, 7 or 6 would depend on how they could be paraphrased by the observer. If the sense of meaning was objectively diagnostic and not recriminatory, a 1 or 3 is possible. The coding given is partly in recognition of the more directive emphasis that the teacher is taking between (70) and (81).

	(Several pupils return to their work) ### (82) Now, we	0
	were just discussing whether or not we (83) could find out	3
	how much it costs to build bridges and houses when we go to	
	the City Hall. (84) Who would like to comment on this? # (85)	3, 4
P:	Well, they have departments in the City Hall for just (86)	9
	about everything. Even the dog catcher has an office. (87)	9
	I think we should make a list of questions we want to have	
	answered. (88)	9
T:	A list would help us to remember all of our (89)	3
	questions and help a committee decide where to go. (90) That	3
	is such an important idea, who would be willing to write (91)	2
	it down on the blackboard? Marie? Good. (92) What are some	4
	other good ideas to help us plan our trip? (93)*	2
P:	I think we should decide who can answer our questions be-	
	fore we go. (94)	9
T:	Yes, it would be silly to ask questions about the cost of	
	houses (95) in the street department, wouldn't it? We have	3
	two very fine suggestions: first, list the questions, (96)	2
	then decide who can best answer them. These are good sug-	
	gestions (97) because if we follow them, we can save time (98)	2, 2
	and we are less likely to forget something we want to know.	
	(99) Are there any other suggestions? (100)	2, 4

SIMPLE HISTOGRAM DISPLAYS

Now that you have coded three episodes, you have divided the verbal communication into separately recorded little "bits." The primary reason for coding little bits is so that you can reassemble them into a composite display which gives a picture of the interaction. More elaborate displays will be discussed later. The procedure for drawing a simple histogram display is discussed at this point. If the word "histogram" is meaningless, glance at Fig. 3–1 to see what one looks like. The histogram has the advantage of illustrating visually the proportional incidence of tallies in each of the 10 categories. The procedure for doing this now follows.

---

*This is a somewhat awkward example of a question which might be coded 2. Such a code indicates the teacher's presumed intent to praise past contributions while asking for further comments.

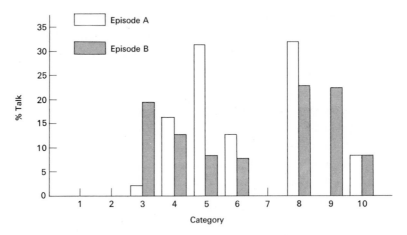

Fig. 3—1.   A Comparison of the Interaction in Episode A and Episode B.

Step One.   Compile all code symbols from one observation into the 10 categories by reading them from your answer sheet and tallying them by category using a form of some sort. It is convenient to use a form like Table 2—2.

     Incidentally, when only a histogram is required or if your only reason for observing is to check your reliability with another observer, you can code directly onto the same form. Each code symbol was recorded separately and in sequence in Episodes A, B, and C, because it was necessary to check your answers and because the data will be used to make a more elaborate display later on in this chapter.

Step Two.   Add all the tallied hash marks for each category separately and write down the sum in the same way that this is done in Table 2—2.

Step Three.   Add the column of figures from Step Two in order to obtain the total number of tallies which were recorded during the observation. Now you could, at this point, draw a histogram and let the height of each bar represent the total number of tallies in that same category. The difficulty here is that it is seldom useful to draw a display for a single observation because insights about classroom interaction more often come from making comparisons, say one display compared with another, or one display compared with a model in histogram form. Thus, there is a requirement which is characteristic of all inter-action analysis displays, namely, it must be in a form which lends itself to comparison with another similar display.

     To stop at this point and draw the histogram means that the height of each bar would be directly proportional to the total number of tallies which, in turn, depends on the length of time you observed. To put it another way, suppose the interaction patterns of two classrooms were identical, but you observed twice as long in one, compared with the other. The bars of the longer observation would be twice as high. By using simple mathematical proportions, the total tallies in each category can be adjusted to some common base, such as 100 tallies as in percent. If all histograms were drawn in terms of percent, direct visual comparisons between histograms would be facilitated. In Episodes A, B, and C there were exactly 100 tallies, so in this case the histograms can be directly compared. But suppose you wished to use histograms to compare two observations from live classroom visits. Except in rare instances, you can be sure that the total number of tallies for one visit will be different compared with the next. Therefore, the number of tallies in each category would not be directly comparable unless they were adjusted to some common base. If one observation consisted of 325 tallies and a second had 486, you have three alternative adjustments in order to make category totals directly comparable. All three alternatives require you to learn how to use simple arithmetical proportions, and most people, including many who are allergic to numbers, find it most convenient to use a circular slide rule for simple proportions. One alternative is to *increase* the category totals in the first observation by multiplying each total by the fraction 486/325; the second alternative is to *decrease* the category totals of the second observation by multiplying each category total by the fraction 325/486; the third alternative is to convert the category totals in both observations to a common base of percent, that is, to 100 total tallies. The third alternative is usually preferred because it permits standardized comparisons.

Step Four.   Convert the raw category totals to the percent of tallies within each category. You can use the procedure below.

a) To find a "common multiplier" divide 100 by the total tallies over all categories. Use this fraction to multiply each category total. For example, suppose there were 56 tallies in Category 8 in the first observation of 325 total tallies:
$100/325 \times 56 = 17.2\%$ (approximately).
If the same *percent* had occurred in the second observation of 486 tallies, there would be about 83 or 84 tallies in that category:
$100/486 \times 83 = 17.1\%$, $100/486 \times 84 = 17.3\%$.

b) Given one observation total, one setting on a circular slide rule will then permit you to calculate the percentage for each of the 10 categories by merely moving the hairline. It takes about 15 minutes to learn how to do this, but it saves a great deal of time subsequently. Learning how to calculate percents quickly is almost a must for interaction analysis observers.

TABLE 3–2
Tallying Code Symbols

Episode A			Episode B		
Category	Total	Percent	Category	Total	Percent
1	0		1	0	
2	0		2	0	
3 ‖	2		3 ЖЖ ЖЖ ЖЖ ‖‖	19	
4 ЖЖ ЖЖ ЖЖ ‖	16		4 ЖЖ ЖЖ ‖‖‖	13	
5 ЖЖ ЖЖ ЖЖ ЖЖ ЖЖ ЖЖ	30		5 ЖЖ ‖‖‖	8	
6 ЖЖ ЖЖ ‖‖‖	13		6 ЖЖ ‖‖	7	
7	0		7	0	
8 ЖЖ ЖЖ ЖЖ ЖЖ ЖЖ ЖЖ ‖	31		8 ЖЖ ЖЖ ЖЖ ЖЖ ‖‖‖	23	
9	0		9 ЖЖ ЖЖ ЖЖ ЖЖ ‖‖	22	
0 ЖЖ ‖‖‖	8		0 ЖЖ ‖‖‖	8	
Total	100		Total	100	

Step Five. Choose an appropriate vertical scale (this is an aesthetic decision), plot the bars of your histogram, and then proceed to make appropriate inferences.

Table 3–2 illustrates the distribution of hash marks which would result from reading the code symbols in the margin of the typescript for Episodes A and B. No calculation of percent is necessary, since the raw tallies of both episodes add up to 100 tallies. It is possible, in a field situation, to skip drawing a histogram if you happen to be the kind of person who can look at the numbers in Table 3–2 and obtain a mental image of the distribution without the aid of a graphical, visual display. Sometimes the histogram is preferred because the person with whom you are working can use a graph more effectively than numbers. Such a graph is shown in Fig 3–1. It is based on the data that can be found in Table 3–2.

Remembering the circumstances of Episodes A and B, we see that it is clear that two different patterns of verbal interaction took place with approximately the same subject matter and lesson plan. These differences are clearly shown in the histogram and, by now, may also be reasonably well established in your mind as a result of reading the two typescripts. Some features which are sharply in contrast when Episode B is compared with Episode A include: more pupil talk in Episode B (45 percent versus 31 percent); eight times more use of Category 3; less lecturing; and the presence of pupil initiation during pupil talk, shown by Category 9. These are relatively simple inferences. Yet in spite of the limitations, it is possible to build toward a general comparison of the two lessons, based on the display only. The teacher in Episode A takes more initiative and the pupils are high in response. The teacher in Episode B responds more often and the pupils produce more initiation. The teacher in A finds it useful to lecture more often; this is less true of the teacher in B. And so on. These are inferences which could be made by any person who knows the category system and who was inspecting the display, even though he was absent when the data were collected.

Assignment Two: Proceed now to follow the same steps in order to make comparisons between Episode B and Episode C. You might note that most of the steps for Episode B have been completed for you, so you can start with Epsiode C. (Do not destroy your master list of code symbols for A and B since we will be using them later on to tabulate a matrix.)

Figure 3–2 is a finished histogram which should resemble your own display. If you prefer to make inferences by looking at the table of tallies, then you would be quite justified in not drawing a histogram. Never engage in clerical tabulation and display drawing unless it is for practice or unless it is a *necessary* step to investigate a problem.

The kinds of inferences which grow out of a comparison of Episodes B and C can follow along the same lines as before. When C is compared with B, it

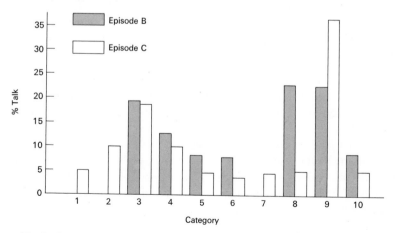

Fig. 3–2.   A Comparison of the Interaction in Episode B and Episode C.

appears that total pupil talk is about the same (41 percent to 45 percent), but there is a higher proportion of pupil initiation; the teacher in C provides much more praise, encouragement, and attention to feelings, more criticism, and only slightly less giving of directions and lecturing.

In carrying out these practice exercises, please note that you are beginning to translate freely between three modes of information (or three languages). First, there is the English that can be found in your inferences; second, there is the code symbol language of the observer; and third, there is the display medium. Facility in shifting from one to the other will sharpen your ability to analyze classroom interaction.

Your next project in this program of self-training is to move on to tape recordings and live classroom observation. You may find it useful to send for and use a kit of recordings and materials which are listed in the Appendix. You can find a current mailing address there, should you care to send for any materials. Another alternative is to make your own recordings. Should you choose this option, some suggestions in the Appendix may help you to obtain clearer recordings with a regular tape recorder under the normally poor acoustical conditions of a classroom. But the most satisfying training experiences will come from live classroom observation. You will find this even more exciting if you plan your observations in terms of some purpose. For example, observe the same teacher, same class, same time of day, for about four successive observations in order to satisfy your curiosity about possible day-to-day changes of classroom interaction under fairly stable conditions. Or, perhaps you have always wondered how a first grade reading lesson differs from "Show and Tell." Perhaps you would like to compare fifth grade, eighth grade, and eleventh grade English teaching in order to speculate about differences of grade level. By selecting the classes to visit with some plan and forethought, you can check out hunches at the same time that you practice.

Assignment Three: Continue your training in observation until you have completed 4 to 6 hours of live classroom observation. You are ready for further work when you feel confident and can "keep up" with your coding.

Don't overlook the multitude of live or quasi-live settings that are close at hand and convenient for coding practice. These include mental coding at the dinner table, or in conversational groups. It is also possible to use paper and pencil coding at a faculty meeting, on the late TV conversation show, and certain other types of radio or TV programs. In most instances, you will gain more training if you designate the person who talks the most as the person who is coded with Categories 1 through 7. Coding practice can occur with just two people who are holding a conversation which you can hear. Designate the most frequent talker as "teacher" and then code all other speakers in the two pupil categories.

Before you go on your first live classroom observation, you may find the next section helpful in scheduling the visit and preparing the materials needed for observation.

FORMALITIES AND FORMS FOR OBSERVATION

This section includes a word or two about the consideration due the teacher who is being observed and then discusses various forms which you may find useful for recording your observations.

FORMALITIES

The arrangements for nearly all observations should be adjusted to the needs and perceptions of the teacher being observed, not the convenience of the observer. An observer has no business being in the room of a teacher who is highly anxious or who mistrusts the observer. The initial step is to contact the prospective teacher, preferably in person, and discuss the purposes and possible arrangements of an observation.

In most instances it is possible to give a complete and frank statement of the purpose of the visit. It helps to point out that the teacher is not being evaluated, studied or even being used as a model, provided that this is indeed the case. Instead, a classroom visit is scheduled in order to obtain a specimen of teacher-pupil interaction. In attempting to gain access in our research projects, we often point out that different kinds of pupils seem to work best with different kinds of teachers and the purpose of the visit is to record some characteristics of class communication by using a kind of shorthand notation. By having enough visits to different teachers we are able to collect a wide variety of classroom communication patterns. The main point is to help the teacher understand why it is more useful to observe what might be called the normal, regular, class interaction. It usually requires especially good rapport with a teacher in order to convince him not to make special preparations because of the visit.

Discussing the following questions seems to help. Why is this visit being carried out? What kind of class activity best facilitates the purpose of the visit? When are such activities likely to occur if the regular schedule is followed? What would be a good time for the observer to come into the classroom? Leave? Should the pupils be notified and/or will the observer be introduced? What are the consequences of acknowledging or ignoring the observer in terms of pupil reactions? What will the observer do while he is in the room? Will there be any discussion about the results of the observation?

This last question can become a bit sticky, especially during early training visits. A teacher is naturally curious and would like to see the results of the observation. However, a beginning observer is hardly in a position to provide a teacher with feedback. During the training period it may be advisable to avoid post-observation discussions with teachers. Principles of feedback and ways to approach teachers with information about classroom interaction are discussed in detail in later chapters.

Besides being concerned with the teacher's perceptions of the observations and being sensitive to the problems which an observer creates, there is also the problem of making the best possible use of the observer's time. It is very frustrating to arrive only to find that the class is viewing a motion picture, working silently at seatwork, or listening to a lecture with little or no opportunity for pupil talk. When you ask the teacher for visiting privileges, find out when class discussions are scheduled. Should you be lucky enough to be exchanging visits with another teacher who is also learning to code, then you can even attempt to provide each other with certain types of statements which are normally very low in incidence, like Categories 1, 2, or 7. The problems of performing and recording low incidence events are usually of benefit to both the teacher and the observer.

FORMS AND MATERIALS FOR CLASSROOM OBSERVATION

Although it may seem silly, a 3-minute dry-run of writing down numbers just as you would in recording code symbols is the best method of checking your preparation. Do you have a clip board or something solid that you can hold on your lap? What will you do if your pencil breaks? How rapidly can you change to the next sheet of paper when the first one is filled up? How much can you write down before you enter the classroom and what do you want to write down after you leave? A few moments consideration of these details and subsequent intelligent action may keep you from wasting a carefully scheduled visit.

Usually the sheet of paper on which raw code symbols are written is a dittoed or mimeographed form. Using a ruler to draw your own recording forms on as many sheets of paper as you think you need, plus a few extra, is a sensible substitute.

We have found three forms useful for regularly scheduled classroom visits. First, a form like Table 2—2, can be used for practice observations. This form is quite satisfactory when you wish to check your coding with a partner by category percents, and when it is not necessary to preserve the original sequence of coded events. Second, a form similar to the one you used for the three episodes in this chapter is necessary when the original sequence of events is of interest. One variation of this second form, used in our research, has a printed box for exactly 33 code symbols per page. This figure was chosen because 33 code symbols were punched on one IBM card. The form provides space for making special notes and comments which are often required in research. Third, there is a form which we use in order to tabulate directly into what is called a *matrix*. This will be discussed later in this book and is mentioned here only to be complete. In designing the first and third forms, it is helpful to anticipate the higher incidence of Categories 4, 5, 8, and possibly 9 and 3. This can be done by allocating more space, either in the rows, columns, or both, for the higher incidence.

There should be space on any recording form for indicating the date, code numbers for the school and teacher, the name or initials of the observer, the time coding started and stopped to the minute, and any other information which will help you identify the visit, as you later stare at a sheet and try to remember where and when it was used 2 or 3 months earlier. It is wise *never* to carry in or out of a school building papers on which are written the names of teachers and schools; use code numbers instead.

OBTAINING MORE INFORMATION BY TABULATING PAIRS OF EVENTS

TEN FOR THE PRICE OF ONE

The more information you collect from a single tally, the more efficient is the observation procedure. Suppose you could realize 10 times as much information from a given set of observation tallies. Your first reaction might be that we seldom, if ever, get something for nothing and you might ask how much the additional information will cost in time and energy. It is the purpose of this section to show how more information can be obtained by employing a different tabulating procedure, even though the same basic 10 categories are used; to perform the extra work involved; and then to let you consider whether the additional information is worth the extra work. As you might expect, there is no clear answer to such an issue, so much depends on the purpose of the observation. There may be times when the additional information is absolutely necessary and therefore any amount of extra work is justified. At other times, the additional information may be useful, but not essential, so it is welcome provided the procedures remain reasonably efficient.

Given any category system designed for classifying events at a constant rate, in sequence, it is possible to increase information by considering a pair of events as the unit to be tabulated rather than the single event. This procedure will more than square the amount of information, so to speak. Let's use the FIAC system you have just learned to illustrate this increase.

Whenever the code symbols are recorded as hash marks and tabulated, it is possible to add the tallies for each category, which provides 10 separate bits of information. By adding these sums together, the total for all tallies can be calculated. This is another single bit of information. Just to keep our thinking straight, suppose we refer to these sums by calling them *primary bits* of information. Given N categories, there will always be $N + 1$ bits of primary information. With 10 categories, there will be 11 such bits.

Now suppose the following was recorded during an observation.

Teacher: "Please take out your geography books and turn to page 137. (Category 6) There is a map on the page which shows the mountains and plains in the United States. (Category 5) You may recall that yesterday Jim was asking how you can tell whether the water in a river (Category 3) will flow into the Atlantic or the Pacific Ocean. Do any of you know the answer to Jim's question?" (Category 3)

Bill: "I know! You look for the continental divide." (Category 8)

Teacher: "What is a continental divide, Bill, and how does it work?" (Category 3)

Bill: "You look for the highest mountains between the Atlantic Coast and the Pacific Coast (Category 8), and since water usually flows down hill, you can decide...." (Category 9)

The sequence from the above conversation, represented by code symbols, will read from left to right:

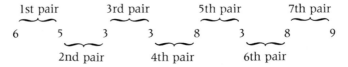

Note that to form a pair, each code symbol is used twice, except for the first and last symbol. A symbol is first used as the second number in a pair and then as the first number in the following pair. In the above sequence there are eight code symbols and seven pairs. When you use this method of pairing, there will always be $n - 1$ pairs, given n code symbols.

How many pairs do you suppose can be formed with 10 categories? When any code symbol can be combined with any other, including itself, it turns out that there are 100 such combinations. Given N categories, there are N^2 pairs. At the same time, we can sum within each category and add these sums to find the matrix total. So that when pairs are chosen as the unit to tabulate, there are $N^2 + N + 1$ bits of primary information. With 10 categories, there are 111 bits of primary information. In effect, we have 100 categories, instead of 10.

You have already had some experience in interpreting the percent teacher talk, pupil talk, and silence. These simple calculations are based on various combinations of categories. Such combinations can be referred to as *secondary bits* of information. Secondary bits of information are obtained by combining primary bits, and when you consider all possible combinations of just 10 categories, this number is very large. Similarly, when you consider the various combinations of 111 primary bits, the possibilities of secondary information become enormous. Thus, when code symbols are paired, the number of primary bits of information is more than squared and the amount of secondary information exceeds what is easily comprehensible and, for that matter, what is psychologically useful.

TABULATING AN INTERACTION ANALYSIS MATRIX

The fastest way to learn how to tabulate an interaction analysis matrix is to do it. It is one thing to read about how it is done, but trying your hand with the procedures provides a much more adequate understanding. After reading this section, you will be asked to tabulate two matrices, one for Episode A and one for Episode B. As each step is described, you will have an opportunity to carry out the procedures.

The general objective of tabulating coded symbols is to arrive at a display of data which is especially appropriate for some problem which is being investigated. The arrangement and procedures about to be described can be applied to many different kinds of problems, but it is obvious that any one method of tabulation will not be equally appropriate to all problems. Feel free, when you investigate patterns of classroom communication, to develop a different procedure which matches your problem or to modify the procedures about to be described.

We have found that a table consisting of 10 rows and 10 columns is a compact and useful arrangement of the 100 pairs which a 10-category system produces. Each column and each row corresponds to one of the 10 categories. There are 100 cells formed by the rows and columns and each has its own name, which is its address. These are shown in Fig. 3—3.

Figure 3—3 makes use of a convention whereby *the first number of any pair designates the row and the second number designates the column.* A pair that consists of Category 2 and Category 5, in that order, has the address 2—5. This indicates that the cell is found at the intersection of row 2 and column 5. It also indicates that a 2 was followed by a 5 or that a 2 preceded a 5; the choice is arbitrary since both are valid. In English, we speak of the "two-five cell" and the name not only indicates where it can be found in the matrix, but also can be decoded by saying, "the teacher shifted from giving praise to expressing his own ideas."

In order to tabulate a matrix, observation code symbols must be recorded in a fashion which preserves the original sequence, just as you recorded code symbols for the three episodes.

Once you have a list of code symbols from an observation, you have to decide whether or not it is reasonable to place all of the code symbols into

Second Number

Cate-gory	1	2	3	4	5	6	7	8	9	10	Row Totals
1	1—1	1—2	1—3	1—4	1—5	1—6	1—7	1—8	1—9	1—10	
2	2—1	2—2	2—3	2—4	2—5	2—6	2—7	2—8	2—9	2—10	
3	3—1	3—2	3—3	3—4	3—5	3—6	3—7	3—8	3—9	3—10	
4	4—1	4—2	4—3	4—4	4—5	4—6	4—7	4—8	4—9	4—10	
5	5—1	5—2	5—3	5—4	5—5	5—6	5—7	5—8	5—9	5—10	
6	6—1	6—2	6—3	6—4	6—5	6—6	6—7	6—8	6—9	6—10	
7	7—1	7—2	7—3	7—4	7—5	7—6	7—7	7—8	7—9	7—10	
8	8—1	8—2	8—3	8—4	8—5	8—6	8—7	8—8	8—9	8—10	
9	9—1	9—2	9—3	9—4	9—5	9—6	9—7	9—8	9—9	9—10	
10	10—1	10—2	10—3	10—4	10—5	10—6	10—7	10—8	10—9	10—10	
Column Totals											Matrix Total

First Number (label on left side)

Fig. 3—3.   Cell Address in a 10 by 10 Matrix.

a single matrix. A single matrix is appropriate if your purpose is to represent the entire observation in a single display. Often classroom activities fit into different time-use periods and should the purpose of observing be to make comparisons between these periods, a separate matrix would be required for each period. Further discussion of this point can be found in subsequent sections of this book, here we will assume that the purposes of the observation can be satisfied by tabulating a single matrix.

Once you have a series of code numbers from an observation, *each pair* must now be tabulated on some kind of form. Figure 3—4 is such a form. It is similar to Fig. 3—3 except that rows 3, 4, 5, 8, and 9 provide more space, since these columns and rows are wider. Drawing the lines of a tabulating matrix unevenly, in this fashion, makes it possible to tabulate more tally marks on a single form because the form is limited by the number of tallies you can squeeze into the cell which will contain the highest frequency. Since higher frequencies are expected in Categories 3, 4, 5, 8, and 9 in most observations, it

	Category	1	2	3	4	5	6	7	8	9	10	Total
Teacher	1											
	2											
	3											
	4											
	5											
	6											
	7											
Pupil	8											
	9											
	10											
	Total											

Category Columns
Teacher — Pupil

Fig. 3—4. Form for Tabulating from a Series of Arabic Code Symbols.

makes sense to provide more space in the cells associated with these categories. On the average the 5—5 cell will have the highest frequency, so if you are drawing your own form, make row 5, as well as column 5, occupy more space on the paper. Sometimes cells other than those mentioned might have higher frequencies; however, the odds favor the suggestions above. Later on you may wish to develop the rather difficult skill of recording directly into a matrix. The form illustrated in Fig. 3—4 can be used in the classroom for this purpose.

It is only fair to provide you with a warning: namely, it is very easy to make errors while tabulating a matrix. Marks simply end up in the wrong cell. There is a way to adjust errors which is not entirely satisfactory, but it is better than repeating the tabulation procedure. This method of locating errors works only when the sequence of code numbers to be tabulated *begins and ends with the same number*. In order to take advantage of tracing errors, the first step in the tabulating procedure is to add the code symbol 10, or simply 0, before the first and after the last code symbol, except in those instances in which the first

Figure 3—5.

or last code symbol is already a 10. This convention is purely arbitrary; any code number could have been used. Ten is chosen because it will affect subsequent interpretation less than any other code number. Although this is true, one of our more cynical neophytes expressed the opinion that, so far as he was concerned, this convention was based on the assumption that the first observation attempted always begins and ends with confusion.

When a sequence of code numbers, which begins and ends with the same number, is entered into a matrix without error, the sum of each corresponding row and column will be equal. When this occurs, the matrix is said to be *balanced*. The way to start checking for errors, then, is to add all the cell frequencies in row 1 and enter this as a row total, then add all the cell frequencies in column 1 and enter this as a column total. The two sums should be identical. Continue, in this way, to check the remaining categories. In order for you to compare the two matrices which will result from coding Episodes A and B, follow the steps below.

1) Add a 10 (or 0) at the beginning and end of your list of code symbols. Draw a blank tabulating matrix, just like the one shown in Fig. 3—4.

2) On the tabulating matrix, make a hash mark (tally) in row 10 and in the column designated by the first code symbol which follows the 10. This mark should be small and fit into the upper left-hand corner of the cell. Since subsequent tallies may be added to the same cell, mark in clusters of five, e.g., ⧄ which helps in adding sums.

3) *While your pencil remains at the end of the first tally stroke*, and before you lift your pencil, move the finger of your free hand to the row which corresponds to the column number of that tally. The next code symbol will be tallied in the row designated by your finger. Now lift your pencil.

4) Now check or cross out the number you just tallied, on your own observation sheet, to indicate that it has been tallied. This helps if you are interrupted because you'll know exactly which code symbols have been tallied.

5) Now mark the next code symbol in the row designated by your finger and in the column designated by the code symbol. Before you lift your pencil, return to

step (3) above, and continue until the entire observation has been tallied, including the extra 10 which you added at the end.

6) Add the hash marks within each cell and write a large arabic number which indicates this sum over the hash marks. A colored pencil helps. An example, without color, is shown in Fig. 3—5.

7) Now add all rows and columns and enter the sum in the appropriate spaces.

8) If there is no tabulating error, each corresponding row and column total will be identical. If this is the case, add the row totals to obtain the matrix total. Given n code symbols, you may remember that you should have $n - 1$ for the matrix total. In the case of Episodes A and B, you started with 100 code symbols and added a zero at both ends of the sequence, giving you a total of 102 symbols. Therefore, your matrix should add to a total of 101. If you have made an error, you may follow the procedures discussed in the next section.

For an example of tabulation pairs, turn to Fig. 3—6 and notice how the 10 pairs were entered into the matrix.

Category	1	2	3	4	5	6	7	8	9	10	Total
1											—
2											—
3							(4th)				—
4				8th	7th		||	(9th)			2
5			(3rd) ||	|| (2nd)							4
6											—
7											—
8				(6th) |				| (5th)		| (10th)	3
9											—
10				| (1st)							1
Total	—	—	—	2	4	—	—	3	—	1	10

Observation Sequence

$$1\text{st} \begin{bmatrix} 10 \\ 5 \end{bmatrix} 2\text{nd}$$
$$3\text{rd} \begin{bmatrix} 5 \\ 4 \end{bmatrix} 4\text{th}$$
$$5\text{th} \begin{bmatrix} 8 \\ 8 \end{bmatrix} 6\text{th}$$
$$7\text{th} \begin{bmatrix} 5 \\ 4 \end{bmatrix} 8\text{th}$$
$$9\text{th} \begin{bmatrix} 8 \\ 10 \end{bmatrix} 10\text{th}$$

Fig. 3—6.   Distribution of Initial Tallies.

These steps will probably seem tedious. They are. However, it is possible to become quite proficient in both observing and tabulating providing you practice. It is even possible to slow down your rate of observation slightly, and with experience, tally directly into a matrix while observing in the class-room. All hand motions, however, must by then be completely automatic and a slightly larger matrix than fits on a sheet of 8½- by 11-inch paper is often desirable for observations lasting longer than 15 to 20 minutes. The most important objective in asking you to tabulate two matrices is to have you learn that transitions from one category to another tend to produce a clockwise rotation when plotted sequentially in a matrix. Or to put it more simply, you have to learn how to put numbers into a matrix before you can learn to take inferences out.

Assignment Four: Draw two tabulating matrix forms like Fig. 3—4. Tabulate a matrix for Episodes A and B, following the procedure outlined above.

ADJUSTING ERRORS DUE TO INCORRECT MATRIX TABULATION

The most helpful rule about errors in a matrix is don't bother errors unless they bother you. Errors usually occur in a hand tabulated matrix, as opposed to matrices tabulated by a computer. The hand tabulation of a matrix is likely to be necessary when it seems important to feed back information within the shortest possible time after an observation. A fellow teacher observes for ½ hour; you wish to discuss the data as soon as possible. Without convenient access to a computer, the quickest way to obtain a matrix is to tabulate it yourself. Since more than 400 tallies are involved, errors are likely to occur, but *a few errors will not influence the major interpretations in most cases.* Under these circum-stances, the errors are not bothering you so they can be ignored.

The discussion of errors which now follows is not recommended for general reading; it will be of interest only to those who have a compulsive interest in tidying up a matrix that is a bit untidy. Many kinds of errors are in-volved with any system of interaction analysis, but a tabulation error is the most irritating. It is purely clerical. You intended to tally in the (4—5) cell, but your accident-prone pencil ended up in the (5—4) cell. Placing a tally in the wrong transition* cell will cause the matrix to become unbalanced. However, the following tabulation errors do not unbalance the matrix: (a) skipping a number, (b) inserting an extra number, and (c) posting too many or too few tallies in a steady state† cell. These last three kinds of tabulation errors can be

---

*There are 90 transition cells; these cells do not have identical numbers in their addresses.
†There are 10 steady state cells; they have identical numbers in their addresses.

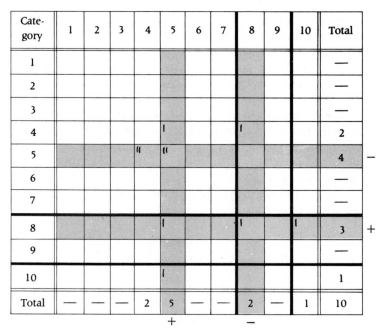

Cate-gory	1	2	3	4	5	6	7	8	9	10	Total	
1											—	
2											—	
3											—	
4					I			I			2	
5				II	II						4	—
6											—	
7											—	
8					I			I		I	3	+
9											—	
10					I						1	
Total	—	—	—	2	5	—	—	2	—	1	10	

+   −

Fig. 3—7.   Distribution with an Error.

discovered only by comparing the total number of code symbols with the sum of all tallies in a matrix.

The effect of placing a tally in an incorrect transition cell can be illustrated by making such a mistake on purpose. Figure 3—6 illustrates a correctly tabulated matrix of the 10 code symbols which are shown to the right. In Fig. 3—7, an error was introduced by tabulating a 4—8 pair in the (4—5) cell, which is the wrong column but the right row. Such an error unbalances two sets of rows and columns. In Fig. 3—7 plus and minus signs have been placed beside each of the rows and columns; plus signs when the sum is too large, minus signs when the sum is too small. The unbalanced columns and rows have been shaded.

Such an error is noticed after the matrix has been tabulated and the sums of corresponding rows and columns calculated. At this point there are usually 400 or more tallies in the matrix, instead of just 10, and deciding what error has been committed is complicated by the fact that there are four alternative ways of adjusting the error. Returning to Fig. 3—7, we find that the first alternative is at the intersection of the row and the column marked with negative signs, cell (5—8). Add a single tally to this cell and the matrix will balance. A second alternative occurs at the intersection of the row and column marked positive, cell (8—5). We could subtract a tally and balance the matrix. Third, we could shift the 4–5 tally to the (4–8) cell, which was the true error in this instance, and balance the matrix. And fourth, we could shift a tally from the (8–5) cell to the (8–8) cell, and balance the matrix.

Given four alternative ways of correcting the matrix and no way to determine which alternative is correct, the most sensible policy is to make corrections which least influence the interpretation. In most instances, this can best be accomplished by altering one or two tallies in those cells which have the highest frequencies. Had the preceding error been buried among 400 or more tallies, the odds suggest that the incidence of tallies from the highest to the lowest for these four cells would be (8–8), (4–8), (8–5), and (5–8). Thus, the best choice for correcting the error would be to shift an 8–5 tally to the (8–8) cell, which is incorrect, but will balance the matrix with the least amount of influence on the interpretation.

TABLE 3–3

Raw Observation Code Symbols for Episodes A, B, and C

Number	Episode A	B	C	Number	Episode A	B	C	Number	Episode A	B	C	Number	Episode A	B	C
(1)	5	5	6	(26)	8	9	9	(51)	5	3	9	(76)	8	8	4
(2)	5	6	0	(27)	8	9	2	(52)	5	5	3	(77)	8	4	8
(3)	5	6	7	(28)	8	9	2	(53)	5	4	0	(78)	6	8	9
(4)	5	6	6	(29)	8	9	9	(54)	4	4	3	(79)	8	5	3
(5)	5	6	6	(30)	8	3	9	(55)	8	8	9	(80)	8	5	3
(6)	5	0	0	(31)	6	3	3	(56)	8	8	9	(81)	5	5	4
(7)	5	0	2	(32)	5	3	3	(57)	8	8	9	(82)	5	4	0
(8)	5	4	4	(33)	4	3	4	(58)	6	3	1	(83)	4	0	3
(9)	5	0	4	(34)	8	6	9	(59)	6	3	1	(84)	8	8	3
(10)	5	8	8	(35)	4	0	9	(60)	0	4	1	(85)	4	8	4
(11)	5	3	8	(36)	8	0	9	(61)	0	9	1	(86)	4	3	9
(12)	5	8	2	(37)	4	0	9	(62)	4	3	3	(87)	8	3	9
(13)	6	8	4	(38)	4	0	9	(63)	8	8	9	(88)	4	9	9
(14)	6	3	8	(39)	8	4	9	(64)	4	8	9	(89)	8	9	3
(15)	6	8	9	(40)	4	8	9	(65)	5	8	1	(90)	3	9	3
(16)	0	3	9	(41)	8	9	9	(66)	4	4	3	(91)	3	9	2
(17)	0	3	9	(42)	5	9	9	(67)	8	8	3	(92)	5	3	4
(18)	4	5	5	(43)	5	3	9	(68)	8	4	9	(93)	5	3	2
(19)	8	5	5	(44)	4	8	9	(69)	0	6	9	(94)	5	3	9
(20)	6	5	5	(45)	0	8	3	(70)	8	6	9	(95)	5	4	3
(21)	0	4	5	(46)	8	9	3	(71)	8	8	9	(96)	5	9	2
(22)	0	9	4	(47)	4	9	3	(72)	8	8	7	(97)	5	9	2
(23)	6	9	8	(48)	8	4	3	(73)	5	8	0	(98)	5	9	2
(24)	6	3	9	(49)	8	9	9	(74)	5	8	7	(99)	6	4	2
(25)	8	9	9	(50)	8	9	9	(75)	6	8	7	(100)	6	9	4

		Teacher							Pupil		X	
	Category	1	2	3	4	5	6	7	8	9	10	Total
Teacher	1											0
	2											0
	3			1		1						2
	4				2	1			12		1	16
	5				5	22	3					30
	6					1	5		3		4	13
	7											0
Pupil	8			1	7	4	4		14		1	31
	9											0
X	10				2	1	1		2		3	9
	Total	0	0	2	16	30	13	0	31	0	9	101

Fig. 3–8. Tabulating Matrix: Episode *A*.

		Teacher							Pupil		X	
	Category	1	2	3	4	5	6	7	8	9	10	Total
Teacher	1	—	—	—	—	—	—	—	—	—	—	0
	2	—	—	—	—	—	—	—	—	—	—	0
	3	—	—	1	—	1	—	—	—	—	—	2
	4	—	—	—	2	1	—	—	12	—	1	16
	5	—	—	—	5	22	3	—	—	—	—	30
	6	—	—	—	—	1	5	—	3	—	4	13
	7	—	—	—	—	—	—	—	—	—	—	0
Pupil	8	—	—	1	7	4	4	—	14	—	1	31
	9	—	—	—	—	—	—	—	—	—	—	0
X	10	—	—	—	2	1	1	—	2	—	3	9
	Total	0	0	2	16	30	13	0	31	0	9	101
	%											

Fig. 3–9. Matrix for Episode *A*.

| | Teacher | | | | | | | Pupil | | X | |
Category	1	2	3	4	5	6	7	8	9	10	Total
1	—	—	—	—	—	—	—	—	—	—	0
2	—	—	—	—	—	—	—	—	—	—	0
3	—	—	8	2	2	1	—	4	2	—	19
4	—	—	—	1	—	1	—	4	5	2	13
5	—	—	—	3	4	1	—	—	—	—	8
6	—	—	—	—	—	4	—	1	—	2	7
7	—	—	—	—	—	—	—	—	—	—	0
8	—	—	5	3	1	—	—	12	2	—	23
9	—	—	6	2	—	—	—	—	13	1	22
10	—	—	—	2	1	—	—	2	—	4	9
Total	0	0	19	13	8	7	0	23	22	9	101
%											

Fig. 3—10.   Matrix for Episode B.

In the assignment of tabulating a matrix for Episodes A and B, there are only 102 code symbols and it is possible to check certain cell frequencies by quickly counting all sequence pairs with the same cell address. In a longer, normal observation, there will be too many code symbols to count quickly, and some method of adjusting errors which is similar to what has been discussed will be necessary.

CHECKING YOUR WORK ON EPISODES A AND B

If you would like to check the clerical part of your work on Episodes A and B, the correct recording of the raw code symbols can be found in Table 3—3. An illustration of just one tabulating matrix, in this case for Episode A, can be found in Fig. 3—8. The final matrices for Episodes A and B can be found in Figs. 3—9 and 3—10.

The interpretation of matrices is the topic of Chapter 4. After you have finished reading it, you can begin the task of making your own inferences from the matrices of Episodes A and B. This way you can discover for yourself just how much more information is available in a matrix, compared with a histogram of the 10 categories.

Chapter Four

INTERPRETING 10 × 10 INTERACTION MATRICES

DECODING IN TERMS OF MODELS

No classroom interaction can ever be completely recreated or repeated. The individual sensations, perceptions, and the instantaneous action-set of the teacher and each pupil are part of a moment in history which passes and then is lost forever. Nevertheless, it is the purpose of interaction analysis to preserve selected aspects of interaction through observations, encoding, tabulation, and then decoding. Contrary to many an argument, *the issue of validity in coding does not rest on the impossibility of recreating what took place*, instead it depends on whether what was encoded did in fact exist and whether these elements of the original situation are recreated in their proper perspective during the decoding process. Validity requires accurate interpretation during both decoding and encoding. In this chapter some of the procedures for decoding and some of the problems of interpretation will be discussed.

The *purpose* of an observation helps to select the comparisons that will be made during the interpretation of a display. Before the observation is scheduled, the observer and the person to be observed should decide what questions are to be answered. These questions will guide the collecting, tabulation, and interpretation of the data. Such questions also help to resolve many other issues such as when should the observer come? Should the teacher try to act in a certain way? Besides classifying verbal statements, what additional information should be collected? What should be the relationship between successive observations? And so on.

Since it is impossible to consider one by one all the various questions which guide different observations, this discussion will consider various kinds of interpretation which a matrix makes possible. This general approach to interpretation in no way advocates that an observer is well advised to drop into a classroom, code behavior, and tabulate a matrix just to see if anything of interest shows up. About the only exception would be a classroom visit for the practice in coding.

LEARNING TO THINK OF INTERACTION IN THREE WAYS

Interpretation and decoding require the skills of thinking about interaction in three ways and the facility to move from one way to another easily. First, there is the English language which you use to think about what a teacher is doing. For example, you may say, "Right now the teacher is conducting drill by asking short questions and the pupils are giving short answers." The second way is to think like an observer. Instead of the foregoing sentence, the observer would say, "There is a 4, 8, 4, 8 sequence occurring." The third way of thinking is to visualize how the pattern would look when tabulated in a matrix. The purpose of this chapter is to train you to translate quickly and easily, back and forth, between any two of these three ways of thinking. The skills involved in shifting from one to another way of thinking about interaction will develop gradually and require practice along with contemplation. If nothing else results from reading this chapter, at least you will learn that the numbers representing code symbols in a matrix are not a cold confusion of statistical symbols, but an interesting source of information for building theoretical speculations. The game is to look at the matrix and then try to reconstruct a portion of the original interaction.

As you read, making your own notations on a matrix form often facilitates comprehension. This form should have 10 rows and 10 columns. The columns are numbered from 1 to 10 across the top, from left to right, and the rows are also numbered from the top to bottom, along the left. Now is the time to stop reading and draw such a form.

A SHORT QUESTION, SHORT ANSWER MODEL

The short question, short answer model of verbal interaction can occur in drill, in review, in checking simple facts, in making inventories, and in some forms of planning in which ideas are proposed, one after another. When a teacher asks a series of short questions, each 3 seconds or less, and the pupils respond with short answers, each 3 seconds or less, and the ideas expressed are curtailed by the nature of the teacher's questions, the best code symbol sequence to represent this type of interaction is, from left to right,

There are only two kinds of pairs in this sequence. The odd-numbered pairs are 4–8 and the even numbered pairs are 8–4. Each time such a pair appears during an observation, a tally appears in the corresponding cell in the matrix, and finally an arabic number appears in each cell which represents the number of times, or frequency, with which that pair occurred. Thus, if the above sequence were to occur quite often during an observation, an above average proportion of tallies would appear in these two cells.

When decoding takes place, an interpretation of short teacher questions and short pupil answers is suggested by higher frequencies in the (4—8) and (8—4) cells. At this time, use a pencil to shade the two cells of your matrix form in which you would expect higher frequencies when this pattern of short teacher question and short pupil answer was present. You will have a chance to check the cells you shaded during the next few pages.

It is almost impossible for a teacher to maintain a pure 4, 8, 4, 8 pattern for an extended period of time, even when this is the intention of the teacher. In practical classroom teaching, when a teacher has many things on his mind, pure 4, 8, 4, 8 patterns seldom, if ever, occur. The two most common embellishments are (a) the teacher takes longer than 3 seconds to formulate a question, and (b) a pupil takes longer than 3 seconds when he answers. Sustained teacher questioning creates 4—4 pairs and sustained pupil response creates 8—8 pairs, both of these pairs can now be added to your matrix, by shading the cells that have these two addresses. Now you have shaded four cells.

The next step is to understand how these four cells are interconnected and how these interconnections can be illustrated by drawing arrows. You can discover this by tracing the movement of your pencil as the symbols would be tabulated in a matrix. Suppose the sequence was

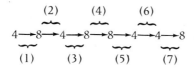

To tabulate this sequence, start by pointing your pencil to the (4—8) cell. You can use the same form on which you shaded the four cells. From the (4—8) cell, your pencil moves directly to the (8—4) cell to reach the location of the second sequence pair. Draw an arrow between these two cells to indicate the direction. The movement for the third pair is back to the (4—8) cell, so draw a second arrow above and parallel to the first to indicate the reverse direction. The fourth pair is tallied in the (8—8) cell, and you will need a third arrow to indicate this direction. Next draw another arrow to the (8—4) cell to locate the fifth pair. Then draw an arrow to the (4—4) cell and another arrow to the (4—8) cell, representing movement to the sixth and seventh pairs. Your drawing should look like Fig. 4—1. The purpose of this exercise is to fix forever in your mind how a sequence of code symbols creates clockwise

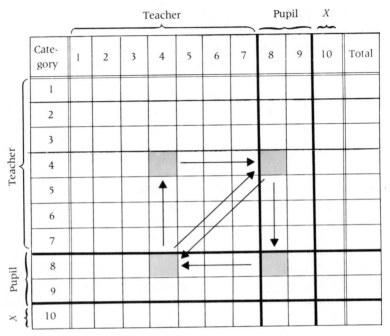

Fig. 4—1.   Clockwise Flow in a Matrix.

entries in a matrix. This orderly procedure will become the foundation of decoding and interpretation later on.

The diagram which you have just drawn would be more helpful if it contained additional information. For example, suppose we added some arbitrary frequency numbers in each of the four cells to show that some pairs occurred more frequently than other pairs. As long as we are building a model we could choose any numbers, but if we preferred percent, then the numbers would have to total 100. The arrows which connect cells that have large numbers could be drawn thick and the cells which had a low number could be connected with a thin arrow. These conventions would suggest a kind of "traffic pattern" at a glance. Suppose, for example, that in this model of drill, it seemed appropriate to assign 70 percent of the time to a 4, 8, 4, 8 type sequence and further assume that the remaining 30 percent would be split equally between the (4—4) and the (8—8) cells. This would mean that almost one-third of the time (30 percent) the teacher or some pupil talked a little longer than 3 seconds. A longer teacher question would produce the 4—4 sequence; a longer pupil answer would be an 8—8 sequence.

Assignment One: Draw a new diagram for a drill model in which 70 percent of the time a 4, 8, 4, 8 sequence occurred and the remaining 30 percent was divided

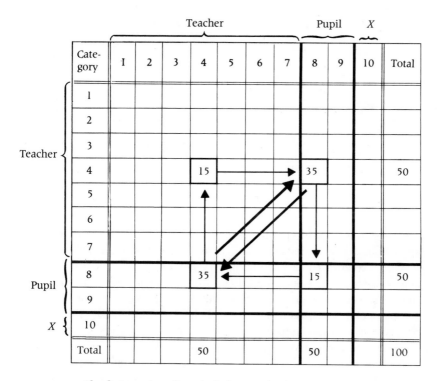

Cate-gory	1	2	3	4	5	6	7	8	9	10	Total
1											
2											
3											
4				15				35			50
5											
6											
7											
8				35				15			50
9											
10											
Total				50				50			100

The first number of a pair designates the row.

The second number of a pair designates the column.

Fig. 4—2.   Flow of Interaction in a Short Question, Short Answer Pattern.

equally between the (4—4) and (8—8) cells. Draw in the six arrows, some thick and some thin, to illustrate the sequence flow. Enter the appropriate numbers into the four cells and then check to see that your model produces a balanced matrix.

The way to solve this problem is shown in Fig. 4—2, and a complete written procedure can be found at the end of this chapter.

By way of review, this exercise starts by considering what a teacher says during a drill, such as in arithmetic or spelling or geography, and deciding that a series of short questions might be asked to which pupils give short responses. In the language of an observer this would be a 4, 8, 4, 8 sequence. Then a minor embellishment was made in which about one out of four questions took longer than 3 seconds, and one out of about four answers took longer than three seconds. So that about one-half of the time there was an extra 4 or an extra 8 in the sequence. We chose to do this in order to have a model which was a little closer to what might happen in a classroom.

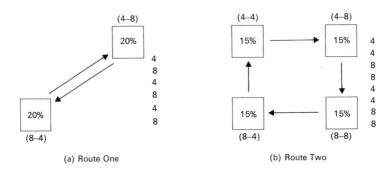

Figure 4—3.

The next step was to visualize how this would look in a matrix display. We drew some arrows to indicate the flow of events. There appeared to be two routes which could be traced on the matrix. One route, which occurred more frequently, is shown as Route One in Fig. 4—3. Another route which occurred less frequently is shown as Route Two. We added numbers to show the incidence of these particular pathways. The numbers helped us draw thick or thin arrows which became a visual indication of the traffic load. When Route One is superimposed on Route Two, our complete model appears in matrix form.

The problem of decoding is that the arrows which you have just drawn are not shown in a tabulated matrix. Merely by looking at numbers, such as those shown in Fig. 4—4, you must imagine the possible sequences which could most reasonably account for those numbers. This is a matter of speculation, since the exact sequences cannot be determined from a matrix. When a decoder has a number of different models in his mind, he can use them to make intelligent guesses about the sequences that must have occurred. If the models just happened to be from another world and had nothing to do with normal classroom interaction, then the inferences reached by using such models would probably be inaccurate. The more a model is like what goes on in a classroom, the more realistic will be the inferences which are based on its use.

In order to make sure that you can recognize this simple pattern when it occurs in a matrix which has many tallies, turn to Figs. 4—6 and 4—7 (pp. 98 and 99) and decide in which of the two matrix displays, Matrix P or Matrix Q, the data suggest that short teacher questions and short pupil responses might have occurred. When you have finished, continue reading.

You may have noticed that Matrix P had a total of 629 tallies, while Q had 448. In spite of the longer observation in situation P, there are higher frequencies—sometimes called *higher loading*—in the (4—8) and (8—4) cells in Matrix Q. Therefore you are safe in guessing that a short teacher question and a short pupil response pattern is more likely to have occurred in Q than in P.

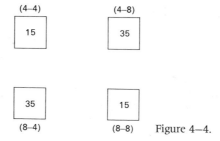

Figure 4—4.

Before moving on to consider another pattern, let's go over the steps which have just been completed. First, there was a somewhat vague description in English, of a classroom activity, such as drill, checking facts, and similar classroom activities. A more behavioral description made use of terms such as "short teacher questions followed immediately by short pupil responses which are limited by the questions asked by the teacher." This last statement made free use of the English definition of two categories. This leads to an observer's way of representing the behavior, namely, 4, 8, 4, 8, 8, 4, 4, 8, 4, and so on. Note that moving between the English description and the code symbol description is made possible by having systematic procedures of observation. Without rules for using code symbols, there can be no translation back and forth. Third, the series of code symbols can be ordered into sequence pairs and then tabulated into a 10 × 10 matrix in such a way that four cells are involved. Arabic numbers within these cells give quantitative meaning to our description. Fourth and finally, the cell frequencies are inspected in a clockwise rotation in order to recreate the sequence of the original events. Placing arrows on the matrix illustrates this sequence and emphasizes the "traffic pattern" of the original events. A person who is trained in interaction analysis can think of these events equally well in any one of the three ways.

We might also note, in passing, that a trained teacher ought to be able to produce particular verbal patterns, in spontaneous situations, once the code symbols are given. Thus, even though it is difficult, a teacher should be able to produce a 4, 8, 4, 8, etc., sequence upon request, or any other pattern which can be described by the category system.

For those who are more ambitious, several problems can now be solved from this introductory experience. For example, how would you represent a silence pause, Category 10, between a teacher's question and the pupil's response? How would this change the model if pauses occurred after every tenth teacher question? How would the model change if the teacher inserted, "Good for you, Jim, that's right," after a pupil response and before asking the next question?

A CREATIVE INQUIRY PATTERN

A creative inquiry pattern is quite different from a teacher-pupil short question and short response drill pattern. To participate in inquiry, pupils must be able to express their own ideas. In turn, these ideas must be dealt with, i.e., the teacher must respond to them and use them in problem-solving. Often, a teacher constructs a question by making use of ideas which have been previously expressed by pupils. These features of inquiry are usually absent in a teacher directed drill pattern.

To be worth its salt, interaction analysis should be able to distinguish between these two types of classroom communication easily. Think, for a moment, and decide what additional categories would be most likely to appear in order to distinguish inquiry from the drill pattern? What two categories are most important?

If you answered Categories 3 and 9, you are on the right track. If you also suggested Category 2, you may be surprised to learn that praise and encouragement by the teacher are usually absent from lessons based on current models of inquiry training. Apparently, whether something is right, wrong, or praiseworthy is a judgment which the teacher does not make arbitrarily, but, instead, it is to be determined by the process of inquiry itself. A better guess for a third category which is present but less frequent would be Category 6.

Often, in the early, introductory phases of an inquiry lesson, the 4, 8, 4, 8, 4, 4, 8, 8, 8, 4, 8, etc., pattern which was just discussed will be present. Certain features of a problem must be brought to the attention of the pupils in order to focus their attention. This is often accomplished by asking rather specific questions. But if the lesson remains within the strictures of the pattern which was shown in Fig. 4—2 after the initial phase, it fails to develop into a true inquiry process. How, then, is this transition made? After the transition has occurred, how will the pattern of inquiry be illustrated within a matrix?

The place to begin is with Category 9, the code symbol which is used when pupils are expressing their own ideas, initiating an expression of their own opinion, such as occurs when they suggest an hypothesis or create tentative explanations. Usually such statements take longer than 3 seconds, so we can expect several 9's in sequence. This locates us in the (9—9) cell of the matrix, which can be a starting point.

You can begin to construct a matrix model by asking what will happen at the termination of a series of 9's. If the teacher recognizes and makes use of ideas suggested by pupils, then the observer will code such teacher responses with Category 3. Thus we might expect 9, 9, 9, 3, 3, 3, 9, 9, etc., to be part of an inquiry process. This involves us with four new cells. They are the (9—9) cell, the (9—3) cell, the (3—3) cell, and the (3—9) cell. You might find it helpful to use your pencil to shade these four cells in your matrix form. At the same time you can draw a series of clockwise arrows connecting the (9—9) cell with the (9—3) cell with the (3—3) cell with the (3—9) cell and back to the (9—9) cell. These arrows form an "outer orbit" around the drill model.

We can now ask the initial question with slightly different terms, namely, "How is the transition made between the inner orbit and the outer orbit during an inquiry lesson?" There are only four possibilities in this simplified model of the problem. The inner orbit contains only 4's and 8's, and the outer orbit only 3's and 9's. This restricts our answer to a 4—3 or an 8—3 transition, or a 4—9 or an 8—9 transition. These sequence pairs are now to be translated into English descriptions in order to consider them more carefully.

A 4—3 transition occurs when the teacher terminates a question based on his own ideas and shifts to the clarification of an idea previously expressed by a pupil. This would occur as uninterrupted talk by the teacher. The second alternative is an 8—3 transition in which the teacher makes use of ideas expressed earlier by a pupil. Should this become an 8, 3, 3, 3 . . . sequence, then the teacher would be making use of ideas expressed by pupils for a period longer than 3 seconds. The third alternative is the 4—9 transition, which is most likely to occur when the teacher asks such a broad question that the observer felt that the question itself in no way restricted the pupil's expression of his own ideas, or a pupil ignores the teacher's question to initiate his own ideas. Fourth and finally, there is the 8—9 transition in which a student shifts from responding to the teacher's ideas and begins to express his own ideas or perceptions, in this case, without interruption on the part of the teacher. Now, which of these four alternatives sounds most reasonable?

Of course, all are possible, but the rank order incidence based on demonstrations of inquiry teaching would place the transitions from most frequently used to least frequently used as follows: 8—3, 4—9, 8—9, and 4—3. The explanation of this rank order begins with the distinction between the first two listed and the third. Both 8—3 and 4—9 involve actions taken by the teacher in relation to a pupil. The teacher is free to react to pupil response talk (8) by reacting to the ideas expressed by the pupil (3). This is the most certain route because the teacher completely controls the transition. If the teacher is clever enough to ask just that kind of question which will trigger pupil initiated talk, then a 4—9 is possible. The 8—9 shift depends on the pupil or pupils and is beyond the immediate control of the teacher. A 4—3 shift is completely within the teacher's control, but it has logical shortcomings and is awkward in terms of syntax.

Figure 4—5 illustrates the inner orbit, or drill pattern, and the outer orbit that is more typical of the later stages of an inquiry lesson. The transition cells which have just been discussed are indicated by a special dotted code. The inner orbit represents a pattern of teacher initiation and direction. This initiation takes the form of asking questions which guide content coverage or the next steps in a problem-solving process. The outer orbit represents a pattern of

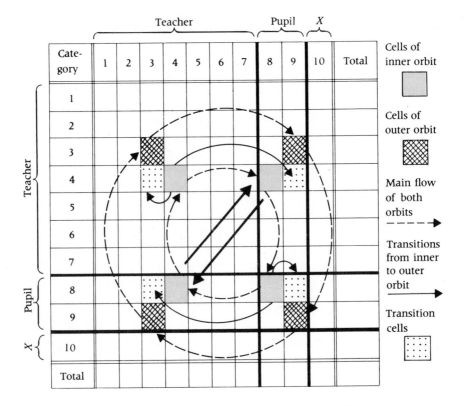

Fig. 4—5.   Shifting from Teacher Initiative to Teacher Response.

teacher response, instead of initiation. The complementary behavior of pupils is to initiate their own ideas and make their own suggestions.

Knowledge of these two patterns and how they can be located in a 10 × 10 matrix provides an evaluative tool for studying the balance of teacher initiation and response during an observation. For example, turn again to Figs. 4—6 and 4—7 and study the two matrices of situations P and Q. Here are some questions which you should now be able to answer.

Assignment Two: Which situation P or Q, shows evidence that the classroom interaction approached an inquiry model of teaching, providing the model of inquiry just presented is accepted?

Assignment Three: If situations P and Q involved the same teacher in the early and later phases of the same lesson, and suppose further that this was an effort to demonstrate inquiry teaching, then which situation followed the other? Was the sequence P then Q or Q then P?

Assignment Four: Assume again that P and Q involved the same teacher, but this time the teacher carried on a discussion to motivate students for a drill session and then followed this with a drill session. Now which is the logical sequence. P to Q or Q to P? List your reasons. (The answers to these questions can be found at the end of this chapter.)

FIVE STEPS TO SET THE SITUATION FOR MATRIX INTERPRETATION

Guessing at patterns that are hidden in a matrix can be fascinating, particularly because it requires constructing a theory that fits the data, but such a theory must rest on certain primary features of the interaction. This section describes five steps which combine primary and secondary bits of information into a background or situational setting out of which theories about patterns can emerge. Two fictitious matrices *P* and *Q* shown in Figs. 4–6 and 4–7 are included so that you can practice making interpretations.

As you start practicing interpretation, there are two assumptions to keep in mind. As soon as any two numbers in a matrix are added or divided, as in the calculation of a percent, the assumption made is that tallying within the category system proceeded at a constant rate and that each tally is presumed to be an equivalent unit. In this case, it represents the mixture of an event and a standard time interval. A discussion of the unit of analysis can be found on page 152. At this point we need only note that the assumption of an equivalent unit is fairly reasonable, given trained observers.

A second assumption appears as soon as an assertion, based on the matrix, is made about the classroom interaction. Here we assume that the total number of tallies and their configuration adequately represent those aspects of the original interaction which were encoded, within the limitations of the category system. What is meant by *adequate* depends on the assertion. In most cases we are on very thin ice if there are less than 400 tallies in the matrix. To illustrate, suppose an assertion is to be made about administrative routine during classroom instruction. The difficulty is that a teacher engages in pure administration during short "bursts," that is, a minute here, one and a half minutes there, and so on. The short segments of administrative routine are separated by long periods of work. Under these circumstances, how can an adequate sample of classroom administration be secured? One solution is to observe for several days, keep compiling the coded data from the short segments into a single matrix, and after this composite matrix has 500 or 600 tallies, you will be in a position to make some inferences about classroom interaction during administrative routine. Because such a procedure lumps many short segments of administrative routine into a single matrix, distinctions about different

Cate-gory	1	2	3	4	5	6	7	8	9	10	Total
1	2	—	—	—	—	—	—	—	1	—	3
2	—	13	—	—	3	—	—	—	6	1	23
3	—	—	61	18	15	2	—	—	22	3	121
4	—	—	—	36	2	—	—	16	17	5	76
5	—	—	—	16	68	4	—	—	7	1	96
6	—	—	—	—	—	3	—	4	—	3	10
7	—	—	—	—	—	—	—	—	—	—	—
8	—	2	22	3	3	—	—	38	2	—	70
9	1	8	38	—	5	—	—	2	145	1	200
10	—	—	—	3	—	1	—	10	—	16	30
Total	3	23	121	76	96	10	—	70	200	30	629
%	0.5	3.8	19.8	12.5	15.8	1.6	—	11.5	32.8	4.9	100

Fig. 4—6.   Matrix P.

kinds of administrative situations are impossible. The purpose of the illustration is to show that repeated observations of short time segments can provide an adequate basis for making limited inferences, inferences which compare administrative routine with other classroom activities.

There are five steps of matrix interpretation which help to pin down some general features of the classroom interaction and which together form a situational setting. These steps are:

1) Check the matrix total in order to estimate the elapsed coding time.
2) Check the percent teacher talk, pupil talk, and silence or confusion, and use this information in combination with ...
3) ... the balance of teacher response and initiation in contrast with pupil initiation.
4) Check the initial reaction of the teacher to the termination of pupil talk.
5) Check the proportions of tallies to be found in the "content cross" and "steady state cells" in order to estimate the rapidity of exchange, tendency toward sustained talk, and content emphasis.

Cate-gory	1	2	3	4	5	6	7	8	9	10	Total
1	—	—	—	—	—	—	—	—	—	1	1
2	—	2	—	—	4	—	—	12	—	—	18
3	—	—	5	—	1	—	—	—	—	—	6
4	—	—	—	16	—	—	—	86	5	10	117
5	—	—	—	5	35	8	—	—	—	—	48
6	—	—	—	—	—	13	3	—	4	4	24
7	1	—	—	—	—	3	7	—	—	4	15
8	—	16	—	96	8	—	—	43	1	—	164
9	—	—	1	—	—	—	4	—	3	5	13
10	—	—	—	—	—	—	1	23	—	18	42
Total	1	18	6	117	48	24	15	164	13	42	448
%	0.2	4.0	1.3	26.1	10.7	5.4	3.3	36.6	2.9	9.5	100

Fig. 4–7.   Matrix Q.

We turn now to a discussion of these five steps and their application to the interpretation of the two matrices shown in Figs. 4–6 and 4–7.

HOW MUCH TIME IS INVOLVED?

The most certain way to know the elapsed time is to have the observer make notations about the hour and the minute he entered and left a classroom and also at the beginning and end of all uninterrupted sequences of code symbols. Such notes permit you to calculate both the elapsed visit time and elapsed coding time. In the event that such notes are not made and your only information is the matrix total, the following equivalents help in making estimates: 20 tallies = 1 minute, 100 tallies = 5 minutes, and 1,200 tallies = 1 hour. These equivalents are based on one tally every 3 seconds. When time notations are available, the coding time in seconds, divided by the matrix total, will give the average rate which the observer used.

A first step, then, to compare these two matrices, is to look at the matrix totals and consider whether the sample of interaction is appropriate for your purposes. Since our purpose here is merely training, we can simply note that there are more than 400 tallies in each matrix, which should provide enough information for simple comparisons. In the event we are concerned with a more stable sample of a teacher's interaction pattern, we would prefer about 6,000 tallies based on six to eight visits which would be spaced according to some logical plan. Should we be concerned with a group of teacher-classroom units, the total tallies per teacher might be reduced from 6,000, but the plan of sampling which guides the schedule of visits should take into consideration the purposes of the investigation.

Assignment Five: How many minutes of coding time would you estimate were required to obtain matrix P and matrix Q? (The answers to all questions in this section can be found at the end of the chapter.)

WHAT IS THE PROPORTION OF TEACHER TALK, PUPIL TALK, AND SILENCE OR CONFUSION?

Monopolizing talking time is one way to dominate and to express one's will. Since power, maturity, authority, and initiative usually lie with the teacher, it is not surprising to discover that the teacher talks more than half the elapsed coding time in most visits.

There are three arithmetic procedures that are commonly used in order to make comparisons between two or more matrices. They all share in common the setting up of proportions so that direct comparisons of numbers can be made, regardless of how long a particular observation lasted. The most elegant method, and one which is generally used in research projects that have access to a computer, is to convert all matrices—usually these are composite matrices involving thousands of tallies—to a common base of 1,000. This is called a *millage matrix*. It might be considered improper to convert a raw tally matrix into a millage matrix unless it contained more than 700 or 800 tallies. A second method, far more frequently used because it is convenient, is to convert all column totals to percent of the matrix total and then calculate certain ratios for which we have normative expectations. These ratios will be explained during the next few pages, since they are useful in field situations where quick interpretations are often desired. A third method is used only when two matrices are involved and there is no need to refer to normative expectations. This method requires a simple ratio based on the two matrix totals. Once such a ratio is set up on a slide rule, a number from one matrix can be increased or decreased, either alternative being available, so that it can be compared directly with another. For example, the numbers in matrix *P* can be decreased by the proportion 448/629 or the numbers in matrix Q can be increased by the proportion 629/448. Most of what is to follow is based on the second method.

Teacher talk, pupil talk, and silence or confusion, converted to percents, should add up to 100. In effect, we are saying that one of three communication states exist: either the teacher is talking, or a pupil is talking, or silence or confusion exists. Knowing these three percents and what one might expect from past observations of many teachers helps to establish the situational setting referred to earlier.

For matrix P, teacher talk is 52.2 percent, pupil talk is 42.9 percent, and silence or confusion is 4.9 percent. The same figures for matrix Q are teacher talk 51 percent, pupil talk 39.5 percent, and silence and confusion 9.5 percent. These figures are quite similar. The only interpretation that might be made by comparing them is that there seems to be fewer pauses in the flow of communication in classroom P, but otherwise they are remarkably alike.

The percents of teacher and pupil talk in both matrix P and matrix Q, while similar, are not very close to normative expectations. After several years of observing, we anticipate an average of 68 percent teacher talk, about 20 percent pupil talk, and 11 or 12 percent silence and confusion.

Assignment Six: Given that the proportion of teacher talk, pupil talk, and silence or confusion is quite similar, matrix P compared to matrix Q, what is your best guess about changes in these three percents in the event that you were able to continue visiting these two classrooms for another six visits and then calculate the same three percents on the basis of all visits?

HOW DOES THE BALANCE OF THE TEACHER'S RESPONSE-INITIATIVE COMPARE WITH PUPIL INITIATION?

Knowledge of how much the teacher or the pupils talked becomes much more useful when it is combined with some index of quality. Simple ratios can be calculated which provide such information in terms of teacher initiative, teacher response, and pupil initiative. We normally expect reciprocal relationships between teacher statements and pupil statements. That is, the more the teacher takes the initiative, the more likely pupils are to respond. The more a teacher responds, the more likely it is that pupils will make statements which show initiative.

In the last section, it turned out that the percent teacher and percent pupil talk for situations P and Q were approximately equal. This comparison suggests that the interaction during the two observations was quite similar. In this section, we will make use of some simple ratios to show that the balance of initiation and response is quite different in situations P and Q, in spite of the similarities noted in the previous section.

In the past, authors writing about the FIAC system of interaction analysis have referred to Categories 1, 2, 3, and 4 as indicative of "indirect teacher influence" and Categories 5, 6, and 7 as "direct teacher influence." It is now being proposed that a more parsimonious way to conceptualize this aspect of classroom interaction is to use the same concepts, initiation and response, to describe both teacher and pupil talk.

Another reason for change is that a problem has arisen in connection with the mathematics of indirect-to-direct ratios which have been used previously to describe interaction analysis data. For example, the i/d ratio, which consists of category frequencies 1 + 2 + 3 divided by 6 + 7, and the I/D ratio, which consists of 1 + 2 + 3 + 4 divided by 5 + 6 + 7, have remained stable and useful statistics when applied to matrices with well over 1,000 tallies. However, matrices from a single visit can contain very few tallies in certain cells and the ratios become spuriously high if the denominator becomes very small. For example, it is possible for the sum of Categories 6 and 7, in matrices with 400 to 600 tallies to provide denominators as low as three, two, one, and even zero. For these reasons new ratios are proposed for making quick comparisons of the balance between initiation and response.

The *teacher response ratio* (TRR) is defined as an index which corresponds to the teacher's tendency to react to the ideas and feelings of the pupils. The formula is designed so that the index will be a percent figure, never higher than 100 and never less than zero. The TRR can be found by adding category frequencies 1 + 2 + 3, multiplying by 100, and dividing by the sum of 1 + 2 + 3 + 6 + 7. One can expect different average TRR figures for different types of classes, but a good estimate of the average of all averages is about 42. Applied to Figs. 4−6 and 4−7, the TRR is, respectively, 94 and 39. This indicates that the teacher responded to pupil talk much more often in matrix P than in matrix Q.

A *teacher question ratio* (TQR) is proposed which is defined as an index representing the tendency of a teacher to use questions when guiding the more content oriented part of the class discussion. The TQR is the percent of all Category 4 and 5 statements which are classified in Category 4. It is calculated by multiplying the Category 4 frequency by 100 and dividing by the sum of Categories 4 and 5. The TQR will vary as the teacher solicits pupil reactions to ideas which the teacher considers important or as he checks on their understanding by asking questions. In matrix P the TQR is 44 and in matrix Q the TQR is 71. This is a radical difference which is created by the unusually high number of questions asked in situation Q. Normally, one would expect the average TQR for a number of teachers, each observed on several occasions, to be close to 26. This aspect of both situations P and Q is well above average, but Q is exceptionally high.

A *pupil initiation ratio* (PIR) is proposed to indicate what proportion of pupil talk was judged by the observer to be an act of initiation. The PIR can be calculated by multiplying the frequency in Category 9 by 100 and dividing by the sum of all pupil talk. One can expect that an average PIR of many different kinds of classes would be fairly close to 34. The PIRs for matrices P and Q are 74 and 7, respectively. This again is quite a contrast. One can conclude that both class interaction patterns were so extreme as to be exceptional with pupils taking much more initiative in situation P.

These three ratios, in combination with the percent teacher and pupil talk, permit us to start describing the situational settings for the interaction represented by matrices P and Q. In situation P, the teacher is unusually responsive to pupil talk, asks an above average number of questions, and the pupils show very high initiative in introducing their own ideas into the classroom discourse. In situation Q, the teacher appears to lead the discussion by asking many questions, is slightly below average in response to pupil talk, and nearly all pupil talk is determined by the questions asked by the teacher. Yet in producing these quite opposite patterns, the proportion of teacher talk to pupil talk is about the same in both classrooms with pupil talk well above average. Whatever theories we may develop later must be logically consistent with these more basic features of the interaction. The contrast stands out quite clearly in Table 4–1.

TABLE 4–1

Ratios in Situations P and Q

Ratio	P	Q	Norm
TRR	94	39	42
TQR	44	71	26
PIR	74	7	34

Although it is a bit premature, at this stage of the analysis, to speculate on the more general reactions of the pupils, try answering the two questions below on the basis of your present hunches. Both answers can be compared with suggested answers at the end of the chapter.

Assignment Seven: In which situation, P or Q, would you expect a gradual increase in pupil restlessness, based on the data in Table 4–1? Why?

HOW DOES THE TEACHER REACT WHEN PUPILS STOP TALKING?

The first things that a teacher says at the instant a pupil stops talking can be studied because the tallies for these statements are isolated and tabulated in separate cells of the 10 × 10 matrix. One might guess that the teacher's reaction at the moment a pupil stops talking is critical because each communication reentry of the teacher sets expectations of what will follow. It seems quite possible that the highest proportion of the class will be paying attention to the teacher, just before he speaks and when he is about to react to something a pupil said. Patterns of teacher talk at this moment may also be more revealing, in the sense that the spontaneous impulses of the teacher are more likely to enter into consideration. Our first task is to locate these cells in a 10 × 10 matrix.

Having read this far, you should be able to identify the 14 cells of a matrix in which are tabulated the first teacher code symbols to follow pupil talk. The way to solve this problem is to think of the original pairs that are involved. The first number of such a pair should represent pupil talk and the second number should represent teacher talk. With this much of a hint, try the following assignments.

Assignment Eight: Take a pencil and shade the 14 cells in which are tabulated the first teacher code symbols to follow pupil talk.

Assignment Nine: Now shade the 14 cells in which you find the code symbols of the last thing a teacher says just before a pupil begins to talk.

The correct answer to Assignment Eight is found by remembering that a sequence pair in which a pupil stops and the teacher starts must have either 8 or 9 as the first number in the pair, and some symbol from 1 to 7 as the second number. Thus, the area you should shade to answer Assignment Eight would be in rows 8 and 9, columns 1 through 7. The answer to Assignment Nine is just the opposite. The 14 cells are in columns 8 and 9, rows 1 through 7.

The isolation of rows 8 and 9 in order to study the immediate reaction of teachers to the termination of pupil talk permits us to develop two additional ratios based on the TRR and the TQR. Both of these ratios can be calculated as they were before, except that the cell frequencies in rows 8 and 9 are combined by addition and substituted for column totals.

Let us define the *instantaneous teacher response ratio* (TRR89) as the tendency of the teacher to praise or integrate pupil ideas and feelings into the class discussion, at the moment the pupils stop talking. The TRR89 can be calculated by adding the cell frequencies in rows 8 and 9, columns 1, 2, and 3, multiplying this sum by 100, and dividing the product by the total tallies in the cells of rows 8 and 9, columns 1, 2, 3, 6, and 7.

Let us define the *instantaneous teacher question ratio* (TQR89) as the tendency of the teacher to respond to pupil talk with questions based on his own ideas, compared to his tendency to lecture. The TQR89 is calculated by adding the frequencies in cells $(8-4) + (9-4)$, multiplying by 100, and dividing by the total tallies in the four cells $(8-4) + (8-5) + (9-4) + (9-5)$.

These two ratios of immediate teacher reaction can now be applied to matrices P and Q. The contrast of P and Q, respectively, for the TRR89 is 100 and 81; for the TQR89, the ratios are 26 and 92. A normative expectation for the TRR89 is about 60 and for the TQR89 about 44. These results permit the following kinds of interpretation. In comparing matrix P with matrix Q, the immediate response tendency of the teacher (TRR89) in situation P is 100, which means that the teacher P always reacted to the ideas and feelings of pupils or else gave encouragement or praise, in contrast with directions or criticism. The teacher in Q found it necessary to react with criticism on four occasions, but due to frequent short praise and encouragement, attains an above average TRR89.

The TQR89 shows that the teacher in situation Q was much more likely to move on to a new question, compared to lecturing, than was the teacher in situation P, although this latter teacher responded with either questions or lecture only a few times.

The results of interpreting the TRR89 and the TQR89 can now be added to the interpretations made from Table 4–1. To what has already been said about situation P, we can now add that the immediate reaction of the teacher was consistent with the high pupil orientation already suggested. The same TRR versus TRR89 trend is present in situation Q. However, the unique pattern of teacher-pupil interchange indicated by the extremely high TQR89 in situation Q suggests that the teacher made use of questions in a most unusual way.

We can now proceed to the last two general ratios which help to round out the situational characteristics of classroom interaction.

HOW MUCH EMPHASIS IS GIVEN TO CONTENT? HOW MUCH SUSTAINED EXPRESSION IN THE SAME CATEGORY IS PRESENT?

The last two general features of classroom interaction to be discussed as aids to interpretation are based on what is called the "content cross" and the "steady state" cells. The *content cross ratio* (CCR) is found by calculating the percent of all tallies that lie within the columns and rows of Categories 4 and 5. The *steady state ratio* (SSR) can be determined by calculating the percent of all tallies that lie within the 10 steady state cells. Before each is discussed in turn, it will help to locate the cells on which each index is based.

Assignment Ten: Use your pencil to shade the 38 cells of the content cross. Just shade columns 4 and 5, then rows 4 and 5.

Assignment Eleven: On another matrix form, or with a different color pencil, shade the 10 steady state cells which have identical numbers in their addresses. These are the (1–1), (2–2), (3–3), . . . , (10–10) cells.

The content cross ratio (CCR) is rather poorly named since many statements in Categories 3, 6, 8, and 9 are concerned directly with content. However, the content cross does isolate those teacher statements which are least likely to be involved with certain process problems which every teacher must solve. The problems of reward and punishment, reacting to the ideas and feelings of the pupils, and the giving of assignments and directions are least likely to be class-ified in Categories 4 and 5. An exceptionally high CCR is an indication that the main focus of class discussion was on subject matter, that the teacher took a very active role in the discussion, and that attention to motivation and discipline problems was at a minimum. A mythical national average for the CCR would be fairly close to 55 percent, probably higher for certain secondary classes in the academic subjects.

The steady state ratio (SSR) reflects the tendency of teacher and pupil talk to remain in the same category for periods longer than 3 seconds. The higher this ratio, the less rapid is the interchange between the teacher and the pupils, on the average. A separate *pupil steady state ratio* (PSSR) is an even more sensitive index to the rapidity of the teacher-pupil interchange when pupil talk is average or above average. The PSSR is calculated by adding the frequencies in the (8–8) + (9–9) cells, multiplying by 100, and dividing by all pupil talk tallies. In the event that you were observing a number of teachers, you might expect the SSR to average around 50 and the PSSR to average around 35 or 40. Apparently, on the average, teachers can extend their talk in the same category more often than the pupils.

In matrix *P* the SSR is 60.8, the PSSR is 71.5, and the CCR is 35.2. The same ratios for matrix *Q* are SSR 31.7, PSSR 26.0, and CCR 61.2. A comparison of these ratios suggests that the interchange between the teacher and the pupils is much more rapid in matrix *Q*, since the SSR and the PSSR are so much lower. The higher CCR of matrix *Q* suggests a more active teacher role and greater emphasis on content.

Table 4–2 summarizes all of the ratios we have been discussing by showing normative expectations for different grade levels, as well as matrices *P* and *Q* in the two columns to the right. You can now review what has been said by seeing if you can make an interpretation for each index ratio listed in the table for matrix *P* compared to *Q*. Can you do this without referring to the text?

USING CELL FREQUENCIES TO SUPPORT
THEORETICAL SPECULATIONS ABOUT TEACHER BEHAVIOR

So far in this chapter, you have read about how the purpose of an observation will determine questions which guide both encoding and decoding. Quite a few pages were devoted to thinking about interaction analysis in three ways: in the English language, as a sequence of coded symbols, and as a pattern within a matrix. And in the last section, the procedural steps to secure several general ratios and other descriptive statistics of classroom interaction were outlined. Now we will turn to certain cells in the matrix which help to support, modify, or refute possible explanations which grow out of initial speculations.

TABLE 4–2

Matrices P and Q Compared to Normative Expectations for Matrix Ratios

Variable	Symbol	8th Grade Math	7th Grade English and Social Studies	6th Grade	4th Grade	Matrix P	Matrix Q
Percent teacher talk	TT	70	61	53	53	52	51
Percent pupil talk	PT	19	28	32	29	43	39.5
Percent silence or confusion	SC	11	11	15	18	5	9.5
Teacher response ratio	TRR	35	41	52	51	94	39
Teacher question ratio	TQR	20	26	26	26	44	71
Teacher immediate response reaction	TRR89	67	75	77	81	100	81
Teacher immediate question ratio	TQR89	39	45	45	40	26	92
Pupil initiation ratio	PIR	35	32	34	35	74	7
Content emphasis	CCR	68	55	47	51	35	61
Total sustained discourse	SSR	52	54	48	53	61	32
Pupil sustained discourse	PSSR	26	55	53	53	72	26
Total of the composite matrix	N	58,614	51,825	77,564	174,140	629	448
Number of teachers observed	N	16	16	30	16	1	1
Parent population sampled	N	85	63	101	72	—	—

	Cate-gory	1	2	3	4	5	6	7	8	9	10	Total
Teacher	1	2	—	—	—	—	—	—	—	1	—	3
	2	—	—	—	—	—	—	—	—	—	—	—
	3	—	—	—	—	—	—	—	—	—	—	—
	4	—	—	—	—	—	—	—	—	—	—	—
	5	—	—	—	—	—	—	—	—	—	—	—
	6	—	—	—	—	—	—	—	—	—	—	—
	7	—	—	—	—	—	—	—	—	—	—	—
Pupil	8	—	—	—	—	—	—	—	—	—	—	—
	9	1	—	—	—	—	—	—	—	—	—	—
X	10	—	—	—	—	—	—	—	—	—	—	—
	Total	3	—	—	—	—	—	—	—	—	—	—

Fig. 4—8.   Entry to and Exits from Category 1,   Matrix P.

JUDGING TEMPORAL SEQUENCE FROM THE MATRIX

One of the most important insights of matrix interpretation is to understand how it is possible to inspect the column frequencies when you are interested in what preceded an event and to inspect the row frequencies when you are interested in what followed, given an event designated by a category number. For example, this kind of understanding is essential to reconstructing patterns from a matrix such as those involving drill or inquiry, illustrated in Fig. 4—5. You also used a similar kind of reasoning if you were successful in completing Assignments Eight and Nine in this chapter.

Suppose we consider, first, the simplest problem which occurs when an entry to a particular category occurs just once. You will see an illustration of this in Fig. 4—8 with respect to Category 1, taken from matrix P.

Here is a rule that you should remember: *subtract the steady state cell frequency from the column total (or row total, since both are equal) in order to determine the number of one-way transitions for that category.* The column and row total of Category 1 is three. The (1—1) cell frequency is two: $3 - 2 = 1$, so there is one transition to Category 1. *The transitions to a category are found in the*

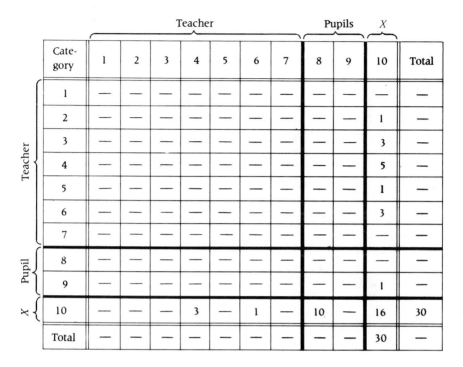

| | | | Teacher | | | | | | Pupils | | X | |
	Category	1	2	3	4	5	6	7	8	9	10	Total
Teacher	1	—	—	—	—	—	—	—	—	—	—	—
	2	—	—	—	—	—	—	—	—	—	1	—
	3	—	—	—	—	—	—	—	—	—	3	—
	4	—	—	—	—	—	—	—	—	—	5	—
	5	—	—	—	—	—	—	—	—	—	1	—
	6	—	—	—	—	—	—	—	—	—	3	—
	7	—	—	—	—	—	—	—	—	—	—	—
Pupil	8	—	—	—	—	—	—	—	—	—	—	—
	9	—	—	—	—	—	—	—	—	—	1	—
X	10	—	—	—	3	—	1	—	10	—	16	30
	Total	—	—	—	—	—	—	—	—	—	30	—

Fig. 4—9.   Silence and Confusion, Matrix *P*.

column; the transitions from *a category are found in the row.* This relationship between a column and row is due to the tabulating convention that designates the row for the first number of a sequence pair and the column for the second number. If we had adopted the opposite convention, the relationship between the columns and rows would have been reversed.

In the simple case of one transition entry, it is possible to state exactly what happened before and after the teacher responded to the feelings or attitude of some pupil. In this case, apparently a pupil was expressing his own ideas or feelings. In any case it was unsolicited by the teacher. Then the teacher reacted to these feelings constructively for about 9 seconds, after which pupil initiation talk resumed. Thus, the sequence must have been 9, 1, 1, 1, 9. What happened before Category 1 is shown by the first sequence pair, 9—1, which is found in column 1. What happened after Category 1 is shown by the last pair, 1—9, which is found in row 1.

Now let's apply these ideas to a more practical type of question. Figure 4—9 shows the entries and exits of Category 10, silence or confusion, also from matrix P. Suppose you wished to answer the question, "Who breaks silence or confusion more often, the teacher or some pupil?" A similar question might be, "Does the teacher tolerate silence or confusion?" For any question concerning silence or confusion, attention centers on the row and column of Category 10.

The question "Who breaks silence or confusion?" focuses attention on the row because we are concerned with an event which follows silence or confusion, not an event which precedes it. A first step is to determine the transitions. In this case we subtract 16 from 30 and find there are 14 transitions, which can be checked by adding 3 + 1 + 10. Now we can reformulate the question with greater precision, namely, "Given 14 occasions on which silence or confusion was terminated, who broke this silence or confusion more often, the teacher or the pupils?" The number for the pupils is found by adding the frequencies in the (10–8) + (10–9) cells; in this case the answer is 10. The remaining four times were transitions to teacher talk, three to teacher questions, and one to teacher directions. Thus, we have accounted for all sequels to silence or confusion and found that pupil talk is more likely to occur than teacher talk by a ratio of 10 to 4.

Assignment Twelve: In which situation, matrix P or Q, is the teacher less likely to interrupt silence or confusion?

Assignment Thirteen: In Fig. 4–9, is silence or confusion more likely to occur after teacher talk or after pupil talk? After what kind of teacher talk is silence or confusion most likely to occur? (Answers are found at the end of this chapter.)

Before leaving the topic of silence or confusion, let us consider the relationships between the type of analysis that has just been explained and several other aspects of teacher behavior. One such aspect is the rapidity of interchange between pupil and teacher. You will recall that the SSR and PSSR ratios are inversely related to rapidity of interchange. When these two ratios are low and rapidity is presumably high, how would you predict the tendency of the teacher to interrupt silence or confusion, compared with the pupils? One answer is to say, it may be conceivable that a teacher working rapidly in a quick exchange, drill type situation might tolerate a pause, silence, or a few moments of confusion, without intervening, but it does not seem probable. Thus, for example, in matrix P, the SSR and the PSSR are above average and the interchange between the teacher and the pupils is presumably slower. We note that the teacher interrupts Category 10 pauses only four out of 14 times. We infer that a pupil usually had all the time he needed to formulate his verbal contribution. The fact that this same system of reasoning does not fit the data in matrix Q will be discussed in the next section. In general, a rapid interchange is more likely to be associated with lower tolerance for silence on the part of a teacher.

TABLE 4–3

Expected and Actual Events Following Teacher Questions, Row 4

Category column	1	2	3	4	5	6	7	8	9	0
Expected frequency	0.4	2.8	14.6	9.2	11.7	1.2	0	8.5	24.3	3.6
Actual frequency	0	0	0	36	2	0	0	16	17	5

Those who have a bent for mathematics can reach slightly more complicated inferences from a matrix by applying probability theory. The formula for calculating the cell frequency that would be expected by chance is

$$(1) \quad \frac{\text{Column total} \times \text{row total}}{\text{Matrix total}} = \text{Expected cell frequency},$$

or, to make use of an equivalent form,

$$(2) \quad \frac{\text{Column percent} \times \text{row percent} \times \text{matrix total}}{10,000} = \text{Expected cell frequency}.$$

To illustrate, suppose we investigate row 4 in matrix P in order to decide whether the events which follow a 4 would be expected by chance. Use formula (1) or (2) to calculate the expected cell frequencies. The results are shown in Table 4–3. One can conclude that in the situation observed, the (4–4) and (4–8) sequence pairs occurred with an incidence higher than would be expected by chance, while the incidence of the (4–5) and (4–9) sequence pairs was lower. These inferences can then be added to the general interpretation of the matrix.

As an additional assignment, those who know how to use a slide rule can quickly calculate the expected incidence of events which precede teacher questions. We might note in passing that the model of chance employed in the above calculations assumes independent events. Since the data fail to meet this assumption, interpretations about chance expectations should be conservative.

THE GAME OF BLIND MATRIX ANALYSIS

The game of blind matrix analysis often erupts spontaneously among members of an observation team, whether they are involved in an inservice training project or helping with some basic research. This game is played in the following way. An observer tabulates his matrix from a visit and provides his fellow observers with a copy, but he hides the additional information which all observers normally collect during a visit. The only information he reveals is the grade level of the class, the sex of the teacher, and the subject matter which was under study. To play the game the other team members study the matrix and slowly build alternative explanations about what happened. Then, as more insight develops, alternatives are eliminated until only one or two remain. On the remaining explanations the decoders rest their case. The original observer then tells them what actually occurred. It is surprising how often the final explanations fit the real facts.

In order to introduce you to this little game, suppose we turn to matrix Q. Several times earlier in this chapter there were suggestions that matrix Q illustrates an unusual interaction pattern. Several of the basic ratios were exceptionally far away from normative expectations. For example, the TQR indicated an excessive use of questions.

In order to illustrate how distinguishing between columns and rows can help suggest plausible answers to a riddle like matrix Q, suppose we turn our attention to speculations in a game of blind matrix analysis. Before beginning, it might be well to point out that most matrices are not decoded through blind analysis—in which there are no supplementary notes from the observer. On the contrary, usually such notes are available and very useful during the decoding process. Blind analysis is just a game that helps decoders and encoders become more sensitive to clues hidden in a matrix.

In Fig. 4–10, letter A points to four cells involving praise and encouragement. Apparently praise always starts right after a type 8 pupil response; see the (8–2) cell. It is usually short because there are only two tallies in the (2–2) cell. It is followed, 12 out of 16 times, by the continuation of type 8 pupil talk; see the (2–8) cell. One might guess that such teacher phrases as, "Good," "Go on," "That's right," "Um hm," etc., might be typical examples. On four occasions—see the (2–5) cell—such statements were followed by teacher lecture type statements. One might conjecture that the teacher said, "Well, you all did well on that, now we are going ...," to illustrate a possible 2–5 transition. There seems to be nothing unusual about the patterns involving praise, except that extended praise is in very short supply.

Letter B points to the extremely high 8–4 and 4–8 transitions, which suggest that short questions and short answers moved along at a fairly rapid interchange. In Category 8, pupils started to talk 121 times (164 − 43 = 121). It is possible that 43 in the (8–8) cell means that a single 8 followed an 8 on 43 occasions, but this is not probable. The most we can say is that on no more than 43 occasions, and probably fewer, did two or more 8's follow in sequence. The entire matrix is now beginning to look like an ordinary drill lesson in some subject matter field like arithmetic or spelling.

Letter C points to further features of questioning. Relatively few questions took longer than 3 seconds; compare the 16 in the (4–4) cell with an expected frequency of about 36. One unusual pattern is that on five occasions—see the (4–9) cell—students initiated their own ideas at the end of a teacher

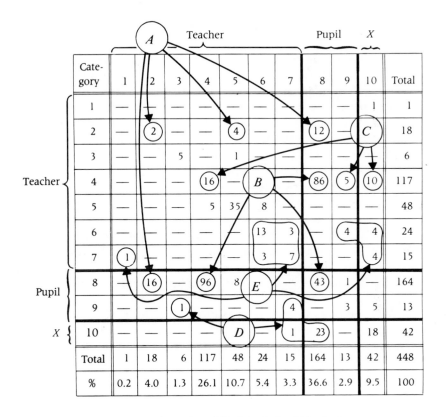

Fig. 4–10.   Blind Analysis of Matrix Q.

question. Broad questions which stimulate pupil explanation are possible, but this conjecture does not fit the drill type pattern or the below expected (4–4) frequency. If these statements were of the type, "Well, wait a minute, let me think," or "I wish you hadn't asked that question," they might be consistent with a teacher directed drill activity. Notice, however, that the teacher never follows 9 with 4. There are no 9–4 transitions. So 4–9 transitions apparently are not logically related to 9–4 transitions. Instead, notice the four tallies in the (9–7) cell. Perhaps the teacher said, "You should have been listening." Yet the (9–10) cell indicates that a pupil might be given more time if he needs it. Also the (4–10) cell indicates that time to think before answering a question did occur.

Letter D identifies how silence or confusion was terminated. In 23 out of 24 transitions, the pupils continued after silence without intervention from the teacher. This raises several questions. Why doesn't a teacher help pupils who fail to respond quickly? Why are the (10–3), (10–4), (10–5), and (10–6) cells zero? In most normal drill or review situations there would be at least some transitions of this sort. Notice also that four out of five teacher reactions to statements showing pupil initiative involve criticism; see the (9—7) and (9—3) cells. It is as if the teacher's role is restricted and requires negative reactions to any kind of initiative.

At this point, anyone playing the game of blind analysis must imagine some kind of activity which takes into account the odd restrictions on the behavior of the teacher. The notion of drill or review does not quite fit the circumstances, although it comes close. There are two types of activities which sometimes occur in a classroom which are like drill, but which require a referee, not a teacher. For example, a spelling bee or any academic quiz game which involves competition between pupils or teams of pupils. Another alternative may be a formal oral quiz. In most such instances, the role of the teacher is restricted with regard to helping pupils. We might note, at this point, that nothing that has been said about the cells designated by letters A, B, and C is in conflict with a competitive game or a teacher directed quiz. One might imagine a spelling bee or an arithmetic drill game between two or more teams.

Letter E identifies transitions and steady state cells involved with teacher directions and criticisms. Directions are most often followed by silence or confusion and statements of pupil initiation; see row 6. The latter sequence does not suggest drill, but it does suggest a pupil making an exclamation about his own performance or an objection to a ruling by a referee during the stress of competition. Also, on three occasions, the teacher voluntarily stopped giving directions and began to criticize; see the (6—7) cell. He also returned to giving directions after criticizing on three occasions; see the (7—6) cell. One possible 6—7—6 transition is, "Sit down, Jim, you're wrong. You should know better. Bill, you take the next question." A 6—9—7 is also possible, according to the frequencies in the matrix, perhaps this was, "Sit down, Mary." To which Mary responded, "But I wasn't ready!" Then the teacher said, "Don't argue with the referee." This kind of speculation is not convincing, but it at least remains in the realm of possibility. The absence of a (10—6) transition tends to rule out the administration of a standardized test or any work period which is followed by further directions. The 7—1 transition is very, very rare. In a quiz or competitive game, however, one can think of possible examples. The teacher might have said, "You should have known better, but don't feel too disappointed when you tried so hard."

The only cell with a reasonably large frequency which has not been discussed is the (5—5) cell. One thing to notice is that this is the only category in which the steady state cell represents such a high proportion of the column total; 35 is almost 75 percent of 48. This means that once the teacher began to lecture, on the average, he was likely to string about three 5's together.

Lecturing was followed by giving directions on eight occasions—see the (5–6) cell—and on five occasions—see the (5–4) cell—by asking questions. Such a pattern of lecture would be consistent with explaining the rules of a game or quiz, then dividing up the class into teams, and so on. On eight occasions—see the (8–5) cell—pupil talk preceded teacher lecturing. This might occur when the teacher chose to express his own opinion about something that was said or decided to explain some aspect of the game.

Perhaps it is time to end this fantasy. It is presented here to illustrate a game that can be played by those who are trying to learn matrix interpretation. A friend or colleague is required to make the observation, tabulate the matrix, and then be the judge who accepts, modifies, or refutes your speculative explanations of what happened. Fortunately, blind matrix analysis can easily be avoided in the scientific study of classroom interaction by simply making sure that observers fill out written reports to be combined with interaction analysis data.

The game has one very important advantage for observer training, whether the trainee is a teacher, research worker, or administrator. It brings the observer into direct contact with the problems of decoding. Issues about how to use a particular category may seem arbitrary or hard to understand during observer training, but as soon as a person attempts a blind matrix analysis and starts to build an explanation of interaction based only on a matrix display, the consequences of placing a tally into a particular category "come home," so to speak, to the prospective observer. For example, observers may argue at some length about the cues that can be used to distinguish between Categories 8 and 9 and finally agree to use a procedure which really should not be used. When this procedure results in a tabulation which is misleading to the decoder, in a game of blind analysis, it appears as a confrontation between the judge, who coded the tallies, and the decoder, who is building the interpretation. Such a confrontation often resolves differences of opinion which, in the long run, is not only likely to increase observation reliability, but improve validity as well.

DRAWING A FLOW CHART FROM A MATRIX

Sometimes it is necessary to provide feedback to teachers who, by some peculiar twist of their personal experience, are totally unable to cope with a matrix. For these people a matrix must be a confusing, conglomerate of numbers rather than an informative display and they probably become uncomfortable whenever they are near a matrix. It may be a kind of allergy. A matrix can be changed into a form which is less toxic for those who suffer from numbers, providing the observer is willing to take the time and energy and providing he knows how to proceed. This section will describe such a procedure.

Category	1	2	3	4	5	6	7	8	9	10	Total
1	—	—	—	—	—	—	—	—	—	—	—
2	—	1	1	1	2	—	—	1	5	—	11
3	—	—	5	1	4	—	—	—	—	—	10
4	—	—	—	23	2	1	—	42	3	5	76
5	—	2	1	22	80	1	2	3	3	3	117
6	—	—	—	1	—	—	1	3	—	—	5
7	—	—	—	—	2	1	1	—	—	—	4
8	—	5	—	22	19	—	—	45	7	—	98
9	—	3	3	3	7	—	—	3	32	—	51
10	—	—	—	3	1	2	—	1	1	—	8
Total	—	11	10	76	117	5	4	98	51	8	380

Fig. 4—11.   Sample of Classroom Interaction.

Suppose an observer comes into possession of a matrix, such as the one shown in Fig. 4—11. A flow diagram can form a visual display which may be a more acceptable form of feedback. In order to make a flow diagram from a matrix, knowledge of the clockwise rotation of events and the differences between columns and rows are essential. In order to follow this procedure, you will need to stop reading and take the time to draw a blank matrix form consisting of 10 rows and 10 columns, each properly labeled.

Copy the cell frequencies from Fig. 4—11 into your matrix and check to make sure that it is accurate. Now search for the highest cell frequency. In the case of Fig. 4—11 it is the (5—5) cell with a frequency of 80 tallies. The highest cell frequency is the starting point of your flow diagram since it is the sequence pair which occurs most often. For example, in Fig. 4—11, 80 is about 21 percent of 380, so the chances are about one out of five that the teacher would be lecturing for longer than 3 seconds should a visitor inadvertently walk into the room sometime during the observation. Circle the (5—5) cell or else draw a square around 80 so that the cell has double lines around it. This marked cell will be the starting point for reconstructing the flow of events.

Most often the cell with the highest frequency will be the (5—5) cell. However, it is possible for another cell to have the highest frequency and become the starting point. For example, see cell (9—9) in matrix P and the (8—4) cell in matrix Q (Figs. 4—6 and 4—7).

Once you have located the starting point, the next step is to locate the event which is most likely to follow. This is done by inspecting the row which is designated *by the second number in the address of the starting cell.* As you glance along this row, locate the unmarked cell with the highest frequency. In the case of Fig. 4—11, the second number in the address of the starting cell is 5, Therefore, you look for the highest unmarked cell in row 5. This turns out to be the (5—4) cell with 22 tallies. The (5—5) cell is not selected because it has already been marked. At this time, circle or square the 22 in cell (5—4) and draw a little looping arrow from the (5—5) cell to the (5—4) cell.

Notice that if you had carried out these two steps in matrix Q (Fig. 4—7), you would now have circled the (8—4) cell with 96 tallies and the (4—8) cell with 86 tallies. Had you drawn an arrow directly from the (8—4) cell to the (4—8) cell, you would have started a diagram similar to Route 1 in Fig. 4—3.

Having circled or squared the (5—4) cell, the next step is to find the event which is most likely to follow a 5—4 transition. To do this, you look in the row designated *by the second number in the address of the cell you just marked.* Therefore, you search row four. The highest frequency is 42, which is in the (4—8) cell, so you circle or square the 42. Draw an arrow from the (5—4) cell to the (4—8) cell and to save later erasure, route it above the two in the (4—5) cell. If you want to peek, in order to choose correct routes for your arrows, look at Fig. 4—12 in which all arrows are shown.

Having circled or squared the (4—8) cell, the next most frequent event will be found, just as before, in the row designated *by the second number in the address of your present cell.* This leads you to the (8—8) cell with 45 tallies. Circle or square this cell, and draw an arrow down to connect the (4—8) cell with the (8—8) cell.

Now look in row 8 for the cell with the highest frequency in an unmarked cell. Continue this procedure until you have traced all possible routes, drawn the corresponding arrows, and then combine routes by using a single arrow wherever possible.

There are two ground rules about this procedure. First, you should choose some minimum number which is the lowest cell frequency that you will mark. In Fig. 4—12, the lowest marked cell frequency is seven. Second, all cells with this frequency or higher must have entry and exit arrows. Sometimes the loop you are working on becomes completed without including all the above minimum cells. Should this happen, simply look for the highest unmarked cell and use it to start a new loop, using the same procedures. Keep tracing loops until all cells to be marked have at least one entry and one exit.

Category	1	2	3	4	5	6	7	8	9	10	Total
1	—	—	—	—	—	—	—	—	—	—	—
2	—	1	1	1	2	—	—	1	5	—	11
3	—	—	5	1	4	—	—	—	—	—	10
4	—	—	—	23	2	1	—	42	3	5	76
5	—	2	1	22	80	1	2	3	3	3	117
6	—	—	—	1	—	start	1	3	—	—	5
7	—	—	—	—	2	1	1	—	—	—	4
8	—	5	—	22	19	—	—	45	7	—	98
9	—	3	3	3	7	—	—	3	32	—	51
10	—	—	—	3	1	2	—	1	1	—	8
Total	—	11	10	76	117	5	4	98	51	8 ·	380
%	—	2.9	2.6	20.0	30.8	1.3	1.1	25.8	13.4	2.1	100
%	58.7							39.2		2.1	100

TT = 58.7	TRR = 70.0	TRR89 = 100.0	PIR = 34.2	CCR = 68.1
PT = 39.2	TQR = 39.3	TQR89 = 49.0	PSSR = 51.8	SSR = 49.2
SC = 2.1				

Fig. 4–12.   Clockwise Flow of Classroom Interaction.

The completed flow diagram should look like Fig. 4–12. The arrows help to clarify sequence and make the matrix display more understandable. In the case of Fig. 4–12, there are 309 tallies in the marked cells. This is 81 percent of the total tallies in the matrix. Thus, you can say that most of the interaction, some 80 percent of it, is illustrated by the arrows.

Ratios based on secondary information are shown at the bottom of Fig. 4–12. Most of the ratios are about average for the sixth grade, according to norms found in Table 4–2, except for the CCR, TRR, and TRR89, which are above average, and SC, which is below. Both TRR ratios are inflated because during this discussion there was no need to give directions. The low percent for silence and confusion (SC) is due primarily to no loss of time due to chang-

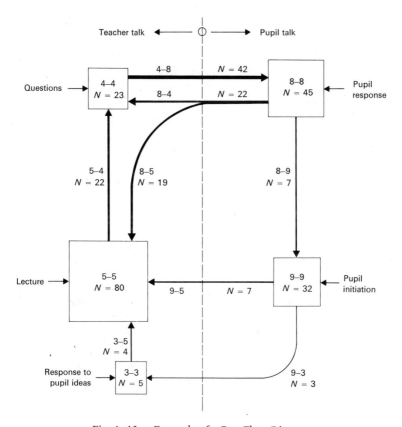

Fig. 4—13.   Example of a Box Flow Diagram.

ing from one type of classroom activity to another, which normally occurs in longer observations.

If this display of data is still incomprehensible to the teacher, it is possible to draw a diagram which looks just a little less complicated primarily because all interaction pairs with a frequency of less than seven are eliminated. Figure 4—13 is such a diagram. It attempts to use space in ways that are proportional to the traffic pattern. Thus, the 4—8 arrow is fat because there are 42 transitions. The 5—5 steady state pair is the largest square, because the frequency of this cell is 80, which is the highest. One way to help teachers who learn faster through participating is to let them draw a flow diagram such as the one in Fig. 4—13 as the observer draws the arrows in the matrix.

You may notice the slim arrow from (9—9) to (3—3) to (5—5) in Fig. 4—13. Drawing these extra low frequency pathways violates the ground rule of minimum frequency, but may serve a purpose during the consultation interview. One communication skill which this teacher may wish to practice is the use of Category 3 during a class discussion. Should the teacher find this to be an acceptable self-development goal, its inclusion in this first observation diagram will help in making comparisons with the matrix from the second observation. These plans for a second visit assume, of course, that you have not (by now) alienated your relationship with the teacher who was observed. During a second observation, the teacher might try to react to pupil ideas with greater deliberation and care. If successful, this would increase the frequency in the (3–3) cell. As an additional self-development goal, this teacher might be interested in trying to formulate questions out of ideas suggested by pupils. If this was successful, we might expect an increase in the 3–9 transitions.

THE OVERALL PROCESS

A teacher or pupil speaks and the observer classifies it into a category and records the code symbol. Code symbols are then considered as sequence pairs and tabulated into a matrix display. This is the process of encoding.

Decoding seeks to recreate those aspects of the original interaction which were encoded by building a description of English. What is to be in the foreground and what is relegated to the background of this description depends on the purpose of the observation. However, there are several features of the process which seem to be present quite often.

First, some kind of comparison is made. Two matrices may be compared in order to find similarities and differences between two segments of interaction. Sometimes a single matrix is compared with normative expectations in order to decide whether a particular interaction specimen is typical or atypical. It is also possible to compare the patterns within a single matrix to a valued model, that is, a desired or preferred state of affairs, described in terms of a matrix, which the teacher is attempting to develop.

Second, inferences about the sequence of events can be made. By understanding the relationships between the rows and columns, probability statements can be made about what precedes or what follows an event of interest. This kind of analysis produces a flow pattern which can be illustrated by arrows within the matrix or by a special flow diagram based on the matrix. The main features of the interaction can thus be highlighted.

Third, three ways of thinking facilitate the encoding and decoding processes. Besides common English concepts which denote behavior events, code symbols provide a "vocal shorthand" for describing the same events, and finally the matrix display exhibits meaning, in terms of communication patterns which can be "read" in a few minutes. The ability to shift rapidly among these "three languages" in the analysis of classroom interaction develops with first hand experience plus reading and contemplation, but seldom with one or the other alone.

Fourth, speculative descriptions of interaction must be logically consistent with situational setting. Basic elements of this situational setting can be identified by calculating percents and ratios which, in turn, are based on primary and secondary bits of information from the matrix.

The over-all goal of interpretation is to reconstruct those features of interaction, which were previously observed, from the display of coded information.

ANSWERS TO ASSIGNMENTS

ASSIGNMENT ONE

The first step is to write in the matrix total, which is given as 100. This number is written in the lower right-hand corner, to the right of the column totals and below the row totals. Since 30 percent means 30 tallies out of 100, and these are to be divided equally between the (4–4) and (8–8) cells, then you must enter 15 in each cell. Next, you must assign the 70 percent 4, 8, 4, 8, 4, 8 . . . in the proper cells. In this sequence there are two kinds of pairs and the tallies are split evenly between the two. Thus, you assign the number 35 to the (4–8) cell and the same number to the (8–4) cell, since only 4–8 and 8–4 pairs are involved. The remaining task is to check your work and find out if the matrix is balanced. This is done by adding the corresponding rows and columns to see if the sums are equal. In this particular case, the sums of rows 4 and 8 and columns 4 and 8 all equal 50. See Fig. 4–2.

ASSIGNMENT TWO

You must remember that one distinction between an inquiry model and a drill model is that the former makes full use of these four cells—the (9–9), (9–3), (3–3), and (3–9). An inspection of matrices P and Q shows extremely low frequencies in these four cells in Q and much higher frequencies in P. Thus, P shows more evidence of an inquiry pattern than does Q.

ASSIGNMENT THREE

If one accepts the model of inquiry proposed in the paragraph describing Fig. 4–5, then the initial short question and short answer pattern shown in matrix Q would occur first, and the outer orbit pattern of matrix P would appear second.

ASSIGNMENT FOUR

Motivation usually requires broad or open questions to which pupils are free to react with their own opinions. In turn, the teacher relates these opinions to the need for drill and to how drill develops skill. Such a pattern would be more similar to matrix P than to Q. Thus, the sequence would be matrix P first, and matrix Q second.

ASSIGNMENT FIVE

To solve this problem you must remember that 100 tallies equal about 5 minutes of observation. In matrix P, the 600 tallies are 30 minutes and the additional 29 tallies are about $1\frac{1}{2}$ minutes; thus the total is about 31 minutes. Matrix Q has a total of 448; 400 = 20 minutes and the additional 48 is close to $2\frac{1}{2}$ minutes, which totals to about 22 or 23 minutes.

ASSIGNMENT SIX

The logic behind this question has to do with estimating the proportion of teacher and pupil talk for two classrooms from the best information you have at hand which, in this case, is very little. For these particular classrooms, the information from a single short visit is shown in matrices P and Q. The only other information in any way related to the question consists of the normative expectations mentioned in the text and summarized in Table 4–2. If you assume that additional visits would provide a better sample of inter-action, then your best guess (even though it could be wrong) is that any changes would be in the direction toward "teachers in general." In this case the best guess is that the percent teacher talk will increase, the percent pupil talk will decrease, and the percent silence and confusion will increase.

ASSIGNMENT SEVEN

Making inferences about pupil restlessness can be based on how long pupils remain in a closely supervised or teacher directed pattern in which there is little opportunity for self-expression. In the 22-minute observation in matrix Q, the (6–7), (7–6), and (7–7) cells indicate the need for some teacher criticism. In matrix P, there is no such evidence during a 30-minute visit. Restlessness is more likely to develop in Q.

ASSIGNMENTS EIGHT AND NINE

The answer can be found in the text, in the paragraphs which follow the questions.

ASSIGNMENT TEN

You should shade rows 4 and 5 and columns 4 and 5 in response to this question.

ASSIGNMENT ELEVEN

You should shade the 10 diagonal cells starting with (1–1) and ending with (10–10), including all cells that have two identical numbers in their address.

ASSIGNMENT TWELVE

The phrase "interrupt silence" means that you are interested in transitions *from* Category 10 *to* something else. The sequence pairs involved must all have 10 as the first number—(10–?), so we inspect row 10. The second number must be a number from 1 to 7, since the question is concerned with teacher talk only. You begin by asking how many transitions from silence exist. To find the transitions, subtract the (10–10) cell from the row total in matrices P and Q. For P this is $30 - 16 = 14$. For Q this is $42 - 18 = 24$. Now look at row 10, columns 1 through 7. For P there are four transitions, for Q there is one transition. Thus, in matrix P the teacher interrupts silence four out of 14 times; in Q the teacher interrupts silence one out of 24 times. Therefore, the teacher is less likely to interrupt silence in situation Q. Arriving at the right answer for the wrong reasons is to miss the point. If this occurs, trace the recommended logic carefully.

ASSIGNMENT THIRTEEN

The phrase "silence after teacher or pupil talk" means that we are interested in a pair which is the reverse of the above problem. The second number must be 10, so we look in column 10. "After the teacher" means that the first number can vary from 1 through 7. "After pupil talk" means that the first number is either an 8 or a 9. An inspection of column 10 shows that silence follows teacher talk 13 times and follows pupil talk just once. The frequency of 5 in cell (4–10) indicates that silence is most likely to follow a teacher question.

Chapter Five

MULTIPLE CODING BY SUBDIVIDING CATEGORIES

THE CHALLENGE OF FLEXIBLE CODING

After a researcher has worked hard to establish a category system for coding some aspect of classroom behavior and has standardized his procedures, it is usually his misfortune to become interested in questions which his system might answer provided it was changed in some way. Responding to the temptation to make changes starts a chain reaction to which there is no end because there are always new and interesting questions to be answered. It is little wonder that a system and its user seem to remain in a perpetual state of flux.

The next two chapters offer a new challenge to anyone whose experience in systematic observation has been restricted to a fixed category system. Such systems involve rigid category definitions, particular rules of coding, standardized procedures of tabulation and display, all to be carried out in a "correct manner." This orthodoxy is probably helpful for early coding experiences, but it also restricts creative applications and innovations. The challenge of this chapter and the next is for you to become technologically flexible, to learn how to adapt coding procedures to a wide range of purposes and problems. In nearly every area of study there is a period of basic training which can then be followed, under the best of conditions, with uninhibited exploration. Skill in coding behavior is no exception.

The challenge in writing the next two chapters is to emphasize the logical steps which lead to the development of flexible coding. How does the nature of a coding problem provide clues for new categories? What coding procedures are necessary to make the new categories practical? How can the data be displayed so as to strike at the heart of a problem? Not all of these questions can be answered in this chapter and most routes to creative innovation are not well known. As writer and reader, you and I will have to work with care in order to emphasize the strategies and tactics rather than the details of the case study illustrations.

RELATIONSHIPS BETWEEN PURPOSE AND PROCEDURE

Modesty of purpose breeds parsimony in conceptualizing a problem. However, the purposes for which we code classroom interaction are seldom modest. Coding procedures have been applied to purposes as broad as "understanding what teaching is all about" by which we mean to study everything that influences classroom learning, as well as to study a particular kind of question asked by pupils.

It might be helpful to visualize a continuum of purposes which could guide coding procedures. Suppose at one end of this continuum purposes are broad and inclusive of all factors which impinge on classroom teacher-pupil transactions. Here we are concerned with the ecology of classroom learning. At the other end of this continuum, narrow, specific and dynamic explanations are sought for some specific pattern of classroom verbal communication. Here we might be concerned with teacher questions, how the teacher reacts when pupils stop talking, or some limited aspect of pupil talk. Researchers who develop radically different coding systems are often responding to purposes at completely different points along the purpose continuum.

An example of research which responds to broad, inclusive purposes can be found in the work of Biddle (11) and his associates. Biddle seeks the major dimensions of classroom behavior which he feels must be conceptualized in order to have a reasonably complete description of what is taking place in the classroom and, subsequently, to develop generalizations about the teaching-learning process. He states:

It seems clear that any reasonably complete study of classroom phenomena should cover a wide variety of classroom conditions and variables. (p. 338)

and later on:

Observer rating [in the classroom] *cannot generate a multifaceted behavior record and hence is unable to study the relationships among the many processes taking place simultaneously in the classroom. Only the audio-visual recording preserves the richness of the classroom for subsequent explorations in behavioral encoding.* (p. 341)

Finally Biddle's associate, Adams (1) states their point of view most clearly:

However, description [of classroom phenomena] *is a selective process which inevitably bears the stigmata of the theoretical orientation adopted by the describer. . . . the orientation most comfortable to us was a sociological one.* (pp. 2 and 3).

It is entirely consistent with this purpose to code the same classroom phenomena into a variety of dimensions, each dimension requiring one or more coding systems. It is not surprising that Biddle and his associates would prefer to code magnetic video recording which can be replayed as often as necessary before as many trained observers as their scheme of conceptualization demands. Progress toward these broad purposes should produce worthwhile knowledge about the complex factors that affect classroom learning. This is an important goal of educational research. However, such knowledge may not lend itself easily to helping a prospective or an inservice teacher alter his behavior in order to improve instruction. This latter goal is more of an engineering problem. The change and improvement of teaching behavior seems more likely to be the product of exploring one's own personal contacts with pupils. This is a more modest purpose and requires less complicated plans. It is the engineering problem which has guided the writing of this book.

The place of a sociological approach at the broad end of the purpose continuum seems relatively clear. It is more difficult to place the 10 categories and matrix display on the same continuum, to say nothing about the flexible coding procedures still to be described in this book. This difficulty arises from the variety of purposes which have been assigned, rightly or wrongly, to techniques of live classroom coding. For example, the FIAC system with a matrix display has been used to describe patterns of teaching behavior for groups of teachers which, in turn, represent larger populations. Generalizations about what goes on in the classroom have been made from composite matrices involving thousands of tallies. In a different application, a single teacher may be involved in two episodes and comparisons are then made in terms of two teaching situations, but the same teacher is working with the same pupils. More recently, matrix interpretations have been made about the interaction in simulated teaching situations in which the only purpose was to see if certain intended patterns did or did not appear. Regardless of these diverse applications, the FIAC system is most appropriately used to study the balance of teacher initiative and response (Chapter 3).

After several years of experience, it now is abundantly clear that the nature of the categories, the observation procedures, and the alternatives for displaying the data, by themselves do not determine purpose and therefore a justifiable placement along the purpose continuum. Instead, it is the combination of the two, the consistency between purpose and the kinds of information quantified that not only locates a particular application on the purpose continuum, but also suggests the misuse or proper use of the technique. A sociologist can look at the FIAC system and decide that the range of phenomena is too narrow, but physiologists studying teacher anxiety may find them too broad and vague.

SUBSCRIPTING CATEGORIES

The word *subscripting,* as used here, means dividing a single category into additional subcategories. The term was probably first used in the early development of coding at Minnesota and Michigan. As members of an observation team for a research project worked toward higher reliability, they often discussed and even argued about how certain teacher statements should be coded. They soon identified various kinds of statements which were given the same code symbol. To keep a record of the different kinds of statements assigned to the same category, subscript notations were used.

In the discussion that follows, any one of the 10 categories could have been chosen to illustrate a case study of subscripting. In this case, Categories 3 and 10 were chosen, but it is the procedure and the steps which deserve your attention. Once these are learned, you can develop subscripts of your own for any category.

THE PROCEDURE OF SUBSCRIPTING

Subscripting can provide additional data. The kind of additional data that would be most useful depends on the purposes of the observation. In order to illustrate relationships between *purpose* and *procedure*, the steps that might be followed to subdivide Categories 3 and 10 are illustrated in a simulated case study.

The procedure of subscripting may be easier to recognize if it is outlined before you read the case study. First, a problem is confronted and its major features identified. Second, concepts will be needed to account for these major features, and the problem itself may suggest relationships among these concepts. Third, each important concept is analyzed in terms of overt behavior which provides the definition of a new subscript or a potential subscript. Fourth, in order to develop a theory and explain the problem, it is often necessary to work back and forth, to consider and then reconsider the nature of the problem, the concepts, the subscripts, and the practical discriminations that an observer may make. Fifth, code symbols for each subscript and methods of displaying tabulated data will require some planning. Sixth, several field trials are necessary to establish the utility of the new category system.

The problem

This problem arose in connection with the analysis of two teaching episodes. It appeared that the use of Category 3 was producing different results. In episode X pupils developed more initiative in expressing ideas, but in episode Y pupils failed to develop this initiative. The problem was to learn more about how Category 3 was used by the two teachers and, if possible, explain the different results. The data concerning Category 3 are presented in Fig. 5–1. In order to practice the decoding skills you were working on in the previous chapter, please complete the following assignment.

Assignment One: Make the following comparisons between episode X and episode Y on the basis of the data in Fig. 5–1. Compare your work with the answers in the next paragraphs.

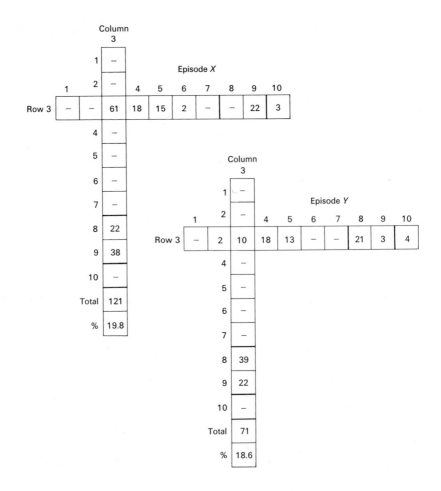

Fig. 5—1.   Columns and Rows for Category 3. (*From two 10 × 10 matrices*).

1) In starting type 3 statements are the teachers alike or different? What is your evidence?

2) Are they alike or different in terms of what follows type 3 statements? What is your evidence?

3) Once a type 3 statement is started, which teacher is more likely to continue and extend the duration of the statement? What is your evidence?

[Hint: *if "starting" and "what follows" are concepts that leave you confused, return to page 108 and read about the differences between columns and rows in a matrix.*]

To begin, note that the *percents* of all tallies coded in Category 3 for both episodes are nearly equal, but the total number of raw tallies are not. The almost equal percent figures indicate that the proportion of total talk that was coded into Category 3 is about the same in the two episodes. It follows that episode X is longer in its period of duration. By simple proportions, you can estimate X at around 600 tallies or about $\frac{1}{2}$ hour. Y involved about 380 tallies or about 19 minutes. If the two episodes had been of approximately equal duration (i.e., had the same total tallies in the matrix), then you could make direct comparisons between corresponding single cell frequencies. However, this is not the case and therefore you are confronted with a problem that requires you to use proportions.

The first question asks you to compare how Category 3 statements are started. The beginning of a new type of verbal event is a transition, so the question centers on comparing transitions *into* Category 3. Should you inspect the column or the row? Knowing matrix tabulation conventions, you should inspect the *column* in order to study events that precede 3's. But to set up a proportion involving column transitions you must determine how many transitions occurred. This is done by subtracting the steady state frequency from the category total. Proportional transitions are then set up as follows:

Category 3 statements begin	Episode X	Episode Y
After 8	$p = \frac{22}{60} = 0.37$	$p = \frac{39}{61} = 0.64$
After 9	$p = \frac{38}{60} = 0.63$	$p = \frac{22}{61} = 0.36$

These calculations show that Category 3 statements *started* in episode X almost twice as often following a type 9 pupil statement, compared with type 8. Whereas in episode Y, the reverse was true. These observations apply to the first question concerned with how Category 3 statements start.

Row 3 of a matrix provides us with information about what follows a type 3 statement which is necessary to answer the second question. Below are some similar calculations to determine the probabilities of teacher talk or of pupil talk (8 and 9) which followed a type 3 statement. You can calculate, if you want the practice, the probabilities of different kinds of teacher talk, following a type 3 statement, by setting up separate proportions for Category 4 and Category 5.

Category 3 statements are followed by more	Episode X	Episode Y
Teacher talk	$p = \dfrac{12 + 15 + 2}{60} = \dfrac{35}{60} = 0.58$	$p = \dfrac{18 + 13 + 2}{61} = \dfrac{33}{61} = 0.54$
Pupil talk 8	Never	$p = \dfrac{21}{61} = 0.34$
Pupil talk 9	$p = \dfrac{22}{60} = 0.27$	$p = \dfrac{3}{61} = 0.05$

These calculations show that the continuation of teacher talk, at the termination of type 3 statements is about the same in both episodes, shown above by $p = 0.58$ and $p = 0.54$. Yet in episode X, when pupil talk does follow type 3 statements, it involves much more initiative.

The third question concerns the duration of a type 3 statement, once it starts. The frequency of the steady state cell, as a proportion of the category total, is our best index of this characteristic of interaction. Once calculated, this proportion is not an exact index in the sense that transitions are exact; instead the decimal indicates the average probability of another 3 following any 3, whether it be the first, second, third, and so on, in a single series. Since it is the only index available, it is used as an "estimate" of average duration of a particular category. The proportions for X are $p = \frac{61}{121} = 0.51$ and for Y, $p = \frac{10}{71} = 0.14$. The comparison indicates that type 3 statements have a much longer average duration in episode X compared with Y.

The answer to the first question indicates that the teacher in episode X starts his type 3 statements in response to pupil initiation (Category 9) twice as often as the teacher in Y. The conclusion about teacher statements is that in episode Y, type 3 statements seldom lead to pupil initiation, but in episode X, pupil initiation always follows a type 3 statement. Given the limited data, only two explanations seem possible. In episode X more type 9 statements follow the 3's because the pupils *have a habit* of emitting type 9 statements; alternatively, the *longer duration* of type 3 statements accounts for more type 9 statements which follow. Of course, there is no way to judge the interaction of habit and duration in accounting for the results.

At best the two conclusions seem unsatisfactory. The first conclusion ignores the possibility that a teacher can cause change during an interaction pattern; the issue of skill in the use of Category 3 is reduced to taking advantage of a type 9 statement when it occurs. The second conclusion is somewhat more satisfactory because it suggests a constructive course of action which the teacher can take, namely, talk longer in Category 3 once you start. This makes some sense in that a fuller development and support of a pupil idea may encourage pupils to initiate their own ideas more often. But notice how this recommendation is devoid of theory. This deficiency tends to produce doubt and skepticism. Extend type 3 statements! Under what conditions? Will it always work? Why does this help? How can these results be explained?

Identifying possible concepts

One way to develop an inventory of possible concepts is to read whatever has been written about a problem and underline those words and phrases which seem to characterize a feature of the problem that stands out and demands recognition. Next make a list of the words or phrases and then see if the meaning of each can be captured in a brief definition. At the same time, see if different ways to quantify the variable can be imagined. A concept must have a meaning that is clear enough to suggest ways by which the concept can be quantified, before it will become a useful thinking tool in the conduct of inquiry.

Suppose you were to try to make such an inventory right now. Read the assignment below and see if you can carry it out.

Assignment Two: To discover the concepts which have thus far been used in an attempt to analyze this problem, read the last three paragraphs of the preceding section once again. Make a list of the fewest number of concepts — words or phrases which stand for concepts — and check to see if their meaning is clear and whether or not they can be quantified. This is not easy! Take your time and think about the alternatives. The error most often made is to include too many concepts. When you are finished, compare your list with those described below.

One response to this assignment is shown in the following outline:

Concepts of Teacher Behavior	Concepts of Consequences
1. when type 3 statements start	4. pupil initiates own ideas
2. what follows type 3 statements	5. pupil responds to teacher ideas
3. duration of type 3 statements	

Each of the above concepts can be defined and can be quantified by reference to category definitions and the procedural conventions of systematic coding and display. Yet the quality of the conclusions which these concepts permit has been found to be inadequate, or at least less than satisfactory.

It is not unusual to find that proposed concepts are inadequate in terms of the task. It sends us back to the drawing boards, so to speak, to design a more powerful and productive attack on the problem. What we need is more information. Not just any kind of information, but information which strikes closer to the heart of the problem and can lead to the development of more effective concepts. The next step is to develop greater insight into the problem of how teachers make use of Category 3 during class discussions. There is one place where this insight is most likely to develop and that is in the classroom. Before returning to the drawing boards *a close, personal, careful, contact with the phenomena to be conceptualized* will help and is probably necessary. At least it is necessary for all except those who are gifted in clairvoyance or who are the type of genius who can sit in their armchairs and somehow think of the right concepts. By my table of equivalents, 1 hour of watching a talented teacher develop pupil initiative by using Category 3 is worth 30 hours of reading in the library plus 30 hours of struggling at the drawing boards. The purpose of such a visit is to observe and describe the different kinds of statements which a teacher uses to accept, to clarify, and to develop ideas which have previously been expressed by pupils. What follows is a summary of findings from such visits by members of our research staff, both at Minnesota and Michigan, who set out to study Category 3.

First, sometimes teachers merely repeat what a pupil has said or they briefly summarize and then move on to another train of thought. Mere acknowledgement is often a statement of short duration and frequently occurs as a single 3 in a sequence of code symbols. Statements of this type can be distinguished from other type 3 statements by the absence of other characteristics which are described below.

Second, a teacher can attempt to paraphrase ideas expressed by pupils and in other ways introduce synonyms to see if they adequately represent what a pupil intended to say. Such utterances might begin by saying, "In other words . . . ," or "I think John is saying . . . " Statements of this type are likely to exceed the duration of a single tally, although this is not always the case.

Statements of this second type represent an active move, on the part of the teacher, to clarify the meaning of pupil statements. Knowledge of meaning is not only a requisite of logical discourse, but it is also a mark of belonging to the problem solving group. As a teacher clarifies the ideas of a pupil he also helps that pupil become a fully participating member of the group.

Third, some teachers have discovered that ideas expressed by pupils can be used. Such teachers may compare the facts, explanations, opinions, or points of view of pupils with those to be found in books and other printed materials, or a teacher may compare pupil ideas with his own. Different ideas expressed by pupils can be listed on the blackboard in order to carry out logical operations such as clustering ideas into a set and then giving that set a label to indicate common characteristics. A teacher may fit a pupil idea into the analysis of the problem and show how its consideration aids in reaching a solution. Making use of pupil ideas in these constructive ways may well be the most potent mechanism of reinforcement available to the teacher who wants to increase pupil initiation and participation. To have an idea used is rewarding; to have it ignored may be a form of punishment or at least suggests indifference. Teachers who make use of pupil ideas are probably directly encouraging the further expression of such ideas. Teacher statements which accomplish these purposes are usually longer and this causes the observer to code an uninterrupted chain of several 3's which increases the frequency of the (3–3) cell.

Fourth, ideas expressed by pupils can also become the basis of questions which the teacher asks. A teacher who asks questions built upon the concepts and logical connectives that a pupil has previously expressed is helping pupils understand the consequences of their own ideas. This is accomplished because the teacher question permits pupil ideas to be tested within the give-and-take of peer interaction. Turning the ideas of one pupil into a question for another pupil expands the base of group participation in a most active way. Such questions may be "open" or "closed," in the sense of Marie Hughes (55), but when they are open, the teacher provides the pupils with an opportunity to express their own ideas.

Concepts and subscripts

The purpose of this section is to make an inventory by selecting concepts from the last four paragraphs in the preceding section, see if each concept can be defined, decide how each suggested concept can be quantified, and then see if the new concepts help in analyzing the problem. One way to start is to nominate each of the four paragraphs as a tentative definition of four new concepts and then create four corresponding subscripts so that each concept can be quantified by coding teacher statements.

Suppose we say that Category 3 consists of (a) mere acknowledgement, (b) clarification of meaning, (c) application of pupil ideas, and (d) questions which make use of pupil ideas. Now we can reconsider this proposal in terms of three questions to which we would like an affirmative answer. First, can these concepts be used to construct a theory that would explain the differences between episodes X and Y? Second, can an observer discriminate between all four types of Category 3 statements during the discussion? And third, to be parsimonious, is it possible to reduce the number of concepts in the theory without eroding the quality of the explanation?

What theory is possible? We might hypothesize that in the Y situation, Category 3 statements were used only to acknowledge and repeat ideas expressed by pupils. When the Y teacher then moved on to make use of his own ideas through asking his own questions and lecturing, pupils were able to relate only to the teacher's ideas and not to their own. In the X situation, Category 3 statements more often clarified meanings and made use of pupil ideas. In addition, the teacher developed questions about these ideas to incorporate them more effectively into the problem-solving process. Note that in this explanation, mere acknowledgment was set apart from the other three proposed categories. This may be a useful clue concerning the minimum number of concepts required by the problem. For example, two categories might suffice: first, mere acknowledgement, and second, collapse (b), (c), and (d) into a single category called "making use of pupil ideas." Let's keep this alternative in mind, but not adopt it too quickly.

Can the four proposed subscripts be discriminated during observation? At this point you may wish to try making these discriminations on some of the materials to be found in the earlier chapters, try it out in a classroom, or simply accept the testimony of those who have tried to use these subscripts. Our research team found that with training, distinctions between the four types of Category 3 statements can be made in live classrooms.

Can fewer concepts be used in the analysis of episodes X and Y? One clue has been mentioned which involved collapsing the four subscripts down to two. In making such a decision, one consideration is the intercorrelations among the four proposed variables. Here, the frequency of each subscript becomes a variable to be taken into account. Any two variables with a high correlation can be combined with very little loss of information. In our exploration of this problem, we found that teacher statements of clarification were highly correlated with making other uses of pupil ideas. Yet the asking of questions, based on pupil ideas, is somewhat less positively correlated and, on an intuitive basis, may be worth recording because of its value during feedback to a teacher. These considerations lead to proposing the following subscripts for analyzing episodes X and Y:

Category 31:   Merely acknowledges or repeats a pupil idea.
Category 32:   Makes use of a pupil idea by clarifying it, making comparisons, or applying it to problem solving steps.
Category 33:   Like 32, except it is in the form of a question with the intent that a pupil answer.

These three subscripts are now applied to the interaction of episodes X and Y to obtain additional information. You may notice that Category 10 has also been subscripted to illustrate how another category can be divided in order to provide additional information. Suppose:

Category 01:   codes non work-oriented pauses, silence, or confusion.
Category 02:   codes work-oriented pauses, silence, or confusion.

Here work is defined in terms of the presumed content objectives of the lesson or in terms of teacher directions. Thus, if the teacher requested that the pupils move to other seats, the resulting confusion is coded 02. But if the teacher stopped the lesson because the noise of pupil movement was disturbing, this would be coded 01. Thoughtful pauses, work at the blackboard, or completing seatwork assigned by the teacher would be coded 02. This embellishment runs counter to parsimony and illustrates the overworked research adage, "be sure and collect as much information as you can, since you have to spend time in the classroom observing." Inquiry efforts should be as efficient as possible, but restraint and judgment are necessary to keep our serendipitous instincts from reducing the quality of data which are collected for analyzing the principal problem.

The subscripts for Categories 3 and 10 provide a total of five categories which are added to eight to produce a 13 × 13 matrix, should this tabulation display be desired. The data concerning episodes X and Y are shown in Fig. 5–2 in the form of the columns and rows of the subscripted Category 3, "lifted" from a 13 × 13 matrix.

Teacher Y

Rows \ Columns	1	2	31	32	33	4	5	6	7	8	9	01	02
1			—	—	—								
2			—	—	—								
31	—	2	5	—	—	15	13	—	—	21	1	2	—
32	—	—	1	4	—	3	—	—	—	—	2	—	2
33	—	—	—	—	—	—	—	—	—	—	—	—	—
4			—	—	—								
5			—	—	—								
6			—	—	—								
7			—	—	—								
8			33	6	—								
9			20	2	—								
01			—	—	—								
02			—	—	—								
Total			59	12	—								
Percent			17.1										

Teacher X

Rows \ Columns	1	2	31	32	33	4	5	6	7	8	9	01	02
1			—	—	—								
2			—	—	—								
31	—	—	5	6	1	12	2	—	—	—	1	—	—
32	—	—	—	25	8	6	13	2	—	—	5	—	1
33	—	—	—	—	16	—	—	—	—	—	16	—	2
4			—	—	—								
5			—	—	—								
6			—	—	—								
7			—	—	—								
8			13	9	—								
9			9	20	9								
01			—	—	—								
02			—	—	—								
Total			27	60	34								
Percent			19.2										

Fig. 5—2. Columns and Rows for Subscripted Category 3. (*From a 13 × 13 matrix.*)

Assignment Three: You are invited to interpret the data in Fig. 5—2 and decide whether it supports, fails to support, or contradicts the explanation which was hypothesized earlier. This is your chance to transfer what you have learned about decoding principles to a different format of data tabulation. Compare your conclusions with those in the next paragraph.

The explanation being tested asserts that teacher Y merely acknowledges pupil ideas whereas teacher X integrates pupil ideas more successfully into the classroom discussion by clarifying and applying these ideas to the problems at hand, and in addition, creating questions based on pupil ideas. Note that finding support for this theory is greatly facilitated by the *close correspondence* between the subscripts and the meaning of the concepts used in the explanation. In fact, this close correspondence makes the interpretation of the data obvious. A mere inspection of the column totals for Categories 31, 32, and 33 confirms the explanation. However, more subtle interpretations can also be made.

The utility of dividing Category 10 into two subscripts appears to be low in terms of comparing episodes X and Y. This is due primarily to the very few tallies in Category 10. Normally we would expect between 10 and 12 percent of all tallies to fall into this category, and in a longer observation which produced more data, inferences about the work orientation could be made. In this case, however, one can conclude that the embellishment does not really add to the analysis of the problem, but might give more data in another observation.

Columns

		31	32	33
Rows	31	✕	A	A
	32	B	✕	A
	33	B	B	✕

Figure 5—3.

There are some interesting transition cells in Fig. 5—2 which deserve some attention. These are the cells with the letters A and B shown in Fig. 5—3. One interpretation of these cells can be based on the following assumption: it would seem both easier and more logical for the teacher to react to pupil ideas according to the sequence 31 to 32 to 33, rather than the reverse. That is, to acknowledge, clarify, make use of, and then question pupil ideas seems more reasonable than when this order is reversed in the teacher's soliloquy. Which cells in Fig. 5—3 indicate the more logical sequence, those with letter A or those with B?

You found the right answer if you remembered how the address of a cell indicates first the row and then the column, which, in turn, indicates the

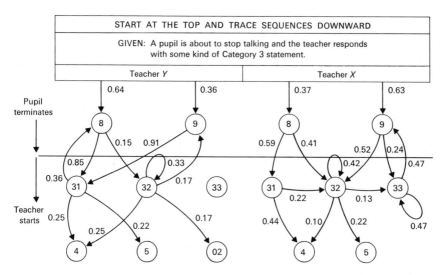

Fig. 5—4. Probability Sequences To and From Category 3 (probabilities less than 0.10 not shown).

sequence. Returning to Fig. 5—2, note that in the A cells of episode X, there are 15 tallies and no tallies are in the B cells. In Y there are no tallies in the A cells and one in the B cells. What can be said here is that the teacher in X did make the logical transitions described in developing pupil ideas. About all that can be said about episode Y is that practically no such transitions occurred and the one that did occur was in the opposite sequence. These cells are mentioned, at this point to show how any theory which involves predicted transitions can be investigated with data tabulated in a matrix display.

The subscript display shows one interesting similarity between the two teachers in X and Y. If you were drawing a flow chart, similar to the procedure recommended in the last chapter, and had reached the (8–31) cell, the arrow in both episodes would be drawn next to the (31–4) cell. Thus, both teachers are most likely to ask questions based on their own concepts, rather than the pupils, following the termination of a type 8 pupil statement. An optimistic interpretation is that both teachers are attempting to alter pupil thinking by soliciting pupil opinions to ideas which the teacher introduces by questions. The results for each teacher, however, are different. A set of subscripts for Category 4 would be necessary in order to analyze this difference.

There is another method of display which can be introduced at this point that is particularly helpful when only a few categories are involved. This display is shown in Fig. 5—4 and involves calculating the probabilities of pathways in a stochastic chain model. This can quickly become rather complicated, but here we will merely look at the less complicated features of the diagram.

The probability figures, shown as decimals, beside the arrows leading to Categories 8 and 9 indicate that teacher Y starts type 3 statements more often after Category 8 and teacher X more often after Category 9. By tracing the sequences along those pathways which have the highest probability, the differences between the two episodes are quickly set in contrast. The most frequently occurring three event sequence in episode Y is 8 to 31 to 8. The probability of this sequence occurring can be calculated by multiplying the probabilities along the pathway; this is $0.64 \times 0.85 \times 0.36 = 0.20$. The most frequently occurring sequence in X is 9 to 32 to 32, which has a probability of $0.63 \times 0.52 \times 0.42 = 0.14$. Perhaps the first inference is that since 0.14 is smaller than 0.20, there must be a greater number of pathways in episode X that are used more frequently compared with Y. A second inference is that the most frequent pathway in Y is mere acknowledgment—a short single 31 between two pupil response statements. In X, the most frequent pathway involves the development of pupil initiated ideas for more than a single 3-second interval by the teacher. Events taken three at a time can be analyzed by this method.

Without bothering with the arithmetic, certain features of a chain diagram stand out and attract immediate attention. For example, look at the absence of pathways involving Category 33 in episode Y. Or, given a type 9 statement in the same episode, look how quickly mere acknowledgment, 31, returns the interaction to the pupil response mode. In episode X, the progression from 31 to 32 to 33 is easily seen and is absent in Y.

Summary of procedure in subscripting

The differences which were found to exist between episodes X and Y are less important, at this point, than understanding the procedures for developing and using subscripts. Two general procedures have been described. In the case of Category 3 the steps leading to subscripts grew out of a particular problem and the need for additional information in order to analyze the problem. In the case of Category 10, the possibility of subscripting grew out of a confusion regarding the meaning of a type 10 tally. Subdividing both categories added more detail to the decoding process.

No matter what stimulates the refinement of a subcategory, its utility depends on the close correspondence between problem element, concept, and category definition. Thus our subdivision of Category 3 was fruitful, but the subdivision of Category 10 was not helpful.

It seems safe to observe that too much care in answering the following questions is almost impossible. What are the major features of the problem being investigated? What concepts will be necessary to analyze this problem and take into account its major features? How can these concepts be quantified? What theory or explanation might explain the relationships among the concepts? Can this theory or explanation be verified?

There are, of course, important questions which are more general. Is the problem directly concerned with educational outcomes? Will success in analyzing the problem make any difference, or can the problem just be forgotten?

SUBSCRIPTING THE BASIC TEN CATEGORIES

A number of different researchers have subscripted the FIAC system in order to increase discriminations among statements. For example, the subscripts developed by Amidon, Hunter, Hough, and others can be found in the anthology of category systems by Simon and Boyer (89). Another example is the work of Honigman (52).

This section will illustrate applications of subscripting by discussing two category systems which were developed at Michigan. But, first, a bit of history helps in understanding how the expanded systems were developed.

Between 1958 and 1963 the 10 categories were used in a series of research studies and introduced to teachers as a theme for inservice training. One advantage of using the same categories was that the data in one study could be compared directly with another. Yet with each successive study, pressure to change the categories mounted as the need for more subtle discriminations was recognized by researchers. The teachers in inservice training programs, on the other hand, found the 10 categories too complicated for quick understanding, but nevertheless objected to lumping so many different kinds of statements or events into the same category. For example, teachers often wanted to change Category 10 by subdividing it into work oriented and non-work-oriented events. Yet these same teachers shuddered at the thought of coding and tabulating even 10 categories, to say nothing about more than 10. The dilemma has not yet been resolved, but the use of computers holds great promise for the future.

A computer can be programmed to accomplish tedious tasks involving large quantities of data, which makes it an ideal resource for anyone interested in analyzing classroom communication. The input data for the first computer programs were decks of cards which had been punched by a keypunch operator, at the research office, from the notations which observers recorded in the classroom. During 1963 and 1964 computer programs for tabulating matrices and making certain basic calculations were developed at the University of Chicago, Cornell University, and the University of Michigan.* It finally became obvious that computer programs could be designed to accept two-digit code symbols, or more than two, providing Category 10 was coded as a zero. At last the door to subscripting was opened.

---

*Perhaps the first computer program was written under the direction of R. Rippey at Chicago; his material was of some use to L. Wightman, who developed a more elaborate program at Cornell. In turn, some of his material was used by M. C. Johnson, Betty Morrison, and U. Smidchens at Michigan. Later programs were designed at Temple, Harvard, UCLA, and other centers.

During 1964 to 1966, efforts to make use of the computer took place at various centers, but at Michigan the emphasis was on a more generalized program. It became possible to design the input so that the first digit indicated one of the original 10 categories, but the second digit could vary from zero to nine according to any preferred system of subscripting. There might be two subscripts for one category, four for another, and no subscripts on some other categories. The computer automatically tabulated the expanded matrix, could collapse the expanded matrix back to a 10 × 10 matrix, could convert all matrices to the base 1,000 (millage), as well as print out raw tally matrices, and calculate ratios, etc. The days of tedious clerical matrix tabulation, converting raw tally matrices into percent or millage, and hand calculating various ratios* were gone forever in the modern research office.

Two examples of subscripted category systems are described in the rest of this section; both were used in samples of self-contained classrooms, one at the fourth grade level and the other at the second.

A 22-CATEGORY SYSTEM: COMBINING PROCESS AND A COGNITIVE ORIENTATION

Purpose

This 22-category system was designed primarily to subdivide Category 3. The additional subscripts were suggested by members of the observing team and are essentially trial and error attempts to explore possible subscripts that might be used in a later project.

The 22 categories

The descriptions below are to be considered additions to the definitions of the original 10 categories. Categories 1 and 7 were not subscripted simply because of their low incidence.

Code
Symbol   Description

10	No change.
21	Superficial encouragement, like "um hm," "good," "right," etc.
22	Provides reasons for praise, or gives special emphasis so that the pupil "really hears it."
31	Merely repeats, very brief summaries, superficial acknowledgement.
32	Pupil's idea is developed in terms of teacher perceptions.

---

*In the 1957 New Zealand project, a class of 18 girls taking a course in secretarial skills at the Wellington Vocational High School, Max Riske, principal, tabulated 38,823 tallies at the cost of two Cokes for each balanced matrix, since two girls worked on each matrix. The process took about 1 week and introduced a piece work rate that not only undercut clerical pay in a research office, but also upset the normal reinforcement techniques which teachers used in New Zealand.

33   Pupil's idea is developed in terms of another pupil's ideas or in terms of ideas expressed earlier by the same pupil.

34   Same as 32 or 33 except it is in the form of a question.

41   Narrow, factual questions, emphasizing recall: what, where, when?

42   Broad, open questions which clearly permit choice in ways of answering.

51   Narrow, factual focus; restricted concepts and purposes; low level in terms of reasoning.

52   Not 51 and not 53.

53   Negative, perhaps critical, but not Category 7 because premeditated intent to misbehave is absent; disagree without comment or explanation.

61   Commands to which compliance can easily be judged; absence of reasons or explanation.

62   Explains directions; how and why something is to be done.

63   Provides alternatives and invites pupil participation in making choices.

70   No change.

81   Like basic Category 8, but not 82.

82   Pupil asks questions which remain within the format of teacher thought or structure, e.g., asks for clarification of teacher directions.

91   Like basic Category 9, but not 92.

92   Pupil asks questions showing freedom of thought and initiative.

01   Nonconstructive use of time.

02   Constructive use of time.

Reliability

After 3 weeks of 6 hours per week training, a team of six observers used this category system for a 2-month research project. Eighteen of nineteen reliability checks produced a Scott coefficient* between 0.70 and 0.86, with the median at 0.79. The one lowest coefficient, 0.56, occurred during a difficult observation and was followed by creating some ground rules which eliminated the difficulty. When all observations were collapsed to the original 10 categories, all reliabilities were about 0.05 to 0.10 higher.

Some results and comments

Figures 5–5 and 5–6 are 22 × 22 matrices of two fourth grade teachers who were observed while teaching a social studies unit for 2 weeks, about 90 minutes per day. The two classes were average or above average in positive

---

*A Scott coefficient (86) varies from a high of 1.00 to a low of 0.00 as an index of reliability. A coefficient of 0.85 or higher is acceptable for research when the 10-category system is used.

Category	10	21	22	31	32	33	34	41	42	51	52	53	61	62	63	70	81	82	91	92	01	02	Total
10	0	0	0	0	0	0	0	0	0	0	0	0	0	0	0	0	0	0	0	0	0	0	1
21	0	0	0	1	0	1	0	2	0	2	0	0	1	0	0	0	1	0	1	0	0	2	11
22	0	0	0	0	0	0	0	0	0	0	0	0	0	0	0	0	0	0	0	0	0	0	1
31	0	1	0	1	1	0	1	9	1	9	0	0	1	0	0	0	2	0	2	0	0	1	30
32	0	0	0	0	4	0	0	1	0	2	0	0	1	0	0	0	0	0	1	0	0	2	13
33	0	0	0	0	0	2	0	1	0	1	0	0	0	0	0	0	0	0	0	0	0	0	7
34	0	0	0	0	0	0	0	0	0	0	0	0	0	0	0	0	4	0	3	0	0	0	8
41	0	0	0	0	0	0	0	19	1	4	0	0	3	0	0	2	63	0	3	0	0	7	103
42	0	0	0	0	0	0	0	1	3	0	0	0	0	0	0	0	4	0	3	0	0	1	13
51	0	0	0	0	0	0	0	26	2	141	4	0	8	1	0	4	6	1	6	1	0	10	211
52	0	0	0	0	0	0	0	2	1	3	14	0	1	0	0	0	0	0	1	0	0	1	22

53	61	62	63	70	81	82	91	92	01	02	Total
6	76	12	3	45	169	5	90	9	2	164	1,000
0	16	2	0	10	6	0	2	0	0	105	164
0	0	0	0	0	0	0	0	0	0	0	2
0	1	0	0	0	0	0	1	2	0	2	9
0	3	0	0	2	7	0	52	0	0	5	90
0	1	0	0	0	0	1	0	0	0	2	5
2	9	0	0	2	68	0	2	0	0	6	169
0	3	0	0	22	4	0	2	0	1	6	46
0	1	0	1	0	0	0	0	0	0	0	3
0	3	6	0	0	0	0	0	0	0	1	12
0	30	1	1	3	9	1	2	0	0	11	76
0	0	0	0	0	5	0	1	0	0	0	6
0	0	0	0	0	1	0	0	0	0	1	22
2	5	1	0	3	18	2	4	0	0	13	211
0	0	0	0	0	2	0	1	0	0	1	13
1	4	0	0	3	20	0	5	0	0	9	103
0	0	0	0	0	1	0	2	1	0	0	8
0	0	0	0	0	0	0	3	0	0	0	7
0	0	0	0	0	1	0	3	4	0	0	13
0	0	0	0	0	22	0	6	0	0	0	30
0	0	0	0	0	0	0	0	0	0	0	1
0	0	0	0	0	4	0	4	0	0	0	11
0	0	0	0	0	0	0	0	0	0	0	1

Total tallies = 12,386

Fig. 5–5. Twenty-Two-Category Matrix: Fourth Grade Social Studies; Teacher K.

Category	10	21	22	31	32	33	34	41	42	51	52	53	61	62	63	70	81	82	91	92	01	02	Total
10	0	0	0	0	0	0	0	0	0	0	0	0	0	0	0	0	0	0	0	0	0	0	1
21	0	0	1	2	4	0	2	6	1	5	0	0	3	0	0	0	1	0	1	0	0	4	30
22	0	0	1	0	1	0	0	1	0	1	0	0	0	0	0	0	0	0	0	0	0	1	6
31	0	2	1	1	3	0	2	2	0	4	0	0	2	0	0	0	0	0	1	0	0	3	21
32	0	0	1	0	13	0	2	4	1	6	0	0	2	0	0	0	1	0	2	0	0	3	37
33	0	0	0	0	0	1	0	0	0	0	0	0	0	0	0	0	0	0	0	0	0	0	3
34	0	0	0	0	1	0	1	0	0	1	0	0	1	0	0	0	8	0	3	0	0	5	20
41	0	0	0	0	1	0	0	12	0	5	0	0	4	0	0	0	29	0	2	0	0	25	79
42	0	0	0	0	0	0	0	0	3	1	0	0	0	0	0	0	1	0	4	0	0	4	13
51	0	1	1	0	1	1	0	17	2	102	3	0	9	2	0	0	11	3	5	1	0	13	171
52	0	0	0	0	0	0	0	1	0	2	7	0	0	0	0	0	0	0	0	0	0	0	11

Total tallies = 10,590

																							Total
53	0	0	0	0	0	0	0	1	0	1	0	1	0	0	0	0	3	0	0	0	0	1	8
61	0	0	0	0	0	0	0	2	0	6	0	0	10	3	0	0	16	1	2	0	0	12	55
62	0	0	0	0	0	0	0	1	0	2	0	0	1	3	0	0	0	1	0	0	0	3	11
63	0	0	0	0	0	0	0	0	0	1	0	0	0	0	1	0	0	0	0	0	0	1	3
70	0	0	0	0	0	0	0	0	0	0	0	0	0	0	0	1	0	0	0	0	0	0	2
81	0	17	1	14	4	0	6	11	1	12	0	0	7	0	0	0	138	1	1	0	0	14	233
82	0	0	0	0	0	0	1	0	0	7	0	0	1	0	0	0	0	1	0	0	0	0	11
91	0	7	1	4	6	0	4	2	1	2	0	1	2	0	0	0	1	0	60	0	0	4	95
92	0	0	0	0	0	0	0	0	0	1	0	0	0	0	0	0	0	0	1	2	0	1	6
01	0	0	0	0	0	0	0	0	0	0	0	0	0	0	0	0	0	0	0	0	0	0	0
02	0	1	0	0	2	0	1	17	2	14	0	0	13	1	1	0	23	3	11	1	0	92	184
Total	1	30	6	21	37	3	20	79	13	170	11	8	54	12	3	2	234	11	95	6	0	185	1,000

Fig. 5–6.   Twenty-Two-Category Matrix: Fourth Grade Social Studies; Teacher L.

pupil attitudes toward the teacher and the schoolwork. The same could be said about content achievement, adjusted for initial ability, in terms of the sample of 16 classes of which they were a part. In turn, the 16 classes had been carefully selected to be representative of all 72 fourth grade classes in an above average suburban school system. The point to be made here is that whatever these two classes represent, the teachers are most likely not below average in their orientation toward pupils. In fact each teacher's use of Category 3, 5.8 percent and 8.1 percent, compares favorably with a fourth grade sample reported by Furst and Amidon (46, p. 169) who found an average of 3.5 percent in this category.

In certain respects, the results displayed in both matrices are disturbing. On the plus side, the subscripting of Category 3 seems to work, in the sense that the column totals for Category 3 indicate that the two teachers react differently to pupil ideas, but the transitions to pupil talk leave only two undesirable alternative interpretations. Either the theory about type 34 statements leading to pupil initiation in categories 91 and 92 is incorrect, or else these teachers do not have the skill to create such patterns.

A second feature of the data can be emphasized by considering the proportion of teacher statements which involve the more subtle nuances of the teacher-pupil interchange. For example, the percent of all teacher statements which were tallied in Categories 10, 22, 32, 33, 34, 52, 62, and 63 is 22.6 percent for teacher K and 14.2 percent for teacher L. Apparently between 78 percent and 85 percent of teacher talk appears to be concerned with a narrow factual orientation toward content, unexplained directions, and superficial reactions to pupil statements. The evidence from these two teachers would suggest that the analysis of what might be called "common practice" in fourth grade teaching does not require elaborate category systems because the interaction is not that elaborate.

AN 18-CATEGORY SYSTEM WITH A COGNITIVE ORIENTATION

Purpose

An 18-category system has been designed by W. W. Measel (66) in an attempt to quantify some of the cognitive processes which have been identified by Hilda Taba (99). Measel observed second grade classrooms. Put as briefly as possible, Measel was interested in distinguishing between three levels of thinking: Level 1 consisted of memory; level 2 consisted of grouping things together; and level 3 consisted of higher reasoning processes (99, p. 11).

The 18 categories

The definitions of the original 10 categories are again accepted as a starting point.

Code Symbol	Description
10	No change.
20	No change.
30	No change.
41	Teacher questions involving concrete objects or events.
42	Teacher questions calling for the mental operation of grouping.
43	Teacher questions calling for the mental operation of inferring.
51	Teacher talk involving concrete objects or events.
52	Teacher talk involving the mental operation of grouping.
53	Teacher talk involving the mental operation of inferring.
60	No change.
70	No change.
81	Pupil response involving concrete objects or events.
82	Pupil response involving the mental operation of grouping.
83	Pupil response involving the mental operation of inferring.
91	Pupil initiation involving concrete objects or events.
92	Pupil initiation involving the mental operation of grouping.
93	Pupil initiation involving the mental operation of inferring.
01	No change.

Reliability

The reliability Scott coefficients for the three levels of subscription for Categories 4, 5, 8, and 9 were calculated separately by Measel (66, pp. 63–64). The range for 12 reliability checks over a 2-month period, after training, had a range of 0.77 to 0.96 with an average of 0.87. During that same period, the coefficients for the 10 basic categories had a range from 0.60 to 0.94, with an average of 0.84. With this sample of teachers and observers, apparently the reliability between levels was higher than for the 10 categories.

Some results and comments

The matrix of one second grade teacher is shown in Fig. 5–7. There is no point in discussing the representativeness of a single case, but this teacher is a fully certified, employed teacher in a school district of above average wealth. The intracategory percentage which Measel has calculated to show the distributions of tallies, at the three levels, within each subscripted category is shown in the bottom row of Fig. 5–7. Note that the teacher's initiating statements, Category 5, and the pupil initiating statements, Category 9, have approximately the same percentage distribution. Most statements, 94 to 95 percent, fall into level 1. If other second grade teachers are like this one, it could be said that the category system shows some promise, but it may be necessary to train teachers before much incidence across levels will be recorded.

Category	10	20	30	41	42	43	51	52	53	60	70	81	82	83	91	92	93	01	Total
10	0	0	0	0	0	0	0	0	0	0	0	0	0	0	0	0	0	0	0
20	0	1	1	2	0	0	1	0	0	2	0	0	0	0	1	0	0	2	9.5
30	0	1	5	8	3	0	8	0	0	3	0	5	0	0	3	0	0	5	43.0
41	0	0	0	16	1	0	5	0	0	3	0	42	0	0	6	0	0	14	87.6
42	0	0	0	1	7	0	1	0	0	1	0	1	17	0	0	1	0	5	36.0
43	0	0	0	0	0	0	0	0	0	0	0	0	0	1	0	0	0	0	1.8
51	0	0	0	16	8	0	113	3	0	19	1	4	0	0	4	0	0	20	189.7
52	0	0	0	0	2	0	1	7	0	1	0	0	0	0	0	0	0	1	12.1
53	0	0	0	0	0	0	0	0	0	0	0	0	0	0	0	0	0	0	0
60	0	0	0	3	1	0	11	1	0	38	2	11	0	0	5	0	0	42	114.4

	1	2	3	4	5	6	7	8	9	10	70	81	82	83	91	92	93	01		Total
70	0	0	0	0	1	0	0	0	0	1	0	2	0	0	1	0	0	0	3	10.3
81	0	3	18	18	3	0	10	0	0	9	1	129	0	0	2	0	0	2	17	210.3
82	0	1	8	1	5	0	3	1	0	2	0	0	2	0	0	0	0	0	2	23.5
83	0	0	0	0	0	0	0	1	0	0	0	0	0	0	0	0	0	0	0	1.1
91	1	2	7	2	1	0	9	0	0	5	1	0	0	0	20	0	0	10	5	51.9
92	0	0	0	0	0	0	0	0	0	0	0	0	0	0	0	1	0	0	1	2.4
93	0	0	0	0	0	0	0	0	0	0	0	0	0	0	0	0	0	0	0	0
01	0	1	2	18	5	0	26	0	0	31	4	16	3	0	10	0	0	88	88	205.0
Total	0	9.5	43.0	87.6	36.0	1.8	189.7	12.1	0	114.4	10.3	210.3	23.5	1.1	51.9	2.4	0	205.0	205.0	1,000
Intracategory percentage	0	9.5	70	29	1	94	6	0		89.5		95	10	0.5	95	4	1			

Fig. 5–7. Eighteen-Category Matrix: Second Grade Self-Contained Classroom.

Columns

	81	82	83
41	42	0	0
42	1	17	0
43	0	0	1

Rows

Figure 5–8.

There is the possibility, in Fig. 5–7, for you to apply a skill of matrix interpretation which was introduced on page 136. There are three cells above and three cells below the set of diagonal cells—(41–81), (42–82), and (43–83) shown in Fig. 5–8. In order for you to practice interpretation skills, the following assignment may prove helpful.

Assignment Four: Suppose the three cells above the diagonal had high frequencies. What would you conclude? Suppose the three cells below the diagonal had high frequencies. What would you conclude? A discussion of these questions can be found in the next paragraph, but you may wish to consider your own answers first.

High frequencies above the diagonal would reveal pupil answers at a higher level of reasoning than was involved in the teacher's question. You might infer that the teacher is not keeping up with the thought level of the pupils. High frequencies below the diagonal indicates the reverse. You might infer that the teacher is advancing to higher levels before the pupils are ready. In the case of the teacher who was observed, there is a consistency of level of thought between the teacher and the pupils. This kind of display may have utility for teachers who are practicing this skill.

In general, this example of subscripting again shows that only a small proportion of the interaction is sorted out into higher levels of thinking. Once more the issue is raised concerning whether more elaborate systems are needed for typical classroom interaction. If the three classrooms which served to illustrate subscripting are indeed typical, they suggest that there is room for a great deal of inservice training designed to help teachers explore more flexible patterns of classroom interaction.

SUMMARY OF PROCEDURES FOR SUBSCRIPTING

Subdividing categories is an attempt to stretch the category system in order to increase the range of problems to which the system applies. Subscripts recommended for general use presumes a single system for many problems, yet a particular set of subscripts can be designed to match the requirements of just one problem. These are such interesting prospects that a researcher with a new set of subscripts is like a small boy with a new hammer—suddenly everything needs hitting.* Subscripting is not so much something that a person invents as it is a natural state of development in thinking about how to quantify significant dimensions of some phase of teaching. There could be as many subscripting systems as there are interested and alert persons working on the analysis of classroom communication.

The one major advantage of subscripting is the ease with which the data can be collapsed back to a standardized category system, yet the subscripts provide distinctions of momentary interest. This means that after investigating the unique problem, the data collapsed to the basic system can be used: (a) to compare the present sample of data with many other samples, (b) to replicate in your own data relationships others have discovered, and (c) to provide others with data for future comparisons and possible replications. If this field of research had three or four basic category systems which could be subscripted in a wide variety of ways it would surely create more progress by facilitating many more comparisons between projects.

Subscripting occurs within the best of category families. For example, the oldest, most well standardized system of interaction analysis was designed by Bales (8) to study small group discussion. This system has been subscripted by Borgatta and Crowther (17) without serious problems for the observers and an increase from the original 12 categories to 18. There are many variations of subscripting the 10 categories which have been presented in earlier chapters, and these 10 categories, in turn, could be seen as subscripts of earlier systems developed by Withall (106) and Bales (8).

Emphasis has been given to using the utmost care in analyzing a problem, developing appropriate concepts, and coordinating these concepts to subscript definitions. These precautions are safeguards against the inappropriate use of any category system. When the inferences you wish to investigate involve concepts which are not at the core of the problem, or if the method of quantifying these concepts is not in tight correspondence with the concepts, then the preliminary analysis of the problem and system of categories has been inadequate.

When common teaching practices in "the average" classroom are the object of study, there is some reason to believe that more complicated, subscripted category systems may be more sensitive to the nuances of teacher-pupil interaction than is necessary. A promising system of subscripts may be discarded

---

*From the apparently inexhaustible supply of Abraham Kaplan.

simply because it showed no variation between visits to several different class-rooms when, in fact, it accurately showed no significant differences. We some-times forget that there must first be differences before a valid instrument can measure differences. On the other hand, in projects which are designed to help teachers change their behavior along lines which have been built into subscript definitions, then a more elaborate category system should provide evidence concerning the presence or absence of change.

One of the interesting by-products in the development of subscripts is increased insight into the capability of the observer in a live classroom. At one time it was thought that as soon as a category system exceeded 12 to 15 categories, it would be necessary to leave the live classroom and depend on some kind of voice or video recording. One way to explain reasonably high reliability coefficients between observers, in spite of more categories, is that cleverly designed subscripts tend to program the decisions that an observer has to make with the original set of categories. Or, perhaps, the subscripts simply program decisions which must be made after an event is fitted into an original category. The net result, in either case, is that observer performance is not only maintained, but might be improved in some instances.

THE EVENT AND OTHER UNITS OF ANALYSIS

How much behavior is to be represented by one code symbol? How long should an observation last? Which data should be tabulated into a matrix? How many different matrices should be tabulated from one visit? All of these questions are special cases of the more general question: What is a unit? The choice of the unit can make a difference, even in a friendly argument. For example, consider the two friends who liked to kid each other about the size of their churches. They met shortly after attending the national conferences of their respective faiths. One, who knew his church had many more members, asked, "And how many attended your conference?" "Shucks, Sam," replied the other, "We don't count heads in our church, we weigh them." The choice of the unit determines the argument. Units in coding are also more or less appropriate for some partic-ular purpose and once chosen, they become the building blocks that are used to construct inferences and reach conclusions.

THE NATURE OF CODE SYMBOLS

Classroom interaction exists *out there*, in the classroom. How it appears in our minds, is described to others, and how it is recorded and analyzed, are things that exist *here* in our heads and not *out there*. What the behavioral unit is and knowing when such a unit begins and ends is less likely to depend on what is going on out there and more likely to depend on why we went out there to look. Thus, we say, purposes determine the choice of the unit to be coded.

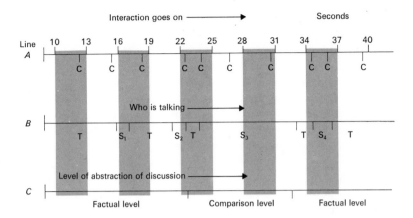

Fig. 5—9.   Elapsed Time and the Unit to be Coded.

Teachers who wish to analyze their own classroom interaction and re-searchers who wish to study the behavior of others may be concerned with different units of analysis, especially when they have different purposes. The point at which the researcher and the teacher share common concerns is that both must know clearly what the units are even though they need not choose the same units.

A teacher who wished to study his own behavior may be satisfied to define an event to be coded as the smallest bit of behavior that can be assigned to a category, regardless of whether 2 or 10 seconds are required to recognize the event. At the instant of insight, he codes the event and simultaneously looks for the next. This definition satisfies a teacher if it helps to solve problems and accomplish purposes.

A researcher may raise several questions about such a definition because he looks at many different classrooms, many different teachers, and what he counts in one situation, he may wish to compare with another. He also has more complex data processing problems. He becomes concerned, for example, when it takes 5 seconds to identify events which fit into one category, but only ½ second for another category. Or to make matters worse, events which are coded in the same category may take a longer period of elapsed time to identify at one moment and a shorter period on another occasion. In most category systems that are used for live class observation, there are fluctuations in the time required to code an event, both between categories and between occasions for the same category. These variations cause error. Perhaps a diagram will help to illustrate the problem (Fig. 5—9).

In Fig. 5—9, the scale above line *A* represents equal 3-second periods, starting with the tenth second and ending with the fortieth. Just below line *A* are points C which indicate when an observer recognized his choice of category.

Let us suppose that he is using a subscripted category system which requires discriminations about the level of abstraction, such as "facts," "comparisons," "explanations and proposals," and "generalizations." In addition, he indicates whether the teacher or a pupil is talking. Let's suppose further that he can average about one code symbol every 3 seconds because he is well trained and very clever, so it is most unlikely that another observer could judge and record any faster. Line B is a true record of successive statements by the teacher and any pupil. Line C represents a valid coding of shifts in the level of abstraction.

In this illustration, error due to rate of coding would involve only a small percent of all error for the categories on level of abstraction because these changes are slow compared to the rate of coding. But his record of the teacher-pupil interchange would involve errors during the more rapid interchanges because they are faster than the rate of coding. However, in this latter case, a slight but significant change in purpose permits coding to remain useful, even when the coding rate is slower than the phenomenal changes. Note that the original statement of purpose was to count the exact number of interchanges. If this purpose is changed so that *making an estimate* of teacher-pupil interchanges is acceptable, then two factors combine to make slower coding profitable. First, the approximately regular intervals between coding points provides us with time sampling that is approximately constant. Second, except upon rare occasions, classroom interactions produce repetitive cycles and fluctuations within cycles tend to become random, the longer the interaction is observed. Thus, if the coding continues an appropriate length of time, the approximation approaches the proportion of actual events which could have been coded had there been perfect accuracy. Incidently, such a change of purpose is quite reasonable, given the other kinds of error which occur, for example, errors of judgment by the observer, the weaknesses between category meaning and inferences made, and so on. There are about 1,200 code symbols per hour, at the 3-second rate, and it would be a most unusual class if the number of interchanges between the teacher and the pupils exceeded 300. These relationships favor the observer when the purpose is to estimate the actual number of interchanges which might have been coded. The error term due to a slow rate of coding decreases with the increasing duration of sampling.*

In the example, there were not wide fluctuations in the coding rate, and as a result the assumption of reasonably constant sampling was tenable, with its resultant advantages. Thus, a researcher might advocate that the best coding rate is one that is relatively constant. It should produce intervals between coding points that are equal to the average elapsed time that it takes to identify the

---

*This is not news to a statistician, of course. Transitions from pupil to teacher and teacher to pupil are estimated by adding Categories 8 and 9, subtracting the steady state pupil talk, and using the difference to set up a proportion with the matrix total, given a 10 × 10 matrix.

more difficult categories in all situations. Observers could be trained, let us say, to maintain a regular coding tempo by slowing down when the coding is easier in order to retain the capability of coding more difficult events at the same rate when they do occur. To make this plan reliable, ground rules would be necessary to guide the observer's choice when several easily coded events happened to occur within the same time interval.

As it turns out, there are areas of agreement between the teacher and the researcher, or more properly, a person whose purpose is to study his own behavior and a person who studies the behavior of others. Both would like to code as fast as possible because this reduces error at transitions, that is, when there is a shift from one category to another. The teacher may be better off to speed up and slow down when his purpose is to count the more rapid events. As long as changes in tempo are consistent in any two situations, meaningful comparisons are possible. The researcher may prefer a more constant rate because he knows that with carefully planned sampling and longer periods of observation, he has nothing to lose and something to gain.

Still unanswered is our question concerning *what is* an event to be coded. For the researcher it is a feature of behavior which is selected by the observer, according to a set of conventions, during a relatively constant time interval which may vary from one category system to another, but which permits coding to occur as rapidly as possible. For the teacher, a coded event may be the smallest bit of behavior that can be assigned to a category.

COMBINING CODE SYMBOLS FOR ANALYSIS

Once the meaning of a coded event is decided, it turns out that observers collect them in very large quantities. The next question is how can they be sorted into manageable bundles for efficient and useful analysis? There are some rules about this, illustrated by the statistics professor who asked, "You wouldn't calculate the average telephone number, in this class, in order to dial the number of the average student, or would you?" "No," replied the student, "I'd use the median." This student had learned some rules about numbers, apparently, but rules alone can be pretty silly when they are not logically related to purpose.

A start toward grouping data can begin by recognizing that different class formations, learning activities, and teaching objectives can occur during a school day, in the same classroom, and with the same pupils—even with a fairly rigid teacher. These factors have a powerful influence on verbal communication and nonverbal behavior. We would expect a matrix display of arithmetic instruction to be radically different from a display of "Show and Tell" simply because these are different activities, occur in a different formation, and have different objectives. Next, it can soon be discovered that even though events are presumed to be all of one kind, they also possess cyclical, sequential variation. Within the arithmetic lesson, for example, there are periods of "getting ready," "going over past work," "introducing new material," "planning new work or just setting assignments," and "individual seatwork or groupwork." Interaction patterns cycle through the school year, the semester, the 2- to 4-week unit of study, the day, the daily lesson, and in terms of learning to spell a particular word in a spelling lesson. To the extent that any coding system is accurate, it would reveal differences in patterns of interaction between one teacher and another, between pupils at different age levels, between different subject matter areas, etc., and also reveal differences within any one of these areas with the passage of time. The relationship between these factors and interaction in the classroom is sufficiently strong to lead to incorrect conclusions if they are ignored. Researchers usually consider these matters more carefully than do teachers who merely wish to study their own classroom interaction.

For the researcher

1) There is some category system with associated procedures for coding small bits of interaction. The FIAC system, with or without subscripts, is an example. Here the basic unit is the event that is defined by the nature of the category system and its conventional procedures.

2) The coded symbols from the above category system must now be combined into groups, and it is here that the purpose of the research becomes a primary consideration. If the purpose of the research is to compare phases of learning like getting ready, introducing new material, seatwork, etc., then a second category system, complete with its own conventions, is used by the observer to record how time is used. He must be trained to indicate the beginning and the end of each phase, make these notations while using the first category system, and thereby indicate the boundary lines of each phase. He does this by identifying the last code symbol of one phase and the first code symbol of the next phase. A shift from one phase to another is likely to be recognized by a change in the immediate purpose of interaction, a change of class formation, or a change in the role of the teacher.

3) Suppose the research purpose permits phases of instruction to be ignored, but is concerned with comparing two groups of teachers. Care must be taken to be sure that differences in the phases of instruction do not bias the comparison of the two groups. This is usually accomplished by extending the total observation time for each teacher.

A different study might have the purpose of comparing interaction for different school subjects within self-contained elementary classrooms. In this case the data are grouped to permit these comparisons, either for a single teacher or for many teachers. There are many different research purposes, but it is the purpose that determines how the data will be grouped.

There are sharp differences of opinion among researchers concerning how different methods of grouping the data will influence the basic unit in statistical analyses. For example, when phases of learning are being compared, is the unit of sampling the original interaction bit, the number of different phases, the number teachers within each phase, or the amount of time spent observing? The conclusion reached in a discussion of the basic sampling unit has two important consequences. First, it provides a logical base for selecting the degrees of freedom in a test of statistical significance. Second, it provides a logical base for extending conclusions so that they become generalizations about target populations.

For the classroom teacher

Teachers who investigate their own classroom interaction are usually less concerned with a more formal designation of the unit of sampling. Yet the logic of inquiry forces at least some consideration of these matters. A teacher may wish to investigate two different ways of introducing a new unit of study. One way to guard against incorrect conclusions is to anticipate the effects of all possible factors and then plan the investigation so that these factors are controlled or measured. It often helps to write down a list which becomes an inventory of possible related factors. Beside each, write down a suggestion or two for establishing control. Some examples are shown below:

Factor	What can be done about it
Controlling the interest of the pupils	A three- to five-item questionnaire could be completed by the pupils at the end of the observed lesson, and a class average calculated. Or split the class into two teaching groups which are known to be equally interested in a topic.
Billy, whose mere presence influences pupil initiation	If he was absent for the first episode, send him to the library for the second. If he is absent at the second, you'll have to wait until he returns.
Stranger in the room	Have him present at both episodes, or keep him away from both episodes.
Intelligence of the pupils	Either use the same group for both episodes or divide the class into two groups of equal ability, one for each episode.

There is little to be gained by extending this list because the inventory of factors would be unique to each investigation and the most practical counter strategy depends on the problem and the plan of inquiry. Perhaps the most generally useful suggestion is to try to replicate the collection of the data by creating several episodes. This can often be accomplished by dividing the class or simply repeating the experiment with similar learning topics.

How the data are grouped determines the unit of analysis. In turn, the unit of analysis in these miniature teacher designed experiments is chosen to provide comparisons which speak most directly to the problem being investigated. In order to be practical, always choose methods of displaying data that take the least amount of time, but still provide enough information. In one case it may be two matrices. In another, it may be most useful to draw out two time line displays, which are discussed in the next chapter. In a more simple contrast, perhaps the interaction can be recorded directly into two histograms.

Chapter Six

MULTIPLE CODING WITH CATEGORY CLUSTERS

TOWARD AN IDEAL FEEDBACK INSTRUMENT

The long range goal of exploring multiple coding is to approach an ideal feedback system for helping teachers change and improve their behavior. There is a description of an ideal instrument in Chapter 2, buried in the middle of a paragraph.

Behaviors of interest are coded accurately, and the code symbols are tabulated into a display which highlights desired comparisons. The entire process must keep up with the tempo of the spontaneous behavior so that at the moment the observation ceases, we have a display of summarized data which could provide instant feedback if this is desired.

Learning how to design and use subscripts is but a small step in the direction of an ideal instrument. The step is the right direction because "behaviors of interest" can be coded by simply subdividing the category in which they appear and then tabulating the tallies into an expanded matrix. It is a small step because the increased information is obtained at the cost of complicating the display. This, in turn, delays rather than facilitates feedback.

The notion that a single category system, with or without subscripts, is an appropriate tool for helping teachers inquire into their own behavior surely underestimates the problems involved. There are many different points at which a teacher might begin his study of teaching behavior. There is a wide range of resources available so that a single system may appear to be too complicated in some situations and too simple in another. The major advantage of a standard set of categories, into which the data from subscripts can be collapsed, is to make comparisons from one study to another or to refer to normative expectations. Such comparisons may be unimportant to a teacher who is interested in his own behavior. They may actually inhibit inquiry into one's own behavior. For example, a teacher might stop studying his own interaction as soon as he finds out that he is asking as many questions

159

or clarifying as many pupil ideas as teachers normally do in classrooms of his particular grade level and subject matter field. For these and other reasons, the topic of subscripting in the last chapter may have been a meagre diet for anyone admonished to be creative in his encoding and decoding. If this was true in your case, have faith. We are about to turn to the topic of multiple coding with category clusters and there are opportunities here for improvising your own categories, your own recording techniques, and trying out different procedures of tabulation and display.

In addition to introducing multiple coding with category clusters, this chapter is also concerned with the design of efficient and useful display procedures. Contemporary researchers have spent very little time and energy on the development of effective display procedures. Perhaps one reason is that when a new category system is developed, attention is first given to investigating criteria of reliability and validity in a kind of eagerness to become academically respectable. *As high as the standards of scientific object-ivity may be, they are not as difficult to achieve as the standards of efficiency which field workers impose in judging the utility of a procedure.* Many observation systems have been developed and tested with enough care to warrant their publication in research journals, but only a few of these systems have captured the interest of field workers. Feedback systems need to be objective or at least show promise of becoming so, but apparently the problems of utility must be recognized from the beginning; otherwise they seem to be ignored.

Much of the material in this chapter describes procedures which have not yet been adequately tested, either in terms of field utility or in terms of reliability and validity. The invention of effective displays for interaction analysis data and the development of category clusters which can be adapted to a wide variety of instructional problems are tasks which offer a challenge to the most talented among us. This chapter will accomplish its intended purposes if it provides a starting point for those who are interested in trying out new ideas which someday may become useful.

You may notice two themes in the pages which follow. At times the emphasis will be on techniques of display and at other times on the problems of designing category clusters. The understanding of one requires knowledge of the other, so both topics are intermixed. In order to start from a point of common understanding, the next two sections introduce time line displays for the FIAC system with which you are already familiar.

URBACH'S INTERACTION SEQUENCE GRAPH

Dr. Floyd Urbach (103), University of Nebraska, has shown creative insight by working on two weaknesses in the 10-category system: First, the matrix fails to provide an exact picture of how interaction varies during the elapsed time of the observation. Second, whenever possible, the act of recording should itself complete a display that can be interpreted without further clerical work.

Urbach planned his study to investigate recurring patterns during classroom interaction, but his unique contribution was stimulated when he disregarded the standard procedures for tabulating a matrix because they did not provide a suitable display for his problem. After exploring many alternatives, he developed a graphical display of interaction analysis data which is most original. Since plotting all 10 categories seemed a bit complicated, he chose to emphasize Categories 3, 4, 5, 8, and 9. This choice indicated that he correctly understood the main thrust of the category system as a method of studying the balance of teacher initiation and teacher response and was prepared to subordinate the display of less essential categories in order to be more efficient. This decision illustrates, once again, how a parsimonious analysis of a problem can and should determine the encoding-decoding procedures. What Urbach has called an "interaction sequence graph" is adapted, in the next section, to the problem of time line displays. Credit for this innovation belongs to Urbach and what follows is a variation of his original thinking.

SINGLE EVENT TIME LINE DISPLAYS FOR FIAC RECORDING

PURPOSE

A single event time line display for the 10 categories provides a visual estimate of the proportion of time in which the teacher initiated and the pupils responded, versus the proportion of time in which the pupils initiated and the teacher responded. This is accomplished by plotting each code symbol as it occurs one after the other with standardized conventions.

PROCEDURES AND CONVENTIONS

Before making an observation, a form for recording the data must be designed and duplicated in sufficient quantity for subsequent observations. On this form dots can be made, squares of graph paper can be filled, ideograms can be drawn, or arabic code symbols can be written, each entry to represent a single coded event. The form could be designed to be used from top to bottom as in columns, or from left to right as in rows. The essential feature is that a particular category is assigned to a constant position, in relation to other categories, so that with a little practice events can be recognized at a glance.

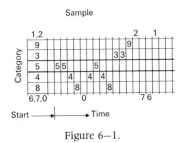

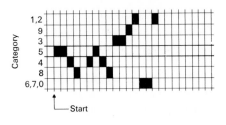

Figure 6—1.   Figure 6—2.

Figure 6—1 shows one arrangement, which places categories of *teacher response* above the horizontal "5 line" and categories of *teacher initiation* below the "5 line." Arabic numbers which represent the code symbols are used as entries. The form involves rows, so that entries are made from left to right in order to indicate sequence and the passing of time. Every event is written down with a code symbol, spaced together as closely as possible, yet clearly indicating the sequence. Light vertical lines, spaced about $\frac{1}{8}$ inch apart, can be added to keep the spacing more accurate. Such lines are mandatory when spaces are to be filled in, as is shown in Fig. 6—2. Some experimentation may be necessary to decide what size graph paper can be used quickly enough to keep up with the tempo of the interaction. The filled-in spaces of Fig. 6—2 require less horizontal length to record the same interaction that was shown in Fig. 6—1. On the other hand, it may be faster to write arabic numbers unless special felt pens are used which can fill a square with one stroke.

A different assignment of categories to the rows can be used for different displays. For example, Urbach prefers row assignments, from top to bottom, of 9, 8, 3, 4, and 5 which highlights who is talking, since pupil talk is found along the top two rows and teacher talk is below.

The complete coding of training episodes A and C, taken from Chapter 3, is illustrated in Fig. 6—3. An interesting sensation of quantitative loading for the different categories can be achieved by tilting the book until it is almost parallel with your line of sight along a row. The code symbols in each row then blur into a solid line which is proportional to the total incidence for each category.

Assignment One: Draw your own form on an $8\frac{1}{2}$- by 11-inch paper and code episode B, from Chapter 3. Write down the inferences the display suggests, episode B compared with A, and see if they are different from your matrix interpretations.

With some trial and error, you can decide what size space you personally need to record accurately and quickly. In my own case, it is possible to place five long, paper-width rows with light vertical lines at $\frac{1}{8}$-inch intervals on

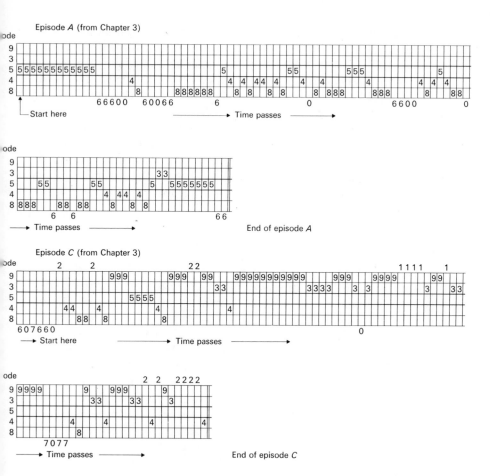

Fig. 6–3.   Time Line Displays and Recording Forms, FIAC System: Episodes A and C.

an $8\frac{1}{2}$- by 11-inch sheet of paper. This provides for 20 minutes of interaction, assuming a recording rate of 20 symbols per minute.

COMMENTS ON INTERPRETATION

The contrast between training episodes A and C can be easily seen in Fig. 6–3. First note the pattern of teacher initiation at the beginning of both episodes. These occurred, as you may remember, when the teacher set the task for the lesson. Sometimes more directive patterns are also found at the end of a lesson such as the one in episode A. All but two of the code symbols in episode A are below the 5 line, which indicates a predominant theme of teacher initiation and pupil response. The opposite stands out clearly in the time line of episode *C*.

This particular method of display has special advantages during preservice and inservice teacher education when certain patterns of interaction are being introduced, practiced, and then used in simulated or real classroom teaching. Any pattern which is being learned has a particular configuration within any standardized method of display. The 4-8-4-8 sequence, discussed in Chapter 4, can be easily recognized in episode *A*. With a longer observation period, a time line display is especially effective in testing hypotheses about the immediate consequences of any particular pattern. For example, if 3's do stimulate 9's, evidence similar to that shown in episodes *A* and *C* in Fig. 6—3 helps to support or reject such hypotheses.

TIME LINE DISPLAYS FOR CUMULATED INTERVALS

The single event time line display accounts for each event in its original sequence; thus it highlights the single event and relationships between single events. Any cumulated display, such as a matrix or histogram, covers any time interval which is chosen. For example, separate matrices can be tabulated for each 5-minute period and comparisons could then be made between such time intervals. Variations between such displays would permit inferences about how the interaction in one interval compared with another, but the original sequence of single events can only be approximated within the matrix and is completely lost in the histogram. Any move toward cumulated displays loses information about single events, but makes comparisons between time intervals more efficient. Teaching strategies which cycle over 20- or 30-minute periods can thus be highlighted in cumulated interval displays. In this section, a cumulated time line display is discussed which combines the histogram and a time line into a direct recording technique.

CHOOSING TIME INTERVALS

The unit of analysis becomes a time interval when data are cumulated. From a practical point of view, there are only two alternatives in choosing the unit of analysis. One alternative consists of selecting a short, standard time period and proceeding with a time sampling approach in tabulating and displaying data. When such time intervals are small, compared with the cycles or natural units which are of interest, then not too much error is introduced. This approach has the advantage that the observer does not have to make snap judgments about the beginning and end of natural units while he is observing. The second alternative is to record certain features of the situation which indicate change, as was suggested in Chapter 5, so that segments of interaction can be grouped into units of analysis while observing or immediately after leaving the class-room. The moment of transition between one unit and another can be located fairly reliably through the development of conventions in much the same way that interaction analysis categories are developed and standardized.

When it is said that the investigator's interest produces the unit of analysis some examples may help to clarify what is meant. Suppose a person was interested in what might be called a role analysis of the teacher's behavior. A first step would be to describe several different roles which the teacher might act out. He may be in charge of the whole class, he may consult with individual pupils, he may act as a roving resource person to workgroups, and he may attend to his own deskwork while the pupils are busy at theirs. It is first necessary to demonstrate that discriminations among these roles can be made in terms of time intervals during an observation. Points at which the teacher shifts his role would be indicated as the interaction analysis was coded. The data could then be cumulated into units of analysis for each role and the behavioral distinctions, if any, between the roles could be analyzed. Another example of units based on time intervals might be to study classroom interaction separately for the teaching of different subject matter topics in a self-contained classroom. In this case the contrast might be between reading, arithmetic, spelling, geography, and any other topics to which time is devoted. Within any one of these subject matter topics, further distinctions of time units might be made between certain learning functions such as "introducing new material," "review," "planning work," and so on. In each case the interest of the investigator determines the nature of time segments.

THE TECHNIQUE OF TIME LINE DISPLAYS FOR CUMULATED INTERVALS

Purpose

The purpose of this technique is similar to those discussed earlier for single events, but the unit of analysis is no longer the single event, but a time interval chosen by the investigator. Within each such time interval, individual coded events are displayed not in their original sequence, but as a frequency distribution for that interval.

Procedures and conventions

The display is designed for direct recording during class observation. Just as before, arabic numbers can be recorded or small squares in a graph grid can be filled. The latter is used in the examples because it requires less space.

As the observation begins, a small square is filled in for each event, but they are additive from left to right, regardless of sequence. If the interaction consisted of 5, 5, 5, 4, 8, 5, 4, 8, then three squares in the 5 line are each

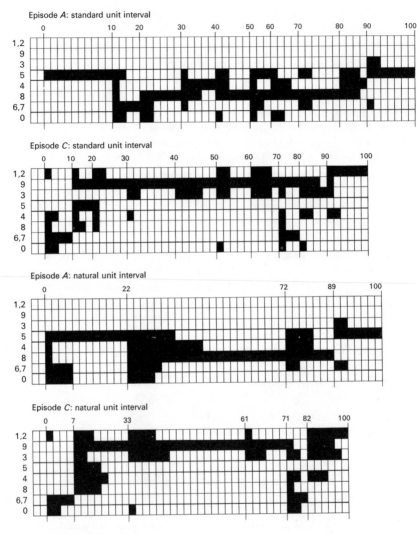

Fig. 6—4.   Examples of Cumulative Interval Time Line Displays for Episodes *A* and *C*.

filled in turn. The fourth event, Category 4, is the first 4 in that time interval, so the *first left-hand square* in the 4 row is filled. The 8 is recorded by a similar convention in row 8. The sixth event is the fourth 5, so it is added onto the existing three squares which have already been filled in. This procedure continues until the end of the interval. A vertical line is then drawn to indicate the end of one interval and the beginning of the next. This vertical line is the beginning point for starting a new display making use of the same conventions. All code marks must be to the right of the most recent vertical line.

Examples and comment

In Fig. 6—4 there are four illustrations of this technique. The top two displays show the interaction for episodes A and C, from Chapter 3, based on a standard time interval of 10 code symbols, which is approximately $\frac{1}{2}$ minute. This type of display has one unique advantage: even though the time intervals are approximately constant, the horizontal distance covered by a time interval is inversely related to the number of different categories used to code events. Thus, when the first 10 code symbols were all 5's, in episode A, the first interval has a horizontal length of 10 columns. Yet the second interval is only a width of four columns because more categories are used. The variation of length in the display highlights differences in the number of different categories used during classroom discourse. It is interesting to note that shorter display intervals appear in the center of episode A, but the center display intervals are longer in episode C. Apparently during the middle work periods, after starting and before ending, the pupils in episode C have more opportunity for expressing their ideas than is true of episode A. The reverse is true for the teacher, when the task is developed at the beginning of the episode. Both of these observations might lead to interesting theoretical explanations which could then be tested in subsequent investigations.

In the bottom two rows of Fig. 6—4, the same interaction is plotted according to natural units. In the case of episode A, intervals based on the topic discussed resemble the steps of problem-solving: code symbols 1 to 22, setting the task and getting ready; 23 to 72, learning how to order; 73 to 91, learning how to figure cost; and 92 to 100, summary and next assignment. In the case of episode C, a similar approach produced six intervals: code symbols 1 to 7, getting ready; 8 to 33, present task is set by reviewing the problem about roads; 34 to 61, the class discusses the alternatives; 72 to 82, some pupils drop out to return to seatwork; 83 to 100, the class continues discussion and makes plans for obtaining additional information. The two displays present a different configuration compared with the top two displays; however, the inferences would not be very different. Perhaps the natural units help to explain the differences of interaction which are plotted by providing information about what was going on. For example, greater teacher initiative in the first and last intervals of episode A suggests that this teacher takes over the setting of tasks and introduces his own ideas in a summary. In episode C, the teacher shows initiative in the first two intervals, when the task is set and the problem clarified. Teacher initiative is also shown during the fifth interval when the class formation changes. But the summary at the end is mainly in terms of past pupil contributions which become the basis of the summary. Higher pupil participation in both episodes, from about the twentieth to the seventieth code symbols, characterizes active work. The major contrast of the display is consistently maintained by the same assignment of categories to the various rows. Thus, teacher initiation in episode *A* and teacher response in episode *C* stand out clearly.

Even though single event and cumulated time line displays on graph paper appear to be quite similar at first glance, the habits of inspecting the first can be misleading if carried over to the second. A solid row of filled in squares for Category 8, for instance, such as appears in the second interval display of episode *A* (natural units), does not necessarily mean sustained pupil talk as it does in single event displays. In fact, the opposite is true in this case. The point is that knowledge of single event sequences is sacrificed in order to make direct comparisons between time intervals, and as a result of using a different kind of display, the rules for inspecting one display do not apply to the other.

Assignment Two: Draw a cumulated time line display for episode B, *first for a standard interval of 10 code symbols and second for natural intervals of your own choosing. Compare episode* A *with episode* B *and see if there are similar interaction changes between "learning to order" and "figuring costs," based on the natural units. Save your analysis of episode* B *for use later in this chapter.*

INTRODUCTION TO MULTIPLE CODING WITH CATEGORY CLUSTERS

Both single event and cumulated interval time line displays introduce recording procedures which eliminate a separate tabulation of the data. Each event, as it occurs, is placed in its final position so that the display is complete when the last code symbol is recorded. By accomplishing both the recording and display at the same time, one more step—or perhaps a long stride—is taken toward an ideal feedback technology.

The purpose of this section is to see if yet another step in feedback technology can be taken by adapting time line displays to flexible category systems in an effort to expand the range of problems to which coding techniques are applicable. Categories might be placed into a limited number of small clusters and then, in turn, clusters might be combined so that encoding is more effectively adapted to the problem being investigated. Should these procedures prove successful, it may be possible to create a general set of rules and principles for creating coding procedures that are custom built to one inquiry. Who knows, someday we may combine instant feedback with disposable category systems— to borrow some terms from Madison Avenue.

CATEGORY CLUSTERS AND SERIAL ORDER

Since an observer can record two code symbols for each event, why not three? Or four? A single event might be coded "341" in order to indicate: "3xx," the third category in the first cluster; "x4x," the fourth category in the second cluster; and "xx1," the first category in the third cluster. Now this simple procedure for writing three-digit code symbols places at least two requirements on what is meant by a cluster of categories.

First, a cluster can include more than one but not more than 10 categories to each cluster. The limitation arises from the use of arabic numbers which can vary between 0 and 9. If letters were used instead, more categories could belong to a cluster. This latter alternative is not necessary for live class observation, however, since this would provide too many category combinations.

Second, the serial ordering of clusters specifies a characteristic which might be called "logical compatibility." This requirement occurs because each category in the first cluster is to be subdivided according to the discriminations possible in the second cluster, and all permutations of the first two clusters are to be subdivided according to the discriminations possible in the third cluster. Categories are logically compatible when redundancy and contradictions are avoided. A code symbol that contains three digits is redundant to the extent that any other three-digit symbol can be used to code the same behavior. A code symbol is contradictory when any two serial digits represent categories which are mutually exclusive of each other and hence produce a meaningless symbol. The trick, then, in designing the categories for three clusters that are to be used in combination is to suffer a minimum loss through logically incompatible permutations. Let's assume, for the moment, that problems of logical compatibility can be solved and anticipate the potential of such a system for making discriminations among events.

Suppose there were five categories in each of three clusters and that all permutations were logically compatible. There would then be $5 \times 5 \times 5 = 125$ possible classifications in coding a single event. This capability is quite remarkable when compared with the 15 to 20 categories which are usually suggested as the category limitation of an observer coding in live classrooms.

Now suppose that the 125 different kinds of events could be considered two at a time in sequence pairs as they are in a two-dimensional matrix. In this case, pairs of events can be tabulated in a matrix with 125 rows and columns or 15,625 cells. The discriminations of a three-dimensional matrix, which considers sequence triplets, would be $125 \times 125 \times 125 = 1,953,125$, if my arithmetic is correct. By any standards, more than one million classifications for coding live communication with a paper and pencil is a pretty rich harvest and one that could be handled only with the help of a computer.

To return to the practical, from this excursion into fantasy, it is clear that we really don't know enough about how to conceptualize classroom behavior to make use of even 15,000 separate classifications, even the 484 cells of a 22 × 22 matrix takes several hours to comprehend. But these speculations involve unnecessary fears because any practical system not only suffers a loss of classifications due to logically incompatible permutations, but the range of behaviors which occur in the classroom is very limited due to the crude and inclusive nature of most categories.

Losses due to redundancy and lack of meaning are products of the overall design of the system. These losses are unimportant if the remaining permutations have utility in the analysis of a problem. Suppose a system of clusters was designed to analyze how a teacher made use of ideas expressed by pupils, the Category 3 of earlier chapters. One possible scheme is:

Cluster A	Cluster B	Cluster C
1. Teacher initiates	1. Repeats ideas previously stated	1. Factual level
2. Teacher responds	2. Uses synonyms of ideas previously stated	2. Higher than factual level
3. Pupil initiates	3. Expands ideas previously stated	3. None of above
4. Pupil responds	4. Applies ideas previously stated	
5. None of above	5. None of above	

This scheme has a potential 5 × 5 × 3 = 75 classifications, but any event which is coded with "none of above" in clusters A, B, and C is not likely to be of central interest in the analysis of the problem. When "none of above" is eliminated, there is really a 4 × 4 × 2 = 32-category system. Furthermore, any event which starts with one (1xx) is logically inconsistent with Categories 1 through 4 in cluster B, so there are probably less than 20 useful discriminations. Yet these may be sufficient to make progress in analyzing the problem.

Perhaps the largest loss in useful classifications is due to events which could be discriminated but just don't occur during the observation. Judging from the observation tabulated in Fig. 4–10, it is clear that in approximately 19 minutes of observation not all of the 10 categories were used equally and not all of the 100 cells were used. In fact, 90 percent of the interaction falls into four of the 10 categories. Glancing at the cells, we can see that all of the interaction is tabulated in 46 cells, 93 percent of the interaction falls into 25 cells and 84 percent falls into 14 cells. In the scheme illustrated in the preceding paragraph, at least two-thirds of the classification capacity is not directly relevant to the problem. So who needs 15,625 cells? Apparently multiple coding with category clusters, in theory at least, has a greater capacity for making discriminations than is needed for most projects. Yet in an application in which the teacher is attempting to produce a certain pattern of behavior, and when two of three clusters focus sharply on these behaviors, as many as 20 of 30 useful discriminations could be made.

At this point in the discussion, we have made a bit more progress in clarifying what is meant by a category cluster. A cluster contains two or more categories, but not more than 10. Clusters are designed to be used in combination with other clusters in the same serial order that the observer uses when he records the double, triple, or quadruple digits of a code symbol. Second ordered clusters subdivide each of the categories in the first cluster and third ordered clusters subdivide all permutations of the first two clusters. Redundancy and/or lack of meaning reduces the total number of discriminations that can be made, but this need not be a serious problem provided the useful discriminations remaining are relevant to the problem under investigation. Probably each cluster should be totally inclusive by adding a catchall category like "none of the above." The most significant limitation to the range of discriminations may be due to the phenomena being observed and their relation to the category discriminations.

There is a strategy issue, as yet unmentioned, about which we can only speculate until it is investigated. It seems likely that clusters which are selected to be first in serial order should involve judgments which an observer can make most quickly and that the second and third ordered clusters are assigned so as to be increasingly complex and, therefore, more time consuming. This strategy is proposed on the hunch that coding becomes fairly automatic after many hours of experience; the easier and quicker the judgments, the more automatic the coding becomes. Perhaps the most successful three-cluster schemes will permit the observer to be thinking about the third digit as he more or less automatically writes down the first two.

BEHAVIOR DISTINCTIONS FOR CATEGORY CLUSTERS

Given the many different category systems currently in use, it is not the purpose of this section to review significant contributions in discovering salient features of classroom interaction and credit the appropriate researcher. In fact, it is sometimes most difficult to decide who originated a particular category. For instance, so many different systems have a category for giving directions that no one can claim credit for inventing it. What does follow is a subjective listing of certain distinctions which seem to be most promising in building clusters. In those instances in which a particular author has proposed a distinction that very few others have mentioned, reference to the author is cited.

Primary distinctions

Before turning to proposed clusters, it may be more helpful to those who would like to build their own clusters to have an inventory of basic dichotomies and trichotomies (see accompanying table).

Some Basic Distinctions

a. Verbal	a. Teacher talk	a. On task (work oriented)
b. Nonverbal	b. Pupil talk	b. Off task (non-work-oriented)
a. Concerned with content	a. New idea	a. Open-divergent*
b. Concerned with process	b. Not new idea	b. Closed-convergent
a. To give†	a. Orientation†	a. Initiate‡ a. Agree
b. To ask	b. Opinion	b. Respond b. Disagree
	c. Suggestion	
a. To advocate (valuing)		a. Feelings (affective)
b. To inquire (objective evaluation)		b. Ideas (cognitive)
a. Indifferent	a. Positive outcome	a. Narrow, factual cognitions
b. Attentive	b. Negative outcome	b. Higher than factual
	c. Neutral	cognitions

There are, of course, many additional concepts which have been proposed and used in one or another classification system. Beyond those mentioned above, there are the dichotomies suggested by Osgood's (72) Semantic Differential Tests, Medley and Mitzel (67) review a number of category systems for classroom observation, including category descriptions (see pp. 274–297), and Borgatta and Crowther (17) who review a number of category systems for group discussions, therepeutic interviews, and mother-child relationships, then suggest subscripts for Bales' original 12 categories. These and other publications on interaction analysis contain suggestions for making behavioral distinctions.

Combining primary distinctions

The primary distinctions can be combined in order to form a single cluster. Two dichotomies, such as teacher talk versus pupil talk, and initiate versus

---

*"Open-closed" after Marie Hughes; "divergent-convergent" after J. J. Gallagher and Mary J. Aschner.
†After R. F. Bales.
‡In the sense of H. H. Anderson, J. Withall, N. Flanders, and others.

response, can be combined to create four categories. In this case, teacher initiates, teacher responds, pupil initiates, pupil responds. A dichotomy and a trichotomy will produce six categories. For instance the six middle categories in the Bales (8) system are based on the dichotomy "to give and to ask" combined with the trichotomy "orientation, opinion, and suggestion," which produces: "to give orientation, to give opinion, to give a suggestion, to ask for orientation, to ask for opinion, and to ask for a suggestion." It is in this fashion that the primary distinctions listed in the preceding section can become the building blocks for category clusters.

The following clusters involve distinctions which may be useful in the conduct of inservice and preservice teacher training. A cluster designated by the letter A is suggested as one which involves relatively rapid decisions and therefore may be nominated for a cluster which is first in serial order. A cluster labeled BC is suggested for a second or third ordered cluster, while the letter C is used when it seems likely that the observer judgments would take relatively more time.

Cluster A1

1. Teacher talks
2. Pupil talks
3. Nonverbal communication
4. Confusion, none of above

Cluster A1 might be called a general cluster and be appropriate when both verbal and nonverbal communication are to be studied. This cluster might be difficult to use efficiently, since the distinctions in the second and third ordered clusters should subdivide both verbal and nonverbal communication equally well and this is not easily accomplished.

Cluster A2

1. Teacher initiates
2. Teacher responds
3. Pupil initiates
4. Pupil responds
5. None of above

Cluster A2 would permit quick judgments for anyone who has used the FIAC system. This cluster would be useful in studying the balance between teacher initiation and teacher response, since it is oriented more to verbal communication.

Cluster *A*3

1. Teacher talk, content
2. Teacher talk, process
3. Pupil talk, content
4. Pupil talk, process
5. None of above

Cluster *A*3 may be of use in the study of teacher-pupil planning. Content and process would take on specialized meaning in such an application: content—what is to be studied, the goals, the questions to be answered; process—actions to be taken, ways that content can be studied, decisions about organization for work, and the like.

Cluster *A*4

1. Teacher talk, convergent
2. Teacher talk, divergent
3. Pupil talk, convergent
4. Pupil talk, divergent
5. None of above

Cluster *A*4 might be helpful in a study of the conditions necessary for pupils to become more creative. Some may prefer to use "open" rather than divergent, and "closed" rather than convergent, since there is some similarity between the two notions. If you are disposed to assign different meanings to the two terms, then you may wish to try separate clusters using the concepts you prefer.

Cluster *A*5

1. Teacher talk, advocate
2. Teacher talk, inquire
3. Pupil talk, advocate
4. Pupil talk, inquire
5. None of above

More and more interest appears to be developing in the effective teaching of controversial subjects. Issues such as sex education, war policies, political parties, the study of religion, and similar matters are often discussed, either on the basis that they should be in the curriculum, or they should not be in the curriculum. Very little analysis has been made of more or less effective teaching patterns. *To advocate* might be defined as making assertions or expressing personal beliefs without qualification and without asking how verification or evaluation might be accomplished. In cluster A5 advocacy means giving very little attention to the careful definition of terms. *To inquire objectively* would mean that terms would be defined, qualifications stated, ways to test or verify are discussed, and personal convictions are clearly separated from the conduct of inquiry but not ignored. In the event that distinguishing between advocacy and inquiry proves difficult, this cluster may require further development and then be labeled BC for placement in a second or third cluster.

Cluster BC1

1. Support
2. Agree
3. Disagree
4. Criticize, reject

Sometimes teachers are interested in tracing interaction patterns in which a distinction is made between cognitive agreement or disagreement and emotional support or rejection of the pupil. Such a distinction might uncover teaching difficulties involving motivation, sustaining interest, and helping younger pupils start to develop more independent thinking. The cluster might be most helpful if categories 2 and 3 applied to objective, nonemotional statements which focus on ideas. Categories 1 and 4 would then refer to the pupil as well as to his ideas. Support would refer to approval of both the person, his ideas, and his actions. Criticism would reject a pupil, his ideas, and his actions; maybe on the grounds of intent, that is, he really knows better and that whatever is being disapproved was done on purpose.

Cluster BC2	Cluster BC3
1. Respond	1. Soliciting
2. Solicit	2. Responding
3. Initiate	3. Structuring
4. Direct	4. Reacting

Clusters BC2 and BC3 are considered together because they accomplish pretty much the same objectives. Cluster BC3 is based on Bellack's (9) pedagogical moves which were identified in a study of communication in secondary classrooms. Bellack distinguishes between responding and reacting by using the rule that responding is always preceded by soliciting and forms a reciprocal relationship. Reacting may follow any kind of action, but it is not directly elicited by the preceding event.

Cluster $BC2$ assumes four basic kinds of action. To *solicit* is to actively request another's participation. To *respond* means to react to either initiation or solicitation. To *initiate* is to be indifferent to the possibilities of response, more like Bellack's structuring. To *direct* is to order with the expectation of compliance—a special kind of solicitation, if you wish. These clusters are helpful in studying the teacher's role and his use of authority. There would arise problems of redundancy if either $BC2$ or $BC3$ were combined with cluster $A2$.

Cluster $C1$

1. Specifics, facts, narrow focus
2. None of above

Cluster $C2$

1. Specifics, facts, narrow focus
2. Not (1) and not (3)
3. Unique insights, generalizations, and explanations

Cluster $C3$

1. Specifics
2. Grouping, labeling
3. Analyzing, structuring
4. Next step, conjecturing
5. Concluding, explaining, theorizing, synthesyzing

Logical functions in classroom discourse are most difficult to code when the purpose of observation is to describe all the logical processes that are used or could be used in the classroom. It is still difficult, but sometimes manageable, to code classroom interaction in terms of a particular model of logic or to see if certain clearly defined events do or do not occur. Thus, cluster $C1$ is useful in order to determine what proportion of classroom discussion rises above a simple concern for specifics. Incidently, early returns from our work with subscripts would suggest that the proportion of time spent on simple specifics is very high, much higher than 60 percent. Cluster $C2$ is the same as $C1$, except that unusual insights, generalizations, or explanations can be coded when they do occur, however infrequently this may be. Cluster $C3$ is offered with some reservations, since the discriminations may be too difficult. To make use of a cluster like $C3$, it is necessary first to adapt the categories to some model of thinking that is directly applicable to the subject matter content. The meaning of each category is probably different, one subject matter field compared with another, such as arithmetic compared with social studies.

Cluster BC4

1. Orientation
2. Opinion
3. Suggestion

Bales (8) has already shown that there are logical changes over time, among the categories of BC4. He studied discussion groups which had the purpose of solving a human relations problem, that is, coming up with a group recommendation at the end of a 30- to 50-minute discussion.

Cluster C4

1. Positive
2. Neutral
3. Indifferent
4. Negative

Cluster C4 illustrates how a kind of affective rating can be made by the observer. In using this kind of cluster, there are several alternatives. It might be restricted to nonverbal communication. It can be used to judge the intent of the speaker. It can be used to make a rating of the consequences, an effect which could be more or less independent of intent. Or it can be a probability rating of the momentary affective tone of the entire class, e.g., if 80 percent or higher show interest, use one, if 50 to 80 show interest, use two, if 50 to 80 are indifferent, use three, and if significant, overt counter dependency is present, use four.

Cluster BC5

1. Accept
2. Clarify
3. Interpret
4. Ask
5. Suggest

In those instances in which particular patterns are expected during interviews, such as a counselor and client interview or a supervisor working with a teacher, the manner of being nondirective can be investigated. Cluster BC5 illustrates certain skills which are presumably practiced in counselor clinic training and may be used by a supervisor working with a teacher.

Cluster *BC*6

1. fight, flight
2. Dependency
3. Pairing
4. Work

Thelen's (101) interesting adaptation of concepts originally suggested by W. R. Bion for the analysis of group discussion may have interesting applications to supervisor-teacher interviews. In such an application, "work" would refer to attending to the client's problem which precipitated the interview. The first three categories of cluster *BC*6 can be used to characterize "emotional modalities" in the conversation. If it seems desirable to code these emotional qualities continuously during all statements, then "none of above" or "neutral" could be substituted for Category 4 and various kinds of work statements would then be placed in another cluster.

Cluster *BC*7

1. Problem (task)
2. Group (we, us)
3. Member (you, other)
4. Self

Cluster *BC*7 can be used to characterize the orientation of a statement with regard to its substantive content, that is, to code events according to what the speaker is talking about. An interesting variation of multiple coding occurs when these same four categories appear in two successive clusters, perhaps the second and third. The first coding is made in terms of what the speaker is talking about, as above, but the second coding is made on the basis of the reasoning or referant in the statement. Thus, to say, "There are two steps in this problem, and they have to be taken in the right order," is to speak of the task in terms of the task. On the other hand, to say "There are two steps to this task, but I don't think I can do the second," is to speak of the task in terms of self. Similarly, one can talk about the group (or us), a member (or the other person), and self, *in terms of* the problem, the group, a member, or one's self.

Cluster *BC*8	Cluster *BC*9 *
1. Gesture	1. Nods, smiles
2. Expression	2. Moves toward pupil
3. Body movement	3. Keeps eye contact
	4. Uses prop

*After Cooper and Stroud who worked with Dwight Allen on microteaching at Stanford University.

Nonverbal communication can be coded either separately or in conjunction with verbal communication. In a particular cluster scheme a catchall category like "none of above" may be necessary. Cluster $BC8$ is a general classification of the type of nonverbal communication and would require a second cluster in order to characterize the nature of the communication, for example, $C4$. Cluster $BC9$ might be used in a sequence after an event has been classified as nonverbal teacher support of the pupil, or at least as nonverbal support. Teachers are given opportunities to practice nonverbal support in certain microteaching exercises at Stanford University. Charles Golloway (47) has shown that it is possible to code nonverbal phenomena.

Perhaps it is time to end this cafeteria line of possible clusters. Anyone interested in multiple coding with category clusters is not only invited to pick and choose in terms of a preferred diet, but to walk right out to the kitchen and "cook up" his own clusters.

STRATEGY IN THE DESIGN OF MULTIPLE CLUSTERS

The introduction to time line displays has helped to focus attention on efficiency in feedback and the discussions of possible category clusters has suggested behavior patterns which might be studied when you first try multiple coding. Now it is time to discuss possible strategies for designing multiple coding schemes for live class observation.

The pioneering work of other researchers, working primarily with sound or video recordings, often supplemented by a typescript, have already shown that multiple coding is possible when there is unlimited access to the phenomena to be coded. An unusually complete coding of different characteristics of verbal interaction can be seen in the work of Bellack (9, p. 16), who made eight different classifications about each codable unit in a typescript. Each classification was made from a minimum of three categories to a maximum of 22, not to mention arabic numbers representing the number of typescript lines. These judgments included: (1) speaker, (2) type of pedagogical move, (3) substantive meaning, (4) substantive-logical meaning, (5) number of lines in (3) and (4), (6) instructional meanings, (7) instructional-logical meanings, and (8) number of lines in (6) and (7).

In this section, the discussion is concerned with the development of design strategies for using category clusters in order to code a single event. Earlier research such as Bellack's helps by showing what can be done when the observer can control or slow down the input rate in order to provide time for a variety of separate judgments. The reverse is now the issue. Can a viable multiple category system be designed to match the natural input tempo of live classroom interaction?

Unrestricted and restricted choice chains

In multiple coding a single event is recorded by a series of arabic numbers, one digit to each category cluster. The code symbol for an event may consist of two, three, or even four digits, depending on the number of clusters. Each digit, from left to right, represents a sequence of choices whereby the observer characterizes an event within the limitations of his alternatives. For the sake of brevity, this sequence can be called a *choice chain*.

It might be possible to design category clusters so cleverly that there are no redundant and meaningless choice chains. In this case, the number of permissible chains exactly equals all the permutations among the categories. In a perfect system, any possible chain is a useful classification. With all chains useful, there is no need for restrictions. A scheme with *unrestricted* choice chains can be illustrated with three simple dichotomies.

Category System

A1—verbal communication	B1—initiation	C1—on task
A2—nonverbal communication	B2—response	C2—off task

Sequence of Coding	Unrestricted Choice Chains
First, is it A1 or A2? ⟶	A1 ⤫ A2
Second, is it B1 or B2? ⟶	B1 ⤫ B2
Third, is it C1 or C2? ⟶	C1 ⤫ C2

The diagram to the right illustrates unrestricted choice because the number of different chains exactly equals all the permutations. There are $2 \times 2 \times 2 = 8$ permutations and there are eight different chains. They are: 111, 112, 121, 122, 211, 212, 221, and 222.

The most *restricted* pattern of choice chains occurs when each choice limits the next alternative choice. The simplest example, shown on p. 181, is again one that presents dichotomies at each choice point. However, note that in order to have eight classifications, when choices are completely restricted, six categories are too few; in fact 14 are required.

From a practical point of view, 14 categories for eight classifications become a bit of an artifact. By writing better category descriptions, eight categories can be formed. The first category, 111, can easily combine three elements into one English description "teacher talk, initiation," and the last category 248 can read "nondisrupting pause, not concerned with the learning task." With such a system, multiple code symbols become a burden rather than a help. Since the system has only eight categories, why not use arabic numbers

Category System and Choice Chains When Fully Restricted

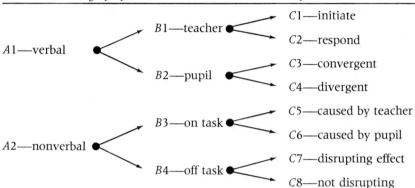

from one to eight? The point is that a fully restricted system involving three category clusters reduces, in effect, to a fixed set of categories similar to the 10 categories which were discussed in earlier chapters. A system of subscripts, such as the two systems which were described in Chapter 5, are examples of fully restricted choice chains involving two clusters which reduce to a single set of categories. Such systems have only the presumed advantage of programming the choices of the observer into two steps. There are no advantages involving permutations which, by their very nature, combine a single category with others to form a greater number of classifications than would otherwise occur.

The unrestricted and the fully restricted systems provide us with two extreme cases which we can use as benchmarks in our thinking. To move from a fully restricted system toward an unrestricted system is like moving from a single cluster in which one category provides for only one classification toward the multiple use of a single category so that it can be used to designate several classifications. There is greater utilization of each category and subsequent greater efficiency in the system as schemes approach unrestricted choice chains. Given the limited total number of different categories which the observer can use in live class observation, greater efficiency could become an important factor in some application. At the same time, as unrestricted choice is approached, the possibility of redundant and meaningless permutations is increased and this necessitates more careful planning and clever design. In the next section, a discussion of semirestricted systems helps to place this discussion on a more practical level.

Semirestricted systems

Most likely, practical multiple coding schemes for live class observation will involve permutations, but with some restrictions. In this discussion, such a scheme is called *semirestricted*. Obviously the smallest restriction that could be placed on a system would involve just one category. A practical illustration might be as follows.

Category System, Semirestricted			Choice Diagram

$A1$—teacher talk $B1$—initiation $C1$—narrow, factual focus

$A2$—pupil talk $B2$—response $C2$—above narrow, factual focus

$A3$—none of above

$$
\begin{array}{ccc}
A1 & A2 & A3 \\
\searrow\!\!\!\nearrow & & \\
B1 & B2 & \\
\searrow\!\!\!\nearrow & & \\
C1 & C2 &
\end{array}
$$

The most useful eight classifications of this scheme are products of the unrestricted permutations. Just as before, they are, 111, 112, 121, 122, 211, 212, 221, and 222, but there is also a catchall category that can be coded 300. This last category is restricted because it forms meaningless combinations with the B and C clusters. The capacity of this system is $2 \times 2 \times 2 = 8$ plus $1 = 9$ classifications and seven categories.

In most applications, category $A3$ would be subdivided because an observer can easily handle more than seven categories. The permutations would be restricted, however, by allowing only those choice chains that are indicated below:

$$
\begin{array}{cc|cc}
A1 & A2 & A3 & \\
B1 & B2 & B3 & B4 \\
C1 & C2 & C3 & C4
\end{array}
$$

To the categories that were described in the preceding paragraph can now be added the following: $B3$ might be "teacher instigated," $B4$ might be "pupil instigated," $C3$ could be "work oriented" (on task), and $C4$ could be "nonwork oriented" (off task). The total number of classifications is $2 \times 2 \times 2 = 8$ plus $1 \times 2 \times 2 = 4$, so that 12 classifications are possible with 11 categories. One might be inclined, at this point, to develop a crude index of efficiency for category schemes whereby the number of classifications is divided by the number of categories. In this case, 12 divided by 11. But such an index is likely to be misleading because the incidence of events would not be divided equally between the two, separate, unrestricted choice chains. It is quite likely that category $A3$ will pick up between 10 and 15 percent only, so that the more efficient eight classifications for six categories will operate 85 to 90 percent of the coding time.

There are, of course, a very large number of category systems that would fit under the semirestricted classification. The design of the system which was described in the preceding paragraph, for example, can achieve the same number of classifications with nine categories, rather than 11, by choosing categories for cluster C which are logically compatible with the semirestricted permutations of clusters A and B. Let $C1$ be "work oriented" and $C2$ be "nonwork oriented." In such a case the choice chains are:

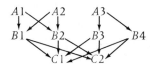

There are still 12 classifications, but only nine categories. While this scheme illustrates a possibility, the utility of the system is not as high because the incidence of "nonwork oriented" events is likely to vary between $2\frac{1}{2}$ and 5 percent. This means that the system would be productive only when the analysis of the small proportion of nonwork oriented events is of interest or in a situation in which their incidence was expected to be much higher than average, such as a nursery school.

Summary of possible strategies for designing clusters

The purpose of this section is largely to illustrate the wide variety of choice chains that are possible. In most instances, semirestricted choice chains will be most practical, but the possibilities are limited only by our creativity and the nature of problems we choose to investigate.

AN APPLICATION OF MULTIPLE CODING

This section contains an illustrative application of multiple coding with category clusters. The purpose is to explain how the nature of a problem enters into (a) planning the analysis, (b) designing the category clusters, (c) inventing a display format, and (d) making inferences from data. The printed word of this book is a limited medium for reaching such objectives. You may find yourself in the position of an apprentice juggler who is told, "Now watch this and maybe you'll learn something." The analogy of juggling is quite appropriate, since the plans, categories, displays, and conclusions must be dealt with simultaneously. The whole system works together, as a single unit, or it doesn't work at all. It would seem quite certain that the skills involved develop best with practice and that the reading may help by suggesting a place to start.

The material below begins with the statement of a problem, one that might occur to someone who is interested in improving classroom teaching. A scheme for coding behavior that is relevant to the problem is developed and then the interaction of episode B in Chapter 3 is analyzed to see if the system works.

PLANNING THE ANALYSIS

Initial statement of the problem

How a teacher makes use of two patterns—(a) teacher initiation coupled with pupil response and (b) pupil initiation coupled with teacher response—ought to be related to (c) the kind of thinking which enters into classroom discourse. It may be that certain patterns of teacher initiation and teacher response are more likely to be present when pupils reach higher levels of cognitive thought processes such as making generalizations and constructing logical explanations, while some other patterns are more likely to be present when these higher levels are not reached, assuming that the requirements of the learning task remain constant.

Besides investigating possible relationships between teaching behavior and levels of thought, it would be nice if the coding procedures were so efficient that they could be used in live class observation with the display completed at the moment that the observation ceases.

Background to the problem

Practically every researcher who has analyzed classroom interaction reports various reciprocal relationships between teaching behavior and pupil behavior. Perhaps the most frequently reported is that persistent, active, direction on the part of the teacher produces a pattern of pupil response rather than pupil initiation. The more teachers structure problems and ask relatively specific questions, the more likely pupils will complement this behavior by following the teacher's lead. In fact, this is the predominant quality of classroom inter-action throughout the world. On the other hand, teachers can stimulate pupil initiation by reacting to and making use of ideas expressed by pupils and by asking more "open" (after Hughes) questions so as to help pupils express their own ideas part of the time. These reciprocal relationships are discussed in terms of matrix models in the beginning of Chapter 4.

It is quite possible that patterns established in the early part of a lesson (or unit, or semester, or year) will have predictable consequences during sub-sequent activity. The hypotheses described by Flanders (41, pp.110–116) suggest that a sequence that begins with extended teacher initiation and pupil response establishes (even fixes) unwanted dependence of pupils on the teacher's initia-tive which subsequently reduces creative pupil participation. Once established, this pattern is difficult to change. A more open and responsive teaching pattern early in a discussion or lesson, on the other hand, curtails overdependence and permits, or at least seems to be associated with, the flexible adaptation of teacher influence to the situation of the moment.

The analysis of logical patterns in classroom discourse has sometimes taken "the level of cognitive thought" into consideration. One such system of levels has been suggested by Hilda Taba (99), who points out that not only are different levels involved, but there are also definite patterns which characterize logical thinking. Two of the patterns involved when children are required to organize information in the classroom are:

1) differentiation ⟶ grouping ⟶ categorizing ⟶ labeling;
2) "reading" points ⟶ establishing relationships between various points ⟶ comparing ⟶ generalizing.

Presumably the sequences in these patterns can be traced providing there are coding categories which can make the necessary distinctions, but the study of sequence means that the method chosen to display the data should include some kind of time line.

Taba has a theory, for example, that in order to guide a total class discussion toward generalizations and explanations that are proposed by the pupils, rather than by the teacher, considerable time must be devoted to citing specifics, clustering these citations into groups, and speculating about possible relationships between clusters. These preliminary steps must be accomplished thoroughly so that as many pupils as possible share an awareness of those problem elements which are logically related to possible generalizations. Only after this "shared apperceptive mass" of information has been constructed can we expect pupils to develop logical explanations and suggest generalizations. An inadequate preliminary development of these logical steps may lead to fewer generalizations and these are more likely to be made by one or two very bright youngsters or by the teacher.

Reformulation of the problem

This brief consideration of background information leads to a sharper description of the problem. We now know that our categories must permit discriminations of (a) teacher initiative—pupil response, (b) pupil initiative—teacher response, and simultaneously indicate (c) the levels of thought, in terms of a model of thinking. Furthermore, the models of teacher influence and logical thinking specify sequence, so that our coding system will be required to display the order of discussion events as they occur, one after the other. All of these requirements seem to suggest some system of multiple coding and a recording technique which produces a time line display so that sequence is clearly displayed. The fact that the time line technique also produces a complete display as coding progresses is simply an extra advantage.

THE CATEGORY CLUSTERS

It is well to remember that there are many ways to code the three aspects of classroom interaction which appear to be central in this analysis. The category clusters about to be described illustrate only one approach; others may be more productive and you are invited to design your own clusters and recording procedures for this or some other problem.

The first cluster

Cluster *A*

1. Teacher responds
2. Teacher solicits
3. Teacher initiates
4. Pupil responds
5. Pupil solicits
6. Pupil initiates
7. None of above

Cluster *A* includes the dimension of who is talking—teacher or pupil—and provides for moments of nontalk with a seventh catchall category. Three types of talk are discriminated: Categories 1 and 4 are *response* actions, 2 and 5 are called *soliciting* and refer to an act which invites the participation of another person, and 3 and 6 are acts of *initiation*, which in this case could also be thought of as not responding and not soliciting. This cluster helps to distinguish between teacher initiation and pupil response by the use of categories 3 and 4, and between pupil initiation and teacher response by the use of categories 1 and 6. Soliciting, especially by the teacher, serves to invite and focus pupil participation.

The second cluster

Cluster *B*

1. Give direction, criticize
2. Use, develop, clarify a teacher idea
3. Cite, acknowledge a teacher idea
4. Cite, acknowledge a pupil idea
5. Use, develop, clarify, give suggestion
   about a pupil idea

Cluster *B* is designed to make additional distinctions between teacher initiation and teacher response. This is accomplished by deciding whether the substance of a statement can be associated more with pupils or with the teacher or book, regardless of who the speaker is. As the category numbers get higher, more and more emphasis is on ideas expressed by pupils. Actually, a sixth category, which is to suggest, to move, or to act on a pupil idea could be added as the complement to Category 1. By using only five categories, the assumption is that most directions and most criticism will be made by the teacher, based on his ideas, and directed toward pupils.

It is sometimes difficult to decide whether an idea can be traced back to the pupils versus the teacher or book or some other written authority, not a pupil. Teachers ask questions, provide orientation, or give directions as they "structure" an activity. Sometimes the resulting interaction leaves no room for pupils to interject their own points of view. When this is true, Categories 1, 2, and 3 are used in cluster *B*. When some degree of freedom is provided by a teacher so that the pupil can react by expressing his own point of view, or when it is unexpectedly interjected by pupils, Categories 4 and 5 are used.

This particular organization of cluster *B* was made with an eye on the problems of display which must be faced in the next step of building a coding scheme. Ordering the categories from 1 to 5 in this particular way will provide a visual emphasis in the display, depending on whether ideas can be associated with the teacher or the pupils.

There are some category combinations of cluster *A* with cluster *B* which are at least awkward and perhaps logically incompatible. A code symbol with the first two digits $34x$, for instance, means that the teacher chose to repeat, cite, or acknowledge the idea(s) of a pupil in such a way that it seemed reasonable to code the action as initiation rather than a response. The same could be said about a pupil reacting to a teacher idea when it is coded $63x$. Both combinations are unlikely to occur. Another awkward classification problem occurs when a question does not reflect any substantive idea. A teacher question, "Would anyone care to comment further?" has no substantive antecedent that is clearly indicated in the statement. One solution is to take into account the teacher's intent to let a pupil cite and develop his own ideas. By this reasoning, the code symbol $25x$ could be used in coding "open" questions.

The third cluster

Cluster *C*

---

1. Specifics, facts, instances, etc.
2. Comparisons and simple contrasts
3. Analysis and more complicated
   comparisons; inferences are
   involved
4. Generalizations, conclusions,
   and explanations

Cluster *C* is designed with the hope that statements that fall into Categories 1, 2, and 4 can be recognized with reasonable reliability. If this turns out to be true, then all other statements are assigned to Category 3. In terms of Taba's model, "reading" points, citing examples, being concerned with specifics, are to be coded into Category 1. This is the category to use for coding classroom discussions about what, where, and when. Category 2 fits Taba's differentiating, grouping, categorizing, and establishing relationships between points, and so on. Category 4 is separated from 3 by the quality of the explanation, conclusion, or generalization. Speculations with reasons, a "string" of logically presented propositions such as those involved in explanations and predictions, and creative synthesis are all relatively rare, tend to be recognized when they do occur, and are assigned to Category 4. Statements not categorized in 1, 2, and 4 would fall into Category 3.

Adding a second chain

Although it would not have much utility for analyzing the behavior specimen of episode *B* in Chapter 3, subdivisions of silences and pauses which are coded in Category 7, cluster *A*, would make these clusters more useful for classroom use. Category 7 can be subdivided into "teacher instigated" and "pupil instigated" (when in doubt use the former) and these, in turn, into "on task" and "off task." The entire system is shown below:

Cluster *A*	Cluster *B*	Cluster *C*
1. Teacher responds	1. Direction, criticism	1. Narrow, factual
2. Teacher solicits	2. Clarify, use teacher idea	2. Comparisons
3. Teacher initiates	3. Cite, acknowledge teacher idea	3. Analysis
4. Pupil responds	4. Cite, acknowledge pupil idea	4. Generalization and explanation
5. Pupil solicits	5. Clarify, use pupil idea or make suggestion	
6. Pupil initiates	based on it.	
7. None of above	6. Teacher instigated	5. On task
	7. Pupil instigated	6. Off task

This system presumably has the capability of making $6 \times 5 \times 4 = 120$ plus $1 \times 2 \times 2 = 4$ or 124 separate classifications. But this gross total is much less important than whether particular permutations will or will not make discriminations which will clarify the problem being investigated.

THE RECORDING AND DISPLAY OF DATA

Three-digit code symbols can be recorded quite rapidly when no display is involved or when the display can be drawn later on from notes recorded during the observation. Simply duplicate some recording forms which provide spaces for the three-digit code symbols, for example, in systematic columns, and then use a pencil and clip board. To make a display while recording in the classroom means that certain conventions about the spatial relationships between the various category numbers are created and followed. The trick is to design the display so that the tempo of recording is not retarded any more than necessary while patterns of special interest are highlighted.

The recording form

The method chosen in this instance involves a vertical display. A vertical time line starts at the top and proceeds downward, arabic digits are written into the squares of a printed form from left to right, and special notations, if necessary, can be made in the margins. An example of this form is shown in Fig. 6—5. There are other alternatives, of course, but I have found the form shown quite useful. One advantage of recording arabic numbers in slightly larger squares, compared with filling in smaller cells or just checking them, is that the number itself indicates what column should be used and should there be a placement error, the number indicates the proper correction. The disadvantage is that fewer tallies will fit on a single sheet of paper, compared with a more compact recording form. The display illustrated in Fig. 6—5 can be drawn so that 100 three-digit code symbols can be recorded on a single sheet of $8\frac{1}{2}$- by 11-inch paper.

INTERPRETING A DISPLAY TO SEE IF IT WORKS

In order to check the utility of the category clusters and the procedures for recording and display, a live observation would be best. In this book an analysis is made of episode *B*. A display of the data is shown in Fig. 6—6.

The code symbols for the first 50 classifications are on the left side of the page, to be read from top to bottom and from left to right. The classifications from 51 to 100 are to the right side, to be read in the same manner. All pauses in this episode were considered to be "teacher instigated" and "on task," so the code symbol 765 is recorded just to the right of each cluster column. Items 6 and 83 are examples. The columns for both clusters *A* and *B* have a double line between the third and fourth category to emphasize the boundary between teacher and pupil.

The display format for each cluster

Early in the development of category clusters, categories are listed in some order and arabic code numbers are assigned. This can be done in terms of the final display format, or at least the problems of display should be kept in mind.

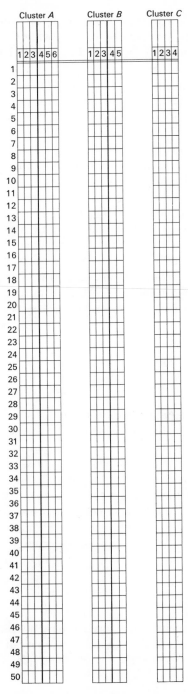

Fig. 6–5.   A Sample Recording Form for Multiple Coding.

Cluster A — Speaker (T P), columns 1 2 3 4 5 6
Cluster B — Idea from (T P), columns 1 2 3 4 5
Cluster C — Level of thinking, columns 1 2 3 4

Row	Cluster A (col)	Cluster B (col)	Cluster C (col)
1	3 (2)	3 (2)	1 (1)
2	2 (1)	1 (1)	1 (1)
3	3 (2)	1 (1)	1 (1)
4	3 (2)	1 (1)	1 (1)
5	3 (2)	2 (1)	1 (1)
6	7 (6)	6 (5)	5
7	7 (6)	6 (5)	5
8	2 (1)	3 (2)	2 (2)
9	7 (6)	6 (5)	5
10	4 (3)	4 (3)	1 (1)
11	1 (1)	4 (3)	1 (1)
12	4 (2)	4 (3)	2 (2)
13	4 (2)	4 (3)	1 (1)
14	1 (1)	4 (3)	1 (1)
15	4 (3)	4 (3)	1 (1)
16	1 (1)	4 (3)	1 (1)
17	1 (1)	4 (3)	1 (1)
18	3 (2)	3 (2)	1 (1)
19	3 (2)	2 (1)	1 (1)
20	3 (2)	2 (1)	1 (1)
21	2 (1)	5 (4)	3 (3)
22	5 (3)	4 (3)	1 (1)
23	6 (4)	5 (4)	2 (2)
24	1 (1)	4 (3)	1 (1)
25	6 (4)	5 (4)	3 (3)
26	6 (4)	5 (4)	3 (3)
27	6 (4)	5 (4)	3 (3)
28	6 (4)	5 (4)	3 (3)
29	6 (4)	5 (4)	3 (3)
30	1 (1)	4 (3)	3 (3)
31	1 (1)	4 (3)	3 (3)
32	1 (1)	4 (3)	3 (3)
33	3 (2)	5 (4)	3 (3)
34	3 (2)	1 (1)	1 (1)
35	7 (5)	6 (5)	5
36	7 (5)	6 (5)	5
37	7 (5)	6 (5)	5
38	7 (5)	6 (5)	5
39	2 (1)	5 (4)	3 (3)
40	4 (2)	3 (2)	1 (1)
41	4 (2)	3 (2)	2 (2)
42	4 (2)	3 (2)	2 (2)
43	2 (1)	2 (1)	3 (3)
44	4 (2)	3 (2)	1 (1)
45	4 (2)	3 (2)	1 (1)
46	4 (2)	4 (3)	3 (3)
47	4 (2)	4 (3)	3 (3)
48	2 (1)	5 (4)	3 (3)
49	6 (4)	4 (3)	1 (1)
50	5 (3)	5 (4)	1 (1)
51	1 (1)	4 (4)	1 (1)
52	3 (2)	3 (2)	1 (1)
53	2 (1)	2 (1)	1 (1)
54	2 (1)	2 (1)	1 (1)
55	4 (3)	2 (1)	1 (1)
56	4 (3)	2 (1)	1 (1)
57	4 (3)	2 (1)	1 (1)
58	1 (1)	2 (1)	1 (1)
59	1 (1)	2 (1)	1 (1)
60	2 (2)	2 (1)	1 (1)
61	6 (5)	4 (3)	1 (1)
62	1 (1)	4 (3)	1 (1)
63	4 (3)	2 (1)	1 (1)
64	4 (3)	2 (1)	1 (1)
65	4 (3)	2 (1)	1 (1)
66	2 (2)	2 (1)	1 (1)
67	4 (3)	2 (1)	1 (1)
68	2 (2)	2 (1)	1 (1)
69	3 (2)	1 (1)	1 (1)
70	3 (2)	1 (1)	1 (1)
71	4 (3)	2 (1)	1 (1)
72	4 (3)	2 (1)	1 (1)
73	4 (3)	2 (1)	1 (1)
74	4 (3)	2 (1)	1 (1)
75	4 (3)	2 (1)	1 (1)
76	4 (3)	2 (1)	1 (1)
77	2 (1)	2 (1)	2 (2)
78	4 (3)	2 (1)	2 (2)
79	3 (2)	3 (2)	2 (2)
80	3 (2)	3 (2)	2 (2)
81	3 (2)	4 (3)	2 (2)
82	2 (1)	4 (3)	3 (3)
83	7	6 (5)	5
84	5 (4)	4 (3)	2 (2)
85	6 (5)	5 (4)	4 (4)
86	1 (1)	5 (4)	4 (4)
87	2 (1)	5 (4)	4 (4)
88	6 (5)	5 (4)	4 (4)
89	6 (5)	5 (4)	4 (4)
90	6 (5)	5 (4)	4 (4)
91	6 (5)	5 (4)	4 (4)
92	1 (1)	5 (4)	4 (4)
93	1 (1)	5 (4)	4 (4)
94	1 (1)	5 (4)	4 (4)
95	2 (2)	5 (4)	4 (4)
96	6 (5)	5 (4)	4 (4)
97	6 (5)	5 (4)	4 (4)
98	6 (5)	5 (4)	4 (4)
99	2 (1)	3 (2)	4 (4)
100	4 (3)	4 (3)	3 (3)

Fig. 6—6.   Multiple Coding of Episode B.

The choices in arranging the categories in cluster *A* can be made in terms of the contrasts to be highlighted. It can be divided into three areas as follows:

Response		*Solicit*		*Initiate*	
T	P	T	P	T	P

This tends to subordinate the contrast of teacher versus pupil, and to highlight the contrast between the three types of statements. The column can also be divided as it is for this problem:

Teacher	*Pupil*
Response, solicit, initiate	Response, solicit, initiate

One advantage of this second format is that tallies representing a sequence of teacher initiation and pupil response will be shown in the two center columns while the opposite pattern of pupil initiation and teacher response is shown in the two outside columns. Since this contrast is central to the problem being investigated, the latter arrangement is the obvious choice.

The design format for cluster *B* places the use of teacher ideas and ideas associated with authoritative sources other than pupils to the left of the double line with the use of pupil ideas placed to the right. The continuum is not as smooth as one might wish, but the relationships between categories do have a rudimentary rank order. From left to right, teacher directs or criticizes with the expectation of compliance, ideas of the teacher or book are developed, the same ideas are cited or expressed, the pupils' ideas are cited, and the pupils' ideas are developed.

The arrangement of cluster *C* is also from left to right moving from the more elementary focus on facts and specifics to the more elaborate explanations and generalizations.

Linking display configurations, behavior patterns, and theory

It is not the purpose of this section to test the utility of this particular scheme of coding, much less its reliability and validity. Such tests would have to take place in a live classroom in close cooperation with a teacher who was interested in the feedback. Before committing the time and energy that is required by a field test, it would be encouraging to find evidence indicating that display, behavior, and theory can be linked together in ways required by the problem. The results of coding episode *B* do provide such encouragement.

The typescript of Episode *B* (see pp. 59 to 63) indicates that one teaching strategy used was an attempt to involve pupils in a discussion of how they could make helpful criticisms of the new instructional book (see items 8 through 32). Two key teacher questions solicit pupil participation, the first is item 8 and the second is item 21. Without looking at the original typescript, the following inferences can be made from the display. The nature of the question at item 8 permits pupils to express their own ideas, judging from the string of 4 in cluster B (see items 10 to 17). The 1-4-1 events which appear as items 11, 14, 16, and 17 show teacher responses to pupil ideas without elaboration. The configuration following the teacher question in item 21 indicates that pupil ideas are not only expressed, but they are also developed, reaching an analytical level of thinking, as indicated in cluster C. Thus, if one had a theory about teaching which suggested that ideas expressed by pupils should be developed early in a class discussion, the present scheme of coding was at least capable of recording such a pattern from a typescript like episode B.

In the study of levels of thinking processes, Taba's theory suggests that a sustained period of citing specifics is necessary to build "an apperceptive mass" of information before pupils can be expected to make generalizations and extended explanations. The configuration of the code tallies from items 51 to 100 show just such a pattern in cluster C. It can be argued, of course, that the pupil statements about the transitivity of numbers while adding are not true generalizations (items 88 to 91 and 96 to 98). However, if they were, the coding system does provide a format which would permit Taba's theory to be studied during class discussions. In this particular case, it can be seen in cluster B that the ideas being cited earlier (items 53 to 76) came from either the teacher or the book (the typescript indicates the latter) because of the heavy use of category two. In a similar development of analytical thinking (items 8 to 32) the ideas are apparently suggested by pupils, since the configuration of the display shows a different pattern. It is in making this last distinction that the three cluster scheme shows advantages over the older 10-category system for a problem of this sort. The clusters permit the recording of a teacher response, based on either his own ideas or those of a pupil, and a pupil response based on ideas mentioned earlier by the teacher or by a pupil.

FIELD TESTS OF MULTIPLE CODING SYSTEMS

The next step in the development of this system of category clusters is to see if problems concerned with teacher-pupil interaction and the level of thinking during class discussion can be analyzed under field conditions. Such a field test would include activities designed to answer the following questions:

1) Can observers be trained to use the three-cluster system under live class conditions? How much practice is required for two observers to reach a point at which 80 to 90 percent of their code symbols reach agreement?
2) What are some of the self-development goals for improving classroom instruction which seem most appropriate to an analysis using these clusters? How can teachers be approached so that they become full partners in the inquiry?

3) During a particular training inquiry, what other kinds of information should be collected and then compared with the interaction data?

4) What modifications or changes in the present three clusters will be necessary when related problems are investigated? Can some substitute clusters be developed which are logically compatible with the present three?

The answers to these and similar questions can be learned only through field trials and cooperative development projects with classroom teachers.

SUMMARY OF MULTIPLE CODING AND TIME LINE DISPLAYS

Both in this chapter and in Chapter 5 there has been an emphasis on the development of many different kinds of coding systems. As a first step, the possibility of subscripting an existing category system was introduced. In this chapter many different behavioral distinctions were listed which could become the building blocks for constructing category clusters designed for a particular problem. These alternatives were presented in terms of seeking an ideal feedback instrument which would abstract and record classroom interaction by creating a display. In turn, the display could be "read" in order to provide an objective English description of those features of the interaction that were of interest. All of this is an effort to study teaching behavior and the effect of such behavior on educational outcomes.

There was a special effort to show how multiple coding with category clusters can be accomplished with equipment no more elaborate than paper, pencil, and clipboard. Granted that these simple tools have their limitations, yet the progress that we can make with these primative tools will prepare us to enter into the world of automatic coding and display procedures which are currently under development and will become available in more and more school systems during the next decade. The next chapter includes a report of current progress in adapting computers to handle the recording, counting, and display problems which have been a burden to those interested in the study of classroom interaction.

Perhaps the major issue which underlies Chapter 5 and 6 is to make the classroom a place in which self-development becomes available to teachers just as opportunities to learn are made available to the pupils. It may well be that when maximum growth does occur, it occurs for teacher and pupil alike.

Chapter Seven

COMPUTER ASSISTED ENCODING
AND DECODING

ESCAPE FROM TEDIUM

Deciding to code little bits of behavior in order to arrange them into a display is a commitment to a great deal of clerical tedium. Anything that reduces the clerical chores and permits teachers and observers to use interaction analysis without being bogged down in tabulating is bound to be an improvement. Since computers thrive on tedious clerical tasks, they are much better adapted to this aspect of interaction analysis than are teachers, not to mention researchers.

Teachers, of course, are accustomed to working long and hard toward goals that have uncertain and delayed rewards. They learned how to do this during teacher preparation, inservice training, and as a part of their teaching. In spite of such experience, we cannot expect teachers to superimpose the clerical work of interaction analysis on an already busy work schedule. The rewards of analyzing classroom interaction are too few and too remote during the more arduous phases of early training.

One alternative is to provide teachers with supporting personnel who can observe, tabulate, and become a partner in the inquiry process. The suggested innovations in the last chapter which provide a display at the moment encoding stops will be a great help for observer and teacher alike if the procedures can be made to work. They require only a pencil and previously prepared forms which are resources that are readily available in most schools.

The second alternative is to have a computer take over the clerical work starting from the moment an observer selects the appropriate code symbol and ending with a completed display. Unfortunately, equipment with this capability is not now readily available in the schools, at least in comparison to pencils and observation forms. However, it seems safe to predict that a few years after this book is published a substantial number of schools will have access to a computer. In 1967 any school with reliable telephone service could be connected on an experimental basis to a computing center providing the cost could be met.

Since the possibility of computer supported interaction analysis is already at hand and the availability of such equipment is rapidly increasing, this chapter will consider some of the introductory problems that are involved.

CURRENT CAPABILITIES OF THE COMPUTER FOR SCHOOLS

Ideas about how to use computers in conjunction with communication media are changing as rapidly as the growth in technology and systems analysis permits, and that is very rapid indeed. T. A. Smith (91) illustrates this rapidly accelerating rate of growth with his observation:

> In all communications, we make use of symbols. The methods which were originally used imposed restrictions on the kind of symbols which could be employed and the speed at which they could be sent. One hundred years ago, for example, only telegraph code symbols could be transmitted over ocean cables at a speed of about five words per minute. Then it became possible to transmit speech—a much more sophisticated kind of symbol. The ability to send television picture information is an even greater advance. Each of these steps represents an increase in the rate of information transfer. At the original rate of transfer over the ocean cable, for example, it would take some 40 hours to send a single television picture frame, which on your home receiver is produced in $\frac{1}{30}$ second (p. 174).

If this rate of growth continues, it is not ridiculous to imagine all recorded knowledge in the world becoming available for fairly quick retrieval, newspapers or instructional materials coming out of a slot at the bottom of the TV set or simply reproduced as a picture on the screen at the touch of a button, and a supporting system of cross country communication channels with their networks criss-crossing other networks. Just how such resources might influence education is difficult to imagine. Either fortunately or unfortunately, depending on your point of view, the more fantastic developments are not likely to reach the schools until after we have a hotel on the moon.

There are some equipment and performance levels which have been achieved, however, that have special consequences for interaction analysis. Prior to 1969 the following had been accomplished.

1) Languages for giving instructions to a computer are rapidly approaching phrases which can be understood as ordinary English.
2) Computers which share time over long distance lines with only one or two customers at the same time have been in use for several years.
3) Computers which share time simultaneously with more than 50 remote stations are now being installed and the necessary programs are being developed.

4) Input assemblies of various kinds, for use by teachers and pupils, are either available or about to be released. These devices call for appropriate programs automatically and incorporate local buffer storage so that the rate of input to the computer can be more efficient.

5) Visual displays by cathode-ray tubes can be used to call from storage any kind of printed material almost instantly, such as the records of a single pupil.

6) Typewriters that type 18 lines a minute and more expensive machines with printout rates measured in lines per second can be placed at remote stations to produce permanent displays of data.

7) Schemes for organizing the information about tens of thousands of pupils, programs for scheduling high school pupils into classes, programs for child accounting, programs for cost accounting, and many other similar developments are now past history and await further development as systems analysts adapt existing functions to equipment with higher capability.

All of this progress suggests that before the 1970's come to an end some remarkable innovations should be operating in our larger school systems, which, in turn, service more than half of our school age population.

As more services are performed, it requires fewer schools to keep a single computing center working full time. The specialist in systems analysis for computer based educational services will become a key person in obtaining the most service at the least cost for his school. This book is concerned with one possible service, which is to help teachers analyze the interaction within their classrooms in order to improve instruction. In a fully functioning computer network, this service will add a negligible time load at the computing center, but could involve several hours per day at the remote station because the inservice input is slow.

THE COMPUTER BASED FEEDBACK LOOP

Suppose an observer was to enter a classroom with a portable encoder. This might actually be the base of a pushbutton telephone with 10 buttons, 0 through 9. Later on, a special unit may be designed for the purpose and include separate start, stop, and error keys. The plug on the end of the cord from the encoder is simply pushed into a jack or receptacle, just as telephones are moved from one room to another in a house. One room in the school building permanently houses the remote station which has some kind of printout facility. The controls on the remote station permit it to be a relay station during the observation, so that the relatively slow initial instructions and subsequent digits of the code symbols will be stored in a buffer and discharged as short bursts of input to the computer from time to time. At the termination of the

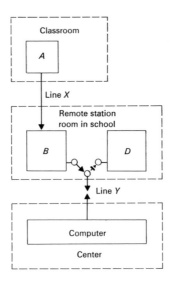

Fig. 7–1.   Feedback Flow Chart.

observation, special signals will start the computer processing the data and the reverse printout function will begin almost immediately. Within a short time the display will be complete.

Figure 7–1 illustrates the input-output loop in a diagram. The characteristics of the component parts might be briefly described as follows.

Unit A.   This unit is a pushbutton, portable encoder in the classroom. The input to this unit consists of buttons pushed by a trained observer. The output includes two kinds of information: (a) process and programming instructions, including choice of displays, and (b) interaction analysis data which is to be processed. It would help if the unit had signal lights to let the operator know whether the circuit was operational or nonoperational. Start, stop, error, and process buttons would also be helpful.

Line X.   It is hoped that a connecting line of telephone quality within the building and probably less than 2,000 feet would be satisfactory. This assumes a tone signal output from unit *A* which would be demodulated at unit *B*.

Unit B.   This unit would probably be equipped to provide processing functions for the entire school program and more than enough for interaction analysis. For observation feedback, it would be necessary to demodulate process control signals and raw data signals received from unit *A*, store these up to the capacity of local storage, and then relay these in batch form to the computer center. A special circuit might be developed, without too much expense, whereby certain types of time line displays could be typed without waiting for the observation to be completed or for a batch of data to be discharged.

Line Y.   The characteristics of this line would be determined more by the other functions of units *B* and *D* that are not related to interaction analysis. Such a line is usually rented from the telephone company.

The Computer and Unit D.   The functions of these two units are to store interaction analysis data according to the program selected by the process instructions. Presumably there would be a variety of programs available. One group of programs for single digit code symbols, another group for two-digit symbols, and another group for three-digit symbols. Each of these programs would have various options which could be chosen with regard to display. For example, if matrix displays for single digit code symbols were required, a process signal requesting a tabulation of portions of the observation as well as for the total observation should be anticipated. Parts of a matrix may be displayed as a program option like the ones on pages 135 or 150. The calculation of millage matrices and various proportions, such as those discussed in Chapter 3, would also be helpful. All of these processing functions could be completed in a few seconds, given currently available computer speeds. The signals for printout would presumably begin within a few seconds of the termination of the observation.

In a school system that cannot afford remote stations it is possible to use telephone lines directly from the classroom to a buffer storage or even a tone operated card keypunch at the computing center. At the end of the observation, the interpretation of the printout by the teacher and observer would be delayed by the amount of time required to deliver the printout. A messenger in an automobile, during the first few years, might be a much more economical solution, even though less elegant. The unanswered question is how soon after teaching does an analysis of the printout provide the maximum benefit? There are no practical research results on this question. Much depends on the display and the other circumstances. It does seem reasonable to discuss a display while the teaching experience is easily recalled in considerable detail. A magnetic video or voice recording, however, might be used to stimulate recall after several days delay, although this would increase the time spent on interpretation.

The preceding material might seem somewhat technical to a teacher, but probably it would be too vague and incomplete for a computer programmer. The past discussion, and what follows in this chapter, are included because the classroom teacher, observer, or supervisor who wishes to use computer based feedback will need to explain to a systems analyst and other computer center personnel just what he wants in the way of a display so they can provide the programs and equipment. He will also be asked to express opinions with regard to how many different systems might be used and to what extent it is desirable to have a library of programs "on call" within the computer memory.

Perhaps some science fiction might help to visualize the possibilities more completely.

CLASSROOM INTERACTION ANALYSIS AND FEEDBACK—1984

Nothing warms the heart of a supervisor faster than a request from a teacher for help on an interesting problem. Jerry Attricks wasn't sure he could help Miss Young, but his concerns were assuaged by the confidence that comes with experience.

"Here are the last two printouts, Miss Young," he said. "Now before we look at them, let's review how all this got started and then restate the exact comparisons we will look for in the data. We might want to dial a different display from storage if your perception of the problem has changed."

"Well," sighed Miss Young, "It all began with Billy. His listless performance on the computer based math program led to our request for an increase in the reinforcement schedule. But, as you remember, that didn't help. In fact, I called you when the second bimonthly report for slow learners showed performance decrements based on last fall's growth rates. That's when this whole matter of maintaining motivation arose and the analysis of my class discussions began. With your help we ran the pupil attitude inventory and found math way down for the slow ones. When Dorothy and Mae complained about the same difficulty in their classes, we formed the team."

"I remember," said Mr. Attricks "and then we had several sessions to design and try out new category clusters which we thought might help."

"Yes," she continued. "We stumbled onto that bit about 31, 32, and 33 transitions in my use of pupil ideas and decided that there was plenty of teacher reinforcement attempted, but you questioned whether it was getting through to the kids. So we've switched to multiple coding and brought in level of abstraction on the hunch that my language involved a shift in concepts that wasn't getting across, and *that* is the sad story to date. Mae was in twice this week to code for me while her class was at the computer stalls."

"Apparently Mae dialed two partial matrices and three time lines for this display," Mr. Attricks said, as he looked at the printouts. "Hmmmm. Exactly what comparisons did you two have in mind?"

"All three time lines are for the full half-hour observation. The first one is a plot of the concept level in teacher talk, the second is the same for the pupils, and that third is a real flyer. Mae thought she could make a crude rating of pupil interest, on a scale from 1 to 5, and we threw it in as the third code digit. We sort of dreamed it up and haven't the slightest idea whether it will work or not. With the time lines we hope to compare the phase relationship between teacher talk and pupil talk, in terms of how abstract the concepts were. Of course, we had to arrange for the computer to summarize the frequency distribution of the second code digit for each minute." Miss Young pointed to show what she meant.

"But how will you use the matrices?" asked Mr. Attricks, becoming more impressed.

"Well, this top one applies to the first 22 minutes of the general discussion. Then Mae dialed a separate tabulation for the last 8 minutes when she saw me move to the blackboard to conduct the review of what we had learned. They are partial matrices because we need only the transitions which occur when the teacher stops talking and the pupils start. You see, since we coded at four levels, these six cells show transitions from a more abstract teacher statement to a less abstract pupil statement, and the cells above show just the reverse. And these four cells on the diagonal cell line show transitions from teacher to pupil which are at the same level."

"What do you expect to find?" asked Mr. Attricks.

"I'm not sure, but this will help us decide whether my concepts are the same as the kids', or whether they are different" said Miss Young. "First, we'll look at the partial displays to see if your theory about my concepts not getting through to the kids fits or doesn't fit. Then we can look at the time lines to check for consistency. If something turns up that we don't understand, I have a voice recording we can always play back. Maybe Mae's low interest ratings will coincide with some of the whispering and restlessness. Suppose it turns out that when my concepts don't match those that the kids are using, the kids get restless. If we can find out just when this occurs, maybe I can start to work on some changes that may help."

"It sounds reasonable," he said, and since they were both very curious, they began to study the data. "With this challenge," Jerry thought to himself, "You'd better be clever, Attricks."

Sound too much like Orwell? Too rich a diet for every day? Both reactions have considerable merit. Active assessment could become oppressive and lead to undesirable Orwellian control. Teachers would have nightmares in which a supervisor or principal chased them down the hall, waving printouts, and demanding changes in teaching behavior. On the other hand, it might be the teacher who chases the principal, waving a printout, and showing how much progress he has made. As for the steady diet, the analysis of problems and efforts to make improvements do not lead to continuous observation. There has to be a judicious schedule when we try to improve teaching in order to have time to think and to attend to other matters. Constant analysis is neither desirable nor necessary even when feasible.

The purpose of the science fiction is to suggest that the verbal communication of an artistic teacher can be analyzed, given adequate resources, and certain patterns in the teaching might be altered on the basis of rational inquiry. With effective feedback, teachers can learn about their own teaching at a faster rate compared to no feedback. As one young, beginning teacher expressed it, after reading the scene in manuscript form, "That kind of teacher is a *real* professional. That's what everybody says we are supposed to be doing." However, before teachers can make use of computer supported feedback, they will have to understand this new resource well enough to make use of it. In the next section, some of the options of feedback display are discussed.

CUMULATIVE MATRIX AND SINGLE EVENT TIME LINE DISPLAYS FOR COMPUTER FEEDBACK

A feedback display is chosen in order to highlight a contrast that is relevant to the problem being investigated. To provide a problem for this discussion, the interaction of episodes *A* and *B* will be used to illustrate various display options (see pp. 56—63).

In the following discussion, suppose a teacher was concerned with the problem outlined in Chapter 6, pages 184 to 193. In order to explore the contrast between teacher initiation and teacher response, suppose the same teacher purposely created episode *A* with half of his class and then produced episode *B* with the other half of his class. Although formal hypotheses might not have been made, let us say that the teacher was interested in the effects of the different teaching patterns, if any, on the development of logical discourse. Suppose further that the category system of three clusters, shown on page 188, is used to code interaction. (Please read these sections again, if you need the review.)

One display that can be used with category clusters makes use of a cumulative matrix in combination with the single event time line. The matrix display deals with sequence pairs and can be used to summarize the entire observation as well as to summarize separately tabulated time intervals. The least complicated matrix display would be to form a single matrix for each cluster. A more complicated matrix would include the permutation of two or even three clusters. The interpretation of the data can start with the time line display of single events and then shift to the matrices for summary comparisons which emphasizes an inductive approach. Alternatively, one can start with a summary matrix and then search for specific patterns within the time line, which is a more deductive approach.

SELECTING THE TIME INTERVAL FOR MATRIX CUMULATION

One advantage of computer based observation is that judgments about time intervals do not have to be made on the spur of the moment, that is, while you are actually observing. Computers can store the raw interaction code symbols in their original sequences and they can be recalled subsequently in any time interval segment.

The storage capability of a computer has a special advantage in the case of episodes *A* and *B*. It turned out that there was a shift, in both episodes, between what might be called "structuring the lesson" which then led to "working toward a generalization about number transitivity" with the change occurring about the midpoint. Taba's theory really applies to the second half of the lesson, while Flanders' theories about teacher influence really apply to the first half. Given this difference, there are advantages to tabulating a separate matrix for each time interval. For each category cluster, there could be a matrix for the first half and another for the second half. What is most convenient about a computer is that even though the observer and teacher might realize that a shift of some kind occurred after the lesson is completed, they could always request a new printout which highlights the desired contrast and receive the display in a few minutes. Not only can this be done in terms of the two episodes now being considered, but if the teacher continues to study interaction for 3 or 4 weeks, special segments of stored observations can be retrieved to form a display that can be compared with any subsequent observation. To give another example, suppose a teacher is trying to increase the incidence of a particular teaching pattern. The ability to retrieve displays of past performance means that a measure of growth is always at hand to aid in the interpretation of the training program.

DISPLAY ARRANGEMENT

The rapid growth of computer technology means that the details of a specific display are likely to change as new innovations become available. Depending on the capability of a remote station, displays may be in printed form or as lines in a cathode-ray tube (CRT) which is like your TV set. In the most econo-

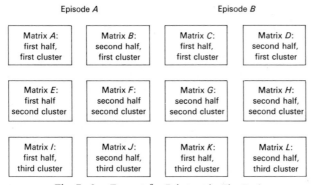

Fig. 7—2.   Format for Printout in Fig. 7—3.

mical installations of today, an electric typewriter might limit displays to typewritten forms. Happily, a computer can be programmed to make decisions about space so that displays do not run off the edge of the paper. Such program routines can be used to decide how many matrices can be printed in the same row. Because of the small size of the matrices, the width of the paper may permit up to four matrices in a single row. The display for episodes A and B is shown in Fig. 7–3, but study Fig. 7–2 first in order to understand the format.

INTERPRETATION OF THE DATA

One way to interpret Fig. 7–3 is to start at the top and work downward, noting only the most prominent features of the data. The task of interpretation may seem difficult at first, but in a surprisingly short time, the initial confusion disappears.

Matrices A, B, C, and D (Fig. 7–3) refer to the speaker and whether the statement is a response, a solicitation, or an initiation. In this case, the most prominent differences can be found in the rows and columns for Categories 1 and 6. There is an absence of pupil initiation and less teacher response in episode A, compared with B. A second difference can be seen by studying the (3–3) cells of each matrix. Statements initiated by the teacher are much more sustained in episode A, compared with B, as shown by the frequencies in the (3–3) cells of 19 and 11 compared with 5 and 3. The low incidence of pupil solicitation is quite common and to be expected. In our classrooms, asking questions and extending invitations to others to participate is usually not part of the pupils' role and is reserved for the teacher.

Matrices E, F, G, and H display the ideas under discussion in terms of whether they were suggested by the pupils, the teacher, or came from instructional materials. It is clear that all ideas in both episodes were made possible by the structure which the teacher created, and in this sense all ideas might be construed as originating with the teacher or from instructional materials. But when teachers structure a problem in such a way that pupils have alternatives and can express some of their own points of view about the topic introduced by the teacher, then such statements are coded with a 4 and 5 in the second cluster. The incidence of statements expressing the pupils' point of view is seen most clearly in the (4–4), (4–5), (5–5), and (5–4) cells. The incidence is much higher in episode B.

Given the eight matrices of the first and second clusters, a number of somewhat more subtle distinctions can be made when episode A is contrasted with episode B. To start, compare the (3–3) cells of matrices A, B, E, and F. In A and B, the sustained initiation of teacher talk is decreasing—first half to second half; in E and F, the sustained citing of teacher ideas is increasing—first half

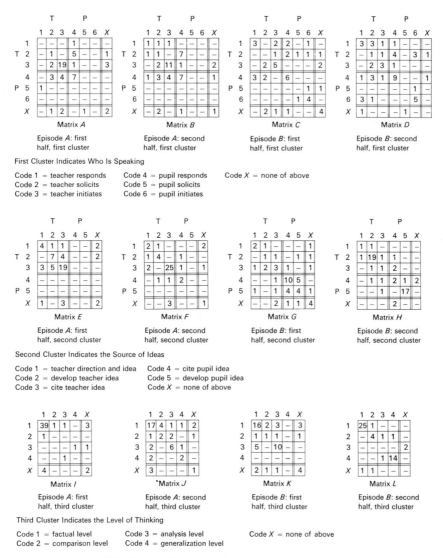

Fig. 7–3.   Cluster Matrices of Episodes *A* and *B*.

to the second half. This occurs in the form of increased pupil talk focused on ideas associated with the teacher or the instructional materials. The increase from 11 to 25 in the (3–3) cell, matrix *B* compared with matrix *F*, is a rough index of this pupil participation. In other words, the initiation of a teacher can be expressed not only by the incidence of teacher talk, but also by the proportion of all talk that deals with ideas associated with his authority. Now make the same comparisons in matrices C, D, G, and H. What conclusions do you reach?

Matrices I, J, K, and L refer to the level of thinking. The most common feature is the high incidence in the $(1-1)$ cell, indicating that sustained interaction at a factual level occurred in all four intervals. Reaching higher levels of thinking did occur, however, in the first half of episode B, as shown by the $(3-3)$ cell of matrix K, and in the second half, as shown by the $(4-4)$ cell of matrix L. It would appear that reaching higher levels occurred almost exclusively in the second half of episode A, but occurred in both halves of episode B.

These inferences can now be given further elaboration by studying the time lines in Figs. 7—4 and 7—5. If you would like to try your hand at interpretation, see if you can locate evidence within the time lines for the following inferences and also use Fig. 7—3.

1) In order to provide the initial structure, teacher initiation and directions extended over a longer period of time in episode A, compared with B.

2) The strategy of the teacher's role in episode B was to choose a discussion problem on which the pupils would be free to express their ideas and once expressed, the teacher helped to support and develop these ideas during the first half. When the teacher then turned to the task at hand, starting with the second half, in spite of heavy concentration on ideas supplied by the teacher or book, pupil ideas were effectively integrated into the class discussion during the last quarter of the observation.

3) On the other hand, in episode A, the teacher established structure by citing facts of his choice in a pattern of teacher solicitation and pupil response. During the second half, pupil initiative and attention to ideas suggested by pupils simply failed to materialize.

A teacher who was interested enough to set up two similar teaching situations in which he could vary his own behavior would find the above display of data a rich hunting ground for hypotheses about his own teaching and its effects. If he was skeptical of the results, as one might hope he would be, the experience with analysis procedures that was gained in the first inquiry would make a replication (with or without innovation) much easier to carry out.

SUBSTITUTING HISTOGRAMS FOR THE CLUSTER MATRIX

A histogram based on a single cluster for the entire observation can be substituted for the first half, second half matrix displays shown in Fig. 7—3. The histograms can then be combined with the same single event time line, just as before. The histogram may be chosen because the more complicated matrix is unnecessary or because it may communicate more effectively to a teacher. The

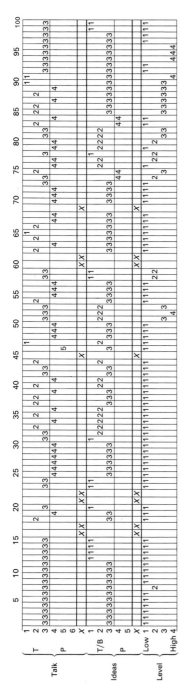

Fig. 7–4. Single Event Time Line Displays for Episode A.

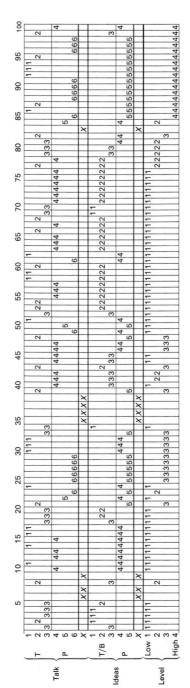

Fig. 7–5. Single Event Time Line Displays for Episode B.

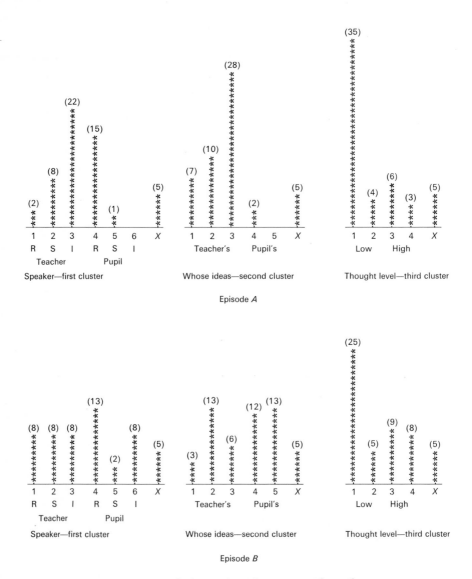

Fig. 7—6.   Total Observation Histograms—Three Clusters.

inferences which are based on sequence pairs, of course, cannot be made from a histogram, but the time line displays help to bridge the gap for the less precise comparisons which histograms provide. A computer, of course, can be programmed to type out histograms, and this form of display can be cumulated over an entire observation or for smaller intervals.

A sample histogram display for the entire observations of episodes *A* and *B* is shown in Fig. 7—6.

Several of the summary inferences previously mentioned can easily be seen in the histograms. For example, it is possible to notice the low incidence of pupil solicitation, the lower incidence of citing and developing pupil ideas (Categories 4 and 5 in the second cluster when episode *A* is compared with *B*), almost twice as many higher level thinking tallies in episode *B* (Categories 3 and 4, third cluster, compared with episode *A*), and other comparisons that were mentioned in the last section.

Incidently, there are program routines whereby the computer considers all graphs in terms of the tallest bars to be made and then proceeds to choose a scale which keeps the display within reasonable dimensions on the printout sheet. In a display, a single asterisk may represent a single event, two events, five events, or some other number, but the same scale is used for all graphs so that visual comparisons can be made. In Fig. 7—6, for example, a single asterisk represents two coded events, except for rounding off errors.

COLLAPSING THE TOTAL NUMBER OF CATEGORIES THROUGH COMPUTER TRANSFORMATIONS

The displays considered in the last section fail to combine into a single display the various dimensions which the three different clusters provide. A matrix for a single cluster ignores other clusters and separate time line displays for each cluster isolate that one set of categories. Yet it was pointed out earlier that a single matrix for all the clusters may be too complex to be practical. If you were a bit overwhelmed when you first looked at Figs. 7—3, 7—4, and 7—5, you can then imagine how a teacher might feel who first looks at a display of data.

Transformations can be made to reduce the number of categories involved, and this provides for a less complicated analysis at the price of having less subtle information. Sometimes this price is well worth paying. Less complicated displays may have advantages: (a) when the teacher is easily overwhelmed by the data, (b) when a preliminary analysis is to be made, and (c) when the data reduction is the only practical means of investigating interrelationships between the different clusters. The great advantage of the computer is that all the original data can be coded and stored, then a more complicated or less complicated display can be requested, depending on the immediate purposes and circumstances. Later on, the complete data can be displayed if the investigation requires more elaborate information.

Before we start a discussion of how transformations can be made, the next section will consider the display problems that are involved in the general case of three clusters, each cluster consisting of dichotomous pairs.

THE GENERAL CASE OF THREE CLUSTERS, EACH A DICHOTOMY

Suppose each of three clusters had two categories to form a $2 \times 2 \times 2 = 8$ category system. One such system might be

First Cluster	Second Cluster	Third Cluster
1. Teacher talk	1. Initiation	1. Facts
2. Pupil talk	2. Response	2. Higher than facts or "nonfactual."
X. None of above		

We will ignore the X category in considering permutations.

In passing, we may note three practical features of such a system. First, the three clusters can be recorded in the classroom in whatever sequence turns out to be the most convenient for the observer. That is, he can write down the three digits in any order, choosing among the six possibilities. If we think of the first cluster as A, the second as B, and the third as C, then the order of recording could be ABC, ACB, BAC, BCA, CAB, and CBA. The "none of above" category X does not enter into a consideration of order since it is used as an independent ninth category. The second feature is that the computer can be programmed to make any preferred transformation of the original code symbols. This means that regardless of how the observer prefers to record, there is a free choice in deciding which cluster, A, B, or C, will be a prominent feature in the display. Third, when the original cluster includes several dimensions, additional dichotomies can be formed with certain category combinations so that the dichotomy contrast combines the dimensions in a new way. This last point will be illustrated later on in the discussion.

Primary Display Position

What is meant by "prominent display" involves the primary division of a matrix. This is shown in Fig. 7—7. In the first matrix, teacher talk and pupil talk form the primary division. In the second matrix, initiation and response form the primary division. And in the third matrix, it is factual versus higher

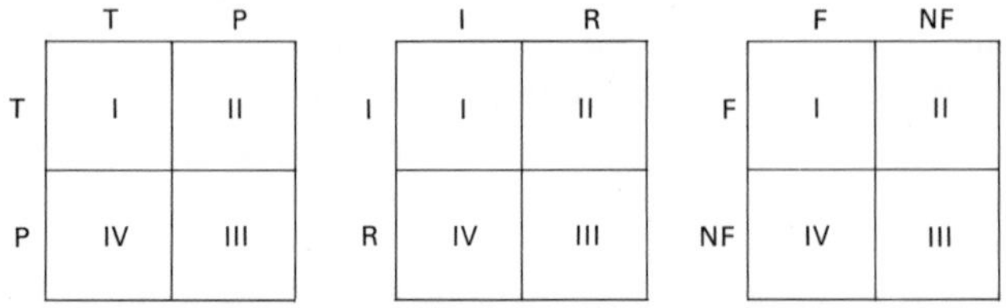

Fig. 7—7.   Primary Division of the Matrix.

than factual (not factual) thinking. The choice that one makes in selecting the primary division dichotomy will determine which characteristic of interaction is to be given the greatest emphasis. This emphasis is the result of assigning more space so as to provide more visual contrast.

If we think of the four quadrants of a matrix, labelled I, II, III, and IV, then each quadrant provides a different interpretation, depending on the primary dimensions of the matrix. For example, in the first matrix of Fig. 7—7, quadrant I locates sustained teacher talk; II is for transitions from teacher to pupil talk; III is for sustained pupil talk; and IV is for transitions from pupil to teacher talk. Similar relationships hold for the other two matrices. Quadrants I and III are sustained events, sometimes called *steady state*, and II and IV are transitions.

It is also possible, of course, to reverse the left to right and top to bottom assignments of quadrants. Thus, in the first matrix, quadrant I could represent sustained pupil talk, rather than sustained teacher talk. These changes would be made in terms of the preferred format for the display which, in turn, would be chosen in terms of the desired contrast that certain spaces provide.

Given three clusters, is there any rationale for choosing one or another as the primary division? There is no simple answer at this stage of computer display development, but there are some features of the problem that can be kept in mind. For one thing, the interchange between the teacher and pupils in terms of talk usually cycles more rapidly than changes in initiation and response, and both of these usually change more rapidly than fluctuations in level of thinking. This is not always true, but it holds in general. It follows that to set up teacher-pupil talk as a major dimension will produce more transitions. Should transitions be of central interest, this becomes a factor in choosing the display format. Another factor, which is more difficult to explain, concerns the amount of relevant information which can be recognized at a glance. Clear contrasts communicate more information without additional study. In analyzing level of thinking, frequencies of higher or lower thinking processes can be assigned to the major quadrants of the matrix so that the comparison of two or more matrices can be more rapid. How these and other considerations enter into the assignment of columns and rows will gradually become more clear when examples are presented later in this discussion.

Secondary display position

The second dichotomy divides each major quadrant into four equal areas, forming four columns and four rows, illustrated in Fig. 7—8. Suppose initiation and response are chosen as the second cluster to subdivide the primary division. There are two nonsymmetrical and two symmetrical arrangements which can

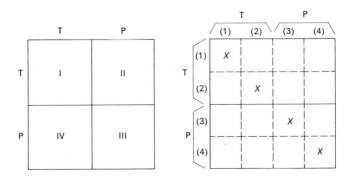

Fig. 7—8.   Assigning the Second Cluster.

be selected in making assignments to rows and columns. In the outline below, let I represent initiation and R represent response.

Column and Row Position	(1)	(2)	(3)	(4)
Nonsymmetrical	I	R	I	R
	R	I	R	I
Symmetrical	R	I	I	R
	I	R	R	I

Which of these four alternatives is to be selected? At this choice point, it becomes necessary to think ahead, as the saying goes, in order to anticipate the configuration if one or another of the four alternatives were selected. In order to do this we have to know how the data will fit into the display format.

The raw material with which we can work are 16 cells, four of which are steady state cells. These latter are (a) teacher continues to initiate, (b) teacher continues to respond, (c) pupil continues to initiate, and (d) pupil continues to respond. The four cells are marked with an X in the second matrix of Fig. 7—8. The remaining 12 cells are transitions among these four steady state conditions. From experience we know that when teachers initiate, pupils are likely to respond and that this pattern has a much higher incidence than pupils initiating and the teacher responding. Suppose that the contrast between these two patterns is central to the problem being investigated. *It is this last sentence, in which a purpose is postulated, that provides a rationale for selecting one of the four possible arrangements.* This purpose permits us to consider the four alternatives

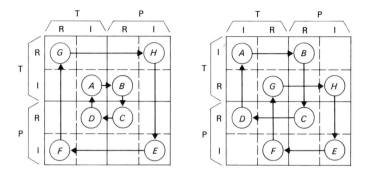

Fig. 7—9.   Assigning the Second Cluster.

in order to select one which gives the best visual contrast of the two patterns, the one that sets them apart so that they can easily be recognized within the format configuration.

Note that the two matrices in Fig. 7—9 have a different assignment of categories to the columns. The first matrix has a nonsymmetrical R I R I assignment and the second matrix has a symmetrical I R R I arrangement. When you check carefully in both column and row, you can discover that the $A \rightarrow B \rightarrow C \rightarrow D$ sequence in both the first and second matrix of Fig. 7—9 represents the pattern of teacher initiation and pupil response. Similarly, the $E \rightarrow F \rightarrow G \rightarrow H$ sequence represents the pattern of pupil initiation and teacher response. Now it simply becomes a question of which of the two arrangements do you prefer? Which one presents a contrast which can be seen at a glance?

Before you make up your mind, you may wish to sketch two matrices based on the remaining two possibilities not shown in Fig. 7—9. What happens to the display with the assignment I R I R or with the assignment R I I R?

Now, if all has gone well, you have your own two sketches as well as the two sketches in Fig. 7—9 to consider. Two of the four displays show concentric, clearly separate patterns; one of these is the first matrix of Fig. 7—9 and the other is your concentric diagram. The remaining two displays show overlapping patterns; one of these is the second matrix of Fig. 7—9. The selection decision goes like this: *If* (and only if) you would like to contrast these two patterns, choose either one of the nonsymmetrical column assignments which, oddly enough, produces the symmetrical display.

To show how the nature of the problem can influence the format to be selected, consider contrasts that involve transition cells instead of steady state cells. Suppose you notice that within teacher talk, shifts can occur from initiation to response and from response to initiation. The same shifts can occur in pupil talk. Let's say that we are interested in comparing teachers and

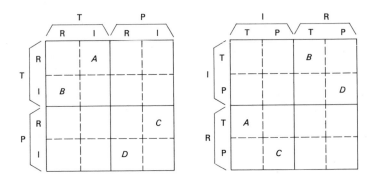

Fig. 7—10.   Comparing Transitions.

pupils in terms of the same kind of shift:

Teacher Talk Transitions	Pupil Talk Transitions
A. $T_R \longrightarrow T_I$	C. $P_R \longrightarrow P_I$
B. $T_I \longrightarrow T_R$	D. $P_I \longrightarrow P_R$

The visual contrast we want to make is A versus C and B versus D. While this comparison could be made in the first matrix of Fig. 7—10, which is the same matrix shown in the first position of Fig. 7—9, a different primary assignment could place the cells to be compared right next to each other. In the second matrix of Fig. 7—10, the primary and secondary clusters have been reversed so that transitions from initiation to response all fall in quadrant II while transitions from response to initiation all fall in quadrant IV. This arrangement would permit the desired comparisons to be made at a glance.

A third illustration involves a case in which the symmetrical assignment of the secondary cluster produces a symmetrical data configuration. Consider, for example, patterns of teacher-pupil interchange at a lower level of thinking as a contrast to the same pattern at a higher level of thinking. Since shifts in level of thinking are expected to be somewhat slower than shifts in initiation-response, a level of thinking once established is likely to be sustained, at least for a short period of time. The display in Fig. 7—11 has a symmetrical arrangement of column assignments, high, low, low, high. The lower level teacher-pupil interchange would appear in the center four cells, while the same interchange at a higher level would appear in the four extreme corner cells. These two patterns would present a concentric, symmetrical (not to be redundant) display. This, then, is an example of a symmetrical column assignment which produces a symmetrical display.

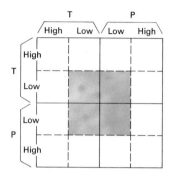

Fig. 7–11.   Symmetrical Secondary Assignment.

A practical application of the format illustrated in Fig. 7–11 would exist in a study analyzing level of thinking. If Taba's theory were being tested, this display would be helpful. A separate matrix could cumulate the first half of the lesson when most class discussion was expected to be at the lower level. A second, and perhaps even a third matrix, each cumulating a different time interval, could be used to illustrate the expected rise to higher levels near the end of the lesson. Such a matrix display, in combination with a time line display, would present clear evidence of creating, or not creating, a pattern of thought development recommended by Taba.

Tertiary display position

Once the primary and secondary divisions of a matrix have been decided, there are still alternatives with regard to assigning the two categories of the third cluster to the columns and rows. As soon as a third cluster is added, the 4 × 4 matrix will expand to an 8 × 8 matrix. There are 192 possible ways to assign six categories to the columns and rows of an 8 × 8 matrix, within the limitations of this problem. Naturally, all of these alternatives will not be discussed in this chapter. It is not an inventory of all the alternatives which is worth remembering; instead, it is the procedure by which one alternative is selected as being most appropriate to your problem.

Our category system is appropriate to a teacher who is interested in three features of classroom discourse: (a) who is talking, (b) does the teacher or do the pupils hold the initiative, and (c) what level of thinking characterizes the statement? In seeking to display these features in a matrix, one might be inclined to anchor the extreme positions first and then set up the remaining assignments. Let's take an example. Below are four conditions listed in a rank order. The

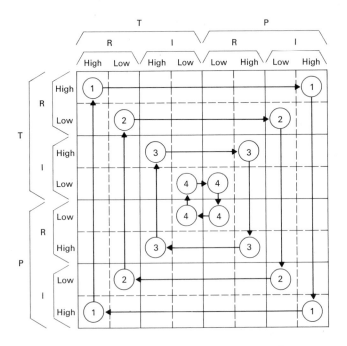

Fig. 7–12.   Concentric, Ordered Pattern Display.

first and last conditions are identical in both lists, but the two middle conditions are reversed in the second and third positions.

Order Alpha	Order Beta
1. Pupils initiate, teacher responds at higher levels of thinking	1. Pupils initiate, teacher responds at higher levels of thinking
2. Pupils initiate, teacher responds at lower levels of thinking	2. Teacher initiates, pupils respond at higher levels of thinking
3. Teacher initiates, pupils respond at higher levels of thinking	3. Pupils initiate, teacher responds at lower levels of thinking
4. Teacher initiates, pupils respond at lower levels of thinking	4. Teacher initiates, pupils respond at lower levels of thinking

Suppose it seems desirable to create a display in which movement up or down the alpha or beta list can be traced in successive time intervals. With a separate matrix cumulated for each time interval, the teacher could analyze classroom interaction in terms of movement along either list and decide whether what went on in his room should or should not be modified.

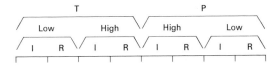

Fig. 7–13.   Arrangement for the Beta Order.

It is possible to provide a symmetrical display in which either the first or the fourth rank ordered combination is placed at the center of the matrix and the other combinations appear as concentric orbits. In Fig. 7–12 the alpha order has been arranged so that the fourth ranked combination is at the center.

The procedure for designing such a display is:

a) Select the condition to be placed in the center. In this case, teacher initiation and pupil response, low level, are conditions which completely specify the innermost columns and rows, provided one starts with the convention of teacher talk to the left and pupil talk to the right.

b) Continue specifying columns, working toward the outside. The rules about permissible combinations will become clear as you try your own hand at the design of formats.

If you wanted to keep the same configuration, but have it refer to the beta order, the assignment of columns—and therefore the rows—is shown in Fig. 7–13. Note that this arrangement requires a reversal of the secondary and tertiary divisions.

Perhaps the most effective display for contrasting the beta order and, for that matter, all three clusters, is shown in Fig. 7–14. This display is more effective because it achieves the simplicity of the first matrix of Fig. 7–9 in contrasting the teacher initiation and pupil initiation patterns, yet uses the major quadrants to contrast higher and lower levels of thinking. The numbers of each ordered combination of the beta order are again shown in circles, connected by sequence arrows.

The few matrix arrangements which have been presented so far are but a small proportion of the total possible. You are encouraged to try your hand at making different arrangements. Note that in order to decide whether or not you like a particular arrangement, you must refer to a problem, a theory, or at least a hunch of some sort. This is what is meant by having the display highlight a particular comparison of interest that is relevant to a problem.

Now that this brief review of 2 × 2 × 2 category display problems is completed, the next section returns to the problem of transforming many categories into a few.

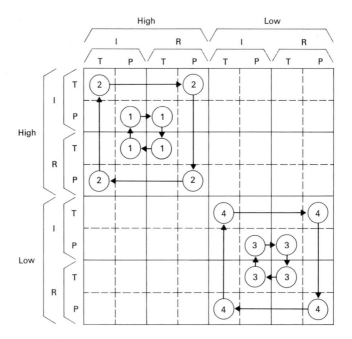

Fig. 7–14.   Double Concentric Displays.

COMPUTER TRANSFORMATIONS TO REDUCE CLUSTERS INTO DICHOTOMOUS DISPLAYS

Just as episodes *A* and *B* were used to illustrate single event time line and single cluster matrix displays, the same classroom interaction will be used to illustrate comparisons with transformed data. The presumption is again made that a single teacher taught both lessons and is interested in analyzing the differences between the two lessons. The raw data consist of code symbols based on the 7 × 7 × 6 category system (page 188) and the topic to be explored is how these code symbols can be transformed so as to fit an 8 × 8 matrix based on a 2 × 2 × 2 set of dichotomies.

Planning the transformations

In order to carry out a transformation, a general computer program is written which can handle any particular set of transformations in order to print out a simplified display. This general program has options whereby any set of transformations can be inserted. Transformations are like a table of equivalents. Just as 5,280 feet can be represented by 1 mile, a set of old categories can be represented by one new category.

The "table of equivalents" to be used in this problem is shown below:

New Cluster and Category Number	Meaning	Old Code Symbols
First cluster 1	Teacher talk	$1xx$, $2xx$ and $3xx$
First cluster 2	Pupil Talk	$4xx$, $5xx$, and $6xx$
Second cluster 1	Ideas from teacher or book	$x1x$, $x2x$, and $x3x$
Second cluster 2	Ideas from pupils	$x4x$, and $x5x$
Third cluster 1	Low level thinking	$xx1$ and $xx2$
Third cluster 2	High level thinking	$xx3$ and $xx4$

For a computer, of course, any combinations of old categories can be made equivalent to a new category, including categories from different clusters. For example, in creating a new category called "teacher initiation and pupil response," not only could old categories $3xx$ and $4xx$ be combined, but $21x$, $22x$, and $23x$ could be added. The resulting composite includes, respectively, "teacher initiation," "pupil response," and "teacher solicitations" based on directions and ideas suggested by the teacher or book. To illustrate such combinations, the following special dichotomy has been created:

Special Dichotomy	Meaning	Old Code Symbols
Category 1	Teacher initiation combined with pupil response	$3xx$, $4xx$, and $21x$, $22x$, and $23x$
Category 2	Pupil initiation combined with teacher response	$1xx$, $6xx$, and $24x$, and $25x$

The results of a transformation of the code symbols from the data are shown in Table 7—1. Opposite each item number, the first three digits represent categories in the simplified first, second, and third dichotomies. The single digit following the slash mark show the code number of the special dichotomy. Thus, 121/2 means "teacher statement about a pupil idea at the low factual level" insofar as the first three digits are concerned. The 2 following the slash mark means "pupil initiation and teacher response."

In the next section, the displays from the simplified transformations are shown and some interpretations are discussed.

MATRIX DISPLAYS BASED ON THREE SIMPLIFIED DICHOTOMIES

There is a division of the data, from episodes A and B, that is determined by the nature of the classroom interaction. Because of the shift at the midpoint of both episodes in the teaching function, the display is again cumulated separately for the first half and second half. The division, incidentally, is actually made

TABLE 7–1

Transformed Code Symbols—Episodes A and B

Item	Episode A	Episode B	Item	Episode A	Episode B	Item	Episode A	Episode B	Item	Episode A	Episode B
1	111/1	111/1	26	211/1	222/2	51	112/1	121/2	76	211/1	211/1
2	111/1	111/1	27	211/1	222/2	52	112/1	111/1	77	211/1	111/1
3	111/1	111/1	28	211/1	222/2	53	112/1	111/1	78	111/1	211/1
4	111/1	111/1	29	211/1	222/2	54	111/1	111/1	79	211/1	111/1
5	111/1	111/1	30	211/1	122/2	55	211/1	211/1	80	211/1	111/1
6	111/1	X	31	111/1	122/2	56	211/1	211/1	81	112/1	121/1
7	111/1	X	32	111/1	122/2	57	211/1	211/1	82	112/1	122/2
8	111/1	111/1	33	111/1	122/1	58	111/1	111/2	83	121/2	X
9	111/1	X	34	211/1	111/1	59	111/1	111/2	84	221/1	221/2
10	111/1	221/1	35	111/1	X	60	X	111/1	85	112/1	222/2
11	111/1	121/2	36	211/1	X	61	X	221/2	86	112/1	122/2
12	111/1	221/1	37	111/1	X	62	111/1	121/2	87	212/1	122/2
13	111/1	221/1	38	111/1	X	63	211/1	211/1	88	112/1	222/2
14	111/1	121/2	39	211/1	122/2	64	111/1	211/1	89	212/1	222/2
15	111/1	221/1	40	111/1	211/1	65	111/2	211/1	90	112/2	222/2
16	X	121/2	41	211/1	211/1	66	111/1	111/1	91	112/2	222/2
17	X	121/2	42	111/1	211/1	67	211/1	211/1	92	111/1	122/2
18	111/1	111/1	43	111/1	112/1	68	211/1	111/1	93	111/1	122/2
19	211/1	111/1	44	111/1	211/1	69	X	111/1	94	112/1	122/2
20	111/1	111/1	45	X	211/1	70	211/1	111/1	95	112/1	122/2
21	X	122/2	46	211/2	222/1	71	211/1	211/1	96	112/1	222/2
22	X	221/2	47	111/2	222/1	72	211/1	211/1	97	111/1	222/2
23	111/1	221/2	48	211/1	122/2	73	111/1	211/1	98	111/1	222/2
24	111/1	121/2	49	211/1	221/2	74	121/1	211/1	99	111/1	112/1
25	211/1	222/2	50	211/1	221/2	75	122/2	211/1	100	111/1	222/1

between the 53rd and 54th code symbols in episode A, and between the 51st and 52nd code symbols of episode B. The reasons for this choice become clear by reading the typescript of the conversation on pages 56 to 63.

Using who talks as the primary division

In this first illustration of the 2 × 2 × 2 category system, teacher talk and pupil talk are selected to make the primary division of the matrix. The completed display for episodes A and B, first half and second half, is shown in Fig. 7–15.

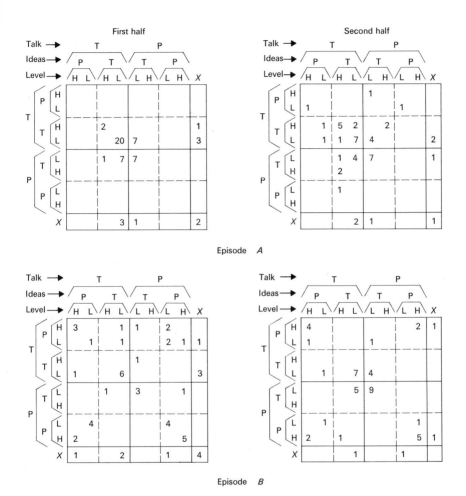

Fig. 7—15. Cumulative Matrices with Simplified Dichotomies—Episodes *A* and *B* (Talk, Ideas, Level).

Knowing what each area in a matrix means helps a great deal in making interpretations. The procedure to be followed involves looking at each dichotomy separately before attempting more complex inferences.

Imagine that you have an overlay which divides each of the four matrices into their major quadrants. Such an overlay for episode *B*, first half, is shown in Fig. 7—16. By adding all of the arabic numbers in each quadrant, it is possible to sense the balance between teacher and pupil talk. In this case it is nearly equal. The totals, in fact, are 23 for the teacher and 21 for the pupils, a sum found by adding all of the figures vertically.

Figure 7—16.

	T	P	X
T	Sustained teacher talk 13	Teacher to pupil 7	4
P	Pupil to teacher 7	Sustained pupil talk 13	
X	3	1	4
	23	21	8

Figure 7—17.

	P	T	T	P	
P	A	C	A		
T					
T	--C--	--B--	--C--		
P	A	C	A		

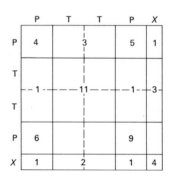

Figure 7—18.

	P	T	T	P	X
P	4	3	5	1	
T					
T	- 1 -	11	- 1 -	3 -	
P	6		9		
X	1	2	1	4	

A second kind of mental overlay refers to "where ideas came from." It is shown in Fig. 7—17. The frequency of sustained discussion of ideas which were suggested by pupils can be found in the four areas marked A. In the center area, B, can be found frequencies of sustained discussion involving ideas which came from the teacher or the book. All areas marked C contain transitions between the two categories just mentioned.

Again referring to episode B, first half, the incidence of tallies within these areas is shown in Fig. 7—18. A comparison of the total frequencies in the A areas with the B areas indicates that the sustained discussion of pupil ideas exceeded teacher ideas at a ratio of 24 to 11. An inspection of the C areas indicates that transitions were made by both the teacher and pupils. It is also clear, by inspecting the X column that silence more often followed the discussion of a teacher idea than it followed a discussion of a pupil idea.

At this point, it would be natural to move on to an analysis of the interaction of the first two clusters with the third cluster, which separates high level thinking

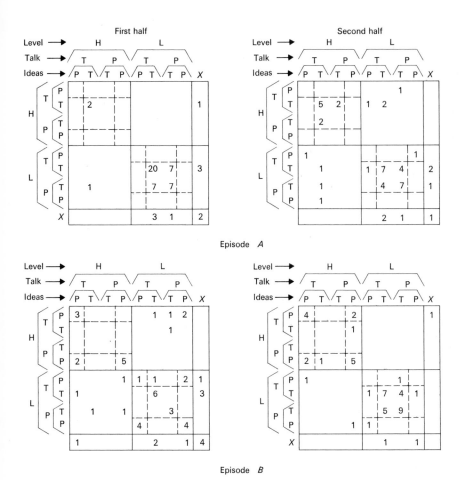

Fig. 7–19. Cumulative Matrices with Simplified Dichotomies—Episodes *A* and *B* (Level, Talk, Ideas).

from low level thinking. However, one of the promises of computer based feedback is that it is more efficient to ask the computer to print out another matrix than it is to work on inferences from the tertiary division of a matrix.

Using level of thinking as the major division

A display which makes use of level of thinking as the primary division of the matrix turns out to be a more powerful configuration than resulted from the format discussed in the last section. It is more powerful because the space relationships permit a visual contrast between the dichotomies of the first and

	H	L	X
H	Sustained high level 10	High to low level 5	
L	Low to high level 4	Sustained low level 21	4
X	1	3	4
	15	29	8

Figure   7—20.

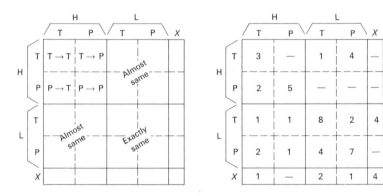

Figure   7—21.

second cluster which is just as effective as Fig. 7—15, but in addition, the separa-
tion of high and low level thinking is superior. The four matrices for episodes
A and *B*, first half and second half, are shown in Fig. 7—19. Note the similarity
with Fig. 7—14.

Once again it is helpful to develop mental overlays which outline the
configurations for each of the three clusters, consider each separately at first,
then proceed to develop more complex inferences. The first such overlay for
episode *B*, first half, is shown in Fig. 7—20. It can be seen that there are almost
twice as many low level statements as there are high level statements. Transitions between levels are, as expected, quite infrequent.

The second overlay, shown in the first matrix of Fig. 7—21, indicates
divisions for who is talking. This is a secondary division of the display even
though it may be the first cluster recorded by the observer. Main quadrant I,
in this matrix, forms a configuration which is identical with Fig. 7—16, although

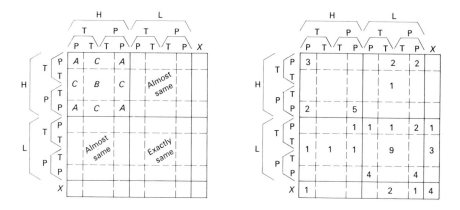

Figure   7–22.

the latter refers to the entire matrix. This is also true of quadrant III, which is labeled "exactly same." Quadrants II and IV have the same configuration but we must remember that only transitions between levels of thinking can be found in these two quadrants, and transitions are single events by definition. Therefore, in quadrants II and IV, there is really no such thing as sustained teacher and pupil talk in the sense that these exist in quadrants I and III. In fact, all steady state cells must lie on the main diagonal of the entire matrix through quadrants I and III.

The figures in the second matrix of Fig. 7–21 are again from episode B, first half. It is interesting to note more sustained pupil talk at higher levels of thinking, compared with teacher talk (note 5 versus 3), which suggests that pupils had the opportunity to develop their own ideas in making analyses or generalizations. We can now also see that the four silences all followed teacher talk, probably the pause before a pupil answers a low level question, although one X is an artifact added to balance the matrix.

In Fig. 7–22, the overlay for the tertiary division is shown in the first matrix. Again note the efficiency which results in similar configurations in each of the four major quadrants. A similar design was discussed in Fig. 7–17. This format refers to where ideas came from, and we must remember that an idea from the teacher or book versus a pupil idea can be the basis of either teacher talk or pupil talk. Thus, in any one of the B areas of Fig. 7–22, both teacher and pupil talk are included.

The second matrix of Fig. 7–22 shows the data for this overlay from episode B, first half. We can now see that all sustained talk at the higher level of thinking, quadrant I, was concerned with ideas which were suggested by pupils. The sustained development of teacher or book ideas, in quadrant III, needs now to be checked in a time line display, to see when it occurred during the first half—at the beginning or at the end? And did the development of pupil ideas at the higher level occur at the same time or at a different time compared with the lower level thinking?

Progress so far

At this point in the discussion, the procedure for making computer trans-formations which collapse the total number of categories has been described. A discussion of the general case of a 2 × 2 × 2 system showed that there is a variety of display formats for an 8 × 8 matrix. Any one of the three dichot-omies can be used for the major division of the matrix, and some of the choices for arranging the secondary and tertiary divisions have been discussed.

You may have noticed that all the examples of "mental overlays" inter-preted the episode B, first half, data. For practice, it may be instructive to sketch your own overlays and make comparisons between two other matrices of your own choice from either Fig. 7–15 or 7–19.

Before turning to a discussion of time line displays for 2 × 2 × 2 category systems, there is one other matrix display which is of interest, since it involves transformations from more than one old cluster to a single new dischotomy.

TRANSFORMATIONS FROM TWO CLUSTERS TO ONE DICHOTOMY

The special cluster described on page 219 attempts to characterize not particular events, but a pattern of events. Instead of collapsing all teacher statements into teacher talk, or all pupil statements into pupil talk, it attempts to ignore who is talking and emphasize certain relationships between teacher and pupil.

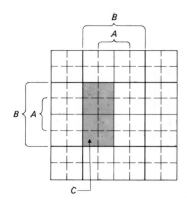

Figure   7–23.

One dichotomy, in the special cluster, refers to "teacher initiation and pupil response" while the other dichotomy refers to "pupil initiation and teacher response." The transformation equates some multiple coded events to a single category as the outline below shows:

Category 1 Teacher Initiation—Pupil Response	Category 2 Pupil Initiation—Teacher Response
Teacher talk, initiation, $3xx$	Pupil talk, initiation, $6xx$
Pupil talk, response, $4xx$	Teacher talk, response, $3xx$
Teacher solicits, directions, $21x$	Teacher solicits, citing pupil idea, $24x$
Teacher solicits, develop own idea, $22x$	Teacher solicits, developing pupil idea, $25x$
Teacher solicits, citing own idea, $23x$	

There are two features of this transformation which were not present in the examples in the preceding sections. First, the basic dimension of who is talking is eliminated, since both teacher and pupil talk enter into the same category. Second, the distinction between the teacher's ideas and the pupils' ideas provides a basis for separating teacher solicitations, so that those which enhance teacher initiation are separated from those which enhance pupil initiation. It is at this point that the categories from two clusters in the larger system enter into the formation of a new dichotomy to form the new system.

Suppose a display is arranged which highlights the contrast between pupil initiation and teacher response compared with teacher initiation and pupil response. One way this can be done is shown in Fig. 7–23. Let A represent pupil initiation based on pupil ideas, and let B represent all statements concerned with pupil ideas, even those that occur under conditions of teacher initiation. This arrangement means that higher frequencies at the center of the matrix indicate a concern for pupil ideas, and at the very center, opportunity for pupil initiative. In addition to considering initiative and whose ideas are being discussed, the full 8 × 8 matrix has a primary division based on high and low level of thinking. This permits special attention to be given to the shaded area (see the arrow from C) in which events at a higher level of thinking are tabulated. The complete display for episodes A and B, first half and second half, is shown in Fig. 7–24.

This transformation and associated display contrasts the differences between the four segments of interaction more effectively, perhaps, than any of the previous arrangements. Should they be shown to a teacher who had purposely created the two different episodes, the displays would emphasize

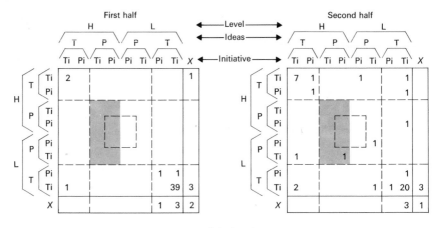

Episode A

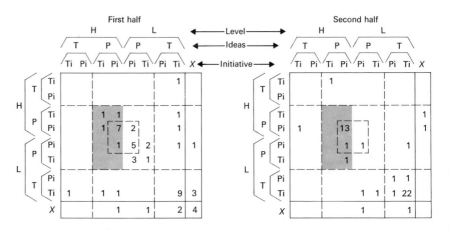

Episode B

Fig. 7–24.   Display Emphasizing Initiation—Response.

the consequences of different teaching patterns on the quality of class discussions.

Matrix displays of the type just discussed would normally be combined with time line displays when providing a teacher with feedback.

TIME LINE DISPLAYS BASED ON TRANSFORMED DICHOTOMIES

One of the most welcome advantages of computer transformations which collapse an original cluster into a dichotomy is that it simplifies the design of time line displays. Besides greater clarity, the advantages include *reducing the length of the time line because it can be based on cumulated intervals rather than single events*. As these two assertions are clarified, it may help to refer frequently to the time line displays shown in Fig. 7—25 (pp. 230—231).

The top three time lines in Fig. 7—25 refer, respectively, to teacher-pupil talk, source of ideas, and level of thinking. The bottom time line is the contrast between teacher initiation—pupil response versus pupil initiation—teacher response, the special dichotomy discussed in the preceding section.

The reference line in all four displays serves a dual purpose. It not only serves to separate vertical bars which are proportional to the incidence of coded events, but arabic numbers inside the bar indicate the number of X type silences or pauses which occurred during that interval. When this arabic number is larger, there are proportionally fewer event symbols above and below, since more periods of silence were coded.

There are, of course, a variety of options in choosing the horizontal time scale. In Fig. 7—25, 10 recorded events have been chosen as the interval to be cumulated. If these observations could be recorded at a rate of 10 per $\frac{1}{2}$ minute (once every 3 seconds), then each cumulated interval represents $\frac{1}{2}$ minute. In longer observations, an interval of 1 minute might be more appropriate.

In most computer printout machines, there are at least 120 letter spaces per line. If a vertical bar was alternated with an empty space, then a single time line could cover 1 hour of observation given the same rate of observation and interval size. This is a great advantage over single event time lines. It remains to be demonstrated, however, that events cumulated during 1-minute intervals will provide a teacher with sufficient discrimination to trace changes in teaching strategies. Given the results of our past research with the original 10 categories, the prospects seem encouraging.

Computers can be programmed to print displays just like those in Fig. 7—25. Three proportions are involved. First, the number of X events, shown by an arabic number within the center line, represents one proportion of all events in that interval. Next, the proportion in Category 1 of the dichotomy is determined, and finally, the proportion for Category 2. The latter two proportions are used to print the proper number of event symbols above and below the reference line. When more than 10 events constitute an interval, for example, 20, yet only 10 event symbols are used, fractions of an event symbol would be more accurate, but not really necessary. In any case, if a full colon was used to build the bar, then a period key could top it off with one-half of an event, if that degree of accuracy seems desirable.

Turning now to the interpretation of Fig. 7—25, the top time line shows a remarkable similarity for episodes A and B. The last time interval is the only striking exception. Apparently the proportions of teacher and pupil talk, one interval compared with the next, is not a feature which really distinguishes episode A from episode B.

Episode *A* Data

Events →	First Half					Second Half				
	10	20	30	40	50	60	70	80	90	100
Pupil Talk		*	******	***	*****	***	****	******	***	
Silence *X* →	0	2	2	0	1	1	2	0	0	0
Teacher Talk	*********	******	**	******	*****	*****	****	****	*******	*********
Pupil Ideas								**	**	
Silence *X* →	0	2	2	0	1	1	2	0	0	0
Teacher or Book Ideas	*********	*******	******	*********	******	******	*******	******	*******	*******
Higher Level Thinking						**		*	********	****
Silence *X* →	0	2	2	0	1	1	2	0	0	0
Lower Level Thinking	*********	******	******	*********	*******	*****	*******	******	**	******
Pupil Initiates— Teacher Responds					**		*	*	**	*
Silence *X* →	0	2	2	0	1	1	2	0	0	0
Teacher Initiates Pupil Responds	*********	******	******	*********	******	******	******	*******	*******	******

Fig. 7–25.   Examples of Computer Printout Time Line Dis[play]

Episode B Data

	First Half					Second Half				
Events →	10	20	30	40	50	60	70	80	90	100

Pupil Talk

| Silence X → | 3 | 0 | 0 | 4 | 0 | 0 | 0 | 0 | 0 | 0 |

Teacher Talk

Pupil Ideas

| Silence X → | 3 | 0 | 0 | 4 | 0 | 0 | 0 | 0 | 1 | 0 |

Teacher or Book Ideas

Higher Level Thinking

| Silence X → | 3 | 0 | 0 | 4 | 0 | 0 | 0 | 0 | 0 | 0 |

Lower Level Thinking

Pupil Initiates—Teacher Responds

| Silence X → | 3 | 0 | 0 | 4 | 0 | 0 | 0 | 0 | 0 | 0 |

Teacher Initiates Pupil Responds

d on Dichotomies Cumulated for Every 10 Symbols.

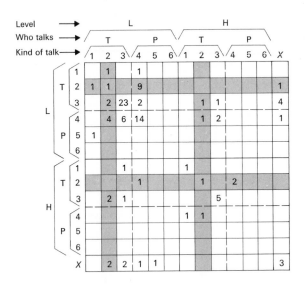

Fig. 7—26.   Types of Talk Combined with Level of Thinking—Episode *A*.

The second time line, displaying the use of ideas which were expressed by pupils versus those which came from the teacher or book, shows that the two episodes were quite different. One difference is that more attention is paid to ideas from pupils in episode *B*. A second difference is that there are more radical shifts, one interval compared with the next, in episode *B* which suggests the notion of flexibility. A third feature of the display, which can be seen only in the variation of the episode *B* profile, is that the flexibility seems orderly. That is, attention to pupil ideas builds gradually and peaks after a period of development in both the first half and the second half.

The third time line indicates that there were more statements in episode *B*, compared with *A*, which were based on higher levels of thinking. The differences in variation, one interval to the next, are not as great in the third time line as they are in the second. And in both halves of episode *B*, and in the second half of episode *A*, there again seems to be an ordered sequence to the variation.

The fourth time line, like the second, indicates sharp differences between the two episodes. During the third interval and the last two intervals, pupils establish initiative and the teacher responds in Episode *B*.

Even a cursory inspection of these time lines leaves the impression that if we are ever to understand the sequential variation of teacher-pupil interaction some method, such as a time line display, will be essential in abstracting, quantifying, and placing into sequence those aspects of the interaction that hold promise of clarifying the teaching-learning process. With computer

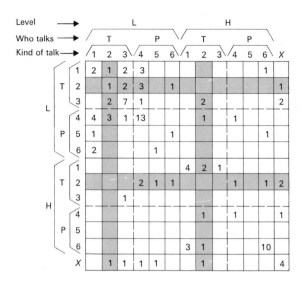

Fig. 7–27.   Types of Talk Combined with Level of Thinking—Episode *B*.

supported observation, it should become increasingly practical "to call" various kinds of sequential displays from a pool of data, either as cumulative matrices or time line profiles, in order to attack the more difficult problem of explaining what laws, if any, account for flexibility in teaching behavior.

PARTIAL TRANSFORMATIONS

Before summarizing the interaction in episodes *A* and *B*, there is one additional matrix display to be mentioned. Suppose it was of interest to study transitions between the six types of teacher and pupil talk that were coded in cluster A, page 188, and a simplified dichotomy for the second or third cluster. Such a comparison may not be readily available within a general library of computer printout options for three-digit code symbols; instead it would be in the library for two-digit code symbols.

In Figs. 7–26 and 7–27, matrices have been developed from what are essentially two-digit code symbols. The first digit is taken directly from the seven-category cluster A of the original multiple coding scheme. The second digit refers to either Category 1 or 2 from dichotomizing level of thinking, cluster C. Such a combination of categories results in a 12 × 12 matrix.

This kind of display might be useful in an analysis of how teacher soliciting moves, to take one example, may be associated with movement from one level to another level of thinking. An inspection of both matrices reveals that episode

A involves fewer transactions with teacher solicitations. By inspecting the two columns and the two rows which have been shaded, in Fig. 7–26, it would appear that: (a) teacher solicitations at the lower level of thinking lead to nine pupil responses at the low level, to one instance of further teacher talk—in the response mode, and once to silence; and (b) teacher solicitations at the higher level of thinking lead to one pupil response at the lower level, and two pupil responses at the higher level.

While episode *B*, shown in Fig. 7–27, is too short to have many different kinds of sequences, it has more than episode *A*. The top shaded row (L-T-2) is similar to episode *A*, with the exception of one pupil statement which expressed the pupil's point of view. The lower shaded row (H-T-2) produced four pupil responses at the lower level of thought—although one was a rare pupil solicitation, and only two at the higher level of thinking. In the event that such a matrix appeared during a teacher's investigation of his own attempts to elicit pupil statements at a higher level of thinking, the feedback information would certainly raise some provocative questions. What is the teacher's function in controlling the level of thinking? When should attempts to shift the level be made? What next steps would represent a practical plan to explore this aspect of the interaction?

The foregoing has been an attempt to illustrate (a) how a partial transformation can produce a specialized matrix display, (b) how such a display can be studied in terms of a particular teacher function, and (c) how a teacher might identify a self-development program involving attempts to control some feature of his own interaction.

SUMMARY OF COMPUTER SUPPORTED ENCODING AND DECODING

Computers are usually first installed in schools to help teachers and administrators with all sorts of bookkeeping and retrieval chores. Their versatility will permit the rapid development of many other important educational functions. Perhaps the least discussed potential capability of a computer installation in a school is supporting the analysis of classroom communication. If computers can help teachers study their own interaction in ways that lead to more effective instruction, this may become one of the more significant contributions.

ACHIEVING COMPUTER SUPPORTED CLASSROOM OBSERVATION

The most intensive work for a systems analyst and computer programmer starts after they have finished a detailed projection of services and functions, ordered the computer, and supervised its installation. Like most electronic gear, a computer seldom performs exactly as you want it to right after you press the "on" button for the first time. In order to provide for classroom observation and feedback to teachers, engineers must secure equipment, install connecting lines, check out equipment interface, design flow charts, and produce the necessary computer programs. At many points, consultation between teachers and engineers will be necessary.

While the computer people are doing their share of the work, teachers will want to develop some experience in observation, tabulation, decoding, and self-directed inquiry. In order to understand what is required, some of the first procedures will necessarily be carried out with the help of pencils and paper. These early experiences will help teachers clarify the functions they would like the computer to perform, to say nothing about increasing their anticipation and appreciation of computer services when they are ready. These early experiences with coding and decoding will provide background knowledge for answering many questions. Will observations be required in more than one classroom? How many such rooms need to be prepared for remote coding? How many hours per week will the local unit be used for this purpose? Exactly what kind of information will be "input"? Exactly what kind of information will be "output"? How many different program options would be necessary, as a minimum, to start? Later on? In what priority should subsequent adaptations be developed? What kind of printout equipment is needed? And so on.

Initial suggestions to develop answers to these questions can be found in this chapter and those that precede it. The initial coding procedures may involve single digit code symbols and make use of a system similar to the 10 categories introduced in the earlier chapters. The need to handle two-digit code symbols may arise first as subscripting helps to focus on specialized instructional problems. Multiple coding with category clusters may or may not be necessary; it will depend on the kinds of instructional problems that are to be investigated.

THE DEVELOPMENT OF CATEGORY SYSTEMS AND OBSERVATION TRAINING

In various parts of this book, some attention is devoted to the kinds of problems that can be investigated. Suggestions and steps for the practical application of encoding and decoding procedures are outlined. Teachers, supervisors, and perhaps even pupils can be taught observation skills. Ways to release time for teachers and provide supporting personnel will be another requirement of self-directed inquiry by teachers. Since there are many ways that such problems can be solved, different solutions are likely to develop.

Among the early problems will be the design of category systems which are appropriate to the initial, then the intermediate, and then the advanced problems which the participating teachers may wish to investigate. This book illustrates how coding systems can become increasingly complex. There are many problems which can be analyzed and useful beginning experiences which can be carried out with the use of a simple, single digit coding system.

The next step is two-digit coding based on subscripting some standard set of categories such as the FIAC system. Multiple coding with category clusters is the most flexible system, but standardizing the observation procedures and establishing observer reliability may prove difficult. These problems would be less difficult if multiple coding is based on a limited number of clusters. These clusters could be combined in many different ways in order to match the requirements of a particular project. Yet if the most frequently used clusters became somewhat standardized, then the system would be both practical and flexible.

Observation training and developing clusters go hand in hand. Practice in observation often reveals weaknesses in the definitions of categories or difficult coding problems for particular categories. As a result, changes in the coding system are made.

Observers need enough training so that the mechanics of recording do not interfere with encoding, the more common events are coded consistently, and the tempo of recording is fast enough to accomplish the purpose of the investigation. But the higher levels of interobserver reliability which are required in research projects may not be necessary for inservice and preservice inquiry projects.

THE TYPES OF DISPLAYS WHICH CAN BE USED

In Chapter 6 and the first part of this chapter, a number of different kinds of data displays were discussed. A brief review of the various displays with suggested advantages that pertain to each type now follows.

The matrix

The matrix is a display of sequence pairs which occurred during some interval of time. By making these time intervals smaller and smaller, a series of matrices approaches a time line display. For the time interval during which the data are cumulated, the matrix is especially useful in contrasting one kind of class activity with another, or for comparing two different classes engaged in the same activity. It is also possible to compare interaction with some model of interaction, provided that the model can be illustrated within a matrix format of columns and rows.

With the help of a computer, many different kinds of matrix displays become feasible. Complicated category clusters can be simplified through transformations that collapse the data into fewer categories. When three clusters are involved and each can be reduced to a dichotomy, the general case of a 2 × 2 × 2 scheme producing an 8 × 8 matrix provides for a variety of interesting displays. Besides reducing the size of a matrix, the computer also facilitates the printing of larger matrices which are required when categories are subscripted. It should also be possible for a computer to print out portions of a matrix, say just the transitions involving four out of 20 categories, as one option in a standardized computer program.

Simple histograms

Simple histogram displays can also be a part of a computer printout. Like the matrix, the data are cumulated during a specified time interval and as these time intervals become shorter, a time line display is approached.

One way to look at histogram profiles is to see them as special cases of the matrix and of time line displays. Besides printing a matrix, a computer could be programmed to print a family of histograms based on the column totals of the matrix or even a particular row, or column, or combination of rows and columns. Thus, for example, besides a normal 10 × 10 matrix, a computer could easily display a histogram profile of the teacher's immediate reactions to pupils by making use of rows 8 and 9, columns 1 through 7. A histogram might provide a profile of the 10 steady state cells, and so on. What is said here about a standard 10 × 10 matrix applies equally well to combinations of matrices, such as those that appear with category clusters.

The cumulative time line display, discussed below, is a special application of the histogram.

Single event time line displays

Single event time line displays position all events coded, or selected types of events, into a spatial arrangement, not unlike music, so as to preserve sequence. The single event time line is particularly useful in demonstrating the presence or absence of particular sequences and in showing when such sequences occurred during the observation. Returning to the FIAC system, for example, comparing the frequency of 4–8–3 sequences with 4–8–3–3 (or more) sequences can be done most efficiently with this type of display.

The single event time line display may always be preferred for short segments of natural or contrived interaction such as might occur in role playing, microteaching, and social skill training exercises. In these training settings, this display can be easily produced without a computer, but the computer can accomplish the task with fewer errors, and like many modern inventions, it may start as a luxury and end up as essential for this purpose.

Depending on the spaces assigned to categories, single event time lines can be used to compare interaction with models, but again, it must be possible to describe the model as a pattern within the same format. An overlay of such a model can be moved across a time line to see how often the interaction sequences fit the model.

Time line displays also have great potential for the direct coding of sub-scripted categories which make use of two digits. This potential will be illust-rated in subsequent chapters.

Cumulative time line displays

Cumulative time line displays refer to a procedure whereby events are stored for very short time intervals and then printed into a display. In general, this type of display stands somewhere between the single event display and a display of the entire observation.

The practical application of cumulative time line displays may have to await the resources of a computer. Two steps in the procedure are difficult for an observer to accomplish by hand. First, the matter of storing events for the time interval selected, while possible, is clumsy with paper and pencil procedures. Second, in some cases, transformations are essential for simplified displays, and this is beyond the capabilities of most single observers. A second observer, of course, might be used for this purpose.

When available, cumulative time line displays are most appropriate to the study of teaching strategies or fluctuations in classroom communication which occur during observation periods of 15 minutes or longer. The rule is that the time interval during which events are cumulated must be small compared with the cycles of the changes which are anticipated.

Chapter Eight

ADAPTING INTERACTION ANALYSIS TO T-GROUPS, SIMULATED SOCIAL SKILL TRAINING, AND MICROTEACHING

A CRITICAL LOOK AT FEEDBACK

Interaction analysis can enrich the feedback information which becomes available to teachers who participate in human relations training. Ways that interaction analysis coding can be used with T-groups, simulated social skill training, and microteaching are discussed in this chapter. First, however, it will be helpful to clarify just what is meant by *feedback*, especially as it applies to helping a teacher change his behavior.

Educators have the habit of calling many events feedback. The teacher decides to ask Mary a question because she appears not to be paying attention. We say that Mary's response provides the teacher with feedback. A principal visits a teacher in order to make certain ratings which are required for a tenure appointment. The results are discussed with the teacher, sometimes because the teacher's signature is required, and the principal may construe these events as feedback. At one time or another, class test results, interviews with pupils, conferences with parents, supervisors, and fellow teachers may be cited as instances of feedback. When we choose, as a matter of convention, to use the word *feedback* in many different ways, its use in a specific instance communicates very little because it can mean too many things. Currently the word refers to most of the information that comes to a teacher in the conduct of his work. Under these conventions it connotes a flavor that is vaguely good, but at best denotes only *something* (?) that a teacher can presumably use.

Feedback is a term which social scientists originally borrowed from the physical scientists. There is not just one, but there are many different kinds of feedback in the physical sciences. In one application, the term can refer to systems in which a part of the output from some process is returned to the input to be reprocessed in order to exert a corrective influence. For example, feedback of this type is an essential feature of a high fidelity amplifier whereby distortion is reduced and the music sounds better. Properly designed,

239

such feedback causes a slight decrement in output and a remarkable increase in quality. Feedback in servomechanisms can be quite different. Here some measure of performance is used to control the process itself. Thus, the thermostat controls the furnace in order to regulate room temperature and the radar guidance system on a missile controls the flight path in order to keep it headed toward a target.

It is important to notice that in physical science applications, feedback is part of a carefully balanced system. This balance is the result of thorough investigation. The choice of not using or making use of one or another kind of feedback is based on overall performance criteria.

When the word *feedback* is used loosely in education, it is not really analogous to the physical science applications. In the case of helping a teacher change his behavior, feedback is only weakly analogous to the physical sciences. The analogy is weak because very little is known about how to help a teacher change his behavior, whereas feedback in the physical sciences can be very precise, very predictable, and systems tend to exhibit very consistent performance characteristics once designed and set into operation. A more thoughtful adaptation of the feedback processes to the social sciences would lead to these questions. What kind of feedback on what kind of schedule would most likely help a teacher improve his classroom instruction? Is there a relationship between the kind of feedback and the kind of change? Here the performance criterion is improvement, and measures of improvement should be used in making decisions about feedback.

IDEAL CONDITIONS FOR SYSTEMATIC FEEDBACK

Since by common usage, feedback to teachers refers to many kinds of information, suppose modifying adjectives are used to clarify meanings. Let *incidental feedback* refer to much of the information which a teacher obtains in the conduct of work. Let *systematic feedback* refer to information obtained by a teacher as part of a carefully designed inquiry in which (a) there are goals for behavior change, (b) these changes hopefully lead to improvement, (c) information about teaching behavior in two or more comparison situations will be fed back to the teacher, (d) decisions about teaching can be made from an analysis of the information, and (e) further explorations of teaching behavior are likely to follow. Since incidental feedback is and has been available to a teacher who begins a program to improve classroom instruction, it is reasonable to guess that new and much more effective feedback will be required for an improvement to occur, something that approaches ideal systematic feedback, described below.

First, the person who is to be helped has requested and may even anticipate the feedback eagerly. His anticipation is based on a plan of inquiry which he helped to design or at least on a commitment he has made. The act of giving a teacher feedback information is but one step in a larger sequence of steps that is called *inquiry*. Feedback alone, not in a context of inquiry, may be too incidental and ineffective.

Second, the *nature* of the information to be provided during feedback is anticipated by the teacher, since he helped to select it earlier from among various alternatives. The selecting was a decision that was made by the teacher, possibly with the help of others, as an earlier step in the planning of inquiry. The reasons why certain types of information were selected are not only known to the teacher, but the procedures for collecting data involve skills which the teacher has practiced or at least understands.

Third, the design of the inquiry leads directly to some planned comparisons. Thus the feedback information becomes systematic because the data are confronted, analyzed in terms of anticipated comparisons, and their meaning determined in terms of logical inferences.

Fourth, feedback becomes more powerful when it is conceptually parsimonious, is objective—in the sense of replicability, and is problem oriented. Earlier analysis of the problem had progressed to the point at which certain features now are of central interest; concepts to represent these features have been selected; and ways to obtain data for each concept are at hand. Information that strikes at the heart of the matter has the highest priority. This is likely to involve just a few concepts. Later there may be time to resift the data through a serendipitous screen.

Fifth, the time and energy involved in collecting and feeding back information are appropriate to the seriousness of the problem, reasonable in terms of expected outcomes, and considerate of existing workloads. Extensive and arduous procedures are inconsistent with superficial or unimportant problems. An elegant matrix should not be tabulated if a quick time line display of the data would suffice. A 1-hour video playback should probably never be carried out except for some very unusual problem.

Sixth, effective feedback information leads naturally to a next phase of inquiry. Feedback information is put to use. The analysis and resulting insight provide clues for deciding which of several courses of action will be followed. The overall process, of course, runs the risk of being ineffective, but even this outcome can lead to subsequent improvements if the problem justifies the work involved.

FEEDBACK IN T-GROUPS

According to Benne (10), the first T-group, or training group, occurred accidentally in a 1946 workshop in which the reports of observers were discussed in the presence of those who had been observed. A year later the National Training Laboratories (NTL) and several universities sponsored a human relations laboratory at Bethel, Maine, in which the central part of the training was to create T-groups that provided delegates with the opportunity to share their perceptions of each other's behavior. Since then, this type of training has been used at many centers throughout the United States and in other countries. There have been many innovations and embellishments to the basic program, but nearly all changes have been efforts to help a person understand his own behavior, how certain patterns of behavior affect others, and to provide opportunities for more intensive interaction. As variations of method have evolved, names such as "laboratory method," "sensitivity training," "instrumented T-groups," and "basic encounter groups" have been used by one innovator or another.

WHAT A T-GROUP IS AND HOW IT WORKS

Ideally, a T-group has from eight to 12 members plus one or two experienced trainers. Groups of this size are large enough to permit one or two members to remain silent for extended periods of time without undue discomfort. This is less likely to be true of groups of eight members or fewer. Yet by restricting size to less than 15, members are more likely to feel that they can talk if they want to.

A single session of the group can extend over 2 or 3 hours. In isolated summer laboratories, like those at NTL's Bethel, all sessions combined may total 20 to 30 hours during an intensive 2- or 3-week period. In some field applications, meetings are scheduled once or twice a week and the entire program extends over longer periods of time.

The substance of the training program arises from the confrontation of members and situation. The members expect that some kind of topical program will be introduced by the trainer. The trainer purposely refrains from providing this kind of leadership, which violates the members' expectations, leaves an authority vacuum, and no agenda. This type of situation is often referred to as "lacking structure." Some members usually express dissatisfaction with the lack of structure, others may try to provide some kind of structure to the meetings, and a few others will resist any leadership action taken by a member. During the initial meetings frustration usually increases.

Individuals are encouraged to express their feelings, to ask why something occurred, to free themselves of more common inhibitions which restrict the range of topics discussed. During subsequent meetings an increasing proportion of the members become more honest, frank, introspective, and thoughtful about their perceptions of the group, the individual members, and themselves. What occurs in the group, literally what is said and done, becomes a legitimate topic of inquiry. The "here and now" becomes the agenda. The trainer will provide thoughtful guidance by selectively supporting certain lines of thought, asking for clarifications, and helping the group return to the analysis of its own interaction when it strays toward other topics. Naturally, much depends on the style and skill of the trainer, the composition of the group, and the course of events which occur. In a very real sense, each T-group is unique and some are more successful than others in helping members obtain self-insight.

TYPICAL PROBLEMS ON WHICH T-GROUPS WILL WORK

Even though each T-group is different, it is quite common for early meetings to be devoted to a consideration of authority and structure. This might include relatively strong criticism directed toward the trainer for not providing leadership or to some member who has attempted to provide leadership. Later the problems of certain members may concern the group for extended periods of time. Carl Rogers (78), who has participated in many such groups, which he prefers to call "basic encounter groups," has tentatively suggested processes which he thinks take place. The entire list of processes can be found in the reference cited. At one time or another a group may mill around, resist personal expression or exploration, describe past feelings, express negative feelings, express and explore personally meaningful material, express immediate interpersonal feelings in the group, develop a healing capacity in the group, (begin) self-acceptance of change, (begin) the cracking of facades, receive individual feedback, (create) confrontations, (establish) helping relationships outside of the group sessions, and other similar processes. Others have described the processes which take place in a T-group differently; the Bradford, Gibb, and Benne (19) book already cited is especially helpful.

THE KIND OF FEEDBACK THAT A T-GROUP PROVIDES

In most T-groups the feedback consists of subjective opinions which one member expresses about the behavior and characteristics of another. "We tell it like it is" becomes the group norm. Any opinion that is expressed, of course, is usually expanded or modified by the opinions of other members. The feelings, perceptions, and opinions expressed in a T-group are historical facts. For example, when member A says that he thought that member B was ignoring the needs of a third member and dominated the conversation, it is a fact that member A thought this, regardless of whether his perceptions were or were not valid. Even though the feelings and perceptions of a member do exist, just how the group or a person can work most effectively with these feelings and perceptions is a matter for thoughtful consideration and sometimes creative suggestions. To explore these matters constitutes work in a T-group.

The subjective quality of the interpretations made in a T-group are a part of its clinical orientation. Time is taken to explore the full meaning of what is being said. This broader spectrum of communication provides the basis of love, empathy, and understanding which can flourish in a successful T-group, giving it the strength to dig into issues that provide new self-insights. A member risks being frank and open because he has developed faith in the group and hopes for constructive outcomes. The feeling of mutual helpfulness can be so pervasive that a few individuals will seek deeper insights even though the experience may involve considerable emotional distress.

At the same time that a T-group works through problems involving self-insights, it is continuously concerned with its own group process. Some more skillful members learn to take the big step from merely sensing a group difficulty to taking constructive action. It is one thing to make a correct diagnosis, it is quite another to act successfully, on the basis of the diagnosis, and help the group move ahead.

From what has been said so far, it is clear that there is considerable incidental feedback available in a T-group. It also seems fair to assert that there is very little systematic feedback in the sense of the ideal conditions described earlier. Yet there is much more to the feedback in a T-group than is captured by the word "incidental." Feedback can develop great intensity and can become very meaningful when the group focuses on one individual, his needs, and his problems. It emerges, almost spontaneously, from the exigencies of the moment and from the unconditional acceptance which the group develops. The experience can never be and is not intended to be replicable. For the individuals involved, moments of insight are remembered as high points in the T-group.

EXPECTED OUTCOMES OF T-GROUP TRAINING FOR TEACHERS

There are some sharp disagreements among social scientists concerning the long range outcomes of T-group training. Right after a successful T-group experience a participant is quite likely to assert that he has new insights about himself, that he thinks that he is now more sensitive to a wider range of cues during his social interaction, and he often resolves to incorporate these new insights into his behavior "back home on the job." Just how much of this kind of learning influences subsequent behavior and how persistently a person will try to approach his human relationships with new insights, say 6 months or 1 year later, is not yet clearly established although some progress has been made. It is at this point that experts differ, some support the more optimistic claims of constructive outcomes while others remain skeptical.

Carl Rogers (78) administered a follow-up questionnaire to 481 participants of encounter groups which he conducted. The information was obtained from 2 to 12 months following the group experience, with most reports in the 3- to 6-months period:

> *Of these individuals, two (i.e., less than one-half of one percent) felt it had changed their behavior in ways they did not like. Fourteen percent felt the experience had made no perceptible change in their behavior. Another fourteen percent felt that it had changed their behavior, but that this change had disappeared or left only a small residual positive effect. Fifty-seven percent felt it had made a continuing positive difference in their behavior, a few feeling that it had made some negative changes along with the positive. (pp. 272–273)*

A review of research on T-group methods and outcomes can be found in Dorothy Stock's chapter in the Bradford, Gibb, and Benne (97) book. Stock points out that most of the research which attempts to discover whether or not individuals gained skill and insight from their training are usually not concerned with the T-group alone. Instead the entire training experience, often called a "human relations training laboratory," is being evaluated. A number of reports indicate that 60 to 75 percent of the participants in such laboratories show evidence of gain. Here, just as in Rogers' results, a self-report provides the primary data and several studies have shown that such data are contaminated by the respondent's attitudes and response set. Only a few of the studies she reviews go beyond mere self-report. Below are two tentative conclusions she reached which seem most relevant to the classroom teacher. (97, pp. 434–435).

First, increases in "sensitivity to the feelings and behavior of others," "role flexibility," "sensitivity to group decisions," "diagnostic ability," and "utilization of laboratory techniques" have been shown to occur for some people under some conditions.*

Second, the characteristics of a person when he comes to a laboratory, especially his expectations and readiness, definitely influence what he is likely to gain. Not all persons are ready; for example, highly anxious people may learn little.

WAYS THAT INTERACTION ANALYSIS CAN BE APPLIED TO T-GROUPS FOR TEACHERS

Not much is known about how participation in a T-Group affects teacher effectiveness. Even less can be reported about T-group activities in which some form of coding behavior is carried out. What follows, then, can only be considered speculation.

---

*This tentativeness is due not only to individual differences, but also to differences among T-group experiences and the difficulties of conducting research in this area.

Clinically oriented T-group trainers might argue that there is no way to implement systematic feedback (as defined on pp. 240–241) in a T-group in which members are struggling to provide structure and learn more about how their behavior is perceived by others. In contrast to this point of view, it might be argued that if teachers came to a T-group with earlier experiences in coding and interpreting behavior patterns, they might use these skills in an effort to understand their T-group experiences.

Some limitations of T-group training for teachers

Surely an outcome like Stock's report of "increased sensitivity to the behavior of others" would benefit a classroom teacher. In the long run, however, the widespread use of T-group training for improving classroom instruction is less likely to depend on what teachers can learn through their participation, but will depend, instead, on the issue of efficiency. Some of the research reviewed by Stock indicates that it takes time for a T-group to move from the initial lack of structure to a point at which maximum effort can be devoted to individual self-development. And after many man-hours have been expended, the positive outcomes, which vary in degree—one teacher compared with another—must still be transferred from the T-group setting to the reality of the classroom. It is not unreasonable to ask whether the resulting changes in teaching behavior could be achieved more economically or whether supplementary activities in a total laboratory program can enhance the effectiveness of the T-group.

Incorporating interaction analysis in the T-group

There are two classes of problems in a T-group experience to which interaction analysis might be appropriate. The first is concerned with analyzing the verbal communication in the T-group itself. The second is concerned with an analysis of classroom interaction as a pre- and post-assessment of a teacher who participates in the T-group experience. Each is discussed in turn.

1) In the event that members of a T-group could learn or already possessed skills in the coding of verbal communication and, in addition, assuming that the group chose to analyze its own interaction, there are some coding categories which are appropriate. The general purpose of coding in a T-group would be identical to its use in the classroom. By coding single events and interpreting an appropriate display, more accurate inferences about what is taking place may occur. The semiobjective data might enhance the subjective interpretations.

Bales (8) has shown that his basic 12 categories reveal differences between more effective and less effective problem-solving groups. Borgatta and Crowther (17) have subscripted Bales' 10 categories so that they would be even more appropriate to the therapeutic aspects of T-group interaction. Either of these two systems would help to show the differences in communication which occur as a T-group moves through various phases of development from its initial lack of structure to more mature work sessions.

It is interesting that both Bales at Harvard and Borgatta at Wisconsin teach courses in which college students learn to code verbal communication in a group. In private conversations with Bales, he reported student testimony indicating that they learned a great deal about *how* individual behavior affects a group by training themselves to code group communication. This is the same testimony that classroom observers report when they say that they learned more about *how* the teacher influences classroom events through extended systematic coding assignments than they learned in their education courses. In both examples, of course, such insight remains to be translated into personal behavior. Yet the possibility exists that learning to code communication with some system of interaction analysis, displaying the data, and then making interpretations is a rich learning experience for obtaining insight into one's own behavior as well as the behavior of others.

Should the members of a T-group become interested in studying the emotional aspects of their communication, there are categories and display methods. For example, Simon and Agazarian (88) have called their system "sequential analysis of verbal interaction," with the pleasant acronym of SAVI. It has a number of categories in each of four clusters: defensive, unsolicited, maintenance, and problem-solving. Matrix tabulations produce four columns and rows which could be used to trace certain phases of T-group development.

It is also possible to develop one's own clusters and try multiple coding as suggested in Chapter 6. Categories similar to those suggested in BC5, BC6, and BC7 (see pp. 177–178) may be useful.

It seems likely that the embellishment of T-group training with some application of interaction analysis would require a total laboratory program. Part of such a program would include the training of the group members in the use of coding procedures during observation skill sessions, but these activities should probably not be superimposed on the T-group sessions themselves unless the members proposed this for later sessions.

2) The second application referred to at the beginning of this section, would make use of interaction analysis to see if participation in a T-group could be associated with changes in the patterns of teaching behavior. This is a research and assessment application. Surely before T-group training for classroom teachers is extensively disseminated, it would be wise to see if participation in this kind of experience influences what the teacher says and does in the classroom.

THE T-GROUP AND THE IMPROVEMENT OF TEACHING

For the college student preparing to become a teacher and the experienced teacher seeking to improve, the T-group offers an opportunity to live through inquiry, that is, actually act it out with one's own behavior. A genuine orientation toward analyzing one's own behavior on a self-directed basis is difficult to achieve. Perhaps the major justification for the many manhours that go into a T-group, insofar as teacher education is concerned, is that we currently do not have efficient ways for creating the readiness and incentive that are required for continued self-assessment. The T-group experience alone, however, is not likely to solve this problem; but set in a context of a human relations laboratory program, the T-group experience may make a teacher more sensitive to cues in social interaction.

For different points of view, consult Miles (68) and other chapters in the Bradford, Gibb, and Benne book. Campbell and Dunnette (22) can also provide an up to date review of projects which evaluate T-group experiences for managerial training and development.

SIMULATED SOCIAL SKILL TRAINING

Simulated social skill training (SSST) can be distinguished from other types of feedback settings by emphasizing the first word. Simulating social interaction has been the basis of role playing, sensitivity training, sociodrama, and psychodrama. The general idea is to place a person in a situation which provides spontaneous interaction to see if he can practice producing certain patterns of behavior. The other adults present may or may not be instructed to present unexpected responses to the trainee so as to control the sequence of training. For example, if the trainee is trying to practice asking certain types of questions, it may be relatively easy as long as expected answers are forthcoming, but as soon as one question is answered by another question unexpectedly, the training task becomes more difficult.

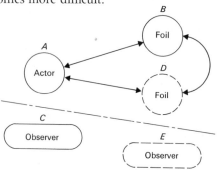

Fig. 8—1.   The SSST Organization.

WHAT SSST IS AND HOW IT WORKS

The smaller the SSST group, the more practice per person when assignments are rotated. From three to five individuals is the optimum group size. The trainee can be called the actor, those who provide the spontaneous setting can be called foils, and one or two observers can code behavior or keep other kinds of records for later evaluation. Figure 8–1 illustrates the organization for a minimum of three and a maximum of five persons.

The purpose

The basic assumption underlying an SSST exercise is that there *are* certain patterns of teaching behavior which are essential in effective teaching. It is further assumed that these patterns can be described, they can be practiced—like any other skill, and their appropriate use in teaching can be discussed and understood. In SSST exercises, the actor is placed in a position to practice a particular pattern of teaching behavior, which can be called a social skill, for a short period of time. The observers can practice identifying this skill and learn how to distinguish it from closely related patterns of behavior. All members of the group have an opportunity to practice controlling their own behavior for professional purposes.

The procedure

The steps outlined below are merely suggestions and need not be followed rigidly. In fact, college students in preparation for teaching and experienced teachers should be encouraged to develop their own procedures as soon as experience with SSST makes this possible.

Step One.   Assign letter designations, *A* through *D* or *E*, to each person in the group and agree on a system for rotating the role assignments by letter so that each individual has a chance to be actor, foil, and observer.

Step Two.   Discuss the skill to be practiced and suggest topics of conversation that fit the skill. Select one topic for the first exercise and decide on additional topics so that each actor can select one that makes him comfortable in his role.

Step Three.   Decide who starts the conversation, suggest a schedule for actor interventions, and decide who will stop the interaction and when it should be stopped.

Step Four.   Speculate on the procedure of evaluation and decide on what kind of data the observers are to record and how their data and opinions can best be presented to the actor when the interaction stops.

Step Five.   Conduct the first practice session, provide the actor with feedback on his performance, and be prepared, if necessary, to alter the procedure for the second session in order to improve the training procedure. As soon as the practice sessions are working smoothly and each person has had an opportunity to be actor, increase the difficulty of the task by privately instructing the foils or restricting the actor's role.

Step Six.   Be prepared to alter the procedure, change topics, and move on to the next skill so as to present a significant challenge to each actor and to keep the interest as high as possible. The task should not be too easy and not too difficult.

An illustration

Suppose practice in asking different kinds of questions is chosen as a skill. For inexperienced participants, a simple task such as asking "open" and "closed" questions may provide an introductory challenge. The actor can be instructed to alternate between these two types, one after the other, while maintaining the same topic of conversation. After several cycles, the criteria for distinguishing between open and closed will become clearer. The effects of "what," "where," and "when" questions can be compared with "why," "please explain," and "what is your opinion" type questions. The dimension of vagueness versus specificity can be investigated in terms of predictable and unpredictable responses.

One way to organize the exercise is to let the two foils start a conversation about some topic which they find interesting. About once every 30 to 40 seconds, the actor intervenes by asking a question. The first question might be more open, the second more closed, the third more open, the fourth more closed, and so on. The observer may be given the task of stopping the conversation when the actor has a chance to ask several questions of each type. Depending on the kind of notes made by the observer, several different issues can be investigated. For example, which kind of question causes the respondent to talk longer? What exceptions tend to arise? Is one or another kind of question more appropriate to such teaching functions as diagnosing pupil difficulties, motivating pupil interest, summarizing, and so on.

For more advanced participants, the actor may be required to practice asking a particular sequence of questions. Perhaps the sequence is to move from the specific to the general, but stay on the same topic. This will involve learning how to shift the level of abstraction of the concepts which form the question. It may also require some attention to the logical connectives which are used to establish relationships among concepts. This kind of training is particularly useful when the actor is restricted to using Category 3 from the FIAC system. This latter restriction means that the concepts and logical connectives must first be mentioned by one of the foils. Such an exercise not only offers a challenge to the actor, it also provides the observers with an opportunity to practice subscripting Category 3. A time line display would be an appropriate recording and display format. For example, before the actor starts, he might sketch his intentions on a time line display so that the sequence of questions is on record as a set of predictions. When the interaction is stopped, the actor's "lesson plan" can then be compared with the observer's record, both displayed on the same kind of time line.

To start the evaluation the actor might be instructed to ask the observer, "Were all the ideas in my first question expressed earlier by the foils?" and then proceed to each additional question that was asked by the actor.

It might also be agreed that before the second actor begins his session, he is responsible for leading a brief discussion about ways to improve the procedure for the next round.

After one cycle in which all members of the group have had a chance to be actor and learn the procedure, the task can be made more rewarding by requiring the actor to use synonyms, rather than the foils exact words. In this more difficult task, the actor succeeds if his choice of synonyms meets the following test. Suppose a second observer (or tape recorder) is used to keep a record of the concepts and logical connectives which the foils expressed. The observer repeats the actor's question and asks the foils, "Do you believe that the ideas in the actor's question are the same as the ideas which you were discussing?" "Do you think he missed some of your ideas or inserted some of his own?" If the foils agree that their ideas were indeed in the actor's question, then that actor has met the requirements of the task.

The purpose of all evaluation discussions is to help the actor. Statements such as, "It seems to me that you (meaning the actor) failed to . . ." should be declared off limits. Instead, an observer or foil should suggest alternatives in the criticism. For example, "Would you (the actor) have come closer to my idea (being a foil) if you had said . . . ?" The idea is not to confront the actor with evidence of failure, but to help find action alternatives which are closer to the task requirements.

When a particular actor is obviously not coming close to the task requirements, it may be helpful to repeat a group discussion of alternatives and then ask that particular actor if he would like to try again before rotating the roles. Alternatively, let other actors try and then return to the actor who was having difficulty for a second try at the same task before moving on to a more difficult cycle.

It is quite possible during an exercise, that an observer may record incorrectly or is subject to some misconception. It is well to remember that both the actor and the observers are practicing skills. The foils might decide that an observer's appraisal of the actor's performance is in error and that it is the observer who needs help in making more accurate observations.

At any time that members of a SSST group believe that the exercise is merely a game and is not rewarding in terms of professional self-development, the activities should either be terminated, altered so as to present a significant challenge to the participants, or embellished as a game in order to have more fun. Perhaps the most common error in serious skill training is the misconception that adults can role play pupils. This is best illustrated by the adult who says, "Teacher, can I go to the bathroom?", in an effort to be humorous. Serious social skill training can be conducted by having adults act like adults, by discussing adult topics, by reacting like adults, and then discussing how the skills would apply to the classroom. Later in this chapter, the discussion of "microteaching" illustrates how contrived practice can include pupils, but in this case each participant is "acting his age." An experienced human relations trainer can be of great help in conducting SSST exercises during the initial training projects. Later, his presence is less essential, providing the participants have had enough experience to direct and alter their own procedures.

PROBLEMS ON WHICH TEACHERS WORK USING SSST

The assumption of three levels of teaching performance, mentioned in Chapter 1, led to the suggestion that certain behavior patterns might help to lift a teacher from one level to a higher level. In this section these patterns of teaching behavior, which might be called social skills of teaching, are arranged roughly in an order of increasing difficulty. Advocating the use of these skills is closely related to the research results that are reviewed in Chapters 11 and 12, but not all of those listed can be specifically supported by a particular research project.

1) *The ability to ask open or closed questions (after Hughes) and to know when each is appropriate in classroom teaching.*   This is a distinction between narrow what, where, when, and sometimes how questions, versus questions which elicit explanation, logical operations, and speculative theory. There is also the element of right and wrong factual answers, contrasted with matters of opinion or value which a pupil can develop without being right or wrong. The skill listed next is also closely related.

2) *The ability to ask a question which lifts the current level of abstraction, or a question which lowers it, and the ability to ask a series of questions which gradually lifts or lowers the level of abstraction.*   A skill such as this is essential to understanding and making use of Hilda Taba's* theories about logical thought processes in the classroom. Another example might involve a talented teacher who wishes to introduce learning goals at a relatively general level, in order to give them greater perspective, but knows that subsequent, adroit questioning must lower the level of abstraction so that individual pupils are talking about

---

*A discussion of Hilda Taba's research can be found on pp. 184 and 300.

tasks and the steps required to complete a task in order that work can start. Finally, teaching the distinctions between opinion, fact, and value by emphasizing the denotative and connotative qualities of concepts requires this skill.

3) The ability to ask questions in which the concepts and logical connectives have previously been expressed by pupils.   At certain times in teaching, it may be useful to build questions on the ideas that pupils have expressed rather than having a teacher express his own idea. Such questions help to build pupil confidence and provide a basis for subsequent independent and self-directed inquiry.

4) The ability to summarize what pupils have said and then end by asking a question which moves the discussion to the next step in a logical sequence of problem solving. This pattern is used in terms of the subject matter being studied and when making decisions about alternative ways of organizing the classroom learning activities. To summarize what pupils say is to acknowledge their contributions, but to relate what has been said to the next step is to make use of what has been said in a constructive fashion. This may be the most potent form of reinforcement available to the teacher, especially when it is directed toward a single pupil.

5) The ability to make constructive use of ideas previously expressed by pupils (a) by acknowledgment or paraphrase, (b) by making comparisons to authoritative sources or task requirements, and (c) by comparing the ideas expressed by one pupil to those of another, or to something the same pupil said earlier.   Insight is most often the product of comparison. The teacher can select key ideas from those expressed by pupils, and ask questions that guide comparison. When this is done skillfully, pupils are more likely to believe that they are solving their own problems rather than just following teacher directions.

6) The ability to make constructive use of positive and negative feelings and the emotional overtones of pupil statements or behavior, especially when these facilitate or interfere with learning subject matter.   Reacting constructively to positive affect (e.g., enthusiasm) helps to reinforce motivation. Dealing realistically with negative affect (e.g., disgust, apathy) helps pupils understand the consequences of the attitudes and to diagnose difficulties. Knowing when and how to shift the attention of a pupil or group away from the learning task and toward feelings in order to enhance the development of both usually has a constructive effect on self-control and discipline.

7) The ability to use phrases which explain the "because" aspects of praise, criticism, and the giving of directions so that reasons for asserting this kind of teacher authority become public and do not remain hidden. The indiscriminate use of praise, criticism, and directions, or their use in ways that pupils cannot understand, merely enhances the unrestricted authority of the teacher and increases unwanted pupil dependence on the teacher. What some have called "a teacher's unconditional regard for the child as a person" means that reasons for doing something must not only be made clear, but they can also be discussed and possibly modified during teacher-pupil planning. Obviously teacher questions to verify the pupils' presumed understanding or to invite pupil participation in giving praise, criticism, and directions including the reasons, should also have a beneficial effect on independence and self-control.

8) The ability to predict the consequences which will follow from alternative actions when a decision is under consideration and to help pupils compare these consequences through speculation before decisions are made.   For pupils, the development of judgment is probably influenced by learning to live with the consequences of action. For the teacher, learning how to help pupils predict consequences requires practice, especially in asking an extended series of questions. To accomplish this effectively, several of the previously mentioned social skills must be combined into a strategy so that the teacher, on appropriate occasions, can guide pupils through the steps of decision-making.

9) The ability to guide discussions which transform more abstract statements of learning goals into less abstract work tasks and clarify the first steps required to start work, in ways that reflect the interests and abilities of the pupils.   Individual or group assignments are tasks which have an end product, usually involve a series of steps, and hopefully match the interests and abilities of the pupils. A skillful teacher knows that to transform the statement of a general goal of learning into a specific task involves less abstract concepts with more denotative meaning. When pupils participate in making this transformation and understand the logical relationships between goal, task, and their own abilities and interests, they are more likely to develop interest in the task and commit themselves to completing it.

10) The ability to listen, to inventory pupil ideas, and to organize them in terms of teaching objectives, in order to reinforce selectively those ideas which are more on-target, yet still encourage all contributions by (at least) acknowledging off-target ideas.   When pupils are confronted with a problem or are reacting to an idea, a wide range of responses are likely to be expressed. Selective reinforcement consists of identifying certain pupil ideas, raising questions about them, paraphrasing them, and asking pupils to develop them. Such activities focus thinking by giving clues to all who listen. The opposite of this skill might be called "the teacher's fishing expedition" in which the teacher often says, "No, Jimmy, that's not what I had in mind. Would anyone else like to try?"

11) The ability both to demonstrate and to explain rules of logic in classroom discourse, including helping to maintain consistency in the meaning of words, and helping to distinguish matters of fact, opinion, and value.   This, of course, is a skill which most of us can work on for the rest of our lives. As stated, this social skill appears to cover all fields in philosophy. What is intended, however, is that an effective teacher realizes that there are different ways to define a term and that the choice limits the term's utility in a logical system. In addition, there are different systems of inquiry which vary in their rules of evidence and thus are more or less appropriate to different kinds of problems. What is often sadly lacking in the discourse of many classrooms is consistency between how terms are defined, applying rules of evidence, and exploring the nature of the issue objectively. A teacher statement which illustrates inconsistency is the question. "What are *the* six causes of the Revolutionary War?"

A curriculum of SSST exercises can be used to introduce concepts about teaching behavior. At the end of an exercise, each participant will have heard a concept described, will have attempted to produce a pattern of behavior to match the description, will have observed others trying to produce the pattern, probably coded acts which were a part of the pattern, and will have discussed how such a pattern might be used in classroom teaching. Introducing only a few concepts in this way seems superior to introducing many concepts by lecturing and class discussion. The result being sought is to have concepts become useful tools for thinking about teaching and to have them trigger mental images which represent behavioral meanings accurately. The assumption is that by acting out a concept, meanings become clear and teaching behavior can be conceptualized accurately—albeit with fewer concepts.

THE TYPE OF FEEDBACK THAT CAN OCCUR IN SSST

The feedback which can occur in SSST consists of opinions and sometimes reasonably objective data which clarify relationships between a person's behavior and the concepts in question. The situation challenges those who are helping the actor in that the subjective needs of the person receiving the feedback are likely to be different, one participant compared with another. Thus, the evaluation phase can provide practice in establishing a constructive, helping relationship in which subjective and objective problems are both involved. Within the same cycle, each person proferring feedback assistance becomes the recipient of feedback later on, thereby experiencing the problems from both points of view. Accepting and integrating information about one's own behavior in terms of a task or goal provides an opportunity to work with one's own defensiveness, control "flight" reactions, and seriously consider consistency between intent and actions.

There is another element in the evaluation phases of SSST that often requires special attention. In one sense, participation requires acting ability; not so much in terms of the theater stage, although such talent might help initially, but in terms of independent initiative that is required to guide interaction. The latter ability is essential to teaching. Yet performance by participants will vary from clumsy, misdirected patterns of behavior to very skillful self-control. It is the task of the entire group to respond constructively to all qualities of performance.

THE EXPECTED OUTCOMES OF SSST EXERCISES

The expected outcomes of SSST will vary according to how it is used in a pre-service or inservice training program. Some examples are now discussed.

Large massed audiences

SSST exercises for audiences of from 500 to 600 participants can be directed by a leader as a way of introducing the technique and as the initial experience to particularly important concepts. The physical arrangements are crucial; the typical lecture hall or theater with fixed seats in rows is an almost impossible setting. The first requirement is a flat floor with movable chairs and tables with enough space to set up four- or five-man discussion groups that are far enough apart so that each group can carry on a discussion. Good accoustics help to make the leader's wireless microphone, connected to an above average public address system, a useful device not only for lecturing, but for interviewing group members. At one time or another, an actor, the foils, or an observer may be asked to report on progress, problems, or conclusions that occurred in his group. It often helps to have several overhead projectors, manned by assistants, so that all can see visual displays clearly.

Problem solving and SSST exercises in massed audiences permits one group to discover whether its experiences and conclusions are or are not similar to those reached by other groups. The leader can provide the directions for the first exercise and after the first cycle, interview an observer to ask what conclusions the group reached. He can then ask for a show of hands in response to the question, "How many other groups reached this conclusion?" This provides for a rather neat opportunity to illustrate how replication enters into inquiry. A group can discover, for example, that it is only one of 20 groups that reached a particular conclusion while 80 other groups reached a different conclusion. The leader may even be able to help the participants see that knowledge about teaching is often expressed more reasonably in the form of probability generalizations. A conclusion might be, "Apparently you can expect to reach a conclusion like yours about 20 percent of the time."

In this application one might expect the following outcomes. Large groups can be introduced to SSST techniques and start to understand what is meant by attention to patterns of teaching behavior. Motivation and confidence might be built for subsequent small group SSST activities. Personal insight into a few patterns can be achieved within the limitations expected in a large audience.

Small building groups or action teams

The place of SSST exercises in a total program for teacher preparation or inservice training remains to be determined. With properly designed instructional materials, it is possible to think of a series of interactive experiments which the participants can investigate one after another. The experiments could be built around some of the social skills already listed. The purpose would be to see if the participants could *discover* tentative hypotheses about teaching behavior in contrast to being told principles of teaching. In a complete program the same hypotheses could be further tested in microteaching and full class settings.

Summary of outcomes

In SSST, participants act out patterns of teaching. This experience helps to connect concepts with overt patterns of behavior and thereby clarifies the behavioral meaning of concepts about teaching. SSST exercises provide an opportunity to practice controlling one's own behavior by simulating spontaneous interaction. Both giving and receiving evaluative feedback can be experienced. Elementary skills of observation can be developed.

COMBINING INTERACTION ANALYSIS WITH SSST

Simulating interactive situations is a natural outgrowth of interaction analysis; the two activities complement each other. In the development of category meaning, for example, observers on a research team often simulate verbal communication in order to illustrate a coding problem. Teachers and college students who are learning the meaning of categories can practice coding in almost any setting in which two or more persons are talking.

Initial observation experiences

A person who is untrained in coding can record with simple written notes certain events which occur in an SSST exercise. He will find this method difficult because talking is faster than writing. Primitive distinctions can then be introduced to speed up observation. For example, the actor's questions can be tallied as "open," "closed," or "can't tell." From that beginning, more elaborate ways of categorizing questions can be developed. It may well be that the place to help a teacher gain the confidence necessary to improvise categories is during successively more complex SSST exercises.

Training games based on categories

At Temple University interaction analysis is taught to college students who plan to become teachers. SSST experiences that train students to understand and use the basic 10 categories described earlier have also been developed.

The actor is given a broad assignment such as "Using only Categories 4 and 3, ask your principal to authorize the purchase of a tape recorder." In this manner various kinds of role restrictions can be placed on the actor which require an understanding of the categories and provide practice in controlling one's behavior. The observer in this case keeps a record of the categories actually used and provides a record to see if the actor met the role requirements.

Types of data displays

The time line display, such as the one shown in Fig. 9—6, is particularly appropriate for SSST. For the analysis of a more complex skill, such as shifting the level of abstraction, a time line display such as the third cluster in Fig. 9—8 would be needed.

In some cases SSST appraisal can be accomplished with simple histogram displays. Especially when sequence of events is of no importance.

Summary

Interaction analysis is not only easily combined with SSST, simulated experience is a means of helping teachers understand category meanings and teaching them how to devise their own category systems. The introduction of multiple cluster coding, for example, would permit the observer to make as many inferences about the foils' statements as he could make about the actor's statements, which is not possible with the FIAC system. In short, observing SSST is one point at which interaction analysis can be introduced and learned as a method of providing systematic feedback.

FEEDBACK WITH MICROTEACHING

Microteaching was developed by Professors Dwight Allen and Robert Bush in the teacher preparation program at Stanford University between 1960 and 1967. It fits quite naturally in the development of feedback techniques in the field of human relations training, but is distinguished by several very insightful innovations including video tape recording, teaching and then reteaching microlessons, and the use of rotating groups of school pupils for each teaching episode. The originators also made full use of average pupil ratings of teacher performance and have been able to show that such ratings are good predictors of subsequent teacher performance.

WHAT MICROTEACHING IS AND HOW IT WORKS

Microteaching, like SSST, is based on the assumption that there are certain patterns of behavior, or perhaps more accurately, strategies which are crucial to effective classroom instruction. By concentrating on these strategies in a program to prepare teachers or to help experienced teachers, it should be possible to improve teaching by practicing certain phases of teaching, one phase at a time.

A microteaching clinic program is organized to expose the trainee to an organized curriculum of miniature teaching encounters, moving from the less complex to the more complex. At each step along the way, a teaching strategy is discussed until it can be incorporated into a short teaching lesson of approximately 5-minutes duration. The trainee then teaches this lesson with a small group of four to six pupils in front of a video camera, a supervisor, and often some trainee peers. The pupils are dismissed after filling out a short rating form, and the video recording is replayed and criticized by those present. Then the trainee is given time to think about this criticism and to make modifications which involve only one or two changes. He then reteaches the lesson with a different group of pupils, under the same conditions and with the same opportunities for feedback, except that comparisons between the two lessons are now possible. A single teach-reteach cycle can be accomplished in less than 30 minutes, but it is the reteach cycle to which microteaching owes its success. Reteaching means practicing, a feature of teacher training that is neglected.

Due to years of creative experience, the Stanford team is a source of useful, logistical information about organizing microteaching clinics. College interns have been trained in the Stanford clinic in such numbers as 150 college students in eight weeks. They have learned how to set up a pool of junior and senior high school pupils and how pupil assignments can be rotated so as not to bias the progress reports of the interns. They can estimate the number of hours that video magnetic recorders require for maintenance and the cost of such maintenance. They have data to show that preintern microteaching training requiring less than 10 hours per week is likely to produce subsequent intern performance which is superior to college students who take a more traditional course of study requiring more than 20 hours per week. They have discovered that at least 15 to 20 minutes are required before the reteach performance, after the criticism of the first teaching, so that the trainee has time to plan meaningful changes. They suggest that supervisor criticism should focus on one or two significant suggestions and not be spread thinly over many aspects of the performance (95).

TYPICAL PROBLEMS ON WHICH TEACHERS WORK IN A MICROTEACHING CLINIC

In a preservice program for the preparation of teachers, microteaching has followed an organized curriculum. For experienced teachers in an inservice training program, projects for personal growth might be selected by the teacher, although even experienced teachers may prefer to have suggestions to guide their initial efforts.

A preservice curriculum

The 8-week program used at Stanford is a summer preparation for a full year of part-time internship teaching. Besides the microteaching clinic, other courses in educational psychology, curriculum theory, history, philosophy, and so on, are required. In terms of teaching behavior, the following topics illustrate the kinds of problems on which students work in the microteaching clinic.

Lectures, demonstrations, and practice through microteaching with reteaching have included such objectives as the following. (1) providing reinforcement for the pupils, (2) ways that the teacher can vary the stimulus, give emphasis, and maintain attending behavior, (3) set induction, which refers to ways that a teacher can interest pupils in a unit of study and practice creative ways of stimulating curiosity, (4) lecturing and use of audio-visual materials with attention to variation, pacing, and appropriateness, (5) illustrating and using examples, which refers to moving from simple to complex subject matter ideas and ways to judge how appropriate an example is, (6) closure, which refers to the skills of summarizing and ways to emphasize the more important learnings, (7) teacher initiated questions, and (8) student initiated questions.

There is some similarity between the list above and the social skills listed in the preceding section. If there is overlap, to this extent it can be said that different educators, working independently, have isolated the same aspects of classroom interaction which seem crucial to effective teaching.

Inservice training projects

Microteaching experiences provide a setting which may be effectively used as a checkpoint just before a new pattern is used in the regular classroom. Suppose a teacher selects the goal of asking questions more effectively. The development of the necessary concepts, and understanding just how these concepts represent patterns of behavior might be investigated in SSST programs. Once a preliminary understanding has been reached, it can be tested within microteaching conditions. Here a teacher can work with high school or elementary age pupils with reference to some content objectives. Yet the concerns of total class management will not interfere because microteaching is a scaled down version of teaching in which the number of pupils, time, and learning objectives have all been curtailed. With the teach-reteach possibilities, teachers can sharpen up their orientation toward questions and their skill in reformulating questions on the spur of the moment. They proceed by analyzing one performance and then trying to improve it.

In considering the range of self-development tasks for experienced teachers in a microteaching clinic, the topics which Stanford has found useful in pre-service preparation and the social skills listed in the preceding section can all be considered. In addition, the individual teacher may have ideas of his own about how best to use microteaching within an inservice training program.

THE KINDS OF FEEDBACK TEACHERS RECEIVE IN A MICROTEACHING CLINIC

Video replay

Seeing yourself on the TV screen for the first time is usually just plain facinating, and for a few a shock to overcome. First impressions are immediately apparent and have the quality of freshness, since we rarely have the chance to see ourselves from a distance. Mannerisms, gestures, mobility, eye contact, and other physical and nonverbal characteristics of teaching can be analyzed. The ease of these first impressions is a great help to start the cycle—teach, look, resolve to change, reteach, see some changes—and just living through such a cycle starts one down the road to self-assessment. A major difficulty arises out of what might be called "hardware fascination." The ease of the first feedback cycles is both a strength and a weakness. One can become so fascinated by the instant replay that this delays developing concepts and systematic analytical procedures which are necessary in order to improve teaching strategies. TV recreates behavior as it appears to a camera, but the task of conceptualizing it remains.

Pupil post-teaching reactions

The programs at Stanford have permitted a continual refinement of paper and pencil pupil rating scales which can be filled out quickly by pupils at the end of a teaching or reteaching period. The average rating of the pupils appears to be a good predictor of subsequent teaching performance during the intern assignment in the public schools which follows the clinic program. Such ratings can also show growth as teaching skills improve. The necessity to train pupils for about 4 hours should not be overlooked. With only four to six pupils, their ratings must be reasonably similar for the average to be meaningful. These forms give the trainee access to the pupils' average perception of "clarity of aims," "planning," "presentation," "interest," and other dimensions of teaching effectiveness.

Supervisor and peer criticism

Video playbacks can be viewed most advantageously with the help of a supervisor. The conclusion reached at Stanford was that considerable restraint is required in order to avoid calling attention to too many different aspects of performance. The supervisor can point out one or two features and the teacher-trainee is able to integrate these suggestions with less confusion. It is possible, however, that when systematic coding is combined with video, the display of data can guide a more comprehensive analysis of the performance. With experienced teachers, coding procedures may be even more important in helping the trainee make his own decisions about what might be altered in the next reteaching performance. In any such feedback setting, there are the usual problems of creating a helping climate, mutual trust, and establishing a problem orientation that is as free as possible from defensiveness. This is not easily accomplished.

Setting up comparisons

A great contribution of microteaching, with or without video, is that the procedure sets a pattern of comparing two or more performances by the same teacher. This innovation has great significance in a profession in which supervisors still confer with teachers after a single visit and wonder why such conferences are sometimes ineffective. The orientation of problem-solving, analysis, and growth develops much faster by repeating teaching-reteaching cycles. The experience of living through a change is acted out and accepted as the normal procedure of self-development.

THE EXPECTED OUTCOMES OF MICROTEACHING FEEDBACK

The expected outcome of a successful microteaching clinic program is not only change in teaching behavior, but changes that lead to more effective classroom instruction. Just how consistently such positive results can be expected will require more research than has so far been completed. The early returns from the Stanford preservice program are in the right direction and statistically significant. Stanford students in the 1963 microteaching clinic were compared with a control group following a more traditional course of teacher preparation; three out of four subgroup comparisons supported higher supervisor ratings for those in microteaching when post-training performance during the intern year was the criterion; the fourth comparison was not significant. There was no control group in 1964, but those receiving higher ratings during summer microteaching practice were more likely to perform more effectively during internship teaching, compared with below average college students (2, pp. 4–7).

Microteaching feedback has the potential to be particularly well adapted to reinforcing the teacher who is attempting self-development. The supervisor critique and pupil ratings can show the trainee when he is or is not making progress. The need to train pupils in making ratings for about 4 hours and a system of pupil rotation that eliminates rater bias were important features of the Stanford training design that were mentioned earlier.

COMBINING INTERACTION ANALYSIS WITH MICROTEACHING

Assume, for the moment, that microteaching is performed not only with a video recorder, but in the presence of a person who could code the interaction on a time line display. If the categories and the display could highlight features of teaching that were being practiced, then there would be several advantages. First, an inspection of the time line display before the video playback could focus attention at particular points. This advantage, for example, might lead the trainee and the observer to agree that it was at the 2-minute point and thereafter that teacher questions began to stimulate pupil initiation. During the subsequent playback, special attention could be given to the questions before and after this point. Second, coding behavior removes some of the vagueness that is inherent in more broadly stated microteaching objectives. For example, "set induction" presumably refers to anything and all things that the teacher can do to interest pupils in school work. There are, however, specific things that a teacher can do to hook the interests and abilities of a pupil to a learning task. A discussion of these teacher actions would be necessary in order to select appropriate categories for coding. In fact, the data in a time line display should take on a particular configuration if the teacher satisfies his own self-development objectives. These discussions and arrangements might help to make microteaching a more potent training experience than would be true without interaction analysis.

Programs which combine systems of coding verbal communication with microteaching have been implemented at a number of centers. According to Amidon and Rosenshine (4) a training program of this type was carried out at Temple University in 1961. In 1967 and 1968 programs were further developed at Temple by Rosenshine and Furst and at the University of California at Davis by Minnis. The major advantage reported by those who conducted the programs was the greater specification of the skill to be practiced and more objective information about the performance itself.

Configurations of interaction analysis data which occurred during microteaching depend on the type of display selected, but the same observation procedures and the identical display format can be used when a teacher attempts to apply the same skills in a total class setting. In moving into the classroom and to longer periods of teaching, video playback becomes time consuming and therefore inefficient. Interaction analysis feedback is faster and can focus on specific skills providing the behavior patterns can be identified in the display format.

It is quite possible that interaction analysis combined with microteaching would provide a potent training procedure for helping to develop and control teaching behavior. For example, consider the following science fiction.

The scene occurs in the video playback room of a behavior analysis laboratory. At the moment, Kathy and Margie, two college students who have yet to start their student teaching, are completely absorbed with large sheets of computer printout. The playback machine is warmed up and ready nearby. Kathy slowly slides a plastic overlay across the rows of computer printout. The two girls had made the overlays to illustrate an interaction pattern in the same form of display which was programmed for the computer. Her hand stops.

"Here's one, Margie! It's a perfect 8, 3, 3, 3, 9, 9, 9! Right here, at 2 minutes out."

Her hand moved on. Now Margie pointed, as the overlay paused.

"Yes. And there are two more. One at about 3 minutes and the other at almost 4. Each pattern ends with a long string of 9's!'

"Let's turn on the recorder," said Kathy, "and see how it happened."

Margie turned on the video, and Kathy started the stop watch. After $2\frac{1}{2}$ minutes their attention intensified. Just after the 3 minute point, Margie stopped the playback.

"You did it with Bobby, Kathy. You compared his answer with what Janet said, and then Bobby took off. His interpretation became almost an extended explanation. That was a good one!" said Margie.

They started the playback again and studied the interaction at both the $3\frac{1}{2}$- and 4-minute points. Kathy was the first to speak.

"That last pattern is an artifact. I goofed, but came up smelling like roses. I introduced my own idea for comparison rather than enlarge on something the kids had said. It isn't a pure pupil idea comparison, so you should have coded it 8, 3, 4, 4, 9, 9, 9."

"I guess you're right," said Margie, "but Jimmie gave you a string of 9's just the same, even if you didn't produce the practice pattern of 3's. You know, that's kind of interesting. Maybe your first two successful patterns established the expectation that kids could introduce their own ideas so that when you introduced your own, they felt free to use them or not, or even introduce their own. Jim must have felt independent enough to incorporate your ideas with his own. *He* was mimicking your behavior by giving *you* 3's! Hey, maybe this is a new principle of teaching!"

Kathy thought for a moment. "You mean," she said, "that attending initially to pupil ideas sets the expectation that they are free to express their own point of view so that when we introduce our own ideas later on, it doesn't hang up the kids?"

"Yeah," said Margie, "it is kind of like a positive fallout."

How could such a scene come to pass? Suppose a week before Kathy and Margie, along with 500 other junior students, had participated in massed audience, simulated skill practice, under the direction of the course instructor. Patterns of interaction which partners were later to practice in microteaching had been introduced and discussed. The instructor illustrates several model patterns, and these are practiced by each student as others act as observers and as foils. The observers learned to use a time line display, how to make overlays, and how to compare expected patterns with computer printouts. During the microteaching, all interaction is coded directly into a computer as well as video recorded. Each college student works with an inquiry partner and they investigate their own interaction patterns.

SUMMARY OF APPLYING INTERACTION ANALYSIS TO OTHER FEEDBACK TECHNIQUES

The procedures of T-groups, simulated social skill training, and microteaching have been briefly described. In each case, speculations were made concerning the possible advantages of using interaction analysis as a part of the feedback. A summary of each procedure is given below.

THE T-GROUP

Nature of the feedback.   There is a direct encounter with how others perceive your behavior. The consequences of attitudes and feelings are explored. Learning how to accept and to provide a helping relationship is practiced under conditions which require considerable initiative. For a few, very intense feedback can provide relatively deep insights.

Advantages.   A successful experience creates a readiness for self-appraisal. Sensitivity to the behavior of others is likely to increase. New concepts for thinking about intent and action are learned. Understanding of self increases.

Disadvantages.   The transfer of subjective insights about self to classroom practice is difficult. A good many manhours are required before potent and skillful feedback occurs. The possibilities of identifying small steps toward more effective teaching are not necessarily altered and reinforcement while practicing each step is unlikely. The qualifications of a competent T-group trainer are quite rigorous.

SIMULATED SOCIAL SKILL TRAINING (SSST)

Nature of the feedback.   One's ability to produce a behavior pattern associated with a concept is evaluated by peer opinion and by interpreting data from coded behavior. Perceptions about what occurred can be compared. Receiving and giving helpful suggestions about behavior patterns are practiced.

Advantages. The difference between talking about teaching behavior and producing it is in contrast. Teaching skills relevant to the classroom can be practiced in an order of increasing difficulty. First attempts by peers to create a helping relationship can occur in a situation that does not affect pupils. Content objectives are not involved.

Disadvantages. The quality of the simulation depends on the ability of group members. Simulation may not be realistic, especially in terms of the classroom. How present activities relate to long range self-development goals must be clearly understood.

MICROTEACHING

Nature of the feedback. Video provides a realistic picture of one's own behavior. Behavior is compared with previously stated objectives. Supervisor and peer opinions about teaching behavior are shared. Criticism can lead to plans for improvement.

Advantages. Teaching objectives and live pupils add to the realism. Total class responsibility is avoided during practice. Teach-reteach permits direct comparisons to assess step by step improvement. Reinforcement after a success is almost immediately apparent. Practice can move from the simple to the more complex skills. Pupil ratings are possible.

Disadvantages. Equipment failure, especially video recording, can be troublesome. Behavior analysis may not be appropriately conceptualized before playback. Organization of the pupil pool and equipment utilization require thorough planning. Microteaching is not appropriate for long teaching strategies.

INTERACTION ANALYSIS CODING WITH CATEGORIES

Nature of the feedback. A coded display of single behavior acts is provided, in some cases as soon as interaction ceases. Summary data or time line displays focus on previously selected concepts.

Advantages. In simple applications it requires only pencil and paper forms. The display can be designed to be compared with a coded model. Observation is systematic, programmed, and its reliability can be determined. Long segments of teaching in the regular classroom can be efficiently displayed.

Disadvantages. Skill in observation requires practice. In some instances tedious clerical work is required. Major aspects of the situation are ignored.

Chapter Nine

ELEMENTS OF A CURRICULUM FOR CONTINUING PROFESSIONAL SELF-DEVELOPMENT

STARTING FROM THE PRESENT

Continuing, professional self-development is a kind of perpetual inquiry, a way of living in which there is a readiness to investigate problems and the will to mobilize the necessary resources. Each of us begins where he is now, designs a project, carries it out, and then pauses to assess progress before starting the next project. These self-development activities form cycles and, if you'll forgive a pun, mounting a cycle is a good way to move from where you are to some point farther down the road.

With increasing skill, each investigation becomes a little better, more rewarding, so that individuals accumulate more than one year of progress during a school year. In order to achieve above average professional growth it is necessary to (a) acquire new tools for analyzing behavior—earlier chapters have been concerned with this topic, (b) design projects of self-inquiry which make use of these tools—this chapter describes ways to organize such projects, (c) create growth opportunities in terms of time, space, and social support—opinions about how these necessities can be nurtured are expressed in subsequent chapters, and (d) find a more potent system of incentives that rewards self-development—each individual has this task to solve in his own way. Perhaps an odd comment, on some page, or even the general impact of this book, can help trigger the personal resolve and commitment that are necessary.

REVIEW AND OVERVIEW

In Chapter 1 it was suggested that the *means* of self-development shape behavior, influence feelings and attitudes, and most directly determine success and failure. In the proposals that follow, the *means* are actions of inquiry in which one's own behavior is an object of inquiry. For this to happen, freedom, self-direction, independence, and the absence of imposed threat seem essential because it is difficult to approach one's own behavior with objectivity under the best of circumstances, much less under conditions of restriction or coercion. In order to have *means* with more favorable characteristics, *the unit of action proposed for self-development is a special partnership in inquiry*, in which two college students or two teachers help each other. A few will prefer to work alone, occasionally trios or quartets may form, and there should be freedom for this to happen. To facilitate and support these action units, cooperative study teams of four to eight persons are recommended which could permit the partnerships to be rotated when necessary. Freedom to form fresh liasons in an effort to improve working relationships probably has more advantages than disadvantages.

In our colleges and universities, it is within the power of the faculty to organize education courses so that self-development through personal inquiry can occur. Student study teams can be supported through large meetings for all the teams. The teams, in turn, can hold meetings to hear proposals, progress reports, and tentative conclusions from the projects that partners investigate. All of these arrangements could also be made in a public school system, even though there would be restrictions to the number of teachers who could participate.

In Chapter 1 three commitments to the development of inquiry were suggested. (1) The procedures which are followed to help a teacher change his behavior should be consistent with those that the teacher will subsequently carry out to help his pupils learn. (2) Both teacher educators as well as classroom teachers may wish to increase the opportunities for independent action during prfessional learning to the fullest extent that is compatible with ability and developing self-control. (3) To correct for misconceptions in our present knowledge, those who inquire into teaching may wish to promote convictions developed from personal experience, values that are open to subsequent reformulation, and habits of self-direction that are deeply rooted in skepticism and curiosity. The proposals in this chapter are designed with these commitments in mind.

Facilitating partnerships for inquiry is most appropriate to studying education because the helping processes which occur during work are, by their very nature, teaching functions. Working with a difficult partner has much of the excitement that can come when gifted pupils cause teachers to learn. Using data collecting tools to gather relevant information and directing one's own investigations are processes which have great value in the classroom. These processes should be experienced as early and as often as possible. To question one's own findings, to compare one's own conclusions with what others have found are activities which spring from a curious and skeptical nature.

THE COGNITIVE AND AFFECTIVE DOMAINS OF INQUIRY

Cognitions consist of thoughts in our head and affective sensations are said to be emotions which we feel. In the history of psychology it has sometimes been more fashionable and sometimes less fashionable to argue about what comes first, the sensation or our perception of it. In a somewhat similar fashion, it has been customary to discuss classroom interaction in terms of its cognitive components and at other times the same behavior is discussed in terms of its affective components—which is to say that we are sometimes concerned with thinking and at other times with feelings. Progress in the analysis of classroom interaction has reached a point at which it is no longer quite so satisfactory to keep our consideration of behavior in such cleanly separated compartments. In terms of the past, Simon and Boyer (89, Vol. I) seem justified in classifying systems of interaction analysis into "affective systems (which) deal with the emotional climate of the classroom by coding how the teacher reacts to the feelings, ideas, work efforts or actions of the pupil" (p. 1) and "cognitive systems, on the other hand, (which) deal with the thinking process itself" (p. 2). They go on to cite observation systems which involve some categories for affective discriminations and others for cognitive discriminations. However, even a cursory inspection of the 26 observation systems which are included in the Simon and Boyer anthology will reveal that this classification is rather arbitrary. For example, almost any set of so called logical categories can deal with feelings and attitudes as objects of inquiry, and strategies of teaching—which by definition have logical elements—can be built from so called affective systems, such as the 10 categories of the FIAC system.

Even though we may continue to theorize about the cognitive and affective components of classroom interaction separately, either one alone is incomplete so that considering both results in theories that apply more realistically to what goes on in the classroom. Teachers and pupils think about their feelings and often feel strongly about thoughts. Researchers and those who would help others improve teaching will have to learn how to take both into consideration. B. O. Smith (90) reminds us that:

In Dewey's view, logic is gounded in inquiry. The rules of successful inquiry are the rules of logic. And successful inquiry is inquiry which resolves perplexing situations. The rules of inquiry are derived by analyzing what is done as perplexing situations are worked out. (p. 7)

With this as a clue, perhaps "learning how to synthesize the affective and the cognitive" will require that both be taken into consideration in our observations and then analyzed logically as best we can. In addition, the process itself, what we are doing, must become an object of inquiry. Later on in this chapter, coding systems which consider both components simultaneously are described and applications are given to illustrate possible approaches.

Classroom interaction as thinking and feeling

We can begin by asserting that *every pattern of interaction has a cognitive and an affective component. To understand what goes on in the classroom is to take both into consideration.* So long as improved classroom performance is the goal of the teacher self-development, the question of how much emphasis is to be placed on either component during the various phases of professional growth becomes a matter for experimentation.

One way to explain the need for synthesizing our analysis of feelings and thinking during classroom interaction is to consider the problem in terms of educational outcomes. Teachers and curriculum consultants are becoming increasingly aware of the need to teach rules for thinking about a particular subject matter rather than be overly concerned with content coverage. This has been due, in part, to such innovations as the new curricula in mathematics, science, and other fields. The argument can be made that the rules of thinking about arithmetic transfer to problems faced in the future more effectively than specific facts and drill in problem-solving. In order to implement this trend, teachers try to make pupils self-conscious about rules for thinking in a particular subject matter field and may even arrange to help pupils discover some of them. The recognition, analysis, and general application of rules for thinking produce interaction patterns which are different compared with a narrow content emphasis.

At the same time, teachers and supervisors are becoming more sensitive to the balance of teacher initiation versus pupil initiation and the skills that are involved in recognizing and making use of ideas expressed by pupils. This trend may be due, in part, to research on classroom interaction. It is possible, but not common, for teachers to solicit the opinions of pupils in deciding how opportunities for initiative and self-direction can be used most effectively by pupils. Such solicitations can also be discerned from an analysis of classroom interaction.

The cognitive and affective components come together when it is discovered that certain teaching patterns may, under one set of circumstances, be seen as teacher initiative, yet under other circumstances, be seen as teacher response. For example, Flanders (41) hypothesized that when a teacher provides the next step in the logical solution to a problem, this may simply produce unthinking compliance when a pupil does not have a clear picture of the end product of the work, but if the pupil knows that he needs a particular kind of suggestion, asks the teacher and receives it, then one result may be to clear the way for more pupil initiative. In other words, a simple cognition, stated by the teacher, can have a different affective component depending on the pupil's readiness.

There have been a number of researchers who have analyzed the logic of classroom discourse. Some category systems used in research on cognitive variables make such elaborate distinctions that an analysis of written typescripts plus video recording is required. Other systems which can be used in live classroom observation make less complicated and more gross distinctions. As long as individuals begin the study of classroom interaction at various levels of skill and with different degrees of understanding, then flexible category clusters have the advantage of permitting a person to choose category clusters which match his skills, whether they be cognitive or affective.

One might begin by distinguishing between simple statements of fact, statements which are known to involve logical relationships other than stating facts, and a catchall category called "unknown." At the same time that some kind of discrimination is taking place in the cognitive domain, it is also possible to make discriminations about feelings, attitudes, and the freedom of pupils to show initiative. Ways of combining both components have been discussed in Chapter 5 in terms of subscripting and in Chapter 6 in terms of category clusters.

Self-development, success, and the inquiring partnership

Feelings of confidence can spring from appropriate, affective reassurance from a partner or a teacher, but perhaps an even more potent source is personal proof of cognitive competence. Such experiences seem possible at any age level. Thus, a teacher can encourage and support the activities of a pupil in order to develop confidence, but this tentative confidence becomes more certain for a pupil when he *knows* that a task can be accomplished because of personal success on a similar task previously completed. Those of us who tend to focus our attention on the affective aspects of interaction, and often see similarities between a teacher and a therapist, may be more prone to overlook the therapeutic value of success in cognitive problem-solving on the individual child. Similarly, one success in the development and control of teaching behavior becomes a potent source of optimism and confidence about the next step when a college student or employed teacher analyzes his own teaching behavior.

In the procedures which are to be described, both the cognitive and affective aspects of self-directed inquiry combine to create confidence or the lack of it. It seems reasonable to suppose that reassurance and mutual support between inquiry partners will be most crucial during the initial and early self-development projects. In later stages of the program, confidence based on competence in analyzing teaching behavior and designing inquiry projects is added to mutual support and reassurance. Thus, incentive and persistent drive in continuing self-development are the result of initial support and are followed by increased competence.

One implication of this discussion for a curriculum of professional self-development is that the early inquiry projects of a college student or an employed teacher should be carefully designed so that task requirements match the skills of the participants. The design of the first projects may involve a rather delicate balance in which the project should be easy enough to increase the chances of success, yet involve experiences and conclusions about teaching which are worthwhile and rewarding.

A GENERAL PROCEDURE FOR PROFESSIONAL SELF-DEVELOPMENT

The general procedure about to be described is very simple and contains just five steps. These steps might be followed during initial, less complicated projects, as well as later on when more complex problems and more difficult skills are investigated. As mentioned earlier, these steps are proposed for partners, even though one person or more than two could be involved. Such small action units, in turn, would be supported by study teams of four to eight persons. Plans for projects, reports of progress, and consultation about tentative conclusions would be possible topics of study group meetings. These study groups, in turn, would be supported at universities by a teaching staff and in the public schools by consultants on inservice training. Large audience meetings of all teams would be useful for original orientation, for learning skills which all participants need, and for providing support, incentive, and a "total perspective" to the activities of the individual.

Perhaps the most important question on which we have no definitive information is: When should data collecting skills be taught to college students and employed teachers who are about to embark on such a program? The teaching of these skills comes as close to a natural learning activity as any of the laboratory experiences in biological, physical, or engineering sciences. Interaction analysis, microteaching, and to a certain extent simulated skill practice can be taught and learned in the context of problem-solving with attendant excitement and interest. This would argue for mastering these skills, at least to a minimum performance, before forming action units and study teams. Professor Douglas Minnes,* University of California at Davis, said that he would "prefer to teach interaction analysis early in teacher education even if the only benefit was the efficiency of the language. But, of course, there are more benefits than just that." Which is to say that a category system permits a great deal to be communicated about teaching behavior with relatively few words, both by the trainee and the person who conducts the training. This issue will be discussed in greater detail in Chapter 11, but there is some evidence to support the notion that training in coding can and should take place prior to self-directed inquiry projects.

---

*Personal communication during an interview at Davis, July 1967.

FIVE STEPS* OF THE INQUIRY PROJECT

Step One.   The partner asks the "teacher" to specify a pattern of *target pupil behavior* he would like to have in his class.

Step Two.   The partner helps the teacher identify two or more patterns of *teaching behavior* which would complement or fit such pupil behavior in order to obtain a reasonable chain of classroom communication events.

Step Three.   The partner would work with the teacher to *practice the required teaching behavior patterns* in simulated social skill training and/or micro-teaching. Interaction would be coded, and if the equipment was available, recorded on video tape.

Step Four.   At the same time that the activities of Step Three were occurring, the partners would *design a way for testing the relationships* which are presumed to exist between the target pupil behavior and the complementary teaching behavior. With two alternative teaching patterns, this test can compare one pattern with the other to see which was more effective under regular classroom conditions. The partner, of course, would help to collect the necessary data and might be called the "observer-helper."

Step Five.   *The plan is carried out* in a regular classroom. During the analysis of the data, the first check would probably be to see if the desired target pupil behavior did in fact occur. Similar analyses would be made to see if the teaching patterns were present. The *results would be discussed thoughtfully* in terms of the relationships between teaching and pupil reactions which were presumed to exist. As unanswered questions arise, plans for testing them through further empirical exploration are considered.

Each of these steps is now discussed in greater detail.

Specifying the target pupil behavior—step one

It appears to be a little easier for all concerned† when the early projects start by talking about pupil behavior rather than teaching behavior. A teacher acts in order to produce desired effects and to start with the target behaviors leads naturally to a discussion of teaching strategies and teaching behavior.

In a well-organized curriculum for college students, the initial explorations might be determined by an instructor or some resource materials, but after a few initial experiences, the opportunity to design inquiry cycles without the

---

*The author is indebted to Dr. Lilburn Hoehn and members of the Michigan-Ohio Regional Education Laboratory (MOREL) for the opportunity of discussing these five steps, 1968.

†Based on the 1968 experience of the MOREL program team.

restrictive suggestions would permit the college student to experience more independent self-development. The same need for initial guidance and increasing independence is probably present in the continuing education of employed teachers.

The target pupil behaviors first suggested for an inquiry project are often too complex for the skills and resources of the teacher in training, and this provides a special function for the partner. He can help by asking the teacher to identify not one, but perhaps a half-dozen target pupil behaviors that are of interest. These initial suggestions will probably vary widely in terms of vagueness, a potential relationship to teaching behavior, and the possibilities for specifying overt pupil behavior. The partner helps the teacher become more and more precise in identifying the behavioral characteristics involved. For example, a teacher might say he would like to have his pupils become more interested in school-work. The partner can ask what the teacher means. In the give and take of conversation, a sequence of concepts showing increased behavioral specificity is identified, starting from more pupil interest, to actively participating, to pupils making their own suggestions (or alternatively, to a higher percentage of pupils talking), to the pupils expressing their own opinions, facts, and conclusions. It is the responsibility of this partnership to arrive at a behavioral meaning that is so clear that the target behavior can be easily identified and coded.

We might note, just in passing, that when both partners are fluent in the three "languages" of behavioral English, observation code patterns, and display formats (see Chapter 4) the planning and execution of these investigations are likely to be much faster and probably more effective due to more powerful inquiry skills. In any case, there are distinct advantages to having the languages and concepts of interaction analysis as early as possible.

The two partners together develop the behavioral meaning of three or four of the target pupil behaviors. *One* is finally selected after talking about the consequences in terms of the activities to follow in steps three, four, and five. Actually, steps one and two are intermixed during the initial phases of planning as we shall see in a moment.

Specifying the complementary teaching behaviors—step two

As soon as either partner asks how a teacher might facilitate the target pupil behaviors, the planning conversation has moved into step two. The dialogue between a teacher and his associate is not always orderly, so that complementary teaching behavior may be discussed before the behavioral meaning of the target pupil behavior has been made clear. Working back and forth between pupil and teaching behavior and then gradually working on the behavioral meaning of both is quite natural. In this way steps one and two are quite often discussed together.

Perhaps the most important function of the partner is to ask the teacher, "Why do you think so?" whenever relationships between pupil behavior and teaching behavior are suggested. Other helpful questions are "Give me an example" or "Let's go over that one step at a time." It is in this fashion that principles of teaching are created in a tentative form, a form that lends itself to investigation.

One purpose of step two is to identify several alternative teaching patterns which would presumably facilitate a particular target pupil behavior. There are several advantages to having alternatives, but perhaps the most important is that they provide greater freedom in reaching the most effective design of the inquiry. Perhaps an example will help to illustrate.

Suppose the teacher proposes that the target behavior is to have pupils contribute their own ideas and conclusions more often during classroom discussion. Both partners then offer suggestions about how a teacher might facilitate such behavior. A number of proposals are made: (a) asking broad questions, (b) merely asking "why?" more often, (c) increase the proportion of Category 3—accepting and making use of ideas expressed by pupils, (d) making use of the special case of Category 3 in which one pupil's ideas are consciously compared with ideas another pupil has expressed, (e) restricting the kind of information (Category 5) which the teacher is allowed to express when pupils are confronted with a problem, and (f) any of a number of more cognitively oriented strategies involving shifting the level of abstraction. These are all features of teaching behavior which can be controlled. Each might facilitate the target pupil behavior, but one or another may be most effective and appropriate in a particular setting. Identifying several target pupil behaviors and then suggesting several alternative patterns of teaching behavior for each target pattern helps by providing more alternatives for Step Four when the procedure is designed.

Sometimes a teacher feels uncomfortable about analyzing his own behavior and will unconsciously reflect this by proposing ways to facilitate the target behavior that are not directly concerned with teaching behavior; for example, the pupils will become more interested if we use different instructional materials. The investigation of this relationship might not involve analyzing teaching actions during class discussion. Another symptom of this concern is to propose that a target behavior can be facilitated by grouping pupils differently, changing seating arrangements, or making use of periods of self-directed activity. With patient questions, the teacher's partner can try to discover whether or not a teacher is ready to study his own interaction. The problem is less awkward when there are several alternatives among target behaviors and in addition, among the suggestions for facilitating each target behavior. In the long run, the best way to help a teacher study his own behavior may be to work through the first investigation on whatever terms the teacher finds acceptable.

The ideal outcomes of steps one and two include (a) having several alternative target pupil behaviors, (b) having several suggestions for facilitating each target behavior that involves teaching behavior, and (c) having several possible settings in mind in which a single relationship between teaching behavior and pupil behavior might be tested. When a teacher is hard pressed to make choices among these alternatives because he is really interested in several, the seeds for the next investigation have already been sown and a step toward continuing self-development has been taken.

Practicing teaching patterns and skills—step three

Awareness of a particular teaching pattern during the discussion of steps one and two does not necessarily ensure that the teacher is prepared to produce the pattern while teaching in the classroom. Practice in producing particular patterns is especially helpful for the inexperienced and the unsure; it improves the quality of the investigation by sharpening the teaching patterns to be compared.

Practice can take place with adults using simulated social skill practice or with pupils in a microteaching clinic. Video playback may not be essential, but some kind of "instant" feedback is necessary to assess behavior. If two patterns of teaching behavior were selected in steps one and two, these two patterns should be consistently performed yet different in character in order to set up a logical contrast which is the product of step four. It is for this reason that steps three and four can take place simultaneously; in fact, one of the best places to carry out the planning of step four is in an active microteaching clinic. During these sessions, the teacher practices and purifies the patterns of teaching behavior which are to be investigated.

Besides the teacher, the partner may need practice in collecting data. The development of convictions from personal experience is facilitated by analyzing data. These data need to be as reliable and objective as possible. The teacher's partner may need practice in coding the relevant behaviors just as the teacher may want to practice performing them. In fact, it is quite possible that the observer is more in need of training than the teacher. Not only is there need to practice using certain categories accurately, but there is often a need to make decisions about the display format. This is particularly true when category subscripts are used or when multiple coding with category clusters is used. Observation training should be continued until the particular pattern of interaction being investigated can be coded with reasonable accuracy.

Progress in self-development depends on feeding back information to the teacher-actor which reflects what actually happened, which shows that certain behaviors did or did not occur, and whether certain predicted relationships are to be accepted or rejected. *The observer, therefore, always codes the behavior patterns that occurred and must carefully guard against recording patterns merely because they were anticipated.* To provide false information is much worse than a waste of time, it leads to invalid conclusions about principles of teaching and to incorrect conclusions about the teacher's progress.

There may be resistance to practice on the part of a self-confident college student or an experienced teacher who feels that it is a waste of time. After social skill practice, I have heard teachers say, "I already use that pattern in my class," or college students say, "I know about that already." This reaction is difficult to understand especially when it refers to certain skills that are known to be of very low incidence in classroom interaction. Those who have these reactions are either unusually gifted teachers or they misjudge the quality of their total patterns while teaching.

Under the best of conditions, step three helps to solve several problems simultaneously. First, a teacher can practice a particular pattern under ideal feedback conditions, notice any improvement in his performance on teach-reteach cycles, develop more suitable lesson plans and subject matter topics, and sharpen the differences between two settings or two patterns that are to be compared. Meanwhile, the observer can become more proficient in coding, particularly if special coding procedures are required, and can settle problems concerned with the display of the data.

Designing a plan of inquiry—step four

Knowledge and skill in teaching can come from accidental insights, but it is more likely to be the product of planned inquiry. Plans for inquiry are made primarily to achieve efficiency, to obtain the maximum insight per unit of energy expended, and to make sure the activities match the interests and abilities of the participants. Inquiry need not be formal, in the sense of precise research, instead, it can be conducted at whatever level of care and logic that can be mustered. Inquiry skills result from experience. To begin is to start experiencing.

The quality of inquiry is greatly influenced by how cleverly *comparisons* are built into the analysis of results. A teacher, for example, may be interested in higher motivation. The behavioral meaning of motivation is that pupils know the first steps of a learning task, find the purposes and activities attractive, and tend to persist in work, once it is started. The question to be investigated may be to decide if motivation is higher when (a) the objectives and procedures for reaching them are first stated clearly by the teacher and then followed by questions from the pupils, versus (b) using general questions first, then shifting to more narrow questions, and ending with a clear statement of the objective and procedures. The way to find out is to conduct inquiry. Plans are made to practice introductions in a microteaching session, learn how the relevant interaction is to be coded and displayed, design some simple observations about pupil persistence, and perhaps some short questions to which pupils can mark their interest in the work. The data are collected and analyzed, and the results are compared with ideas which can be found in books and with the opinions of colleagues which are expressed in thoughtful conversations.

The by-products of these activities may be as important as the immediate results. A teacher will have designed and then tried to implement a strategy which calls for self-control in asking and sequencing questions. A partner learns skills of data collecting. They both may learn that some unanticipated factor turned out to be more important and that the design did not permit logical conclusions. No matter how it turns out, the activities comprise professional inquiry into interaction events.

Perhaps the biggest difficulty in self-directed inquiry is that college students and teachers alike often expect to be told how best to teach. A frequent request from many sincere teachers and students is to be taught how to do something by a person who is qualified to give the advice and instruction. The "expert" is asked to come by and see if "I'm doing it right." Value judgments of right and wrong are very pervasive and can dominate the development of skills. Whenever inquiry designs fail to provide for interesting comparisons and only one set of events is in focus, then no logical plan guides the analysis. The questions most likely to be asked are, "Was it satisfactory?" "What did you think of it?" "Was it all right?" Our long adherence to the apprentice system in education has left us with a legacy of high dependency when a subordinate works with a superior. Our nearly universal desire to maintain this dependency is not very well hidden by the old adage—say something nice first before you make critical suggestions, a psychology that is probably more deluding to the supervison than it is to the teacher. It is hardly a surprise when teachers carry this same emphasis on value judgments into the classroom in their work with pupils.

There is a problem of efficiency, of course, when one sets out to discover an insight, compared with simply asking an expert. Some educators believe that experienced teachers, research workers, and knowledgeable persons can save precious time and energy by simply providing their advice. The position taken here is that most inquiry experiences can be organized so that each generation of new teachers builds on the knowledge already available rather than starting from scratch and still preserve the learner's right to rediscover.

At this point it can be said that step four, intermixed with step three, has as its purpose the design of a creative plan of inquiry which strikes at the heart of a problem. Many features of this design were illustrated in the discussion of subscripting categories, to be found in Chapter 5. In brief, a logical comparison is created to test the consequences of two different interaction patterns. Certain target pupil behaviors are identified, complementary teaching behaviors which facilitate pupil behavior are suggested, and the plan of inquiry is designed to provide information which can be the basis for forming judgments about the relationships being investigated. Perhaps more important, the participants have the experience of attempting to develop and control particular patterns of teaching behavior, to conduct inquiry about teaching, and to develop attitudes which are associated with independence while learning.

Collecting and analyzing the data—step five

Once the plans are completed and all preparations made, the teacher and his partner carry out the inquiry in the classroom. Interaction analysis data and perhaps information from the pupils' point of view are collected and arranged for analysis.

The analysis can begin with the basic questions identified in steps one and two. Did the target pupil behavior occur? What is the evidence? Did the complementary teaching behavior occur? What is the evidence? Can any inferences be drawn from the comparisons which were built into the design? For example, was there a higher incidence of the target pupil behavior when one or another kind of teaching behavior was present?

Perhaps the best reason for suggesting that two or more persons conduct inquiry together is that each person can help the other clarify the more subjective aspects of the experience. Besides attending to the cognitive problem of analyzing teacher-pupil interaction, step five provides an opportunity to identify and discuss how the teacher felt about his teaching role, how the partner assisted the teacher in gaining self-insight, how the *process* of this kind of working relationship might be improved, and similar matters. In the same sense that a teacher seeks to be somewhat self-conscious about his own actions so that his self-control in the classroom has a professional orientation, the partnership in the conduct of inquiry exists to add perspective to the subjective elements of self-development. One way to facilitate this aspect of conducting inquiry is to set aside time near the end of step five to recapture feelings and perceptions, to discuss and explore their meaning, and to interpret them in terms of what was or was not accomplished. The *process* of self-development can also be an object of inquiry!

SUMMARIZING THE STEPS OF A CYCLE OF SELF-DEVELOPMENT

These five steps of inquiry into teaching behavior represent a cycle that can be repeated. Initial efforts may be very informal, perhaps unsuccessful, and limited by the experience and skill of the participants. In subsequent cycles the quality of the experience should improve. One begins, however, by trying. The objectives are increased skill in the control of teaching behavior, increased knowledge about teacher-pupil interaction, and strengthened attitudes and convictions about independence and self-direction during learning.

CURRICULUM ELEMENTS FOR PROFESSIONAL SELF-DEVELOPMENT

Perhaps the best curriculum for learning anything is one which is custom built for the person who carries out the learning activities. It is here that the maturity of an adult and his potential for self-direction are advantages. Rather than use this maturity as a rationalization for lecturing, the teacher-educator can demonstrate his confidence in it by creating opportunities in which judgments about what to study next are made by the learner, especially after the initial self-development experiences. The guidance function of the teacher-educator can be expressed in providing alternatives, giving suggestions based on experience, and supporting inquiry projects by directing the training which the observation and data collecting skills require.

Three levels of teaching patterns were mentioned in Chapter 1, consisting of level one—lecture, narrow questions, and giving directions; level two—responding to pupil ideas and asking a wider variety of questions; and level three—using patterns of more advanced social and cognitive teaching skills and making use of models for longer range teaching strategies. It would be unfortunate if this division and the numbering of three levels led to the conclusion that self-development starts at level one and proceeds upward. Although level one patterns predominate in current, average classroom interaction, they are not necessarily the best point at which to begin the analysis and improvement of teaching behavior. It can be recommended that the study of level two patterns has the advantage of using the less complex FIAC system, centers on teaching problems which the participant is more likely to find challenging, but lies within the participant's reach in terms of the skills that are required for investigating the problems.

LEVEL ONE PATTERNS

Level one patterns are concerned primarily with subject matter content and with learning activities which the teacher initiates, directs, and actively supervises. The dominant role of the teacher is characterized by high participation while the pupils are either passive or respond when asked. Most adults already know and seem prepared to perform the teaching behavior which is a part of this level, but as the discussion of level three will reveal, improvement at level one is very urgent and most difficult. As a result, level one patterns are simply described in this section. A discussion of possible self-improvement projects is delayed until level three is discussed.

The lecture pattern

The lecture pattern with narrow questions is illustrated in Fig. 9–1. This pattern might deal only with the subject matter content or it might be concerned with

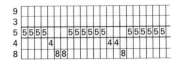

Fig. 9—1.   Time Line Display of Lecture with Narrow Questions*

a topic such as how the class is to be organized in order to accomplish its work. In this pattern it is presumably appropriate for the teacher to be the major spokesman and he checks pupil understanding by asking specific questions from time to time. It is the pupils' responsibility to listen and to provide answers when asked. The structure is created and expedited by the teacher.

The most constructive use of this pattern is likely to occur when the learning goals are clear and attractive, when most of the pupils need the information which is provided by teacher lecture and look forward eagerly to hearing it, when what is said by the teacher is of high quality, and when the information is being applied by pupils in some kind of problem-solving activity before and after the lecture period.

The least constructive use of this pattern occurs when it predominates nearly all total class discussions, is sustained throughout the school day, week, or year, and is not intermixed with situations in which pupils can express their own ideas and opinions.

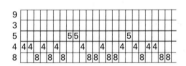

Fig. 9—2.   Time Line Display of Drill and Review.

The drill-review pattern

The drill-review pattern is illustrated in Fig. 9—2. This pattern, like the one above, might be devoted to subject matter content or to the directions which have been given with regard to some class learning activities. The interchange consists of fairly short, narrow questions by the teacher and equally short and rapid answers by the pupils. This drill pattern was discussed in some detail in the first part of Chapter 4.

The most constructive use of this pattern is likely to occur when the pupils understand the purpose of either drill or review, when a game or fun format creates excitement, and when no pupil is made to feel embarrassed

---

*See pp. 161—68 for a discussion of time line displays using the 10-category system.

because of his ability. It is this pattern that most closely approaches the more simple forms of programmed learning materials. It is, therefore, a teaching function which is most likely to be replaced by some form of automation.

The pattern is used least constructively when the opposite conditions prevail, that is, pupils are uninterested, do not understand why they should participate, and when competition is unnecessarily vicious, hurting those who are least able and who are probably most in need of support.

The giving assignments pattern

The giving of assignments fits a pattern which is illustrated in Fig. 9—3. The teacher gives directions and makes assignments in the belief that the pupils will comply. When used properly, it is considered to be a legitimate use of teacher power and authority. The pattern appears as directions or commands which most often determine the kinds of group work, seatwork, and homework which the pupils carry out. The pattern occurs with relatively low incidence except when directions are vague or inappropriate; in which case, they often have to be repeated.

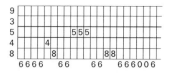

Fig. 9—3.   Time Line Display of Assigning Class Work.

This pattern is used most constructively after some kind of teacher-pupil planning or developmental orientation has created positive anticipation and an acceptable context for the work from the pupils' point of view. This understanding not only includes the nature of the work involved, but is extended to reasons why the teacher chose to initiate the directive rather than arrive at agreements which the pupils see as next steps.

This pattern is used least constructively when it represents an arbitrary use of power, is connected with punishment, and involves work which is not suitable to the abilities and interests of the pupils. A condition that always occurs when the same assignment is given to the entire class.

Summary of level one patterns

One reason that level one patterns have not been the target of programs to improve classroom interaction on any widespread basis is the lack of practical category systems for analyzing the teacher soliloquies which we call "lecture."

The difficulties were made all the more apparent by Smith's (90) scholarly, extensive, and basic investigations of logical thought processes in the classroom. It seems very unlikely that teachers can make direct use of these existing systems for live observation without modification, although reading reports of such investigations would be well worthwhile. Ways around these difficult problems are not yet available, but promising projects are under way.

Meanwhile, there are educators who prefer to view level one problems in terms of teacher domination, rigid patterns which suppress pupil independence, and lack of pupil initiated participation. Those who prefer this point of view can find useful suggestions in the next section where level two is discussed.

LEVEL TWO PATTERNS

Level two patterns appear at those moments when a teacher chooses to extend opportunities to pupils for more self-direction and self-expression. For these patterns to be authentic, the invitation to participate is extended in a way that it can be accepted and acted upon. That is, judging whether these patterns are present or absent depends not only on what a teacher does, but also on how pupils respond.

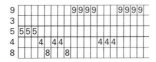

Fig. 9—4.   Time Line Display of Open Questions.

Open questions

One way to loosen up a rigid pattern of interaction, providing this is to be the teacher rather than a pupil prerogative, is to ask questions which invite participation by the pupils. Questions can be very narrow and restrictive; on the other hand they can be very open. The latter offer the respondent alternatives. Perhaps the most open question is, "Would anyone care to add anything?" When the invitation is authentic, any kind of comment is logically acceptable.

The pattern of open questions is illustrated by the 4—9 and 4—8—9—9 transitions in Fig. 9—4. These questions stimulate pupils to express their own ideas and to contribute their own suggestions.

This kind of pattern is most effective when seeking to lift the level of abstraction in order to set an issue in a broader context, when the opinions and reactions of pupils are solicited during the planning or work, and when speculation and explanation is to come from the pupils.

. These patterns are least effective when the details, specific facts, and particular steps of problem-solving are to be designated by the teacher. In "show and tell" or "current events" or "casual conversation about what happened yesterday" pupil talk can be encouraged by open questions, but these questions alone fail to provide logical structure, clarify the meaning of terms, and fail to move the discussion from one logical phase to another. Their *exclusive* use means that the teacher is withdrawing his guidance and influence in the control of thought processes.

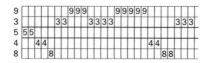

Fig. 9—5.   Time Line Display of Developing Pupil Ideas.

Developing pupil ideas

A teacher can react to the ideas pupils express by acknowledging, clarifying, and using them in the problem-solving process. This pattern is the straight-forward Category 3 and is illustrated in Fig. 9—5. The use of Category 3 was the topic of an analysis problem which began in Chapter 5, and ways to make use of this pattern were discussed in detail on pp. 42, 94, and 127. It might be wise to review these pages at this time. The use of this category involves several skills and it is for this reason that it might be subscripted in more advanced inquiry projects.

The use of this pattern is most effective when a teacher wants to support and reinforce pupil participation, when the ideas expressed by pupils are to be selectively developed during problem-solving, and when a shift from teacher initiated structure to pupil initiation is about to take place. The simple coding system of Categories 3 and 9 is limited and the full development of the skills of making use of ideas expressed by pupils requires more subtle distinctions and more advanced teacher inquiry projects. These are discussed in the section devoted to level three.

This pattern is least effective when the teacher wishes to guide class discussion more actively, rather than less. There are times when he wishes to express his own opinions and ideas, give directions, and take a more active part. There are also moments of readiness when pupils request or in some way need specific information or when pupils solicit a particular action from a teacher. On such occasions this pattern should either be modified or not used.

The skills involved in making use of pupils ideas are, in general, under-developed, in what might be called average teaching. However, the commitment to understanding the pupil and making use of his ideas is usually highly valued by the average teacher. The result is that *this particular pattern is a good point of entry into the analysis of classroom interaction and in helping start a teacher or college student along the path of inquiring into his own teaching behavior.*

"Because" extensions

Perhaps the single most important word in a teacher's lexicon is "because." There are several reasons for this assertion, and considering some examples may help to make them clear. In the examples, notice that the word "because" may not be used literally, but is implied by a "because clause." It is also possible to see that both a dimension of logic and a dimension of reasonableness appear to differentiate the contrasting examples. The logical dimension is discussed separately in a later section.

Praise extension.   There is quite a difference between looking over the shoulder of a pupil at work and saying, "That's a good job, Mary," compared with, "That's a good job, Mary, because you are following the form we discussed earlier," or "That's a good job! Notice how vivid your opening sentence is!" The distinction is that in the first statement no criteria about praise were made public and, to judge only from the teacher's statement, the pupil can conclude only that when he is lucky, the teacher gives praise. This kind of reinforcement does not provide clues for future decisions about behaving. It enhances the authority of the teacher, makes his use of this authority capricious, and some-times interrupts the train of thought of the pupil. Praise without explanation or when given inappropriately led Farson (29) to suggest that praise does not motivate—it may more often threaten rather than reassure a person of his worth—it establishes the superiority of the praiser, and praise may constrict creativity rather than free it. There is much food for thought in the analysis of teacher praise, especially when the reinforcement to pupils may be more effectively given in terms of Categories 1 and 3.

No diagram of extended praise is shown here in order to illustrate a time line display because extended praise appears simply as *more than one* 2 unless some system of subscripting is used. The self-development goal which might be investigated is to reduce the randomness in the incidence of Category 2 and extend a series of 2's whenever praise is given by always clarifying the criteria which makes something praiseworthy. Asking pupils to participate in providing praise is an interesting and worthwhile variation, especially when the pupil explains "why."

Criticism extensions.   Many of the comments made about praise can also be made about criticism. It is one thing to say, "Stop talking!" in an angry fashion and quite another to discuss either rules of conduct that were agreed to earlier or the tasks at hand and how they would be affected by unnecessary talk. Criticism can also be made more effective by at least acknowledging its causes; this can sometimes be done so effectively that it might not be properly coded with Category 7. For example, "Jimmy, you are so enthusiastic and eager to talk that you sometimes forget and interrupt others," is a statement that would be coded with a 1—7 transition, and under certain circumstances and tone of voice, as a 1—1.

The time line pattern of extended constructive criticism usually involves code numbers other than 7, such as 1—1—7—7, or 7—3—3—7, and similar sequences except when subscripts are used.

Extending directions.   Providing reasons for a direction softens the arbitrary use of authority. For example, there is quite a difference between "Please open your books to page 67" and the same direction with the explanation, "Please open your books to page 67 so we can find out how the author describes that part of South America." Extensions of this sort are oriented to a purpose in problem-solving and frequently are concerned with subject matter. It is also possible for extensions to explain why a teacher decides to use his authority, for example, a teacher might say, "Put away your books and materials, boys and girls," or he can say, "Look at the time! We have only a few minutes to clean up before the recess bell."

The time line display models for the extensions of directions would require subscripting, given the basic 10-category system. A series of 6's or shifts from Category 6 to some other category do not provide the information needed. Multiple coding with category clusters can be recommended for this kind of analysis.

Summary of level two patterns

All level two patterns either tend to invite more active pupil participation or tend to soften the use of teacher authority by making it more reasonable, understandable, and less arbitrary. The rationale by which a movement from level one to level two can be considered to be an improvement in instruction runs along the following lines.

While the main business of learning is concerned with subject matter— the knowledge, skills, and attitudes associated with it—*how* the teacher controls the learning activities and manages his own interaction establishes a common expectation among the pupils in spite of their individual differences or differences between classes. These expectations that are held in common have been called "classroom climate" in earlier studies (41) and can be measured by pupil attitude inventories. In groups of comparable classes (e.g., same age level, subject matter, and hopefully of about the same ability) classrooms with higher average class scores on such an attitude inventory are more likely to average around 15 percent level two patterns while classes scoring significantly lower average attitude scores would involve about one-half or $7\frac{1}{2}$ to 8 percent level two, based on teacher talk only.

What needs to be emphasized is that a relatively small increase in level two patterns, from $7\frac{1}{2}$ percent to 15 percent, seems to be associated with more positive pupil attitudes. About the only conclusion from these comparisons that seems warranted from our present knowledge is that a teacher who seeks to move from level one to level two, given our present classroom practices, is attempting to make a small increase in patterns which invite more active pupil participation and tend to soften the use of teacher authority. Yet in *both* high and low attitude classrooms, level one patterns predominate, easily exceeding more than one-half of the interaction.

A second point to emphasize is that any teacher or college student who sets out to alter the balance between level one and level two patterns of classroom interaction, *in the same classroom with the same pupils*, expecting to produce more positive pupil attitudes, is proceeding into unknown territory insofar as our present knowledge is concerned. We do not have objective evidence to show that a teacher can expect to alter pupil attitudes simply by shifting this balance, even though there is a good possibility that this can be done. However, this absence of evidence should make the prospects of the inquiry more rewarding, not less, provided, of course, that there is a genuine spirit of adventure.

Keeping the two foregoing limitations in mind, one might risk experimenting with his own patterns of classroom interaction by attempting to increase the incidence of level two patterns. It would seem reasonable that such a program of self-development might involve finding "safe" settings in which a teacher can practice asking more open questions, clarifying and making use of ideas expressed by pupils, and learning how to extend praise, criticism, and directions during spontaneous interactions with pupils. He then might consider which classroom situations would be most appropriate for trying out these new patterns. Finally, he might try to introduce them into his own classroom with his own pupils. If he has a partner in inquiry and a plan of self-development, he may be in a position to decide for himself whether or not such shifts in classroom interaction patterns do or do not have a perceptible effect on the reactions of pupils.

LEVEL THREE PATTERNS

Level three patterns of classroom interaction can be distinguished from those in the two lower levels because they are more complex. Level three patterns are more complex because the affective and cognitive components of the interaction require some kind of synthesis in order to reach improvements. It is the purpose of this section to clarify what is meant by the affective and the cognitive components of instructional problems by giving examples of inquiry projects, by showing the kinds of interaction analysis data that can be collected, and by suggesting relationships between teaching behavior and pupil behavior that can be investigated.

Independent pupil behavior in the classroom

In our culture, classroom behavior practically invites the interpretation that all pupils and students from kindergarten through graduate school possess a built-in dependence on the authority of the instructor. The maturity and power advantages of a teacher, reinforced by social expectations, are such that the pupil anticipates teacher direction and supervision. Most pupils and students expect to comply to teacher directions, a few expect to resist, and still fewer are indifferent, depending on their past experiences with other authority figures. Pupil self-direction, independence, and initiative are features of learning behavior which run counter to the prevailing patterns of dependency.

When a pupil does what he is asked to do, such as to open a book or close a door upon request, this is an act of compliance. There is a great deal of conditioning along these lines in the life experience of young people, starting with parents and continuing with teachers. This kind of behavior is considered highly desirable by most adults since compliance to the laws of society and conformity to social customs are considered necessary. This pattern of growth presents difficulties to a teacher who would like his pupils to respond to the objective requirements of a problem in creative and independent ways. It is time to question the extent of pupil conformity and compliance which exists in our classrooms. In particular, it is time to investigate how different degrees of compliance match optimum growth toward different educational objectives, to learn how to recognize excessive compliance, and to do more than just speculate about the consequences of maintaining present levels of compliance from one year to the next, throughout the school experience.

One way to describe teaching is to say that the teacher strives to change response patterns of a pupil from mere compliance to more appropriate independent action which is determined by the pupil's own analysis of the problems he confronts. Skillful teaching helps pupils learn to accept responsibility for their own actions. The goal is to have pupils learn to identify problems rather than have them "given," to analyze the problem and plan a tentative course of action rather than follow "a recipe," to carry out the plan with some feelings of responsibility rather than just "follow directions from the teacher or a book," and then to consider the results with some degree of personal judgment rather than "asking the teacher if it is satisfactory." In short, the goal is to help pupils conduct inquiry in a way that is similar to the inquiry being advocated for the self-development of teachers.

At this time not very much is known about the consequences of providing more opportunities for independent and self-directed learning activities in the classroom. When can this be done? How often? How does the teacher design an organized curriculum of increasing self-direction and incorporate these plans into the classroom activities? What about pupils who are excessively dependent prone? Definitive answers to these questions are not available. A teacher who is interested in them can proceed to conduct his own inquiry, but to start he needs a target, such as—*classroom learning activities should involve as much self-direction and independence as the maturity, self-control, and self-directing skills of the pupils will allow; keeping in mind the necessity of total classroom coordination and organization.* On the pages which follow there are suggestions about inquiry projects which will help those who can accept this value.

Teacher responsiveness and pupil initiation

One way to know that you exist is to have your ideas recognized; one way to force another to question the relevance of his presence is to ignore what he says. Often the way this works out in the classroom is illustrated by the following: Teacher: "Billy, what is three times three?" Billy: "Six." Teacher: "Jimmy?" Right after Billy said "Six," he apparently disappeared! Judging by communication, Jimmy simply vanished. Teachers and college students often react to this illustration by saying, "Yes, I know that." But what teachers usually do not realize is how often something like this happens, under what circumstances it happens most often, and whether it happens more often to some pupils than to others.

The problem is not only to hear what pupils say more conscientiously and accurately, it also involves learning those skills of communication which convey to the pupils that his ideas were heard. The teaching behavior which is most likely to achieve this goal is categorized in Category 1, for feelings and in Category 3, for ideas. Successfully used, these statements help a *pupil to know* that his ideas do make a difference because they are being heard and reacted to. Under these circumstances a pupil can begin to learn that there are consequences to expressing ideas and can start practicing the responsibilities that belong to any person who expresses ideas. In the next section, subdivisions of Categories 1 and 3 are listed. This list is similar to the subdivisions made on pp. 133–36, but here the analysis is carried just a bit further.

Types of teacher response.   Verbal statements about pupil feelings and ideas can be either declarative or they can be interrogatory. Both types of statements can be further subdivided according to the following scheme. The teacher can make a statement or form a question which

1) *Acknowledges* the idea or feeling; that is, he merely repeats the nouns and logical connectives that the pupil has just expressed or he simply identifies an expressed feeling.

2) *Modifies* the idea or feeling; that is, the pupil's ideas are rephrased by using synonyms or the pupil's feelings and actions are conceptualized by using the teacher's own words. To fit into this category, the synonyms or concepts must pass the test in which the pupil says, "Yes, that is what I meant," or "That is how I feel."

3) *Applies* the idea or feeling; that is, the teacher uses it either to reach an inference or to take the next step in a logical analysis of a problem. With feelings, he might speculate on how an attitude or feeling could influence work on a task.

4) *Compares* the idea or feeling; that is, the teacher relates what a pupil said or feelings he expressed to what the teacher thinks, to written material, or to the ideas and feelings that another pupil has expressed. In some cases a relationship can be drawn to something the same pupil said earlier.

5) *Summarizes* the ideas or feelings; that is, the teacher makes an inventory of what was said or feelings that were expressed during a preceding period of time. In this case, the activities of several pupils may be involved.

Possible inquiry projects. The above subdivisions of Categories 1 and 3, from the FIAC system, can be used to form new category subscripts. An observer can learn to record these subscripts, making special notations to indicate questions. A possible direct coding time line display, discussed in the next section, can be used with the subscripts. Here we are concerned with the possible inquiry projects which would require such categories.

The first activity would be to practice coding with the subscripts. The partners of an inquiry team could visit each other's classroom; they could jointly visit a third teacher's classroom; they could listen together to voice recordings. No matter which alternative is chosen, the purpose is to practice subscripting in a teaching situation in which the teacher is likely to make above average use of Category 3 type statements. A classroom session of drill, for example, might provide so little practice that the observation would be a waste of time.

A second activity might include some kind of exploratory microteaching. Four or five pupils could be asked to discuss a story they had just finished reading and in this setting the teacher could practice making different kinds of Category 3 statements. During these sessions, the inquiry partner could be invited to practice coding. This second step, then, would move the inquiry project toward three objectives: (a) both partners learn to perform a wider variety of Category 3 statements, (b) each partner learns to code these same statements with the subscripts, and (c) the two partners can begin to speculate about the kinds of pupil behavior which different kinds of Category 3 statements tend to support.

Now it is time to turn to the five steps of inquiry which were described on p. 273. That is, after completing the "warm-up" activities above, the partners would be in a position to identify target pupil behaviors, suggest supporting teaching patterns, and proceed to design inquiry comparisons, and so on. The nature of these projects would depend on the grade level, the interests of the partners, the time and energy available, and so on. One partner might prefer to explore the consequences of these teacher statements when above average pupils are compared with below average. In a self-contained classroom, one participant might be interested in seeing how such statements would fit into an arithmetic lesson compared with reading. At the high school level, it might be instructive to compare the effects of these statements in a class that meets during one period with a class that meets at some other period. Or the use of such statements during the introductory phases of a new unit of study might be compared with their use in the middle work period of the unit, or the terminal phases of the unit.

Fig. 9—6.   A Possible Time Line Display for Subscripting Category 3.

Coding and display.   A direct coding time line display like the one illustrated in Fig. 9—6 could serve for interaction segments which are 15 minutes or less in duration. Longer periods might require a histogram or expanded matrix tabulation. The coding conventions for the time line in Fig. 9—6 would be to place a check ($\sqrt{}$) in all rows except row 3. In this row the arabic numbers are used to indicate the subscript number. A circle around the symbol in rows 9, 3, and 8 would be used to indicate questions. The zero below the last column, to the right, would be used to indicate Category 10.

Collecting data from pupils.   When pupils are old enough to read and fill out rating forms, data in addition to interaction analysis data can be very helpful. With very young children, it may be possible to design nonverbal checklists which pertain to such pupil reactions as being distracted, persisting in work, and so on. If the project was concerned with how Category 3 statements affected the motivation of pupils, then a little questionnaire like the one shown below could be used to gather pupil reactions. The administration time would be very short, on the order of 2 minutes. Older pupils can help tabulate the answers for the total class, displayed separately for each item. Each item shown below could be written beside a five-point scale and each pupil responds by marking one of five points for each item. Below the 5 and the 1 at the extreme ends of the scale, key words could be written. The suggested key words are shown to the right of each item.

Sample Pupil Questionnaire

Item	Five-Point Scale						
1. Today's class discussion was very interesting.	all of the time	5	4	3	2	1	none of the time
2. I'm looking forward to doing the work that we planned with . . .	high interest	5	4	3	2	1	low interest
3. I know how to start my task as soon as we begin work.	very well	5	4	3	2	1	not at all
4. The teacher seemed interested in our ideas today.	all of the time	5	4	3	2	1	none of the time
5. I really liked the class discussion today.	all of the time	5	4	3	2	1	none of the time

Short questionnaires can be filled out quickly by pupils in the fourth grade or higher. Second and third grade pupils usually perform more effectively when someone reads each item and shows the pupils how to mark the answer of their choice with an illustration on the blackboard. Pupil rating scales of this sort are of value only when two class sessions are to be compared. A single administration provides no basis for interpretation.

Asking questions to stimulate pupil initiative

All teachers ask questions. For some, this is a highly developed skill which provides pupils with a genuine opportunity to express initiative. A few teachers use questions to establish and maintain control. Questions can be cruel and vicious, routine and boring, or the basis of exciting inquiry. Most teacher questions are perceived as acts of initiation by pupils who must answer. Questions can easily reinforce superior-subordinate relationships with at least overtones of "expertness" or greater maturity.

The expected response to a question is an answer. In our society, however, an unanswered *pupil* question is an accident or planned indifference, but an unanswered *teacher* question can easily be impudence and sometimes may even be considered a crime.

Improvement in asking questions may fit into one of three conditions: first, questions are now asked that were previously ignored; second, questions are formulated and then arranged into sequences which are more effective in terms of the teacher's purpose; and third, the quantity and pacing of questions are altered in order to become more consistent with some model of teaching behavior. An example of the first two now follows.

Questions frequently ignored. Most teachers can double or triple the number of questions asked about attitudes, feelings, and perceptions which pupils have *at the moment*—not to be confused with questions about how a pupil felt during some past experience—and still not come close to 1 percent of all questions asked.* Since a teacher is not a therapist, the value of such a change in teaching behavior can be questioned. There are, however, appropriate circumstances for such questions in the classroom. Two illustrations are discussed below.

First, a teacher can learn how to deal constructively and realistically with negative feelings which develop when a learning task is blocked or is not progressing satisfactorily. Carefully chosen questions can help a pupil get back on the track more efficiently by attending to feelings first and then dealing with the cognitive aspects of the problem second. This was done rather bluntly once when one pupil asked another, during a group-work committee meeting, "Well, how do you expect to get anything done if you feel *that* way about it?" The teacher who can ask a youngster with genuine concern and with not even a trace of malice, "Do you feel upset?", "Are you bored?", etc. and then says, "Maybe it would help if you told me about it," can help "open up" communication so that emotional difficulties can be taken into consideration. In these instances, it is the teacher who makes a judgment about whether stopping work on arithmetic, in order to discuss feelings about arithmetic, is or is not the most promising approach. In most classrooms, the judgment is usually against opening up communication to include feelings, or at best the teacher expresses an optimistic "flight" statement away from feelings by asserting, "I'm sure you'll get through, cheer up."

Second, a teacher who can identify and support positive feelings of enthusiasm and excitement when learning tasks are being planned may be able to mobilize much more energy than teachers who ignore this aspect of planning work. The identifying requires questions, or at least neutral statements about feelings which elicit responses, and once attitudes and reactions have been expressed, the consequences are then discussed in terms of the learning task.

Setting up microteaching practice and classroom applications of questions which deal with feelings and attitudes sometimes becomes less authentic because it may be necessary for the teacher to role play feelings when the situation makes it awkward. Nevertheless, a coding system for observing patterns

---

*Such a question would be coded in Category 1 and the incidence of all Category 1 statements is below 0.5 percent in the average classroom over an extended period of observation. Call the statement an informed guess, since the data are not available.

of this type can be improvised from the basic 10-category system almost on the spur of the moment. For example, a "+" sign can be used to indicate positive feelings. A "−" sign can be used for negative feelings. Either symbol could indicate the quality of feelings expressed by pupils, or it could indicate the teacher's reaction to a pupil. The addition of an "=" sign for neutrality, and a "?" sign for a question are other alternatives. Figure 9–7 provides an example.

		1+1+			1+			1=1=		
9		9	9		9+	9+		9−	9−		9	9	
3													
5													
4	4	4											
8													

Fig. 9–7.   Time Line Display of Feeling Questions.

Formulating, arranging, and sequencing questions about feelings.   Suppose that an inquiry project is designed to go beyond the mere identification of positive, neutral, and negative feeling tones. Two partners in inquiry may wish to investigate how a model of inductive reasoning might be applied to diagnose feelings. This will involve asking questions to identify and clarify feelings. When the purpose is to deal realistically with the consequences of these feelings, several logical steps are often helpful, steps that are similar to those which Taba (99) proposed for inductive thinking. For example, the teacher can ask, "You seem upset, Jimmy. Can you tell me how you really feel about this?" The purpose here is to help the pupil identify his feelings and this usually requires several questions and several answers. This first step produces a list, or more formally, an inventory of present perceptions. Following Taba, these can be grouped, given labels, and then any discussion of consequences would produce functional relationships constructed out of the labels. To illustrate, suppose the pupil's responses and clarifications can be characterized as "angry at himself," "dislikes the task," "so upset he can't think," and these might be well laced with rationalizations such as "I'm no good at this" and "it isn't worth doing." Statements such as these can be grouped into clusters that refer to the difficulty of the task, the inability to proceed, how one feels about this, and what can be done about it. The functional relationships are of the sort— "when I can't proceed with a difficult task, it makes me angry," or "I would feel better if I could figure out what to do next." The purpose of helping a pupil formulate such functional relationships is to help him use his negative feelings as a stimulus for constructive plans and subsequent action. The purpose of teachers who are in training is to conceptualize the inductive model, associate appropriate questions with each logical step, plan a sequence for these steps,

TABLE 9–1

Categories for Classifying Questions About Affect

Logical Process	Intended Openness of Alternatives		
	Only one	Two or three	Open
Citing present feelings, attitudes, and perceptions	11	12	13
Grouping, conceptualizing, and naming emotional or attitudinal states	21	22	23
Applying, comparing, interpreting, and explaining relationships among conceptualized states	31	32	33
Making generalizations, predictions, reaching conclusions, synthesizing about consequences	41	42	43

Examples:

11—"Are you interested in your arithmetic homework for tonight?"

12—"Do you think tonight's homework is more or less interesting than last night's?"

13—"What are your reactions to homework?"

21—"Well, if this assignment is too long and too hard, would you call it unfair?"

22—"Which assignments illustrate hard and easy homework?"

23—"Do you see any way to group these assignments in terms of your reactions?"

31—"What is a first step to take when you face an assignment that you dislike?"

32—"Do you think that your feelings help or hinder how hard you might work?"

33—"If you think an assignment is fair, but difficult, what effects might this have on your work?"

41—"What happens to 'work accomplished' when most pupils in the class really like their homework?"

42—"Which of these two conclusions do you think applies more appropriately to the pupils in our class?"

43—"Can you explain why you think that your prediction is likely to occur?"

and then practice performing and coding the interaction during the inter-change.

In order to accomplish this training task, it will be necessary to design a set of categories which have both logical and affective dimensions. Next an appropriate setting for microteaching and classroom discussions will be necessary, a setting which is realistic and which will evoke authentic behavior so that a genuine expression of feeling is likely to occur. Such a setting might become available, for example, when pupils become upset about a difficult arithmetic assignment given as homework.

The categories and code symbols in Table 9–1 might be used for this training problem. The logical processes shown to the left are based on Taba's (99) steps of inductive thinking. The affective dimension, shown by the columns to the right, is based on Hughes' (55) notion of open and closed questions. A closed question to which only one response is appropriate is shown in the left column. A partially closed question which involves two or three options is shown in the center column. An open question to which any kind of response is ap-propriate is shown in the right column. Two digits are used for each code symbol: the first number indicates one of four levels of logical process; the second number indicates one of three degrees of openness. This gives a total of 12 categories. Questions which illustrate each of the 12 categories are listed following Table 9–1.

In a practical microteaching episode and especially in a total class discus-sion, it is quite likely that all 12 of the categories would apply to statements other than questions. The way that this can be handled is to consider the 12 categories (Table 9–1) to be subscript notations of the FIAC system. A form for direct time line coding could be designed which had columns spaced wide enough for two digits per column. An example is shown in Fig. 9–8. This direct coding procedure would require a rate of coding single events which un-doubtedly would be slower than one tally every three seconds. With practice, a talented observer might approach one notation every five seconds. Should this estimate be optimistic and the rate for a particular observer turns out to be too slow for practical use, then another option is to collapse the 12 categories to a smaller number. One way to collapse the 12 categories into 4 which would require only a single digit symbol for each subscript is the following. Let the first category consist of 11 and 12 (Table 9–1); the second of 13 only; the third of 23, 33, and 43; and then let all the other combinations from Table 9–1 fall into a fourth category. Suppose the 12-category system was used and produced data like the configuration in Fig. 9–8. How would this display be decoded?

The pattern in Fig. 9–8 starts with the teacher expressing his opinions about a specific attitude and then shifts to a more open view (13) of the topic. This leads to an open question (13) which asks for any kind of reaction. Pupil

reactions of their own choice fall in row 9, which the teacher briefly acknowledges. Then the teacher asks a more specific question (11). The pupils' response
is again acknowledged, which leads to some self-initiated additional comments
by pupils. The teacher expresses his own views and then asks for any reactions
(33) to the application or consequences of the attitude or feelings being discussed.
There is then an open teacher question (43) soliciting level four generalizations
or conclusions to which there is a pupil response.

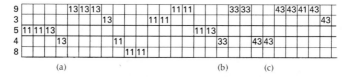

Fig. 9–8.   Time Line Display of a Model for Diagnosing Process Problems.

This model has two dimensions. First, all shifts of level in the logical dimension are introduced by open rather than narrow questions; see columns a, b, and
c, Fig. 9–8. Subsequent questions at the same level, which is illustrated only
once after column a, may be more specific. A second dimension is shown by all
first digits in the columns which proceed from 1 to 3 to 4 or from the specific
to the general, moving from left to right. Alternative models can mix up
these two dimensions into several combinations. Movement from left to right in
the time line can be from the specific to the general or vice versa. Each phase
shift can be introduced by open questions or by narrow questions. More complex
models could involve three shifts in the specific to general levels. It might be
argued that in diagnosing individual difficulties, to choose one example, the
first questions should be open, followed by specific, ending with open, and
that this sequence should be superimposed on a gradual shift from the specific,
row 1 in the category arrangement, on toward the general or row 4. In terms of
strategy, the teacher would begin by asking open questions so that a pupil
could express his own specific attitudes. The teacher then clarifies one particular
attitude (or more) and helps the pupil cite it, name it, apply it, and predict the
consequences. The sequence could end at the (43) levels, when the teacher
asks, "What reactions do you have about how discussions of this sort might
help boys and girls who have homework?"

Some project suggestions for building pupil initiative

Although making use of pupil ideas and asking questions in order to support
pupil initiative and independence have so far been discussed separately, the
two go together, hand in glove. What the teacher does when a pupil stops

talking and how the teacher solicits pupils' participation are essentially parts of the same instructional problem.

One place to begin is to investigate what happens to the ideas which pupils express during classroom interaction. Are they acknowledged by the teacher? By other pupils? Are the ideas used in some constructive fashion? A next step might be to become concerned with feelings and attitudes. How can feelings be acknowledged? Can the attitudes and feelings which pupils develop about learning be used constructively? How does one decide when to take the time to confront feelings, interpret them, and relate them to the main business of learning? In what ways can feedback to pupils about attitudes and feelings be most constructive? Which patterns of teaching behavior are most effective in accomplishing a constructive use of attitudes and feelings? Throughout our concern with ideas and feelings, the function of teacher questions is a central issue. How can the range of questions be increased? Which questions serve particular purposes?

There is a strategy for sequencing questions which might be called "selective reinforcement." A teacher can ask broad, open questions about subject matter, or about plans for action, or about feelings and attitudes. By acknowledging ideas and feelings that are expressed and by encouraging other pupils to express their own point of view, many different opinions can be gathered. A teacher can focus the attention of the class along lines of thinking and feeling that he thinks will be most productive by selectively reinforcing what some pupils say. That is, when opinions or feelings are expressed which may move the discussion toward desired objectives, a teacher can ask the pupil who spoke, or some other pupil, to elaborate. By asking any number of questions such as, "Why do you think so?", "Tell me more about what you have in mind?", or "How do you see this idea fitting into our discussion?" the teacher turns the attention of the class upon a particular emphasis that the teacher has selected, but a pupil has suggested. When this is done skillfully, the pupils progress in their analysis of a problem, but achieve this in such a way that their own actions and points of view are actively expressed. In this way a teacher can exert his authority and more mature judgment without unnecessary imposition and without generating unwanted, excessive dependence. Attention which is focused in this manner can proceed along lines of thought that the teacher thinks are most productive, yet the pupils will experience a sense of independence and ownership with regard to the matters under consideration.

When questions are used for selective reinforcement, there are usually predictable shifts in the concepts used. The teacher's questions and immediate acknowledgments are likely to be more abstract—in terms of generality and broadness—during the early phases of the discussion. As the conversation achieves more focus, comments and questions become more specific. At times the meaning of words is clarified, particular comparisons are made, and the thrust of the conversation is judged in terms of the original problem. These are essentially logical procedures, even when the topic is concerned with feelings and attitudes. So let us turn to an analysis of these logical processes, discussed in terms of pupil initiative.

Level of thinking during classroom interaction

Very crude guesses about the level of thinking involved in teacher questions and lecture in an above average socio-economic, suburban school district can be made by referring to some data from a fourth-grade unit on social studies involving 16 experimental classrooms. The matrices of two classrooms within this sample are shown in Tables 5—1 and 5—2, in which Categories 41 and 51 designate questions and lecture which are restricted to facts and the more limited mental processes connected with citing facts.

The proportion of narrow questions and factual statements to all questions and all lecture, teacher talk only, is an astonishing 89 percent! Apparently current teaching practices in these two classes not only involve teacher domination through teacher initiation and pupil response, but in addition, the logical quality of the verbal interchange more often consists of narrow questions and simple factual relationships. The proportion of discourse which is concerned with inductive and deductive reasoning, synthesizing, predicting, and generalizing probably reaches an incidence that is below 15 or even 10 percent during subject matter discussions.

One way to acquire at least an orientation to the concepts describing the range of thinking which might take place in the classroom is to consult Sanders' (84) adaptation of the six levels of thought developed by Bloom (13). Sanders made small modifications of the Bloom levels of thinking that can be presumed to characterize educational objectives. Sanders was interested in questions asked by teachers, primarily, and thinks that questions can be classified as (1) memory, (2) translation, (3) interpretation, (4) application, (5) analysis, (6) synthesis, and (7) evaluation. Sanders' paperback is a handy book for those who would like to start thinking about the teacher's role in the improvement of the logic of classroom discourse. It may well be that the best place to start is by increasing the kinds of questions asked, just as it was recommended earlier that the best place to start improving pupil initiative was by responding more thoughtfully to ideas expressed by pupils.

There is some evidence to suggest that an increase in the kinds of questions alone would underestimate the problems and that besides reformulating questions, practice in timing and sequencing questions is also essential to improving the logic of classroom discourse. Bellack (9, p. 212) showed that only three out of 21 possible teaching cycles in his category systems accounted for more than half of all the interaction. They were: teacher solicits and a pupil responds,

19.3 percent; teacher solicits, a pupil responds, a pupil reacts, 27.6 percent; and teacher solicits, pupil responds, a pupil reacts, a pupil reacts, 10.2 percent. These data indicate that a single idea is given a relatively "short ride" in classroom conversation before it is dropped in our eagerness to get to the next idea.

On Hilda Taba's San Francisco team, McNaughton (65) compared six experimental classes with six controls and then cross validated the study on a similar population in an effort to locate generalizations expressed by fourth, fifth, and sixth grade pupils. The experimental teachers had been trained to ask those questions which would more likely stimulate pupils' thinking and cause them to state generalizations, in contrast with a teacher making generalizations. What seemed most interesting was the difference between isolated higher level pupil statements and the same higher level pupil statements when they appeared in a more complete logical context. The *isolated* higher level pupil statements occurred at an incidence of 76 for six experimental classes and 60 for the six control classes in the cross validation study. Here there was not a large difference. But when the high level pupil statements which occurred in the context of a logical "module" were counted, the experimental class incidence was 59 while the control classes showed only five. Here the difference is large. This shows very promising results when teachers are trained to understand logical thought modules which provide a more logical context for the ideas which are being discussed.

Unfortunately we do not have enough studies to make generalizations about the quality of logic in classroom discourse. What can be said, from the studies so far reported, is that when and if a representative survey is made, we should be prepared for a devastating indictment, especially in those classrooms which are below a mythical national average with regard to logic in classroom discourse. Our uneasiness should be sharpened when we realize that about half of our youth could be found in such classrooms.

Improvement will not be easy. Surely at least these steps will be necessary. First, pupils are not likely to have opportunities for developing and practicing higher logical processes until teachers have learned the skills themselves and are in a better position to teach them. Second, something like a national convulsion may be necessary in order to free teachers from the pressure of covering facts and to slow down the tempo of instruction so that intellectual skills are more likely to grow and flourish. Third, specific strategies of teaching behavior which facilitate higher logical processes for pupils must be identified through research on what is the best teaching, not what is common practice, and teachers will need opportunities to experiment with these strategies. Fourth, given our present conditions, the initial training experiences should be rather simple, primitive, self-development projects in which the more rudimentary skills are involved. Fifth, a genuine appreciation of the problems must surely involve reformulating questions, sequencing these questions, and developing skill in patient timing, in order that most pupils, not just the brightest, can show more initiative in thinking at higher levels of logic.

Possible approaches to improved teaching patterns

In considering the speculations which follow, it would be well to remember that teachers need practice *during interaction* in order to develop useful skills for guiding thinking during classroom discourse. Lectures either at a university or in a program for employed teachers can reach only very limited objectives. The procedures already outlined which involve microteaching, simulated skill practice, and classroom practice with interaction analysis feedback are more likely to be effective, given our present knowledge. The goal is to provide opportunities for pupils to take the initiative in higher level thinking.

Asking questions.   One way to start is to read pages 184 to 185 regarding Taba's steps of thinking. Questions which support these steps are:

Function	Example
Differentiating and citing	"What would happen if ...?" "What other things might happen?"
Grouping and categorizing	"What things on the board go together?" "What else goes in this group?"
Labeling	"Who can suggest a name for all of these things?"
"Reading" points and relationships between points	"How does a *cold climate* affect building houses?" "Why do you think that would happen?"
Explanations and generalizations	"Who can put all these ideas into a single sentence which says what we mean?"

Questions of the type suggested by Taba can be open as shown above or they can be more specific in order to focus pupil observations and thinking toward particular facts or relationships. A first step in developing skill in asking questions which guide pupil thinking is to increase the repertoire of questions, to know of more kinds of questions, and to be able to ask them on the spur of the moment.

Taba's ideas also require that questions be asked in a sequence that is purposeful. In Fig. 9–9, inductive processes leading to generalizations and deductive thought processes which test generalizations are illustrated in diagramatic form. Citing instances and facts, using labels, finding relationships between points identified by conceptual labels and forming these into generalizations emphasize an inductive sequence. To start with generalizations and explore their meanings through illustrations and applications usually

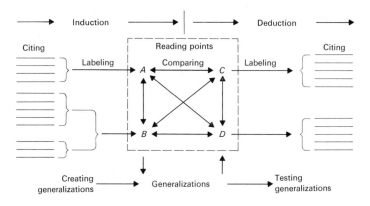

Fig. 9—9.   Sequences in Logical Thought.

involves a more deductive emphasis. The teacher guides these sequences by asking questions according to a strategy.

Besides repertoire and sequence, the teacher is concerned with timing, especially when as many pupils as possible are to participate and when the pupils and not the teacher are to make generalizations, give examples, and make applications. For instance, to reach generalizations inductively, Taba (99, p. 114) recommends that a large proportion of time be spent citing ideas without moving on to grouping them so as to encourage the participation of many different pupils. This aspect of pacing requires patience and judgment about when to shift from questions which elicit "citing" to questions which stimulate "grouping" ideas. The most frequent teaching error may well occur when one or two bright pupils leap to generalizations before the rest of the class is ready and the teacher enthusiastically reinforces such behavior. The point is to teach most of the pupils to reason carefully and to protect the opportunities for practicing such skills.

Those who are seriously interested in these cognitive characteristics of classroom discussion are urged to first read the references cited and then proceed to ask how systematic observation coding systems can be used to display the processes involved. Several of the coding systems described in Chapter 6 and in the present chapter can be used to assist a teacher who wishes to practice sequence and pacing in asking questions.

In passing, a moment of consideration should be given to teachers inquiring into their own teaching patterns in ways that are consistent with how they expect to teach in the classroom. Please notice that Fig. 9—9 could also be presented as an illustration of the five steps of inquiry which have been recommended earlier for professional self-development. Citing particular pupil behaviors and citing complementary teaching behaviors are the initial steps to the left. Concepts describing both pupil and teaching behavior are labels which refer to these behaviors. Reading points, making comparisons, and explaining then occur through data collection, feedback, and interpreting the data. This then leads to generalizations about teaching patterns and the effects of these patterns on pupil participation. Inquiry into one's own behavior can also start with a generalization and through practice and observation lead to specific applications through a process of deduction. In other words, the problems of understanding teaching strategies involve thinking processes which are very similar to the thinking processes which pupils carry out in their own intellectual growth.

Teacher lecturing.   One of the few experimental studies on the effectivenesst of teacher lecturing, conducted with exceptionally high standards of research design and control, has been conducted by Rosenshine (79). Variables in 21 categories were identified in one experimental group and then cross validated in two additional groups. Variables in three categories were finally identified as features of a lecture performance which distinguished those situations in which pupil comprehension and understanding was high, contrasted with situations in which these measures were low. Each of the three are briefly discussed below.

Gesture and movement to emphasize points were found to have a higher incidence when pupil comprehension was high. Such movements tend to emphasize points.

"Rule and example pattern of discourse" was also a significant predictor. This refers to the use of summary statements before and after a series of examples. Although it may be an oversimplification, this characteristic means to tell someone what you are going to tell them, then tell them, then remind them of what you said. Stating a point, illustrating it, and then restating it was the sequence which occurred with high incidence in the high scoring classes.

"Explaining links" were also higher in incidence with above average comprehension. Explaining links are such words or phrases as "because," "in order to," "if . . . then," "therefore," and so on. Such links could be labeled "logical connectives." Some are stronger and more vivid while others are weak or may be missing. Their use helps, apparently, to fix relationships in memory and may assist in giving emphasis.

There are two types of interaction analysis coding which might help in the analysis of teacher lecture. First, categories which apply to the subject matter itself can be used. For example, the topics of the lecture can be organized into a content grid or simple outline and each major division of the content can be assigned a code symbol. The record would show how much time was spent on particular topics during the lecture and the sequence whereby one topic follows another. Second, some system of classifying the kinds of knowledge, such as the seven types of questions which were suggested by Sanders, could be used as a second classification. A third cluster might consist of first statement, illustration or application or explanation, and then restatement and summary. By using three code digits, the topic, level of abstraction, and restatement emphasis could be traced during a lecture.

Initiative in pupil thinking

The traditional method of encouraging pupil initiative in thinking has centered on individual projects, homework, seatwork, laboratory experimentation, creative writing, and similar activities. Thoughtless preparation for such activities can result in suppressing initiative and limiting the experience to following directions, completing highly structured assignments, and simply doing what the directions say to do.

Curriculum revision with new instructional materials has been one answer to this problem. It is not yet clear whether such innovations will achieve pupil initiative in thinking. For example, in an extensive five-state field study to assess any differences in classroom interaction when new mathematics materials were used, the evidence (107, pp. 1−12) is not very convincing. The new materials were designed to elicit more pupil initiative in thinking such as creating unusual solutions to problems. Theoretically, the new materials were expected to show a higher incidence of four types of statements. The categories representing these statements were (a) pupils—independent, active, (b) teacher—confronting, seeking, (c) teacher—challenging, jolting, and (d) pupils—curious, creative. There were not enough (c) and (d) events in either the experimental or control classes to be worth noting. There were statistically significant differences in the expected directions for the first two categories, but the incidence in percent was extremely low. The contrast from "experimental" to "control" for (a) was 2.4 percent to 1.9 and for (b) 1.4 to 0.9. In other words, the vast majority, some 97 percent of the classroom interaction, was more or less the same when the new materials were used. In this project, the experimental teachers attended a summer workshop prior to attempting to use the new materials. What is disturbing, then, is that even with widely disseminated mathematics curricula involving materials designed and developed at four centers,* the hoped for effects on pupil initiative in thinking did not appear during classroom interaction. Although there was more attention given to "the structure of mathematics" in the experimental classes, there was no corresponding change in the thinking of pupils. Teachers still tended to dominate, asked narrow questions, and the pupils responded in a highly controlled fashion.

---

*The materials came from Ball State University, the University of Illinois Committee on School Mathematics, the School Mathematics Study Group, and the University of Maryland Mathematics Evaluation Project.

Programmed instructional materials might be another response to increasing pupil initiative in thinking. At this time, however, no data indicating whether pupils can show more initiative in thinking, as a result of using such materials has come to my attention.

With the present evidence, no firm conclusions are possible concerning how to increase the initiative of pupil thinking. The most promising leads appear to be untested and these would occur when a teacher has learned how to facilitate this kind of behavior and has the time and materials to help in forming the necessary cognitive skills.

RECONSTRUCTING WHAT HAS BEEN PROPOSED

This chapter began with a "call" to inquiry and by suggesting that the *means* of self-development demand as much attention and careful planning as the subject matter outcomes. Throughout these activities the analysis of classroom interaction, the desired behavior of pupils, and the complementary behavior of the teacher become the focus of nearly all activities. A generalized procedure included asking:

1) What target pupil behaviors would you like to have occurring in your classroom?
2) What patterns of teaching behavior, in each case more than one, are most likely to support the desired pupil behavior?
3) How much practice do you need to be sure that you can produce the proposed teaching behavior patterns, and can you be sure that your partner can code these patterns?
4) What plan of investigation will give you the most information in comparing each alternative teaching pattern?
5) After conducting the investigation, what conclusions have you reached about how best to produce the desired target behaviors?

These five questions formed a cycle of inquiry which could be used equally well by the least skillful as well as the most advanced teachers. In fact, self-development of teaching skill was seen as the result of recycling these five steps through a series of increasingly complex problems, each adjusted to the present interest of the participants and incorporating procedures which match current skills of inquiry.

In order to protect independence and self-direction, yet obtain a degree of objectivity greater than one person can normally create, a partnership was proposed as the unit of action. These partnerships were the products of working liasons formed in a study group of four to eight persons. A director for these activities would arrange large audience meetings for the study teams, help to

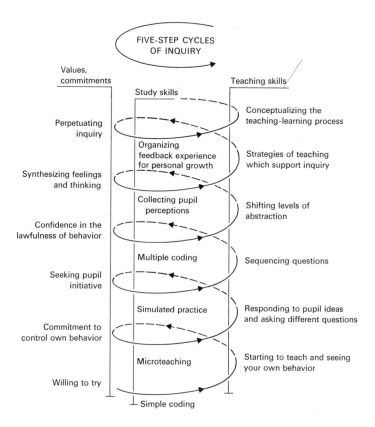

Fig. 9–10. Curriculum Elements in Professional Self-Development (after Hilda Taba).

secure instructional materials, and work to resolve the many problems that would arise.

A schematic organization of these curriculum elements has much in common with Hilda Taba's (98, p. 11) conception of spiral concept development. Such an organization is illustrated in Fig. 9–10. Each spiral consists of a five-step cycle of inquiry. The values and commitments listed on the left are all a part of each cycle and are not necessarily arranged into an expected sequence. The phrases on the right suggest increasingly complex teaching skills which become the objectives of study and self-development. The study skills, or at least some of them, are listed in the center, showing an increase in the ability of the participants to work on their own problems and to help others.

The main thrust of these self-development activities is toward more independence and self-direction on the part of pupils. The activities include the study and control of teaching behavior which facilitates the desired pupil behavior. The starting point is at whatever level of interest and ability the participants may possess. The activities can be maintained at whatever level the available energy and resources permit. Thus, with beginning teachers, a project may center on simple notions—such as, a teacher can provide opportunities for a pupil to answer by keeping his mouth shut after asking a question so that there is a reasonable opportunity for an answer to be formulated and expressed by a pupil. Such a problem can be investigated with the five steps of inquiry, including alternatives, other than tolerating silence, which a teacher can use to help pupils formulate thoughtful answers. The same five steps can also be used to study very complex teaching strategies in which shifts in teaching behavior follow models of thinking and the advantages, or disadvantages, of several different strategies can be compared.

The propositions in this chapter are considered equally relevant to college students who seek to become beginning teachers as well as to experienced teachers who participate in continuing professional education.

Chapter Ten

STRATEGIES OF TEACHING WHICH PROMOTE PUPIL INITIATION

CONCEPTS FOR THINKING ABOUT TEACHING STRATEGIES

Suppose a teacher leads a class discussion in order to find out what substantive issues the pupils would like to study. All contributions are written on the blackboard, but some of the suggestions are explored in more detail than others because the teacher asks pertinent questions. The class then divides into small discussion groups to select and plan separate learning tasks on which one or more pupils may choose to work. As the selected tasks become clarified, the teacher asks rather specific questions about plans for work, availability of resource materials, when the work might be finished, and what kind of an end product is expected. During the work period the teacher assists each group that requests help, acts as a consultant at decision points, helps to locate hard to find materials, and sometimes sits in during the diagnosis of difficulties. When most of the groups are nearly finished, the teacher solicits suggestions about how the learning activities are to be terminated and how products of learning might best be shared. Should these events take place as described, an observer might assert that the teacher was following certain teaching-learning strategies in order to facilitate learning.

In another classroom, or the same classroom at a different time, the class may be busy at seatwork. Worksheets and book assignments provide a series of individual learning tasks. At times the teacher uses total class discussion to explain a problem when a substantial proportion of the class can benefit. If some pupils become bored, misbehave, or disturb others, the teacher intervenes promptly with directions, occasional reprimands, or changes the seating arrangements; at other times he calls the attention of the class to work well done and praises progress when appropriate. There is a strong element of teacher control; the pupils seem to be responding to the teacher's initiative. Just as in the first scene, the activities seem to follow a purposeful strategy of teaching and learning.

There are wide differences in the classroom interaction of the above two scenes with many more variations available, for your observation, at the nearest school building. The purpose of this chapter is to propose concepts for talking about teaching-learning strategies, even those that result in quite different patterns. What concepts would be needed to explain essential differences in teacher-pupil relationships in the two scenes? Could these same concepts be used to clarify relationships between the style of teaching and its consequences in terms of educational outcomes? Are these same concepts useful in predicting conditions which are more likely to produce pupil initiation and self-direction in the classroom? These are some of the questions which guide the writing of this chapter.

Another way to describe this chapter is to say that it presents tools for thinking about teaching during a particular lesson or perhaps an entire unit of study. Short interactive events have been the focus of interest in earlier chapters. In the last few chapters, we have studied these events after they have been combined to form patterns. Now it is time to look at the flow of pattern sequences from an even greater conceptual distance. In this chapter the concepts will refer to long strings of events and thereby explain strategies which occupy extended periods of time. To do this the concepts proposed refer to (a) perceptions of learning goals which pupils develop, (b) shifts in teacher initiation complemented by changes in pupil response or initiative, and (c) the characteristics of social access in the classroom. Hypotheses are developed which associate different configurations of these dimensions with classroom interaction as well as other outcomes such as pupil achievement and pupil attitude.

These concepts will be useful to the extent that they facilitate additional inquiry. Just as college students and experienced teachers can conduct inquiry into the shorter patterns described in Chapter 9, it is also possible to investigate longer teaching strategies. To illustrate the similarity between these two kinds of inquiry, compare the following questions about teaching strategies with the five steps (see p. 273) proposed for studying patterns. First, what pupil behavior specifies the content objectives, problem-solving skills, or changes in pupil attitudes? Second, what learning activities lead logically to these behaviors? Third, what teaching behaviors are involved at each different phase of instruction? Fourth, how can data be collected in order to compare what happened with what was intended? Fifth, what improvements can be made as a result of analyzing the data?

The main thrust of these theoretical formulations is to understand how a teacher can promote more pupil independence and self-direction in the classroom. The strategies to be discussed are based on several hypotheses about teaching behavior and its consequences. These hypotheses are not meant to be memorized as generalizations about teaching. This would be most unfortunate for two reasons: first, the hypotheses may later be disproved even though there is some evidence to support them; second, knowledge about teaching should be experienced through planned inquiry, not memorized and stored for later retrieval.

Some readers may profit from comparing the conceptual development which occurs in this chapter with earlier published statements. For those who respond to such curiosity, earlier references by Flanders (34, 37, 39) are available.

CONCEPTS FOR DESCRIBING FOUR DIMENSIONS OF CLASSROOM INTERACTION

There are four dimensions of classroom teaching and learning to be taken into consideration. Here each dimension is briefly introduced; then it is described in more detail on subsequent pages.

First, pupils perceive classroom learning activities in terms of a presumed purpose, and these perceptions should be clear enough so that pupils can decide what to do next. This dimension is called *goal orientation* and consists of pupil perceptions, not those of the teacher. When goals are not clear to the pupils, they have less opportunity to direct their own behavior and are more dependent on teacher directions.

Second, how the teacher uses his authority influences a pupil's independence and his feelings about trying to become more independent. This dimension is called *authority in use*. The "in use" is added to distinguish the teacher's potential power from his present, active influence. A teacher always retains his authority, but with discretion its active use can vary from one situation to the next.

The third and fourth dimensions can be described by asking "who can talk to whom?" and "how many different topics can be discussed?" Both of these dimensions are a part of *social access* in the classroom. The first question refers to what might be called *social contacts* and is concerned with how often and under what circumstances one pupil contacts another in the classroom. The second question is called *range of ideas*. Here we are concerned with what is said, once there is an opportunity to say it.

There is an interesting serial order associated with the third and fourth dimensions which is illustrated in Fig. 10–1. There has to be an opportunity to talk before pupils can decide what things can be said. Using the new labels, we would say that usually pupils must be free to contact each other before they can freely test the full range of ideas that they may wish to discuss.

These four dimensions—goal orientation, authority in use, social contacts, and range of ideas—are each to be characterized by several concepts. These concepts will refer to different types of goal orientation, different conditions of authority in use, different kinds of social contacts, and various conditions that

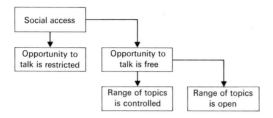

Fig. 10–1. Two Dimensions of Social Access.

control the range of ideas. Together these concepts are used to describe a *configuration* among the four dimensions at some point in time. The concept *variety* refers to the total number of separate configurations that can be distinguished. The concept *sequence* refers to how one particular configuration follows another. It seems quite likely that both variety and sequence should be considered in any strategy for controlling the independence and self-direction of pupils.

GOAL ORIENTATION

The presumption of purpose

The classroom is a place in which practically all teachers and most pupils expect "to do schoolwork." The notion that you can do anything you want in a classroom has been explored in various experimental programs* and in most of them, pupils are inclined to choose voluntarily what most of us would call schoolwork. These programs have served more to illustrate what can be done in terms of a philosophical position rather than to prove that one educational program is superior to another. It can be argued, however, that some form of pupil participation in making plans for schoolwork would be logically related to the degree of independence and self-direction which characterizes the learning activities. It must be conceded, however, that the evidence necessary to support this assertion lies beyond the skill and resources previously available to educational researchers. Progress in the development of interaction analysis may be prerequisite to an analysis of this problem.

The presumption of purpose merely means that so long as we have required attendance, professionally trained teachers, and the desire to provide for the educational development of youth, there are educational purposes which we seek to implement. In the contemporary scene, an example of a sharp conflict between purpose and pupil response appears when underprivileged, inner-

---

*The history of having pupils select their own learning activities and goals is quite extensive. Rousseau's *Emile*, A. S. Neil's *Summerhill*, and the more recent writing of Carl Rogers are all examples.

city pupils are exposed to what is alleged to be an inappropriate "middle class" curriculum. Any substantial mismatch between the abilities and interests of a pupil and the learning tasks he is to accomplish becomes the basis of such conflict. The resolution of this conflict has a profound effect on the independence and self-direction of pupils during classroom instruction.

The characteristics of goals

A vague orientation "to do schoolwork" does not provide a pupil with criteria for deciding how to act, unless it suggests that he should wait for the teacher to tell him what to do. Not knowing what to do because the goals are not clear is referred to as *goal ambiguity* in this discussion.

Goals are broken down into learning activities, and the activity for a particular pupil becomes his *learning task*. A learning task provides criteria for deciding how to act when the pupil can picture the end product, has a general idea about how to reach the end point, and knows the first few steps that are required to start work. When this state of affairs exists, it will be called a condition of *goal clarity*. At this point, work could begin if the pupil wanted to start.

Goals are not only relatively clear or ambiguous, a pupil's motivation reflects his perception of how attractive or unattractive the task is. This characteristic of goals and their associated learning tasks will be referred to by using the adjectives *positive* and *negative*. Positive goals lead to tasks that are interesting and match the abilities of pupils. Negative goals are not interesting and pupils would prefer some other activity. Sometimes goals stimulate a negative reaction because the pupil perceives them as too difficult and beyond his abilities.

A question can be raised concerning whether ambiguous goals can be positive or negative. One might prefer a convention whereby goals are assumed to be neutral until they are clarified, at which point a pupil would see them as attractive or unattractive. This convention is adopted in order to avoid unnecessary elaboration. It is quite clear, however, that many pupils have positive or negative anticipations even when the learning tasks are unknown. Extreme negative anticipations require special attention by the teacher and more properly belong to the field of special education.

Notice that in choosing to distinguish only the three conditions of ambiguous goals, clear positive goals, and clear negative goals, many more complicated conditions are being ignored. For example, given a single assignment to an entire class, some pupils may perceive ambiguous goals, some perceive clear positive goals, and others clear negative goals, due to individual differences in interests and abilities. More complex individual perceptions might include a pupil who likes the subject matter area and the goals associated with it, but resents the teacher or dislikes the methods by which schoolwork is organized. While these more complex situations are interesting, could be conceptualized, and probably could be distinguished, they are not essential to explaining the simple teaching strategies which are discussed on subsequent pages.

These three conditions of goal orientation will permit us to consider how goal ambiguity changes to clear positive and clear negative goals. How goals become clarified is an essential feature of teaching which affects pupil independence and self-direction.

The measurement of goal orientation

Instruments or procedures for quantifying a concept like goal orientation are not very well developed. Anyone who wants to assess the change in goal orientation which takes place during the period between starting to plan schoolwork and the time when pupils are busy at their work faces the task of developing his own measurement techniques.

The problem is difficult because many teachers and nearly all pupils have had no training in emphasizing the behavioral aspects of educational goals and learning tasks. Teachers can start to practice this skill by reading and using a short programmed booklet by Mager (62). If a questionnaire is used to assess goal orientation, pupils will have to be taught how to use it. It has been my experience that without practice pupils do not consciously distinguish degrees of goal orientation. When you ask a pupil, "What are you doing?", he is likely to say, "I'm doing arithmetic," or "My homework," or even "My schoolwork." With care and training, relative scores on goal clarity and ambiguity can be obtained by interview, observation, or from a questionnaire. Items such as those illustrated below can be used in a questionnaire:

Item One.   How many steps are required for you to complete your present work?

Item Two.   Which step are you on now?

Item Three.   How certain are you that you know how to complete the next step?

Item Four.   Do you check your work with your teacher before starting something new?

Item Five.   Do you know when you will be finished with your present task?

The above items would require a space to write an answer or an appropriate scale to indicate the degree of certainty, clarity, or confidence, on some response dimension. To repeat, pupils need special training before they can mark such instruments consistently in terms of their perceptions of the moment.

AUTHORITY IN USE

The presumption of authority

In our culture teacher-pupil relationships are superior-subordinate in terms of authority. By law, maturity, expertness, or even by accident, a teacher is paid to be responsible for what occurs and is therefore accountable. By inclination, past experience, age difference, or lack of another alternative, a pupil is most often prepared to defer to this authority in the long run, with the possibility of passive or active resistance for shorter periods of time. The power to influence another person varies among pupils, in the sense of peer leadership, but resides with the teacher in terms of classroom management.

The teacher, however, can exercise discretion in his use of authority. While he retains ultimate authority, his authority in use can vary from constant, direct teacher initiation with pupil compliance, to periods of pupil initiation with teacher response.

Characteristics of authority

Teachers can take the initiative in specifying learning tasks, the steps and methods of completing tasks, start and stop learning activities, and retain the perogative of deciding when one step is complete so that the pupil seeks permission before moving on to the next. The more actively the teacher initiates in these ways, the more pupils will comply. When this condition exists, we will refer to it as *teacher initiation*. The teacher assumes a position of power and the pupils are forced into a uniform position of subordination.

On the other hand, when individual differences among the pupils are encouraged and pupil initiative is supported, then pupils no longer remain in a position of uniformly low power. Instead, they become spread along a continuum from most to least influential, with regard to influencing each other, and enjoy a uniformly higher degree of self-control and initiation with regard to their own work. When this condition exists, it will be referred to as *pupil initiation*.

Measuring authority in use

Pupil perceptions of authority can be gathered by a questionnaire at the end of any time interval, but immediate past experiences color pupil responses. Items can be constructed which refer to how often a pupil checks his work with the teacher, whether he can decide when to go on to the next step, whether he feels free to consult another pupil, and so on.

Interaction analysis is probably a more effective method of assessing authority in use. Categories 5 and 6, lecturing and giving directions, characterize teacher initiation. Category 9 indicates pupil initiative, but unless this coincides with the above average use of Category 3, then inferences about pupil initiative and teacher response are in question.

SOCIAL CONTACTS AND RANGE OF IDEAS

The presumption of social access

The presumption of social access for communication merely means that most of what takes place in the classroom depends on communication. Who talks to whom forms a network of communication which is closely related to physical access, such as the seating arrangements in a classroom. The range of ideas which can be communicated openly in a classroom is quite a different matter. Most statements about the subject matter are acceptable, but not all, in the normal classroom, yet there are acknowledged prohibitions about certain kinds of pupil statements which covertly or overtly limit the range of topics which are discussed. Both of these aspects of communication are a part of social access in the classroom.

The characteristics of social contacts

Who talks to whom is primarily a function of seating arrangements, teaching style, and whether pupils occasionally commit transgressions against the authorized communication patterns of the classroom. When the desks are placed in straight rows, facing the teacher, the formation facilitates communication between pupils and the teacher, yet inhibits communication between most pupils, since talking to the nearest pupil is merely convenient, at best. We will refer to such a formation as *restricted*. This means that opportunities to contact other pupils are at a minimum.

On the other hand, pupils may be free to move about the room, may form small discussion groups, or otherwise show initiative in communicating with others. Such mobility permits pupils to select their communication contacts and we will refer to these conditions of pupil contacts as *free*.

The characteristics of the range of ideas

With free social contacts and movement around the room, a pupil can talk without teacher restrictions. Thus, in most instances, free social contacts also permit a wide range of ideas to be discussed. Yet with a persuasive and trusted teacher, the pupils might be encouraged to consult with their neighbor, even in the most rigid seating arrangement, and then express any ideas which they may think important about some topic. It is interesting that in the last analysis, it is the real or imagined fear of the teacher that inhibits pupil expression, with peer approbation coming in a close second. For whatever reasons, there are degrees of freedom or restriction to self-expression which may be independent of classroom seating arrangements. A separate analysis of "freedom to talk about whatever comes to your mind" seems appropriate. When the ideas discussed are determined primarily by the teacher, we will call the range of ideas *controlled*. When anything can be discussed, we will call this *open*.

Measurement of social contacts and range of ideas

The most efficient measurement of social contacts can be achieved by having an observer make a separate assessment of the class formation, recording notes whenever this formation changes. Inferences about openness in expressing ideas must remain a guess, when contacts are free, unless ways to code conversations among individuals can be arranged. It is relatively easy to determine the degree of control exercised by the teacher during a total class discussion because it can be coded.

Pupil questionnaires can be used at the end of a learning activity period to determine whether the pupils' perceptions about expressing ideas is controlled or open. Items concerned with "feeling free to talk," "feeling free to bring up your own ideas," and "free to express attitudes and feelings—as well as opinions" can be constructed and administered to quantify this dimension.

SEQUENCE AND VARIETY

At this point in our thinking, a particular configuration might consist of some combination of the alternatives shown in Fig. 10–2. Variety refers to the total number of different configurations which occur in a classroom. The concept of sequence refers to how many different configuration pairs occurred in a given time period. Knowing the more frequently occurring sequence pairs of configuration helps to predict what will happen next. Perhaps an example will help to illustrate this last point.

Suppose goals are ambiguous as a new unit is started. Let's say the teacher believes in strong teacher initiation and therefore uses straight rows and total class discussion. This makes it easier to restrict pupil contacts and control the ideas discussed. Learning tasks are identified, discussed, and finally either assigned by the teacher or selected by the pupils. Goals are becoming clear when the planning stops and work starts. A new configuration emerges because of the change in goal orientation. It is quite possible to keep other changes from occurring so that only goal orientation is changed. Suppose worksheets were handed out so that the teacher's authority is now expressed through this type of highly structured task. Pupil contacts would be highly restricted if the pupils were required to complete their assignments without talking. The range of ideas would obviously remain highly controlled. In this case, the sequence pair would consist of a first configuration consisting of goal ambiguity,

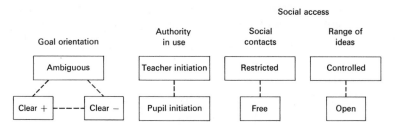

Figure 10–2.

high teacher initiation, restricted social contacts, and controlled range of ideas; the second configuration of the pair would be the same except that goals would now be clear instead of ambiguous, the other three conditions remaining the same.

CONCEPTS FOR DESCRIBING EDUCATIONAL OUTCOMES

Concepts describing educational outcomes, however limited they may be, are a part of a teaching strategy. They are necessary because a teaching strategy is concerned with establishing relationships between actions and consequences, between classroom activities and what pupils learn from these activities.

CONTENT ACHIEVEMENT

One consequence of teaching is learning, and those interested in teaching strategies are required by this interest to assess what the children learned. Those who object to an assessment of pupil achievement for the purpose of relating the data to teaching behavior are quite justified when the design of the investigation fails to control the factors, other than teaching behavior, which influence achievement. Those who claim that content achievement tests fail to quantify all the important educational outcomes are also quite justified; anyone who has constructed a test knows that only a small portion of learning is sampled by the test items. Those who believe that achievement testing adversely affects a teacher's philosophy and psychology of education may also be expressing a valid opinion. Nevertheless, given an appropriate research design, inferences about *relative* learning can be made between two groups of teacher-classroom units by sampling content achievement with a carefully designed test.

Much more will be said about evaluation problems in Chapters 11 and 12 which are concerned with research. Our purpose here is to define one educational outcome as *content achievement*. In one degree or another, pupils learn what is being taught and estimates of learning can be secured by the careful use of tests.

PUPIL ATTITUDES

Pupil attitudes are perceptions of the teacher and the classroom activities which are held in common by pupils in spite of their individual differences. A class average on a pupil questionnaire is a fairly stable and useful measure of this educational outcome.

The pupil attitude inventories which have been most successful in the research on teaching effectiveness in projects under my direction consisted of more than 50 items to which pupils react on a four- or five-point scale. An inventory can be divided into subscales. The most successful subscale in our research might be called "teacher attractiveness." It contained items like:

"I'd like to have this teacher next year."
"This is one of the best teachers I have ever had."

The teacher attractiveness scale was judged to be more successful because it had higher reliability and the average scale scores correlated with classroom inter-action measures at higher levels.

Other scales in our inventory include "fairness of rewards and punishments," "interest in schoolwork," "pupil independence," and "absence of disabling anxiety." The last two subscales correlated least with the first three subscales. Teacher attractiveness, fairness of rewards and punishments, and interest in schoolwork were all three positively intercorrelated (34, p. 45).

Measures of pupil attitudes do fluctuate from one teacher to the next and less frequently from one class to another with the same teacher. The class average is a useful measure of an educational outcome when the testing conditions are standardized and only comparisons within a careful research design are made.

INDEPENDENCE-DEPENDENCE AND SELF-DIRECTION

Given the power advantages and greater maturity of teachers, all pupils are dependent to some extent on teacher initiation. In general, teachers initiate, pupils respond. The actions of the teacher can influence this characteristic of pupil behavior, although the personality traits of the individual pupil also play a part. What is meant here by independent behavior is the tendency of the pupil to take the initiative when the opportunity exists, to be more self-directing in his work, and to be less concerned with teacher authority when busy on a learning task. What is meant by dependent behavior is the preference of the pupil to comply to teacher initiative, to solicit it when it is absent, and to react much more to teacher authority while working on learning tasks.

One measure of pupil initiative can be secured from the ratio of pupil initiation statements to pupil response statements* when the FIAC system is used to code classroom interaction. Such ratios are more meaningful when the data collected during the planning work and the supervision of work are isolated for separate analysis.

Another measure might come from any system of observation which records how often pupils solicit teacher directions, go up to the teacher and ask, "Is this the way you wanted it?", or "Can I go on to the next step, now?" and any other behaviors which solicit teacher approval and direction.

EXPLAINING VARIATION IN TEACHING BEHAVIOR

Variety and sequence of teacher-pupil influence enter into strategies for controlling the development of pupil independence and self-direction. In order to specify the "if ... then" conditional relationships in a given strategy, the concepts which have just been discussed are to be used. A particular set of conditional relationships can be expressed as an hypothesis. Strategies for controlling independence and self-direction consist of a series of hypotheses, each to be acted upon according to the turn of events. So that teaching becomes the exploration of probable conditional relationships between teaching behavior and the reactions of the pupils.

It would be nice if teaching could be more definite than merely exploring hypotheses stated in the form of conditional relationships. For example, someday principles of instruction may be stated as laws which operate with a known probability. Knowledge about teaching with this degree of specification is not now at hand and will require many years of research of a quality that is much higher than our present efforts.

To be realistic, any laws about teaching behavior must take into account why some characteristic of teaching behavior varies, one episode compared with the next. A proposition such as "teacher warmth and kindness are associated with higher achievement" fails to take into account why teachers who are usually warm and kind are sometimes distant and demanding. Or to give another example, an inflexible law to the effect that pupil initiative with teacher response produces more positive pupil attitudes fails to explain why periods of teacher initiative with pupil response can also be found in classrooms in which pupil achievement is above average. Teachers sometimes act one way and sometimes act another and it is quite possible that such variation is lawful.

---

*See pupil initiation ratio (PIR), Chapter 4.

In this section some hypotheses about teaching behavior and pupil independence are presented and discussed. In each case, the relationships are specified for conditions which are known to change over time. Thus, these hypotheses are attempts to explain why *variation* in teaching behavior can be expected to be related to pupil independence and self-direction. Taken altogether, they cast doubt on the old admonition that above all, a teacher should be consistent if by consistent we mean that a teacher should try to make use of the same teaching patterns in the same way in all or nearly all situations.

HYPOTHESES ABOUT EDUCATIONAL OUTCOMES

In this section we are interested in using the concepts which have just been described in order to form conditional relationships which predict educational outcomes. These conditional relationships take the form shown below:

If . . .   a certain goal orientation exists
                                      (here we begin with the pupils' goal perceptions)

And . . .   classroom interaction is characterized by
                                      (a) certain authority in use
                                      (b) certain social contacts ⎱ social access
                                      (c) and range of ideas   ⎰
                                      (here are features of the interaction)

Then we *probably* expect . . .   certain educational outcomes, in terms of
                                      (a) pupil initiation and self-direction
                                      (b) average pupil attitudes
                                      (c) average subject matter achievement.

If we had a number of conditional relationships, all verified through research and experimentation, we would be well on the road toward a theory of instruction. Notice that the proposed relationships begin with the perceptions of the goals that are held by the pupils. Educational outcomes are then specified.

Variation in teaching behavior enters into consideration because goal orientation always changes with the passage of time. Even when pupils are brought into a room and told that they can do what they want and, for purposes of discussion, let us assume that the pupils are convinced; some unique goal clarification is developed by each individual. Goal ambiguity is an unstable social condition and is not likely to persist for an extended period of time. As goals become clearer it is reasonable to expect that the configuration of authority in use, social contacts, and range of ideas would be altered in order to maximize desired educational outcomes. This may be especially true of the teacher's authority in use. As goals become clarified, we can expect the balance of teacher initiation and pupil initiation to change.

In this section some hypothetical relations among these concepts are proposed. A college student or an experienced teacher who is interested in exploring teaching strategies which control pupil initiation and self-direction may find it instructive to test these hypotheses in terms of their own teaching behavior and classroom conditions. It is through personal inquiry that each of us can decide whether to reject or accept the proposed relationships.

AMBIGUOUS GOALS

As defined earlier, goal ambiguity occurs when the end points of learning activities and the procedures to reach them are not clearly perceived by the pupils. A pupil may know that arithmetic comes after recess, but he may not know what arithmetic process is to be studied and he may not be sure how he can start to work. In a first grade, the pupils may know that they are going to study the farm or the city, but will the learning tasks to be built around a sand-box model, will there be pictures to paint, or will trips be taken?

Goal ambiguity is not only present before work starts, it can occur later when difficulties arise in the conduct of work. When these difficulties occur and a pupil does not know how to overcome them, he no longer can guide his own problem-solving.

The presence of goal ambiguity is unstable because both adults and children become uncomfortable when they don't know what to do. Lack of purpose makes teachers especially nervous and they sometimes respond by acting hastily and without very much thought. When goals are not clear, the cooperative pupils may feel guilty and seek to verify the situation with the teacher; the troublemakers usually begin making trouble; the impatient teachers usually become impatient.

Alternatives

When goals are unclear, the teacher acts. How he acts is the issue. A hasty action might be illustrated by the teacher who says, "Take out your geography books and start reading on page one." Most pupils will comply to such a request, but this compliance is not evidence that pupils perceive clear learning goals. It takes time to clarify goals and the important decisions made during this period determine the degree and quality of pupil participation. Keep in mind that goal clarity is a pupil perception, not just a teacher perception.

In analyzing this problem, our model for thinking is based on the four dimensions of classroom interaction which were described in the last section. As ambiguous goal orientation moves toward goal clarity, how will the teacher vary authority in use? How will he arrange the social contacts in the communication

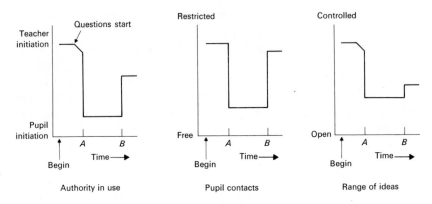

Fig. 10—3.   Clarifying Learning Goals with Pupil Participation.

network and control the range of ideas expressed? Just how do sequence and variety enter in? One way to guide our thinking is to suggest several hypotheses about ambiguous goal conditions. We will consider just two, although more are possible:

1) When goals are ambiguous, sustained teacher initiation with restricted pupil contacts and teacher controlled ideas is less likely to produce positive goal attraction and more likely to produce compliance with high pupil dependence on teacher supervision.

2) When goals are ambiguous, increasing pupil initiation and maintaining flexible social access are more likely to produce positive goal attraction, pupil independence, and more sustained self-direction.

An example will help to give these hypotheses more meaning. Let us assume that 10 or 15 minutes are to be spent clarifying some schoolwork which will keep pupils busy for a reasonably long period of work. The teacher decides to start by describing general goals for learning and then suggests one or two illustrative individual projects. In a total class formation the teacher asks for suggestions from the pupils. After a number of suggestions have been written on the blackboard, discussion groups are formed with approximately five pupils in each group. Individual learning tasks are discussed as each pupil reveals what he thinks he would like to do. When the class comes back together some of the more interesting projects are shared. Those who are ready start work while the teacher continues to help other pupils who are still unsure about their plans. The three graphs shown in Fig. 10—3 illustrate an idealized model of this kind of teacher-pupil planning.

Notice that all three graphs have a time line which begins to the left, is followed by point *A* when the discussion groups were formed, and by point *B*

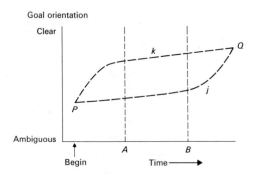

Fig. 10—4.   Goal Orientation.

when the pupils returned to a total class formation. In the left graph for authority in use, the teacher begins by taking the initiative. Soon questions permit some pupil initiation. At point *A*, pupils express their own ideas in groups, and after *B* these are shared with the teacher and class. Pupil contacts, illustrated in the center graph, are restricted by a total class formation at the beginning and end of the planning session, with free access within each group occurring during the discussion period. In the right graph, the range of ideas is initially controlled by the teacher, but after point *A*, the range of ideas is more open, especially in the privacy of a pupil discussion group.

Sequence enters in when the three time intervals are considered. The initial more structured period is followed by higher pupil self-direction, and this, in turn, is followed by a teacher led summary discussion in which pupil ideas can be supported or modified by the teacher. Variety consists of three levels of authority in use, two levels of pupil contact, and two, or perhaps three, levels in the range of ideas expressed.

As a result of these three periods of activity, each with its own configuration, the goal orientation of the pupils is becoming clearer. In Fig. 10—4, the initial ambiguous goal perception is shown as point *P* and a clearer perception at a later time at point *Q*. Whether the growth of clearer perceptions would be best illustrated by a straight line between *P* and *Q* or a nonlinear curve like *j* or *k* is unknown. If measurements of pupil goal perceptions could be made at the end of each time period, it would be possible to judge which curve best illustrates how goals gradually become clear.

Teacher inquiry into situations with ambiguous goals

The purpose of varying authority in use, social contacts, and the range of ideas as goals are being clarified, is to produce clear, attractive goals which permit increasing pupil self-direction and independence. How this is to be achieved is likely to be different, one teacher compared with another, or one situation compared to the next. The way a particular teacher finds his optimum strategies is to conduct his own inquiry. There are a number of factors which appear to be in conflict with each other and which require creative solutions.

First, there is a curriculum. To some degree, the classroom activities are to be associated with this curriculum. Some form of teacher initiation is required in order to influence the nature of the learning activities. Yet when goals are ambiguous, teacher initiation increases pupil dependence. This is a conflict which must be resolved in some optimum manner.

Second, there is a problem of efficiency. With too much time spent in planning, the period of time for accomplishing work decreases. Yet more careful and effective planning may produce interest and motivation which will persist for longer work periods. This is a conflict which must be resolved.

Third, each combination of task and pupil produces its own balance of dependence-independence, more attractive—less attractive, quickness in clarifying goals—slowness in clarifying goals, and so on. Some pupils are ready to go to work before others. Some optimum point for starting work must be found.

There are other conflicts which grow out of the nature of the learning goals, the maturity of the pupils, and the teacher's preferred style of interaction. Perhaps enough of them have been mentioned to indicate that here is a rich area for professional inquiry. There is one point of view, however, on which there should be more agreement—it would seem unlikely that a single assignment for the entire class, administered in a standardized fashion, is likely to resolve the conflicts which are present. Once this assumption is made, some kind of teacher-pupil planning becomes necessary.

A teacher can explore different strategies for dealing with goal ambiguity by adapting the five steps of inquiry which were recommended in the last chapter. Instead of investigating patterns of interaction, longer strategies are the object of study. For these longer teaching periods interaction analysis is more efficient than video recording for systematic feedback. Observer notations or ratings which permit inferences about pupil motivation and persistence in work can also be a helpful adjunct to interaction analysis coding.

CLEAR GOAL ORIENTATION

Ambiguous goals give way to clear goals and more time is spent in a classroom with the pupils at work than is spent in planning that work. In any strategy of teaching, it is quite possible that teaching behavior which is more appropriate for work and summarizing work may be of a different quality compared with planning work. Teachers adjust their behavior from one phase of teaching to another, and hypotheses about teaching strategies should be able to explain these differences.

Clear positive goals

The second hypothesis predicted that some form of pupil initiation during the planning of work is more likely to result in positive clear goals for subsequent learning. Suppose pupils are at work on learning tasks that they understand and teacher-pupil contacts under these circumstances are to be explained. Although the first hypothesis predicted that sustained high teacher initiation and rigid social access produces compliance and dependence, there may be other times during teaching when these characteristics of teacher initiation are appropriate. One hypothesis might be: *When goals are clear and positive, high teacher initiation is less likely to produce dependence to the extent that the pupil sees this initiation as helpful in satisfying the learning task requirements.* A teacher who judges accurately how to help a pupil complete his learning task can initiate suggestions and directions which may expedite learning. Teacher initiation, under these circumstances, may even be more helpful when it is followed by conditions in which pupils can resume an appropriate degree of self-direction.

Clear negative goals

When the pupils are at work on tasks which they find unattractive, a special system of rewards and punishments is required to maintain work. This condition, by its very nature, creates pupil dependence and decreases self-direction. One hypothesis might be: *When goals are clear and negative, modifying the valence of the goal requires diagnosis based on increasing pupil initiation, attention to attitudes and feelings, leading to either a change in the learning activities or a change in the pupils' perceptions.* The implementation of this last hypothesis requires considerable social skill on the part of a teacher and might best be achieved by following the model suggested for ambiguous goals.

Another hypothesis about clear negative goals refers to those situations in which a teacher decides to force work with some system of surveillance. *When goals are clear and negative, high teacher initiation with restricted social access and with rewards and punishments controlled by the teacher are necessary to maintain pupil compliance and dependence.* There is a growing evidence that this last configuration is less effective in producing content achievement than other configurations and is more likely to increase negative pupil attitudes.

SEQUENCE AND VARIETY

Regardless of current teaching practices, the researcher seeks conditions which improve the educational outcomes. This means speculating about ideal patterns of teaching and investigating strategies for supporting pupil independence and self-direction. These longer strategies take into consideration sequences which occur during different phases of learning, including the time that goals are first introduced, learning tasks are identified, work occurs, and learning is summarized. The purpose of discussing these strategies is to consider and study alternative ways to support greater independence and self-direction for pupils who work on learning tasks.

Suppose strategies are considered which apply to patterns of teaching behavior which occur during a 2-week unit of study. In this case, variations of teaching behavior which might occur in a 2-hour or 1-hour period of instruction can be ignored, even though these short cycles may have much in common with longer cycles. During the first two days of an organized 10-day unit of study, it would seem reasonable to assume that the goals of instruction were least clear and that a major purpose of instruction would be to clarify the goals by developing individual learning tasks. During the middle 6 days of such a unit, it could be assumed that work was underway on the learning tasks and that greater goal clarity would be present. The last 2 days of such a unit of study would represent the terminal activities of summarizing and hearing reports from pupils who have been working on individual learning tasks.

A study of this type has been conducted by the author (35) and is reported in detail in the reference cited. The next three sections briefly describe parts of this study, especially the parts that have to do with sequence and variety.

The design of the study

Sixteen 1-hour, eighth grade mathematics and fifteen 2-hour, seventh grade core classes (English and social studies) and their teachers were selected for this project. The methods of selection helped to increase differences among the classes with respect to classroom interaction. The math classes studied a unit containing content not normally taught in the eight grade and the core classes studied a unit on New Zealand; both units were selected so that learning would be least influenced by previous schoolwork and by the environment outside of the classroom. All the instructional materials were supplied, were the same for each teacher, and were provided in enough quantity and had enough variety so that each teacher could use his own natural style of instruction regardless of the size of his class.

Pretests and posttests of achievement were administered just before and just after the 10 days of instruction. A posttest of pupil attitude was also administered. All tests were carefully designed and improved through pilot runs and item analysis. The achievement test not only required recall of facts, but presented problems which demanded skill in the transfer of learning. Trained observers coded classroom interaction with the FIAC system during the first 2 days, the last 2 days, and 2 days near the middle of the 10-day period. The posttest achievement scores were adjusted through analysis of covariance in terms of pretest scores in order to compensate for differences in initial ability between classes.

The hypotheses about sequence and variety

Although this study has been widely quoted to indicate that achievement is higher with "indirect"* teaching, the main purpose was to study variation in teaching behavior during a 2-week unit of instruction. Within the limitations of observing only 6 of the 10 teaching days, the hypotheses about sequence and variation were as follows.†

First, in high achieving classrooms the teacher's initiation will be low and his response high when goals are ambiguous. As goals become clarified, the teacher's initiation will increase and his response will decrease.

Second, in low achieving classrooms, the teacher's initiation will be high and his response low when goals are ambiguous. As goals become clarified there will be less variation in these classes compared with the higher achieving classes.

The results

Before turning to the results, a word to those readers who are qualified researchers. The conclusions about to be stated are in what might be called "popular form" and are pushed to the edge of being overstated. Should you wish to compare these conclusions with the original data, please read the footnote.‡

In making comparisons with earlier references, remember that "indirect" is here called "teacher response with pupil initiative" and "direct" is called "teacher initiative with pupil compliance." Here the two treatments are called "high and low achievement," whereas they were originally called "indirect" and "direct." Also the sharpest readers may note a discrepancy between the graphs on page 107 of the Monograph, compared with similar graphs on page 217 in Biddle and Ellena, and page 232 in Amidon and Hough. The monograph graphs were for all teachers; the later two graphs were from data that were reworked for the "most indirect" and the "most direct" teachers—both slightly smaller groups.

A first step in the analysis of the data was to rank the teachers in each subject field according to the teacher's tendency to make use of teacher response

---

*"Indirect" teaching, mentioned on page 102, refers to combining teacher response with pupil initiation and is quantified by the i/d ratio: Categories 1 + 2 + 3 divided by 6 + 7. Thus, this measure depends entirely on the quality of teacher talk, excluding Categories 4 and 5.

†The words used to state the hypotheses in this book are not the same as the original monograph, but the theoretical import is identical.

‡The original Cooperative Research Monograph (39) is difficult to locate in libraries, but can be secured from the author at cost. Summaries of this project may be more easily located in two other references (38) and (40).

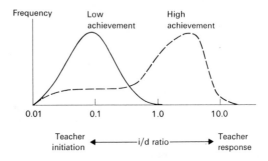

Fig. 10–5.   Range of i/d Ratios Showing Variation in Teaching Behavior.

to pupils' ideas. At the top of this rank order were those teachers who responded more often to pupil ideas; at the bottom end were those teachers who more often used teacher initiation. The list was then split at the median and the adjusted achievement of the top group was compared with the low group. In both mathematics and social studies classes, the adjusted achievement of the top group (those whose teachers were more responsive), was significantly higher than the other group. The same significant differences also occurred when average class scores on positive pupil attitudes were compared. Put most simply, in those classrooms in which the teacher responded to pupil ideas more often, the pupils appeared to be learning more and liking the learning activities better.

The interaction analysis data were tabulated separately for different classroom situations; for example, administrative routines like passing out or collecting materials were time intervals tabulated separately from introducing new content materials or planning work, and so on. A separate i/d ratio could be calculated for each type of activity so that five or six ratios were available from each teacher. Fig. 10–5 shows a smoothed frequency distribution of these ratios for the high and low achievement classes separately. The most important feature of the graph is the *range* for each distribution. In both social studies and mathematics, the low achievement classes exhibited a range from about 0.01 to just above 1.0, while the range from the high achievement classes was from about 0.01 to above 10.0, almost 20. Our first conclusion, then, is that variation of teacher initiative and response during the different teaching conditions in a 10-day unit was much greater in the high achievement classes. In fact, any particular balance of teacher initiative and response which appeared in the low achievement classes also appeared in the high achievement classes, but the reverse was not true. Teachers in the high achievement classes were able to achieve ratios, during some periods of instruction, which were much higher and which never appeared in low achievement classes. Apparently the

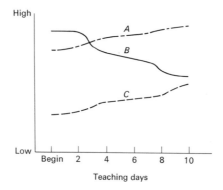

Fig. 10—6.   Variation in High Achievement Classes.

variety of interaction patterns was greater in those classrooms in which pupils learned more and liked it better. These data also support the distinction between level one and level two patterns made in Chapter 1. There are more level two interaction patterns present in the high achievement classes.

Our second concern is with sequence. The question is whether variation in teacher initiative and response followed sequences such as those suggested in our hypotheses. By assuming that goals are least clear during the first 2 days, the data from the high achievement classes showed teacher response to pupil ideas was highest when goals were unclear and then tended to decrease afterward. These data also indicate that teacher initiative was lowest when goals were unclear and then became higher during subsequent teaching days. In Fig. 10—6 the solid line B illustrates a smoothed curve that shows the decrease in teacher responsive behavior. Line C shows an increase in teacher initiation which might be typical of situations which arise in social studies. Line A, which is higher at all points, might be more typical of teacher initiation in a subject like mathematics.

In the low achievement classes, the sequences were quite different compared with high achievement classes. Also the social studies low achievement classes were quite similar to the low achievement classes in mathematics. One might make an educated guess that variation in teacher initiative in low achieving classes, regardless of subject matter, may be more similar than between high achieving classes. In Fig. 10—7 the smoothed curve D for teacher initiation is more variable and more interesting than curve E which illustrates relatively constant, low teacher response. Note that teacher initiation is highest at the beginning and end of the unit, when the teacher is more likely to work with the class as a total unit. These teachers are also more likely to respond to goal ambiguity by giving assignments and directions in order to have work

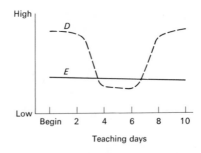

Fig. 10—7.   Variation in Low Achievement Classes.

begin. They also provide more teacher initiation during the terminal activities at the end of the unit such as review and summarization. Teacher response in the low achievement classes is uniformly low and has very little variation.

Those who wish to compare these smooth curves with the original data will notice that there is variation between different phases of instruction among low achieving classes. The changes are small,* but they do show pattern tendencies in terms of i/d ratio.

Summary of sequence and variety

For the classroom teacher, this discussion of variety and sequence suggests that variation in teaching behavior and special arrangements for social access are features of classroom instruction which are worth investigating. Inquiry projects for a teacher may be most rewarding when they concentrate on those phases of teaching in which goals are clarified and learning tasks for individual pupils are specified. It may well be that a teacher's natural impulse to "move in and set things straight" or in other ways to combine teacher initiative with pupil compliance are patterns which should be questioned, at least when goals are ambiguous.

The variety of classroom interaction patterns and the sequence with which they occur may someday prove to have significant differences between more effective and less effective teaching. The study just reported contains only two examples of variety and sequence in the patterns of teacher initiation and response. With such a complex topic, one research project is no basis for making generalizations about teaching. Future investigations of this topic face several unresolved issues. First, how shall we define a pattern which presumably will

---

*The issue of variation in the low achieving classes must be considered unresolved. A log transformation of the i/d ratios would show that variation does exist in these "more direct" classes, but it is still not as great as in most high achievement classes. How best to transform these data and what would result are not known at this time.

vary from one phase of teaching to the next? Does it exist for less than 5 minutes? Or is the unit of investigation to be a full period of teaching which can vary from one day to the next? Second, this is surely a research topic which requires true experiments in contrast to field studies. Controlled field studies face the problem of locating classrooms in which there will be reasonably large variety and flexibility in sequences. Unless research variables vary, hypotheses about variation cannot be investigated. True experiments might follow the design of training some teachers until the variety of classroom interaction patterns and the use of different sequences can be guaranteed in an experimental treatment. Such experimental classes can then be compared with more representative teaching.

PUPIL INDEPENDENCE AND COGNITIVE FUNCTIONING

If variety and sequence of teacher and pupil initiative are related to pupil achievement and attitude, as the two studies reported in the last section suggest, then it may also be related in some way with the logical aspects of classroom discourse. Why would these relationships hold? How can the results be explained? In answer to these questions, this section contains a discussion about the teacher's use of broad questions, Category 3, and pupil initiation; speculations are then made about how all three of these events might be related to the development of longer thought units during classroom discourse.

RESEARCH ON THE COGNITIVE ASPECTS OF CLASSROOM DISCOURSE

Deciding what a unit of thought is, how it can be defined, identified, and taken into account in analyzing thinking have been major stumbling blocks for those who have been concerned with logic in the classroom. For example, Smith (90), Bellack (9), and Taba (99), and their associates, have all spent considerable time trying to decide how a unit of thought can be defined and identified.

A unit of thought can be defined in a number of ways. It may be that a unit should be concerned with one topic or one idea. On the other hand, a series of statements about different topics might be considered to be within a single thought unit because they serve a common logical function. In any case, a unit of thought begins with some event and terminates sometime later with another event. Figure 10–8 illustrates a string of events, and a unit of thought may terminate after any one of the events in the chain, depending on its definition.

An initial event might occur when a teacher asks a question which focuses the attention of the class on possible answers. If it is a narrow question, a

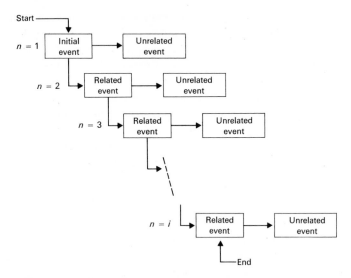

Fig. 10—8.   Thought Units as a String of Communication Events.

single, correct answer may be given and then the teacher asks a second question. The first question and answer forms a two-event string in the chain of classroom interaction. The third event, in this example, may be unrelated to the initial question or answer and therefore becomes the first event of a new string.

A larger string might occur, simply because the researcher has a different system of deciding what is or is not related to the first event. For example, a series of different, narrow questions might be considered to be part of a strategy whereby certain facts are assembled. Once assembled, the teacher may then ask a question which requires the pupils to speculate about relationships among the facts. In this case, what is a unit of thought? Should the unit include the first phase of assembling facts *plus* the interpretation or application of these facts to a larger problem? Researchers who follow Smith attempt to consider all possible combinations of these sequences in terms of an elaborate and comprehensive set of logical categories. Those who work with Taba would prefer to consider those sequences which fit their models of how children think. For them, a string of events is judged as present when the characteristics of the string match certain logical steps which are a part of the teaching objectives. Bellack and his associates have four basic moves in their category system, two initiatory and two responsive, which produced a total of 21 admissible strings in the data they studied.

Another factor which enters into defining a thought unit is that the sample of classroom interaction on which a preliminary investigation is based may be of poor quality in terms of logic. In fact, our efforts to subscript logical aspects of classroom interaction at Michigan would lead us to the conclusion that common practice is severely limited in terms of logical thought units. A system may be able to code and explain the logical aspects of common teaching practice, but this procedure may produce a system of classification that cannot code the more effective, ideal patterns of interaction that are to be found only in exceptional classrooms. Taba's response to this issue was to train teachers in certain skills of logic along with the development of her category system.

From the progress so far in analyzing the logical aspects of classroom communication, it appears that deciding what is a thought unit looms immediately as a difficult problem that has not yet been satisfactorily resolved.

SUSTAINING LONGER THOUGHT UNITS

It seems reasonable to infer from the work of Smith, Bellack, and Taba that high levels of thinking do require long chains of interrelated statements. This may be especially true if we accept Taba's assertion that the pupils should be practicing high level thought processes. The teaching skills required to create circumstances in which pupils can make generalizations, for example, may be much more difficult and require long chains of statements, compared with situations in which only the teacher makes the generalizations.

Let us assume that definitions of what is meant, in Fig. 10–8, by "related" will continue to be investigated for many years. Furthermore, even when satisfactory definitions have been developed, applications may require typescripts, voice recordings, and much more time, compared with coding for immediate feedback. This assumption seems fairly reasonable, given our present knowledge. Events form short chains, these short chains form larger clusters, and teaching strategies may involve creating certain sequences among clusters.

Taba, more than any other researcher in this field, has attempted to break out of this conceptual difficulty by postulating models of how children think and then ask how the teacher can act in order to facilitate logical thought. She emphasizes the asking of good questions (similar to those on p. 301) asking them in the proper sequence, and pacing the asking so that more pupils can keep up with the cognitive processes that are involved. Many of the teacher questions she uses as illustrations would be classified in Category 3 in the FIAC system, since the pupil is asked to explain and the teacher to support ideas previously expressed. It is at this point that a possible relationship might exist between "indirectness" proposed in this book and logical thought in classroom discourse.

When questions are open, but introduce a new idea or train of thought, they are likely to appear as a 4–9 transition in the 10-category system. Enlarging and developing the ideas suggested by pupils involves 9–3, 3–3, and

3—9 sequence pairs. When a teacher follows the teaching strategies suggested by Taba, an above average incidence of the four sequence pairs just mentioned must occur. However, the reverse is not necessarily true, since the following reasoning applies. A longer chain must involve the use of Category 3* and 4—9 transitions. A high incidence in any cells involving this category must be present with long chains of thought. Thus, we can say that the below average incidence in the use of Category 3 precludes the above average use of long thought chains. The reasons the reverse statement is not true, namely the above average incidence in Category 3 is evidence of long logical thought chains, rests on the argument that pupil ideas can be reacted to in a nonlogical fashion. This presents a "necessary versus sufficient" distinction. The above average incidence in the 4—9, 9—3, 3—3, and 3—9 cells is necessary to long logical thought chains, but this evidence is not sufficient to prove the existence of such chains.

This discussion does emphasize the key position of the teacher in creating and maintaining long chains of logical thought. Remember that the teacher talks more than the pupils, structures most of the inquiry problems, and has a greater opportunity than pupils to control the ideas discussed and the order in which they are discussed. The teacher is in the best position to maintain a chain of related statements, no matter how they may be related, such as the chain illustrated in Fig. 10—8. Knowing how to ask open questions and respond to ideas suggested by pupils is a first step toward performing the strategies suggested by Taba. The presence of these teacher behaviors, then, is a necessary but not a sufficient condition for creating long chains of logical thought.

SUMMARY OF CONCEPTS FOR THINKING ABOUT PUPIL INDEPENDENCE

The chapter began with the consideration of goal orientation in terms of authority in use, pupil contacts, and the range of ideas expressed in the classroom. These concepts were suggested as tools for thinking about how pupil learning could become more independent and self-directing. Should a teacher become interested in investigating long teaching strategies with these concepts, some attention to variation and sequence in teacher initiation and response patterns appears to be justified. These inquiry experiences might lead to an increase of levels two and three interaction patterns which were first described in Chapter 1 and again in Chapter 9.

---

*There is a subtle issue here, which pivots on the definition of "related," as illustrated in Fig. 10—8. The issue is that "logically related" must be included in the definition of Category 3. In most cases this is probably true.

The hypotheses discussed in this chapter can be combined to form teaching strategies which seek to promote pupil independence and self-direction. For example, emphasizing teacher response when goals are not clear and then increasing teacher initiation after work gets underway appears to be a promising variation of teaching behavior. Shifting back to emphasizing teacher response when diagnosing learning difficulties may be another helpful strategy. There is a possibility that teacher response to pupil ideas is an essential feature of discourse which reaches higher levels of logic during classroom discussion. These propositions are tentative and the first two were illustrated by evidence from classes which were involved in a 2-week unit of study. In order to move from these rather primitive and somewhat general propositions to more explicit strategies, a teacher is encouraged to conduct his own inquiry. Before there can be any laws about variation in teaching behavior, a great deal more research must be accomplished.

Chapter Eleven

HELPING OTHERS CHANGE THEIR
TEACHING BEHAVIOR

SHOW AND TELL IN TEACHING TEACHERS

The emphasis throughout this book on consistency between intentions and teaching actions is most appropriate when we consider how one person helps another change his teaching behavior. It is most appropriate here because those who teach teachers have their own teaching behavior on display. There is a kind of show and tell going on continuously in which teaching behavior is shown at the instant that the instructor talks about it. Showing teaching behavior as you talk about it makes preservice and inservice education literal examples of show and tell. Even though some professors and supervisors think primarily in terms of "telling," their more mature students may be equally if not more impressed by what they see rather than hear.

The fact that teaching behavior occurs when we help others shape and reshape their own teaching behavior leads directly to obvious consequences. If we want our classroom teachers to be concerned with their pupils' goal orientation, we can help by assessing the goal perceptions of college students or experienced teachers as they are being taught. If we want our adult students to adjust their authority in use, arrange different social contacts, and expand the range of pupil ideas when they teach, then we can demonstrate the required analytical techniques in our own teaching. If we urge adults to support pupil initiative and self-direction, then the place to begin is where we are, in *our* classroom, with *our* students. Anything less than a reasonable consistency between what is said about teaching and the events that comprise this instruction creates a charade in which those involved pretend to believe, but really have no conviction. For the more mature adult student, "show" usually wins when there is a conflict between show and tell.

OVERVIEW

The material in this chapter is divided into two sections: first, the characteristics of a change environment are discussed; second, some of the research reports which evaluate efforts to help others change their teaching behavior are reviewed. The first section looks ahead to some of the problems of creating more effective programs to improve teaching. The second section reports past efforts. Taken together, it is clear that the state of the art in teacher preparation and inservice programs is still exploratory. In spite of the progress of the last 10 years, there is much more to be learned than has, so far, been accomplished.

THE CHANGE ENVIRONMENT

Suppose a change environment could be created which did, in fact, help teachers alter their teaching behavior and then helped them discover whether the modifications were or were not improvements. What would such a change environment look like? In isolated programs, one element of a potent change environment or another has been tried out. Some innovators have tried microteaching, others have taught interaction analysis, and still others have introduced simulated practice, T-groups, or simply more intensive observation and field work. Only a few innovators have tried two or more of these techniques in a coherent and potent curriculum.

THE OBJECTIVES OF PROFESSIONAL SELF-DEVELOPMENT

The objectives listed below are concerned with developing and controlling teaching behavior with independence and self-direction. These objectives seem just as relevant to inservice education as they are to preservice education. After all, most of the teachers employed today have had no more opportunity to study teaching behavior systematically than have the college students who are preparing to enter the profession.

First Objective.   A competent teacher can identify different patterns of teaching behavior, code them, assess them, perform them, and string them together into strategies of classroom instruction.

Second Objective.   A competent teacher can design inquiry projects and carry them out in order to compare different patterns of his own teaching behavior and different strategies of teaching.

Third Objective.   A competent teacher can control the balance of pupil initiation and his own initiation so that it varies purposefully during the planning, conduct, and evaluation of schoolwork.

Fourth Objective.   A competent teacher can design and use instruments for assessing pupil attitudes and achievement and is able to relate measures of these outcomes to various teaching strategies.

Fifth Objective.   A competent teacher can guide the logic of thought processes during the teacher-pupil interchange, including defining terms, grouping them, labeling them with appropriate concepts, then using these concepts to make comparisons, explanations, or predictions, and formulating and testing generalizations.

Sixth Objective.   A competent teacher can help his colleagues develop analytical skills, provide consultation during inquiry, and can accept the responsibility for analyzing his own teaching behavior as well as helping others do the same.

Seventh Objective.   A competent teacher continues to build his theory of instruction, to develop principles of instruction, and to study his own teaching behavior in terms of its consequences.

Eighth Objective.   A competent teacher develops commitments and convictions about his own teaching behavior in terms of preferred patterns of classroom interaction and desired educational outcomes through personal experience and evaluation.

It would be redundant to take the space, here, to show how objectives one through four can be translated into inquiry experiences. Previous chapters have been devoted to these topics. Objectives five through eight are special products of the learning activities associated with the first four objectives. The last two objectives, for example, refer to convictions that are products of personal experience and experimentation. Objectives five and six involve the application of logic to classroom teaching and to one's own inquiry.

THE DENSITY OF A CHANGE ENVIRONMENT

The intensity of forces toward investigating one's own behavior is not well understood. This *intensity* of forces in a change environment, will be referred to simply as the density of the change environment. We do not understand how to increase the density of a change environment because the social inventions that are necessary have been developed separately and not combined. We have experimented with T-groups, microteaching, interaction analysis, and simulated skill training as separate means of achieving corrective feedback, but these techniques have seldom, if ever, been organized into a single integrated curriculum of professional self-development.

What passes for preservice and inservice education in different parts of the country is highly variable. At colleges and universities there are education courses covering a variety of topics. During a particular week of instruction a college student will hear, read, or discuss one or another principle of instruction and the evidence which supports it. A thoughtful discussion may take place, under better than average circumstances, in which there is an opportunity to examine a principle, decide what is meant, and speculate about the classroom conditions which would have to be present for the principle to operate. Only on rare occasions are these conclusions products of contemplation, shared opinions, and imagination. Being exposed to this level of meaning in a course of professional education is an example of what is meant by low level density. The insights are not products of intense experience and personal meanings are not carefully differentiated according to the behavioral skills required. In such circumstances, it is not easy to distinguish the consequences of a correct conception compared with a misconception. When organized in this way, the experiences are spread thinly over time, an hour's lecture here, a book that is read in the evening, an hour in writing on another day, a seminar discussion two days later. This is not the kind of experience which mobilizes extra energy and raises the tension of concentration. There is not enough drive to reduce a dissonance which may develop. Most of all, the learners do not personally explore new conceptual meanings in terms of their own behavior in anything like a systematic fashion.

Now suppose we could wave a magic wand and simply double the density of the change environment. Such a change might require considerable effort for both the students and the instructor. For example, observations in live classrooms, motion picture or closed circuit TV, more frequent tests and experiments in animal learning; suppose all these are added to the curriculum. Let's say that although everyone is working twice as hard, change in beginning teaching behavior is only slightly more effective, compared with the old curriculum. How could we explain such disappointing results? How could working twice as hard make so little difference in beginning teaching performance?

In an effort to answer these questions, suppose the relationship between input effort for professional development and output performance was not linear. Suppose, instead, a relationship such as the one illustrated in Fig. 11–1 represents the relationship between effort and progress. Let point L' represent the amount of progress that a college student would make by taking no special courses in education. Let point A represent the input level of the training experiences just described. When the activities are doubled, twice the input is represented by point B. Now look at the consequences of this effort. On the vertical output scale, ordinary living, input L, produces L' performance. Add some education courses and input increases to A, but performance increases merely to A'. Double the input effort to B and again performance increases only slightly to point B'. When these relationships hold, the presence or absence of effort at levels A or B makes very little difference in teaching performance, and one could question the wisdom of having education courses. A critic might say, and this is certainly not unknown, why not just eliminate education courses? One might point out, however, that specific courses not in education, probably would have the same relationship to any measure of beginning performance in classroom teaching, but eliminating noneducation courses is a suggestion that is very seldom made. It seems to me that most of the innovations

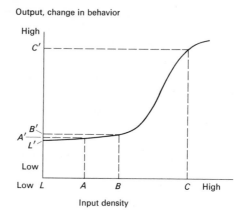

Fig. 11–1.   Input-Output Curve.

and curriculum changes which have been tried out in professional education prior to 1960 could fall somewhere between *L* and *B* in Fig. 11–1.

If the curve in Fig. 11–1 is correct, then increasing effort from *B* to *C* will create significant improvements. The question seems to be: What kind of experiences can be shown to make a difference in the performance of a beginning teacher? A difference, incidentally, that stands out so clearly that calculating its statistical significance would be a waste of time because it is so obvious.

SPECULATIONS ABOUT A HIGH DENSITY CHANGE ENVIRONMENT

The most speculative thing about a high density change environment is the idea itself. Since one has never existed, we don't know what it looks like, how it runs, or how effective it is. Perhaps the most relevant observation is that if it works, we need one; but if it doesn't, we don't.

The words which may help to imagine a high density change environment are grouped into four major dimensions in Fig. 11–2. These words, however, refer to the perceptions of the person whose behavior is to be modified and not necessarily to the perceptions of the person who is trying to help. This distinction can make quite a difference. Quite often college professors and inservice supervisors can explain the characteristics of the learning situations which they create. Such efforts are likely to loom large in the minds of those who are in charge. Yet the real issue is whether the college students or the participating teachers whose behavior is to change can recognize the main features in the change environment; indeed, whether these main features stand out and demand to be noticed.

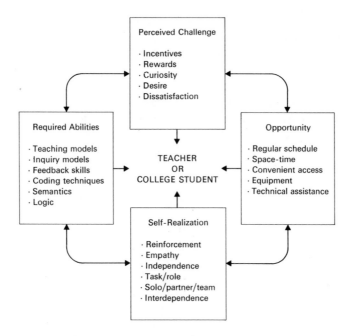

Fig. 11—2.   Forces in a Change Environment.

Opportunity

Opportunity to participate is illustrated in the right-hand quadrant of Fig. 11—2. Here we are concerned with the time-space-equipment-access features of the setting.

How much time should be allocated to a behavior clinic? One answer is to suggest full time participation. This may not be as impossible as it first appears at a college or university. For example, a fifth year for a teacher's credential is quite common and was offered without benefit of the M.A. degree before 1936 at the University of California at Berkeley, as I know from my own preparation for teaching. Full time to concentrate on the development and control of teaching behavior is quite possible during the summer and fall of a fifth year program, with practice teaching to follow. Scheduling full time participation in a behavior clinic in a 4-year program may be limited to periods in the summer, but it is not impossible.

In the public school systems there are at least two ways to arrange for full time participation. Summer periods are available, but there are possibilities during the year which may be less expensive. First, it is possible to set aside blocks of time for self-improvement on a regular weekly schedule through radical curriculum revision that leads to variable grouping, team teaching, and ungraded individual progress. At least this is one of the claims of those who propose such innovations. Second, and probably more certain for schools using a traditional class organization, class size can be increased. A school with 600 pupils and 20 teachers has an average class size of 30. It is possible to divide 600 by 19, rather than 20. One man-year of teaching time is released by increasing the average class size from 30 to just below 32. The released man-year could be divided into about $\frac{1}{2}$ month per teacher per academic year, or a full month every 2 years. Alternatively, the released teacher could spend his time continuously as an inquiry partner to each teacher who wishes to have the help.*

In any case, the goal is to locate periods of time which are not cluttered with regular responsibilities for either the college student or the employed teacher. The schedule should permit regular, planned, self-development activities.

Opportunity in terms of equipment, space, and access refers to a well designed laboratory, easily accessible, and provided with the equipment necessary to study and analyze behavior. Someday the specifications for such a facility will be as common as those required for a chemistry building or a high school shop. There is need for a large meeting hall for all study teams to meet together with good audio equipment, video recording, and playback facilities; small rooms for team meetings; equipment to facilitate coding, access to a computer, multicopy machines for data collecting forms, and the usual audio-visual equipment. Perhaps most important is the capability of scheduling pupils for microteaching sessions. The study and analysis of teaching behavior are activities that require highly specialized space and equipment.

Abilities and skills

The left-hand quadrant of Fig. 11—2 refers to the abilities and skills which are to be developed by participating in a high density change environment or which are prerequisite and should be developed before participating.

The study of semantics and logic might be recommended as prerequisite type skills. At universities and colleges the difficulty is to interest qualified instructors, usually from departments other than education, and to free them for the development of a service course designed primarily for teachers. Yet the use of language and the primary elements of logic are surely as important to teaching as a basic understanding of psychology, which has long been a prerequisite to teacher preparation courses.

Practice in coding techniques and feedback skills might be learned most effectively by investigating teaching models. These activities themselves can

---

*Negotiations between school boards and teachers' unions may include class size. However, unions are usually in favor of experimentation. When offered a choice that is carefully explained, teachers may vote to release a teacher to serve as an inquiry partner even though this results in a slight increase in average class size.

be understood in terms of self-directed inquiry and the models associated with inquiry. Just how these elements of a change environment can best be developed remains to be determined.

Perceived challenge

The top quadrant in Fig. 11–2 is meant to suggest that an essential part of a change environment is some kind of perceived challenge. Perhaps a person is curious about possible inconsistencies between his intentions and his actions and this curiosity stimulates his desire to analyze his own teaching behavior. Perhaps he enters the change environment with some dissatisfaction with his present performance and this dissatisfaction, when combined with opportunity, creates a challenge to which a constructive response is possible. Perhaps the most difficult function of those who are in charge of a change environment is to create challenge in a potent and constructive form. Pressure and coercion are not likely to be as effective as mutual planning which helps the individual create and recognize his own motives for participation. It is at this point that a teacher of teachers may find that his actions are inconsistent with his values. The methods he uses to create challenge in any learning situation speak louder than his professed values so that consistency between intent and action assumes critical importance.

Self-realization

The bottom quadrant of Fig. 11–2 contains words that refer to a variety of socialization processes. It may be that assisting a person to obtain that degree of self-realization which impels him toward self-improvement is a feature of a change environment which is most difficult to achieve. Adults differ in their need for independence and interdependence. In working alone, with a partner, or on a team, each individual seeks that "mix" of socialization that gives him the greatest satisfaction. A flexible program within a change environment will permit each person to make a unique adjustment, while working with others, so that his reinforcements and incentive are as high as possible.

A good deal that is accomplished in the name of professional preparation for teaching simply does not really involve the individual. This is equally true for those experienced teachers who participate in inservice programs. In one study involving the dissemination of innovative practices, Chesler and Flanders (24) found that forces such as "scientist gives dogma," "client becomes dependent," and "scientist takes responsibility" are found to be false facilitators of effective collaboration. More involvement in the partnership for inquiry is necessary in a high density change environment, whether the collaboration takes place in the field or in a college preparation program.

Creating the change environment

Those in charge of helping others change their teaching behavior are, by definition, required to take the initiative in creating an appropriate environment.
One of the first ways to meet this responsibility is to ask whether creating the
opportunity, organizing experiences which develop abilities and skills, facilitating challenge, and supporting self-realization is or is not a full time job. Professors of education and supervisors in school systems are alike in that demands
are made on their services which can interfere with creating an experimental
change environment of the type being described. Resolving these conflicts of
interest so that full time participation is possible may be the first step toward
creating an effective change environment.

An environment which has sufficient power to stimulate the analysis and
development of one's own teaching behavior, tentatively illustrated in Fig. 11—2,
consists of a mix of four interrelated forces: an *opportunity* is provided in which
skills and abilities can be developed in response to a perceived *challenge*; the
tension system of this challenge is resolved through social processes which
enhance the *self-realization* of each participant. What would make this change
environment radically different compared with the usual preservice and
inservice situation would be to have all four of these forces impinge on the
participant at the same time and that the quality of each force is such as to
stimulate self-direction, openness, skepticism, and a willingness to analyze one's
own behavior. Most college students and employed teachers do not face such
situations very often, if at all, and to provide it would be a creative exploration
of how adults can work together more effectively.

Since there is so little experience that can serve as a guide to creating
potent change environments, the only proposal that can be made at this time
is to consider the task to be an inquiry project in itself. That is, the steps of
inquiry, which were discussed in Chapters 9 and 10, may form the only viable
method of operation during the experimental development of change environments. One might ask those in charge to specify the conditions and participant
reactions they desire and what might be done in order to reach the desired
behaviors. Practice, a plan, and an evaluation at appropriate intervals may be
steps which can be recycled so that such an environment is created, not all at
once, but through a series of approximations.

THE ETHICS OF SHAPING ANOTHER PERSON'S BEHAVIOR

The choice of the verb "to shape" is quite intentional. It not only catches the
eye, but introduces issues that all teachers face. What set of presumptions justifies
one person setting out to change another's behavior? And in the next breath,
what naive presumptions are necessary in order to believe that one person's
behavior *does not* influence another's? As surely as behavior has consequences,

teaching behavior *does* influence pupil behavior. Indeed, over an extended period of time, much of what a pupil does in the classroom is literally shaped by the teacher. The teacher's only choice is how much influence will he share, under what conditions, and for how long? These issues are a part of professional ethics.

Ethical standards are involved in the professional behavior of a teacher which are quite different compared with nonprofessional contacts. Casual social interaction involves a type of amateur standing whereby one person is relatively free to be influenced or to influence another. Because we act one way rather than another, we are liked or disliked, receive approval or disapproval, and the individual can even pretend to be indifferent to the social consequences of his behavior if he so chooses. On the other hand, classroom teachers and those who teach teachers are not amateurs; they are professionals. They are paid to influence the behavior of others. Pupils are required to be in the classroom by law, and older students by degree requirements. The give and take of amateur interaction is not present in the classroom because the teacher has power advantages that limit pupil reactions and often provide the teacher with a system for rationalizing some degree of indifference. For example, pupils may not feel free or capable of countering teacher influence in the classroom, and a teacher usually believes that "he knows best" about how to deal with pupils. The first ethical commitment of a professional teacher is to evaluate the consequences of his professional behavior in a fashion which is as objective and constructive as possible. To ignore this responsibility is to act unethically.

There are sharp differences among educators about how to conceptualize the influence processes present in the classroom. Given the current domination of the classroom teacher in contrast with his own personal convictions, Carl Rogers* believes that *teaching* is a vastly overrated concept, especially when it means to instruct, to impart knowledge or skill, to make to know, or to show, to guide, or to direct. He rejects this conception of teaching and prefers to think in terms of facilitating learning, of trusting and believing that pupils can control most of the learning process. The depth of Rogers' conviction is partially explained when he asserts that when these attitudes about teaching are understood and the necessary skills implemented effectively, "they do not simply modify classroom methods—they revolutionize them!"

Different points of view are not difficult to locate. B. F. Skinner (87, p. 5) asserts that teaching consists of arranging contingencies of reinforcement. Or consider the assertion in the first paragraph of this section to the effect that pupil behavior is literally shaped by the teacher.

---

*From a presentation at Harvard University in 1966, or the keynote address at the ASCD Convention, Dallas, Texas, 1967, and from a forthcoming book to be published in 1969, called *Freedom to Learn: A View of What Education Might Become.*

It is too early in the analysis of teaching behavior to know the consequences of choosing to think about teaching with one or another set of preferred concepts. The issue of how to conceptualize teacher influence in order to improve it is not yet resolved. Few would question that the point of view expressed by Rogers needs to be heard and understood. At the same time, very few teachers are likely to start revolutions in their classrooms. Teachers can make use of Rogers' ideas to begin an exploration of new ways of relating to pupils, especially when particular activities permit the pupils to act more independently and become more self-directing.

Along with using new and different concepts to think about teaching, very active learning experiences are undoubtedly necessary because a shift in thinking does not ensure different teaching behavior. If a teacher prefers to think about facilitating learning rather than instructing pupils, then the next steps are to practice the required behaviors, to try them out, and to compare one performance with another. The problem is *to learn how to act differently* while teaching.

Given a teacher who wants to learn more effective teaching behavior, does thinking about shaping and reshaping behavior help or hinder the process? Would a different set of concepts be more useful? Again there are no clear answers to these questions. It is possible to argue, however, that teaching involves an element of control and that control tends to shape and reshape behavior. Teachers need concepts that refer to control if they are going to study and analyze this aspect of their performance. This is equally true of one teacher who wants to increase his active control and another who wants to decrease it. One can assert that the phrase "teacher influence shapes pupil behavior" is essentially neutral because there are different degrees of active influence and different kinds of pupil behavior. Yet some educators reject this assertion and argue that by conceptualizing control a person commits himself to a kind of teacher manipulation which has undesirable consequences. For my own part, I would prefer to have a teacher use these concepts, because they are realistic in terms of present influence processes in the classroom. A teacher influences no matter how he acts, and the more ethical position is to investigate the influence processes.

In a well organized behavioral clinic there are certain essential teaching skills to be learned such as responding to the ideas pupils express, and learning to classify, pace, and use different kinds of questions. Beyond specific skills there are attitudes about evaluating patterns of teaching and values to be established about the teacher's balance of initiative and response. These attitudes and values are likely to be influenced by the teaching behavior of the instructor. It is just as unethical for the instructor of adults to avoid evaluating his teaching behavior as it is for one of his students who will be working with younger pupils.

SUMMARY

In this first part of Chapter 11, our attention has centered on the objectives of helping adults improve their teaching behavior and on the features of a change environment. These ideas are possibilities not yet evaluated in a college program for prospective teachers or in an inservice program for experienced teachers. As a result, the implementation of these ideas is itself a matter of inquiry and exploration.

In the next section we turn to published research reports which evaluate innovations in teacher education. We turn from future possibilities to experimental programs which have already been tried.

RESEARCH ON CHANGE IN TEACHING BEHAVIOR

Four techniques—T-groups, simulated skill training, interaction analysis, and microteaching—have singly or in some combination provided innovations for preservice and inservice programs in education. These techniques emphasize teaching behavior because it is conceptualized, performed, and information about the performance is made available to the actor. But these innovations are relatively new and not yet well accepted. A 1968 survey of teacher education programs by Johnson (58), for example, showed that some 30 institutions make use of microteaching extensively, 17 report using Flanders' interaction analysis extensively, out of 847 reporting. These figures represent, respectively, about 4 and 2 percent of all teacher preparation programs in the United States. Whether this indicates remarkable dissemination or whether this shows the usual high resistance to change, is difficult to decide. In either case, thousands of college students are learning to use both techniques.

These innovations are taking place with some evidence to justify the program changes, but the evidence is tentative and not yet complete. However, there is very little evidence that the existing, more traditional programs actually influence teaching behavior, one way or another, in spite of the confidence with which state certification requirements are established. Collecting evidence about the teaching behavior of those who complete teacher education as a way of evaluating the teacher preparation curriculum is itself very uncommon. For example, in 1964 Cyphert and Spaights (26) reviewed 188 fairly recent studies on teacher education. The poor quality of research in this field of study is reflected by the following observations. Only six projects included a measure of teaching behavior; most of the projects were surveys; none of the studies included a measure of the college instructor's teaching behavior. Apparently the instructor's behavior is not perceived as a significant variable in the effectiveness of a teacher education program.

Faced with incomplete knowledge about how best to help others change their teaching behavior or how such behavior might be most effectively developed, it would seem prudent to evaluate all existing programs as well as innovations and try to find out if they lead to any changes in teaching performance. Research on helping another change his teaching behavior has bearly begun. Most of the work lies ahead. It is little wonder that the review of research which follows is sketchy and, in some ways, relatively inconclusive.

VEXING PROBLEMS TO BE FACED IN CONDUCTING RESEARCH ON CHANGING TEACHING BEHAVIOR

Research on how to help others change their teaching behavior is a curriculum evaluation task. The curriculum, in this case, consists of experiences designed to help another understand and develop selected teaching skills. The objectives of teacher education which have been emphasized in this book (see p. 337) are concerned with classroom communication skills. Research on program effectiveness seeks knowledge that consists of functional relationships between learning these communication skills and program characteristics.

Some of the treatment differences might be:
1) Different strategies for selecting and sequencing learning activities.
2) Different systems for providing feedback about performance to participants.
3) Alternatives for selecting and grouping the participants.
4) Different roles which the instructor can implement.

Some of the learning outcomes might be:
A) The ability of participants to perform skills while teaching.
B) The attitudes and perceptions of the participants during learning.
C) Increments of growth during the learning period.
D) The development of personal commitment to particular values and the relationship of these commitments to overt teaching behavior.

The various combinations among treatment differences and learning outcomes are not meant to be totally inclusive, but quite a variety of studies would fit into the scheme. For example, if one group is taught microteaching and a second isn't and then supervisors make ratings of beginning teaching performance, the purpose is to establish a functional relationship of the 2A type. The weakness of such evaluation research is immediately apparent when it is compared to a more complex study in which the relationships analyzed include 1, 2, 3 versus A, B, C. That is, the treatment differences might compare two ways of sequencing interaction analysis and microteaching in large group and small group sessions and then analyze outcomes in terms of teaching performance, shifting attitudes and perceptions during training, and evidence of growth from the specimens of interaction which were part of the feedback.

A major problem in this kind of curriculum research consists of selecting the learning outcomes to be evaluated. Once they are selected, it is particularly difficult to design a fair and effective test of the hypotheses which guide the project. A few of the most difficult problems are briefly described below, primarily to foster a skeptical attitude prior to presenting the research results which follow.

Contamination of treatment differences

Just because some individuals participate in a T-group combined with simulated skill practice and other individuals follow "the traditional curriculum," there is no assurance that two reasonably homogeneous and different growth and development experiences have been created. The treatment differences expected may not appear. The reasons why these differences fail to appear are almost endless and this is not the place to start an inventory. The point is that in this kind of research, establishing proof of treatment differences is a research problem in its own right, a subproject within the larger design. It is usually helpful to collect evidence from each participant, which is independent of the outcome assessment, in order to specify the treatment differences from his point of view. In other words, the assumption that the individuals in a particular treatment had the experience which was intended merely because they were a part of a group is weak and needs to be verified.

Contamination of outcome assessment

Very creative decisions are required in selecting methods of assessing outcomes in research on change in behavior. There is a spectrum of measures which need to be sampled instead of using a single measure. For example, suppose the teaching behavior sought involves asking questions. A simple measure which counts only the number of questions asked before and after learning is not likely to provide enough useful knowledge. First, a simple achievement test can be used to discover whether there has been any change in the participant's ability to distinguish one type of question from another. Second, it will be useful to know the intentions of a participant before he enters a performance situation involving questions. Third, both the quantity and sequence of questions used provide more information than either measure alone. Fourth, it may be useful to obtain, in addition to the perceptions of a trained observer, pupil perceptions of the teacher's use of questions. An average rating by several pupils can be very helpful.

Some contamination can occur when the learning experiences provide the participant with enough cues so that he can unintentionally or intentionally bias his performance in terms of the assessment technique. For example, inter-action analysis is a very useful tool for training teachers, and so it becomes a part of the curriculum treatment, but what happens if the same coding procedures are used for the performance assessment? The prelearning assessment occurred when the participant had no idea what an observer was doing or how a sound recording might be analyzed. The postlearning assessment occurred after the participant had developed his own skill in making use of the same coding procedure. The more knowledge the learner has about the assessment techniques, the more capability he has to alter his performance in ways that will influence the assessment. The same knowledge is supposed to be absent in the control group.

Countermeasures which help to control bias in the assessment of outcomes are expensive. It may be necessary to use additional groups, some with only posttests, and some with both. One type of microteaching or interaction analysis may be used for learning practice, a different type for assessment. If it is desirable to check the persistence of behavior change, a single year project may turn into a longitudinal study covering several years.

Specifying a dynamic explanation

Perhaps the most common shortcoming of research on behavioral change is lack of concern with explaining why the results turned out the way they did. In research on microteaching, what aspects most influence teaching behavior? What are the consequences of altering the sequence of learning tasks? Are there different schedules of feedback to achieve optimal change? Is there a different schedule for each type of learning? Is video playback essential in all phases of learning? Why? Finding the answers to such questions is quite different than merely reporting that individuals studying microteaching were given higher ratings on teaching performance than individuals who did not study microteaching. The same criticisms apply to research on interaction analysis.

A point of view

Curriculum research would probably improve if innovators were less sensitive to the clamor of critics who demand "research evidence" about an innovation. Each question about an innovation has its own season. The first challenge should not be a full scale evaluation. The problems of helping any person change his teaching behavior are so complicated and so important that any promising innovation should be protected from being tested too early. Before such proof can be provided there are preliminary questions. How does it work? How can it be improved? Can it be made more efficient? More parsimonious? What resource materials and equipment are needed? Can any of it be programmed? What aspects of the program require sensitive, humanistic treatment? How much release from other responsibilities will be required for different types of participants? After all these questions and many others have been answered, the season for a series of field tests is at hand.

TABLE 11–1
Projects Using Interaction Analysis to Help Modify Teaching Behavior Which Include Evidence of Program Effectiveness

Date Collect Data	Publish Results	Author(s) and Reference Number	Location
		Preservice Programs for College Students	
1963	1964	Hough and Amidon (53)	Temple University
1963	1965	Zahn (108)	Glassboro State College (N. J.)
1964	1965	Kirk (59)	Temple University
1964	1965	Furst (44)	Temple University
1964	1965	McLoed (64)	Cornell University
1965	1966	Hough and Ober (54)	Ohio State University
1966	1966	Lohman, Ober, and Hough (61)	Ohio State University
1966	1967	Finske (31)	St. Mary's College, Notre Dame
1966	1967	Moskowitz (71)	Temple University
1968	1968	Borg, et al. (16)	California
1968	1969	Bondi (14)	Florida State University
		Inservice Programs in Field Settings	
1960	1961	Bowers and Soar (18)	North Carolina
1960	1963	Flanders (36)	Minnesota
1962–'64	1966	Soar (93)	Pennsylvania
1965	1966	Hill (51)	Ohio State University
1966	1967	Emmer (28)	Michigan
1967	1968	Jeffs, et al. (56)	Las Vegas, Nevada
1968	1968	Borg, et al. (15)	California

RESEARCH ON HELPING OTHERS CHANGE THEIR TEACHING BEHAVIOR

The projects to be reviewed are listed in Table 11–1. Some of these studies are based on college programs for the preparation of teachers, and others evaluate inservice programs for experienced teachers. Most of the projects investigated make use of interaction analysis, a few use microteaching, and two report the results of participating in T-groups.

The absence of research on simulated skill training is due partly to the lack of standardized meaning which is associated with such a label. However, the Hough and Ober study made use of dyadic programmed human relations training which consists of a series of simulated skill training exercises, and Borg's studies use programmed, instructional material.

It should come as no surprise that practice in conducting this kind of research helps to improve the quality of the next project. Except for unusual circumstances, experience in several earlier projects seems to be a prerequisite for a well conceived and conducted research project on changing behavior. For example, the special attention given to the studies of Hough, Ober, and Lohman, Moskowitz, Flanders, and Soar and Borg (16) is partly due to the fact that there was at least one person on the staff who had previous experience in helping to change another person's teaching behavior prior to the project reported here.

Special mention should be given to the long series of research studies which were carried out at Temple University, largely inspired and directed by Edmund Amidon. The work at Temple is a classic example of how a team can explore various alternatives in the preparation of teachers through the evaluation of curriculum innovations. It also shows the unusual position of the faculty member in a school of education who can conduct research on his own teaching effectiveness and then publish it in journals of teacher education. This response to the "publish or perish" forces at a university is an ideal way to combine teaching and research that is uniquely available to education professors.

The consequence of analyzing behavior

If there is any common bond which cuts across all of the projects listed in Table 11–1, it is that they all provide some support for the following proposition. *Attention to teaching behavior, practice in analyzing it, and performing it with feedback, tends to incorporate such behavior in the teacher's repertoire.* At first glance, this generalization seems about as weak as "studying and practicing the German language tends to increase proficiency in that language," hardly a proposition which would prompt us to telegraph the Library of Congress. Yet there is a great deal we don't know about how to teach German and even more to be learned about helping another person change his teaching behavior. In a field in which very few generalizations have any empirical basis, it is of value to cite support for even a relatively weak assertion.

To illustrate the value of investigating so general a proposition, it is possible now to specify some qualifications based on research evidence. Judging from the Bowers and Soar (18, p. 137), study, it appears that experienced teachers who score high in the MMPI scales of (Pd) psychopathic deviate, (Pt) psychasthenia, and (Sc) schizophrenia, are less likely to change their teaching behavior from level one toward level two (see p. 280) when exposed to a human relations program which includes sensitivity training and T-group discussions. In the Zahn and Amidon and Hough studies, there is some evidence that college students scoring high on the Rokeach "Dogmatism Scale" are less likely to make the same changes in teaching patterns as a result of studying and using interaction analysis compared with those scoring low. In the Flanders inservice training project there were different results from the study of interaction analysis for teachers who were above and below the median in the use of level two patterns before they started to study interaction analysis. Those above the median made even further gains in the use of level two patterns when the inservice instructor's behavior was consistent, that is, also contained more level two patterns. Teachers in the same group actually decreased their own use of level two behaviors after training when the inservice instructor's behavior was inconsistent. Those teachers below the median in the use of level two behaviors before training made small, insignificant gains in the use of level two behaviors when exposed to either kind of instructor behavior. Finally, Emmer reported that the skill of a teacher in estimating certain features of classroom interaction, such as percent pupil talk and the proportion of initiation in such talk, was not related to their ability to change their teaching behavior, although his sample was small.

These studies confirm that not all individuals can be expected to make significant changes in their teaching behavior by studying and analyzing behavior with the currently available techniques. Again, the inference is not earthshaking, but please note that there are several small increments of progress. First, further research in this area might identify individuals who are most likely to profit from special learning activities either through the use of personality trait scales or through pretraining observation of classroom interaction. Second, the most promising personality trait scales appear to be the Rokeach Dogmatism Scale or perhaps some new scale constructed from the MMPI subscales (Pd, Pt, and Sc) which Soar used. Third, it now seems very worthwhile to separate individuals whose pretraining assessment suggests a poor prognosis for behavior change and explore change environments which are especially designed for such individuals.

The effects of studying interaction analysis

At this time more research projects have been completed which make use of interaction analysis than any of the other three techniques, a condition which is likely to change. The conclusions from these studies provide variations on the theme that the study of behavior may change it. Each of the numbered generalizations which follow has some evidence to support it. However, the evidence is so variable that it is appropriate to read the material as you would a list of recommended restaurants: you have more confidence in four stars, less in three, or two, and you may prefer to reject those with the dubious distinction of a one-star rating. Furthermore, in one or another study, a particular generalization may not be supported, just as on a particular evening a four-star restaurant may prove disappointing. We must constantly remind ourselves that a probability coefficient of less than one is associated with knowledge about teaching which indicates how often, in a large number of instances, the generalization is likely to be true. About all that can be said about our poorest generalizations is that the coefficients are greater than could be expected by chance. On the other hand, when the same finding appears in successive replications and when the strength of the relationship seems to be increasing, then our confidence can be greater.

1) *An individual becomes more responsive to pupil ideas (level two) by learning how to code with categories of interaction analysis and by interpreting displays from specimens of his own teaching and the teaching of another person.* At the college level this generalization is supported by Lohman, Ober, and Hough, by Moskowitz, by Kirk, by Furst, by Finske, and by Bondi. It was not supported for secondary science teachers (but not rejected) by McLeod. During inservice programs this generalization is supported by Flanders, Emmer, Hill, Jeffs,* and by Soar.

Although this may be the most replicated finding of those to be discussed the evidence from one replication to another is not entirely consistent. For example, Emmer reports that when the same teacher and same class experiences a change of teaching behavior that involves an increase in Category 3, Category 9 also increases. Furst failed to find this increase in student initiated talk, but Kirk, Hough-Ober, Lohman-Ober-Hough, Jeffs, and Finske did. Only Emmer studied change in the same classroom unit. Not all studies report the same trend with respect to Category 4; for Jeffs it decreased with training; for many others the change was not statistically significant. For that matter, the quality called "indirectness" which is quantified and described on page 102, is not always a significant change in teaching behavior.

This lack of consistency raises disagreeable problems for those who would like to have firm and consistent consequences from replications, but the "science" is too young and our knowledge too primitive for this kind of accuracy. The generalization tends to be true, most of the time, and at the moment of writing this manuscript, it stands with more independent verifications than most inferences that are concerned with helping another change his teaching behavior. Perhaps the next paragraph will help clarify some of the issues.

In the event that our goal is to have the same cells of a 10×10 matrix and the same ratios be consistent indices of program outcomes, then the following standards are probably minimum necessities. First, the goals of the training program should be clearly understood by all concerned and be identical from one study to the next. Unfortunately, the behavior goals of the studies cited in Table 11–1 are not the same, yet in one degree or another, the participants

---

*Jeffs' project involved four volunteer teachers who met approximately once a week for a school year. There was no control group and no statistical analysis; therefore it cannot be counted as a research replication. A composite matrix for all four teachers is reported, based on data collected at the beginning of the year. There is a second composite matrix for the end of the year. A Darwin chi-square test calculated at Michigan indicates that the differences between the two matrices are greater than would be expected on the basis of chance alone. The project is unusual because none of the individuals connected with it were trained at any of the recognized centers at which interaction analysis is taught. It is a truly independent, "do it yourself" type of project.

became more supportive of pupil ideas as a result of their learning experiences. Second, the curriculum, the sequence of learning experiences, and the instructional experiences should be the same, one study compared with another. This was not true. Third, the coding of interaction should be reliable from one study to the next; and this is simply unknown. Fourth, the method of quantifying the concept "more supportive of pupil ideas and initiative" should be exactly the same for each study. This is also not true of the studies reviewed. In spite of these differences, it can be said, in general, that the learning experiences increased the incidence of Categories 1, 2, 3, and sometimes 9, in most of the studies. The incidence of Categories 5, 6, 7, and 8 more often decreased. Given these outcomes, the generalization made at the beginning of this section tends to be confirmed more often than not by relatively independent researchers, working in different locations, who conducted their own separate studies.

The common outcome causes us to search for a common explanation. Here it would be helpful if the researchers had reported the events of the learning curriculum in greater detail. As the reports stand, the most common element is learning interaction analysis. In one study, interaction analysis might have been a tedious, unwanted assignment and in another, an exciting new world of insight into teaching. From the reports there is no sure way to make this determination. With the wide range of conditions which could exist, it is rather remarkable that there was a common element in the outcomes.

2) *Teaching behavior becomes more flexible (or variable) as a result of studying interaction analysis.* This is a weak generalization supported primarily by the Moskowitz (71) and Finske (31) studies. Moskowitz reported that both the student teachers and the cooperating teachers who had studied interaction analysis appeared to have significantly more variability. The interpretation was (71, p. 279), "Not only did the trained groups of teachers use more indirect teaching patterns, but they used these patterns in a wider range of ways." Whether this variation was between visits or some other unit of time is not clear. In the Finske study, the variation was greater for those college students trained in interaction analysis. Flexibility was measured in the Finske study by comparing the matrices for one lesson in which the teacher was instructed to conduct a discussion and a second lesson involving spelling or rules of grammar in which more teacher initiation could be expected. The two lessons were taught during the second week and again in the eight week of student teaching. A flexible teacher would presumably alter his behavior more radically, one lesson compared with another, than would an inflexible teacher. The significant results are rather interesting since only nine matched pairs or a total of 18 student teachers were involved. Finske concluded (31, p. 69), "student teachers trained in interaction analysis (1) were more flexible at the beginning of student teaching; (2) were more flexible at the end of student teaching; (3) used more extended indirect influence in the discussion lessons; (4) used more lecturing in direct influence lessons; and (5) elicited more pupil-initiated talk."

There is no firmly established procedure for quantifying the concept "flexibility" or "variation" and until there is, replications cannot occur. The weakness of the generalization rests on the lack of replications. Since this second generalization is theoretically sound, it is quite possible that subsequent replications will appear.

3) *The attitudes of college students toward teaching and programs for the preparation of teachers become more positive for those who study interaction analysis compared with those who don't.* This conclusion was reached by Zahn, Furst, and Moskowitz. Researchers who made use of the MTAI (Minnesota Teacher Attitude Inventory) long ago reported that the scores of college students on this test increase during professional training, reach a plateau during student teaching, and then decline to about the original level after 2 years of teaching. Here a high score indicates positive attitudes. The differences referred to in this second generalization apparently mean that the study of interaction analysis elicits a response from college students which is even more positive than these established patterns.

This third generalization is reported here without much confidence. In both the Zahn and Moskowitz studies there were no pretraining measures of attitude. In the Furst study, there were no differences between treatment groups in both the pre- and post-measures, but there were significant differences when difference scores were compared. The generalization is limited by the personality characteristics of the individual. Apparently the more rigid types (high in dogmatism) are less likely to be significantly more positive according to Zahn. Moskowitz reports that the supervising teacher can influence the student teacher's attitudes. Flanders' analysis of attitudes during inservice training, to be discussed in the next section, indicates that the behavior of the inservice training instructor influences the participants' attitudes. While it is true that replicated findings help to eliminate reservations due to the lack of pretraining measures, the main conclusion seems to be—the more an individual likes what he is doing and thinks he is making progress, the more positively he views teaching.

Changes in attitudes and perceptions will become important when we know more about how they are related to teaching behavior. There is some evidence (Hough, for example) that the Teacher Situation Reaction Test is related to teaching behavior. Less is known about the Cooperating Teachers' Attitude Questionnaire and the Student Teachers' Attitude Questionnaire used by Moskowitz. When these tests are used in subsequent research, more information will become available.

We might note in passing that positive testimony from college students who make use of microteaching has been reported by Allen and Fortune (2, p. 10) who state that "Microteaching is accepted and regarded as valuable experience by interns, during the training process and after teaching experience." Stock (97) reports that positive attitudes toward T-group experiences are quite common among the majority of participants. These reports are constructive, but the more significant issues are concerned with teaching performance.

PROGRAMMED SIMULATION AND INTERACTION ANALYSIS FOR COLLEGE STUDENTS

So far the most complete analysis of the effects of using interaction analysis and programmed simulation in a college curriculum has been reported by Hough and Ober (54) with a follow up study by Lohman, Ober, and Hough (61). These studies occurred at Ohio State University.

Plan of the two studies

Five treatment groups with 84 subjects in each participated. The five curricula followed were various combinations of human relations training and the study of teacher-pupil verbal interaction. There were three kinds of human relations training: first, readings, lecture, and classroom discussion of human relations in teaching; second, programmed instruction for pairs of students with simulated exercises; and third, pairs of students who discussed educational case studies. There were two ways to study teacher-pupil verbal interaction: first, skill training in interaction analysis using Flanders' 10 categories; and second, analysis and discussion of classroom teaching behavior but no instruction in the skill of interaction analysis.

The control of the personality differences between groups was excellent. Three separate measures of personality traits and perceptions of teaching were used to demonstrate the equality of the groups before training.

The main outcome variable in both studies was an analysis of teacher-pupil interaction assessed by a 13-category system developed by Hough. In the case of a Hough and Ober study, the interaction occurred in a stimulated $\frac{1}{2}$-hour teaching lesson at the end of training. In the Lohman, Ober, and Hough study, samples of interaction during student teaching, 4 to 12 months after the training, were gathered for 30 college students who were shown to be representative of the total group in the earlier study.

The major results

In the Hough and Ober study the most change in teaching behavior occurred in the treatment which combined the programmed simulation of human relations training with actual practice in using interaction analysis. The change was toward level two interaction patterns. When all treatments were split between those who learned interaction analysis versus those who didn't and between those who followed programmed simulation and those who didn't, the significant differences were larger in the former split than in the latter, suggesting that training students to use interaction analysis was more potent.

In the Lohman, Ober, and Hough follow up, the main comparisons were between those who studied interaction analysis and those who didn't. The interaction analysis data, using the 13-category system, showed that the tendency to use level two patterns of interaction persisted into the following academic year during the student teaching assignment. Those who had learned how to use interaction analysis a year earlier responded more to pupil ideas, gave more sustained reactions to these ideas, and were less likely to maintain the traditional high level of lecturing and other kinds of teacher initiative.

Summary

This project comes at the end of more than 6 years of fairly consistent results in assessing the consequences of teaching individuals to use interaction analysis. It is a well designed project and confirms that the active analysis of teaching behavior tends to make teachers more responsive to pupils.

It is important to place these changes in teaching behavior into a reasonable perspective. The increased use of Category 3, for example, is only a matter of 4 or 5 percent. A control group might average around 8 percent Category 3, while those who study interaction analysis are more likely to average from 3 to 5 points higher. In other words, as interaction analysis has been taught in these studies, there has been no really radical change in the format of the teacher-pupil interchange. It remains teacher dominated. Pupil talk, for example, ramains within the limits of 25 to 30 percent for both groups in the Hough, Ober, and Lohman studies. But there is a slight shift in the quality of teacher talk by those who study interaction analysis, and this slight shift tends to make pupil attitudes more positive and tends to increase measures of content achievement. This last assertion is the topic of Chapter 12.

Points of special interest

The Hough, Ober, and Lohman studies mark a growing sophistication in the design of research on helping to change another's teaching behavior. Returning to the list of variables on page 348, instead of relating one independent variable to one outcome variable, these two studies investigate relationships between several treatment and several outcome variables in the same research design. These studies illustrate a 1, 2, 3 versus A, B, C type of relationship. Note that:

1) Personality traits and perceptions of teaching situations were measured.

2) Five learning sequences were involved for the college students' curriculum, each roughly equivalent in terms of time.

3) Both change in teaching behavior and persistence of these changes were assessed.

4) College students were acting differently as a result of their training while teaching, and the nature of these changes was specified within the limits of the category system which was used to make the assessment.

TRAINING BOTH THE COOPERATING CLASSROOM TEACHER AND THE STUDENT TEACHER

The study by Moskowitz (71) is an example of investigating situational factors which can influence teaching behavior. A significant feature of the student teacher's assignment is his relationship with the cooperating classroom teacher, the closest representative of the teaching profession. Moskowitz designed an experiment with four treatments that created different qualities of this relationship.

Plan of the study

Some student teachers were trained to use interaction analysis and others were taught learning theory principles. In this study, half of the cooperating classroom teachers, who supervise student teachers, took a two-credit education course in interaction analysis as it applies to supervision, while others took a course in learning theory principles. This meant the 44 secondary student teachers in the study could be assigned to one of four treatments. First, the cooperating teacher and the student teacher had both learned to use interaction analysis. Second, only the student teacher had learned interaction analysis. Third, only the cooperating teacher had learned interaction analysis. Fourth, neither the cooperating teacher nor the student teacher had learned interaction analysis.

Moskowitz was unable to collect pretraining data on attitudes and perceptions of teaching. She writes (71, p, 274), "The attitude questionnaires were administered the last week of the semester and the classroom observations were made during the last few weeks of the spring term." The assumption that the treatment groups were equal before training must be made without verifying data. This weakness in research design should be kept in mind when reading the comments which follow.

Major results

The results of the first treatment were different from the fourth in two ways. First, the attitudes of both parties were more positive and the teaching behavior of both was closer to level two type interaction patterns, compared to the fourth treatment. The shift of teaching behavior on the part of the cooperating teacher would be expected in terms of previous inservice training results, but its verification in this study helps to make the results from the second treatment more interesting. The student teachers in the second treatment used more level two patterns than their cooperating teachers did. In the third treatment, the student teachers were not significantly different from the cooperating teachers. A tentative hypothesis is suggested by these results. It may be that the training in interaction analysis, which included a total of 60 hours for the college students, was sufficiently convincing that the student teacher was prepared to implement more level two interaction patterns in spite of the model set by the cooperating teacher who did not have this training. Yet an untrained student teacher in both the third and fourth treatments was more likely to imitate the interaction patterns of the cooperating teacher.

Summary

In spite of the lack of pretraining measures, this study is reported here because the results are consistent with other similar studies and because it illustrates another factor which influences the performance of a person who is attempting to change his teaching behavior. Two contributions merit special note. First, training the cooperating classroom teacher to use interaction analysis is associated with an increase in level two interaction patterns when the student teacher teaches; and second, training the student teacher in interaction analysis may create a sense of independence such that the student teacher produces more level two interaction patterns than the cooperating teacher normally does. Greater confidence can be placed in the second of these two conclusions due to a partial replication by McLeod (64). He also found that student teachers in secondary science trained in interaction analysis were less likely to mimic their cooperating classroom teachers' interaction patterns.

A point of special interest

One of the most persistent problems in education is that neophytes are introduced into the profession by experienced colleagues. If improvement is to come, all neophytes cannot mimic their experienced colleague perfectly, but must strive to introduce new elements into their own development. One of the most encouraging conclusions in the Moskowitz study is her finding that training in interaction analysis may help a neophyte to develop personal convictions and associated skills which affect his behavior in spite of the model provided by the profession.

SOME EFFECTS OF THE INSTRUCTOR'S TEACHING BEHAVIOR DURING INSERVICE PROGRAMS

Opportunities to trace the reactions of teachers as they participate in an inservice training program are relatively rare. A modest example of this occurred in Minnesota in 1960–1961 when Flanders (36) made his first attempt to help teachers change their teaching behavior through the study of interaction analysis. The question guiding this discussion is, "Does the teaching behavior of the instructor influence the perceptions of teachers during inservice training?"

The plan of the study

The original project was designed to investigate four hypotheses about helping teachers change their behavior. In order to accomplish this purpose, it was necessary to conduct two, concurrent, 9-week inservice programs for junior high school teachers. The four hypotheses, while interesting, are not at issue in this discussion. Instead, evidence is discussed that shows certain relationships between instructor behavior and teacher reactions.

In terms of the original design, the two inservice programs became experimental treatments. In treatment A, the instructor purposely created more level two interaction patterns during the verbal exchange; in treatment B, there was no attempt to create such patterns. It was expected that there would be more independence and self-direction among the adult learners in treatment A compared to B.

In order to permit the instructor's behavior to become a variable, other features of the curriculum were as similar as possible. The following statements apply equally to both treatments. All of the instructional materials, the film strips, the assignments, and the topics to be investigated were identical for the two groups. Most of the meetings were multiple sessions lasting 4 hours each. During this extended period it was possible to meet for part of the time as a total group for lectures and demonstrations. At other times skill training could occur in groups size four, small group discussions could be held in separate rooms, and the teachers could spread all over the school building for work sessions in which they practiced coding with voice tape recordings.

In order to compare the two treatments, a trained observer coded the larger, total group sessions which were conducted by the same instructor in both treatments. It was expected that a display of the interaction analysis data would show whether the instructor was successful in controlling his own behavior in terms of the required treatment differences. At the end of seven sessions, skipping the first and sixth weeks, the teachers filled out a questionnaire which was designed to assess their perceptions of their own initiative and responsibility. Ten of the items in this questionnaire were in the form shown by the example at the top of the next page. This type of item gives three scores. The mark from item (a) indicates the respondent's perception of what occurred. The mark from item (b) indicates what the respondent would have preferred in retrospect. The difference between the (a) and (b) score is a

Assuming that the *approach* to ideas or problems before our group could be determined either by the instructor (staff) or by the teachers participating, where did the approach come from TODAY?

a) Mark your appraisal of TODAY'S session, as you saw it.

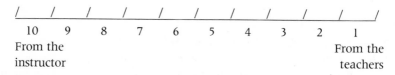

/	/	/	/	/	/	/	/	/	/	/
10	9	8	7	6	5	4	3	2	1	

From the
instructor
                                                              From the
                                                              teachers

b) Now indicate what you would have preferred TODAY.

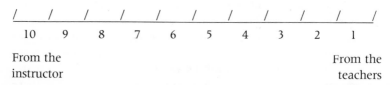

/	/	/	/	/	/	/	/	/	/	/
10	9	8	7	6	5	4	3	2	1	

From the
instructor
                                                              From the
                                                              teachers

fairly reasonable operational definition of *dissatisfaction*. One meaning of dissatisfaction is the difference a person sees between what is going on and what he would prefer.

The results of the interaction analysis

The data from coding the verbal interaction during the general sessions are shown in Tables 11–2 and 11–3. Some of the ratios which were discussed in Chapter 4 are shown in Table 11–4.

Several similarities and differences can be inferred from Table 11–4. In treatment *A*, compared with *B*, the instructor talked less and the teachers talked more, the response and question ratios were higher, the content emphasis and total sustained discourse were lower, and the sustained discourse by the teachers was higher. The proportion of initiation in teacher talk was the same and very high for both groups. With the exception of this last feature, the differences show that the instructor was more responsive in treatment *A*. The equal proportions of teacher initiated talk may be reasonable for mature adult students who felt free to talk and were actively involved in learning.

An inspection of the two matrices in Tables 11–2 and 11–3 indicates how the instructor altered his behavior. The (3–3) cell is about four times higher in treatment *A*, indicating that the instructor responded more fully to ideas which were suggested by the teachers. There were probably more three-event 9–2–9 chains in treatment *A* which would occur when the instructor nodded and said, "Um hm," in order to encourage teacher participation. Compare the (9–2) and (2–9) cells in each matrix. A comparison of the combined column totals for Categories 1, 2, and 3 shows 73.5 for *A* and 28.0 for *B*. The difference

TABLE 11–2

Interaction Matrix for Treatment A

Category	1	2	3	4	5	6	7	8	9	10	Total
1	0.7	—	—	—	1.8	—	—	—	0.2	0.2	2.8
2	—	1.8	1.9	2.1	2.5	0.2	—	—	16.4	1.2	26.2
3	—	0.5	34.5	1.9	3.2	0.5	—	0.4	2.3	1.2	44.5
4	0.2	1.2	0.4	11.1	5.7	0.7	0.2	12.4	12.4	5.5	49.7
5	1.4	9.9	4.2	18.0	485.9	3.7	1.6	0.9	10.4	5.5	541.5
6	—	—	0.2	1.4	2.7	3.2	—	1.1	2.5	2.5	13.4
7	—	—	—	0.5	1.1	0.4	1.2	—	—	—	3.2
8	—	—	0.9	2.1	4.6	0.9	0.2	8.1	8.3	0.2	25.3
9	0.4	11.7	2.1	9.0	26.0	2.1	—	1.2	193.0	10.1	255.6
10	0.2	1.1	0.4	3.4	8.3	1.8	—	1.2	10.1	11.5	37.8
Total	2.8	26.2	44.5	49.7	541.5	13.4	3.2	25.3	255.6	37.8	1000.0

$N = 5658$

TABLE 11–3

Interaction Matrix for Treatment B

Category	1	2	3	4	5	6	7	8	9	10	Total
1	0.6	—	—	—	1.5	—	0.2	—	0.2	0.2	2.5
2	—	—	0.5	0.8	0.9	—	—	0.2	9.9	0.2	12.3
3	—	0.3	8.4	1.2	1.2	—	—	—	1.8	0.3	13.2
4	—	—	—	7.5	3.7	0.5	0.2	9.6	5.2	5.8	32.5
5	2.0	6.6	1.4	13.5	694.7	3.4	2.1	0.6	14.2	5.5	744.0
6	—	0.3	—	—	2.1	3.4	—	—	1.8	1.7	9.3
7	—	—	—	0.2	2.2	0.2	2.5	—	1.1	0.2	6.3
8	—	0.3	0.5	2.0	4.9	—	0.2	2.4	3.4	0.3	13.9
9	—	4.5	2.5	4.3	25.1	0.9	1.2	—	96.8	1.8	137.2
10	—	0.3	—	3.1	7.5	0.9	—	1.2	2.8	13.0	28.9
Total	2.5	12.3	13.2	32.5	744.0	9.3	6.3	13.9	137.2	28.9	1000.0

$N = 6682$

of 45.5 events per 1000 is about 4.55 percent of all tallies. There is also a slight increase from A to B in the use of criticism, Category 7.

By way of summarizing the interaction analysis data, lecturing and emphasis on content were main features of both treatments. The intent of

TABLE 11–4

Basic Ratios in the Two Inservice Treatments

Type of Ratio	Symbol*	Treatment A	Treatment B
Percent instructor talk	TT	68.1	82.0
Percent participating teacher talk	PT	28.1	15.1
Percent silence or confusion	SC	3.8	2.9
Instructor response ratio	TRR	82	64
Instructor question ratio	TQR	8	4
Instructor immediate response ratio	TRR89	82	77
Instructor immediate question ratio	TQR89	27	17
Participating teacher initiation	PIR	91	91
Content emphasis	CCR	67.	83
Total sustained discourse	SSR	74	82
Sustained discourse (for the teachers)	PSSR	72	66

*See discussion starting on p. 97.

the instructor to involve the treatment A teachers in planning work, in expressing their own ideas, and to have these ideas taken into consideration did result in differences that could be coded. These differences, however, appear as small shifts of percentage in the response categories, more talk by the participants, and less lecturing.

Teacher reactions and the growth of independence

The 10 items in the teacher questionnaire referred to the following features of the program.

    a) How did you see TODAY?
    b) What would you have preferred for TODAY?

1) Would you rate our work today as very theoretical or very practical?
2) Was the approach to problems determined by the instructor or the teachers?
3) Were "feelings-attitudes" or "ideas" about teaching emphasized?
4) Did we cover material "too fast" or "too slow"?
5) Did the instructor or the teachers control the activities today?
6) Were your relationships with the instructor formal or informal?
7) Were you motivated to work today primarily by the instructor or yourself?
8) Were you "free enough" or "not free enough" to speak out today?
9) Was any progress made today due to instruction or to self-determination?
10) Was the material covered today difficult or easy to understand?

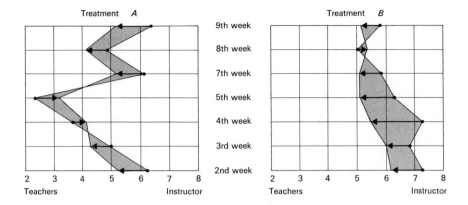

Fig. 11—3.   Item 2: Who Suggested the Approach to the Ideas Discussed?

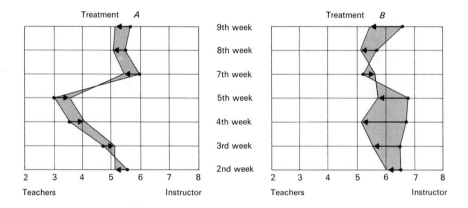

Fig. 11—4.   Item 5: Who Controlled the Learning Activities?

The teachers' reactions are presented in graphical form. Our main interest centers on items 2, 5, 7, and 9, which were designed to scale the independence and self-direction of the teachers. The results for each item are very similar (they are positively intercorrelated) and are shown in Figs. 11—3, 11—4, 11—5, and 11—6, respectively. The way to read these graphs is to notice that successive weeks are arranged from the bottom to the top of each graph. The "solid dot" opposite the arrowhead indicates the average perception of what occurred. The arrowhead indicates the average rating in response to what the teachers would have preferred. The shaded areas, between the solid dots and the arrowheads, illustrate the magnitude of dissatisfaction. Treatment A is always on the left, treatment B to the right.

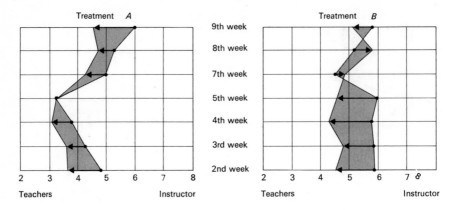

Fig. 11–5.   Item 7: Who Motivated Most Class Participation?

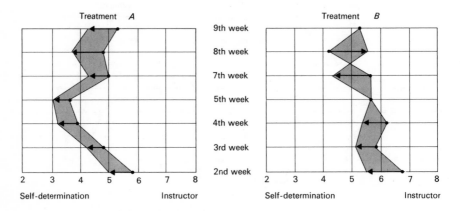

Fig. 11–6.   Item 9: Who was Responsible for Progress?

For all four items, there is a consistent growth of independence for the teachers in treatment A during the first 5 weeks of the program. The growth is less consistent and remains instructor oriented in treatment B. It is interesting to note the effect of having a different instructor take over during the seventh week in both treatments. The sense of independence was reduced and its regular growth pattern altered when the teachers were no longer reacting to the regular instructor, but were confronted with a new authority figure. Since the teachers' reactions to these four items are fairly consistent, especially for the treatment A teachers, that is, positively intercorrelated, they can be combined to form a single four-item scale. A statistical analysis of the differences between treat-

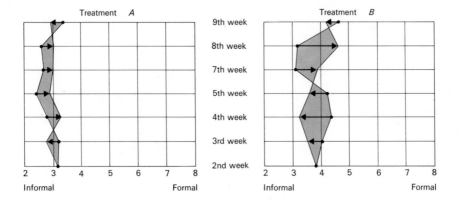

Fig. 11–7.   Item 6: What was the Relationship of Teachers to Staff?

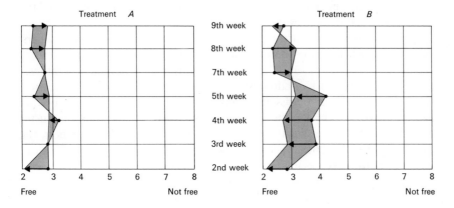

Fig. 11–8.   Item 8: Did the Teachers Feel Free to Express Ideas?

ment *A* and treatment *B* indicates that the differences could not be expected to occur by chance, no matter whether the analysis is one item at a time or all four combined.

The graphs for items 6 and 8 are shown in Figs. 11–7 and 11–8. Here we see that contrary to the growth of increasing independence, the teachers in treatment *A* feel quite free to speak out and consider their relationships with the instructor to be informal. The teachers in treatment *B* also feel the same way, but not to the same extent. Furthermore, there is clearly more dissatisfaction. During the last three weeks, when individual progress and work are being summarized, the teachers in treatment *B* desire more formal relationships.

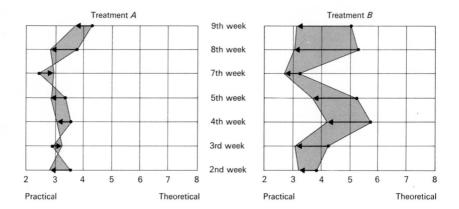

Fig. 11—9.   Item 1: Were the Ideas Discussed in Class Practical or Theoretical?

This shift might suggest the need for distance between the participant and the instructor when work is evaluated.

The last item to be illustrated in this report is concerned with the teachers' estimate of whether the material and ideas being learned are practical or theoretical (see Fig. 11—9). Teachers apparently prefer the practical; at least this is true in all but two administrations, both occurring in the treatment *A* group. It is the degree of dissatisfaction that can be found in treatment *B* that is impressive. Except for the seventh week, when the substitute instructor presided, there is extensive dissatisfaction among the treatment *B* teachers. The possibility that "practical" became "good" and "theoretical" tended to mean "bad" is an attractive speculation.

We might note in passing that this study, like the Moskowitz study, does not have pretraining measures of teacher perceptions. However, when successive assessments are available, the initial base rate serves the same purpose. There are no statistically significant differences between the groups at the second week administration. If there had been a first week administration, it would appear from the existing data that even fewer differences between the two groups would exist. This guess can be reasonably made by extrapolating toward the first week, using the existing line slopes. The use of successive questionnaires eliminates the need for pretraining measures of the attitudes and perceptions of the teachers.

Summary

This section began by asking whether the instructor's teaching behavior influenced the reactions and perceptions of adult teachers during an inservice training program. In spite of a heavy content emphasis, some associations are evident which are a first step toward explaining an influence process. Higher responsiveness on the part of the instructor is associated with stronger feelings of independence, self-direction, and perceived satisfaction. This small shift in the interaction data may not point up the real differences which occurred between the two treatments. For example, the individual contacts which teachers had with the instructor and other staff members are not reflected in the interaction analysis matrices. Given these conditions, it is not surprising that the teachers in treatment *A* designed and carried out almost twice as many individual projects during the fifth, sixth, and seventh weeks as did the teachers in treatment *B*. The treatment *A* teachers simply generated more man-hours of work in learning and using interaction analysis in their own classrooms.

One wonders whether similar relationships occur between an adult teacher and younger pupils.

THE EFFECTS OF SENSITIVITY TRAINING LABORATORIES, INCLUDING T-GROUPS

To my knowledge the only evaluations of T-group training for classroom teachers that include a pre- and post-assessment of teaching behavior are studies conducted by Robert Soar, now at the University of Florida, Gainsville. His 1961 project report with Bowers (18) and his 1966 report (93) include personality data about the teachers, interaction analysis data collected in the classrooms, and both attitude and achievement data for the pupils. Both reports were concerned with sensitivity training in a laboratory type experience. In both studies the trainees were experienced teachers.

Plan of the study

The 1961 and 1966 projects have many central features in common. In both studies some teachers participated in human relations training; in 1961 there were 23, and in 1966 there were 14, while other teachers were in a control group. Both studies were large and extensive since two purposes were combined. First, relationships between teacher personality, teaching behavior, and pupil attitudes and achievement were investigated. These results are reported in the next chapter. Second, after the first year of data collecting, a small sample of the participating teachers were invited to participate in a summer inservice training program. The rest of the population then served as control. A second round of data for all participants was collected during a second year.

Detail about the research design is not necessary in this review because specific research findings are not discussed. Anyone interested can refer to the references cited. Instead, the contributions of these two studies to the problems of helping others change their teaching behavior occupies our attention.

The results

The results with regard to change in teaching behavior are not definitive, and at the risk of tremendous oversimplification, might be summarized as follows. First, with the cirriculum used, some teachers made constructive changes toward intended objectives and the evidence was reasonably clear that an equal number of teachers did not. There are some personality scales that help to predict those who will and those who will not gain from this kind of training. The error of prediction is likely to be tolerable only at the more extreme scale deviations. Second, no simple relationships exist between teacher personality measures, classroom interaction, and effects on pupils.

The training curriculum

The objectives of the training program (93, p. 74) included understanding leadership styles, such as democratic, laissez-faire, and authoritarian; studying and practicing the skills of group leadership; and becoming aware of what is going on in a group and becoming more sensitive to feedback information.

The training activities included "theory sessions" which approached lectures in form; T-group meetings; and skill practice sessions based on role playing or directed observations. Among the topics dealt with in the skill sessions were some concerning communication, sensitivity to feelings, clear versus unclear goals, group cohesiveness, force field analysis, and group problem-solving.

The laboratory workshop was held over a period of 3 weeks with 4 to $4\frac{1}{2}$ hours scheduled in the morning.

Contributions to the field

The two studies suggest that what is learned in T-group training in combination with skill sessions may not transfer to the classroom easily. If there are any suggestions to be made here, they might be that the objectives of the training were generally abstract. The curriculum, as reported, varied from force field analysis to role playing. The value of these activities to a teacher may depend on how the problems are conceptualized and how readily these concepts transfer to the control of teaching behavior.

Soar has shown, once again, that teachers who are already reasonably skillful in their human relationships usually benefit from this kind of training, but those who need help most desperately may fail to find it. One conjecture is that more specific skill exercises, related to the classroom by some technique like microteaching or interaction analysis, might help the average to below average teachers.

Concepts about teaching behavior which are general, like authoritarian, force the trainee to move from the general to the specific. The addition of microteaching or interaction analysis to the curriculum would present opportunities for reaching generalizations from specific events. It may be that opportunities for both inductive and deductive insights are necessary.

EARLY RETURNS FOR MINICOURSES INVOLVING MICROTEACHING

The Far West Laboratory for Educational Research and Development, one of the U.S. Office of Education's regional laboratories, has been experimenting with what is called a "minicourse," designed to help change teaching behavior. The team of Borg, Kallenbach, Kelley, Langer, Morris, and Friebel (16, 15) has reported one evaluation for experienced teachers and one for college students who were starting their student teaching. The results need further testing in a total class setting for experienced teachers because the evaluation of performance made use of pre- and post-microteaching video tapes. The initial results, however, are very encouraging.

Plan of the studies

A minicourse was completed by 48 experienced teachers. There was no control group. In the second project, the minicourse was taken by students at three colleges. At each of two colleges there was an experimental group and a control group. The two experimental college groups and all of the experienced teachers made full use of video playback in their minicourse. The two control groups made use of the minicourse, practiced teaching skills in a microteaching format, but did not see themselves in a video playback. The third control group, at the third college, were given some course materials, but many students in this group failed to find the time to complete all phases of the minicourse. There was also no video for this group. The college students in all groups were exposed to the insights which are gained during student teaching.

The curriculum

The minicourse consists of printed instructional materials as well as sound films which instruct the trainee. Both of these media were used to give the trainee directions for making his own video recordings during microteaching.

A minicourse includes the following lessons. First, there is an introductory film which gives directions for a first, practice microteaching experience. Second, the teacher completes the practice lesson and views an instructional film which describes three specific questioning techniques. Third, the teacher views a model film in which these three techniques are illustrated by an experienced teacher. Fourth, several microteaching episodes are carried out with reteach cycles by the trainee. Fifth, the microteaching lesson is again repeated and, if possible, evaluated with the help of a fellow teacher who is also taking the course. The above complete cycle, less the introductory lesson, is then repeated three times in order to introduce and practice additional teaching skills. A minicourse is closely related to the steps of microteaching, but is also distinctive because of the self-instructional format and a high proportion of programmed material.

The results

The preliminary evaluation of the minicourse indicates that college students and experienced teachers can make changes in their behavior. There were more significant differences among the 48 experienced teachers, and fewer among the various college student groups.

In the experienced teacher project, 11 out of 13 separate measures showed significant changes, the pretraining microteach compared with the posttraining microteaching. For example, teacher talk dropped from about 52 percent to 28 percent. The number of times a teacher used *redirection* (a particular method of asking questions) increased from an average of 27 to an average of 41 for a 20-minute recording. Other significant differences were: the teachers increased the number of times they used prompting; they used clarification more frequently; the teachers repeated their own questions less often, the teacher repeated pupil answers less often; the number of times that the number of questions could be answered with one word decreased; and so on. It was possible to analyze an additional microteaching video recording which each teacher completed 4 months after finishing the course. Eight of the 11 significant differences were maintained without erosion. Three differences, namely, prompting, clarification, and not repeating own questions, continued to show the same trend so that there were significant differences when the 4-month tapes were compared with the posttraining tapes. In this project, two skills showed no significant change: these were the number of times the teacher used refocusing and decreasing punitive teacher reactions to incorrect pupil answers. The last finding could easily be due to the low incidence of that kind of teacher statement on the pretraining video tapes.

The results of the preliminary investigations with college students were impressive because the final performance tapes were made while the student teacher was teaching the entire class, and because comparisons could be made with different control groups.

The third control group, at the third college, was the group which did not complete the course, for the most part, did not engage in microteaching, and therefore did not see themselves in a video recording. This group made statistically significant changes of the following sort. First, the number of one-word remarks by pupils decreased; second, the number of times a teacher repeated a question decreased; and third, the percentage of teacher talk decreased. Presumably these changes would be the result of experience with regular student teaching. But it is interesting to note that these changes involve doing less of something, not doing more of something.

In the two experimental groups, each at a different college, one made five and the other made seven significant changes in teacher behavior. Six of these 12 significant changes involved increasing the incidence of skills that were taught in the minicourse. These two groups completed the minicourse, carried out microteaching, and viewed their own efforts on video playbacks.

The two corresponding control groups at the first and second colleges made four and six significant changes. Two of these 10 significant changes were skills which were supposed to increase as a result of taking the minicourse. These two groups completed the minicourse, carried out microteaching practice, but did not view their own performance on video playbacks.

These results raise some interesting questions about the effects of video playbacks as a source of feedback. Each of these last two control groups achieved only one less significant change than the companion experimental group at the same college. Yet they were less likely to make changes which required a higher incidence of some teaching skill. It is clear that we need to know more about the effects of video feedback. For what kinds of skills is it essential? For which skills does it help? And for what skills is it of no assistance?

Summary

The team members at the Far West Laboratory probably would wish to make it clear that these two projects merely supply preliminary results. A more extensive evaluation will become possible with more cases. Yet the notion that instructional materials for a minicourse can be packaged, sent out to teachers or to college students, and produce changes in teaching behavior is an intriguing possibility.

THE PRESENT STATUS OF HELPING ANOTHER CHANGE HIS TEACHING BEHAVIOR

The first part of this chapter includes a description of a behavior clinic in which college students or experienced teachers could learn to identify, perform, and explore patterns of teaching behavior. The second part contains a review of projects concerned with helping others change their teaching behavior. In selecting studies for this review, some assessment of teaching behavior was prerequisite and at least one of four different techniques was a part of the training program. Thus, there are one or more examples of evaluating T-group training, microteaching, interaction analysis, and simulated skill exercises. What now follows is a summary.

WHAT WE KNOW ABOUT HELPING OTHERS CHANGE THEIR TEACHING BEHAVIOR

What we know is very little compared with what we need to know. We know that teaching behavior can be changed. We know that it can be influenced during its growth and development. And we know that when teaching behavior is actually practiced and analyzed, that the probabilities that a change will occur are increased.

We know that evaluation research is complex and difficult, requires a careful design, and more resources than are usually brought to the task. The most definitive studies have been part of a program of research and development and not single shot efforts by one or two individuals. Experience in this kind of research appears to be associated with the more successful contributions.

Interaction analysis

Most evaluations of programs in which interaction analysis is used as a learning experience show that the trainees will increase their responsiveness to pupil ideas and initiative. The results are not entirely consistent, the circumstances of teaching these coding techniques are quite variable, and the controls in different research designs are difficult to maintain. In spite of these difficulties, there is evidence to suggest that efforts to improve this kind of training are likely to be productive.

Microteaching

The early research at Stanford indicated that training with microteaching provides college students with a curriculum of learning tasks, that students respond positively to the training, and that students so trained receive higher ratings during their intern year (2). Additional research, reviewed here, indicates that certain teaching skills can be studied in a minicourse, practiced with microteaching, and then applied after training. These results are tentative and more evidence is needed, including understanding of how important video feedback is to the training process.

Simulated skill and T-group training

The least amount of evidence is available for these two techniques. Part of the difficulty is that the curriculum of both techniques is not standardized, varies from one program to another even with the same program directors, and has seldom been evaluated in terms of teaching behavior.

Combinations

Microteaching, T-groups, and interaction analysis have each been combined with various forms of simulated skill exercises. Judging from the results reported by the Hough team at Ohio State and the Far West Laboratory team in Berkeley, simulated training combined with interaction analysis or with microteaching have both proven helpful in single projects.

PROSPECTS FOR THE FUTURE

Continued progress in creating programs that result in changing teaching behavior will require a balance between the design of more effective learning experiences—which is largely a matter of insightful inquiry—versus the considered use of research evaluation—which is largely a problem of research design. When research requirements are overemphasized and place limitations on insightful inquiry, the result may be an elegant analysis of an inconsequential innovation. When creative training strategies are not adequately evaluated, then the evidence of effectiveness fails to be persuasive.

Besides balance, there is the question of timing. Curriculum innovations that are developed through insightful inquiry should not be evaluated in a comprehensive research design until the smaller inquiry cycles have resulted in improvements through pilot runs and a certain amount of trial and error. For example, the minicourses which were reported by Borg et al. were developed by submitting parts of the course to trial runs. Different ways to combine interaction analysis with simulated skill exercises should be explored before a full scale research evaluation is attempted. Much more preliminary research on microteaching should be carried out before we can understand just how this fascinating feedback medium functions most effectively. Running counter to this plea for pacing research and development activities are the pressures to prove that one or another innovation is better than a traditional curriculum, the desire to gather evidence in preparation for assaulting the *status quo*, and the need to develop "promising leads" in order to apply for "outside funds."

Some ways to combine our present technologies are outlined in the first part of this chapter. What we need are fewer converts to one or another technology and more creative combinations of existing techniques built around practical programs. Perhaps the most productive efforts will occur when T-group training, microteaching, interaction analysis, and simulated skill exercises are relegated to the position of techniques and the steps and procedures of inquiry become the main framework for helping others change their teaching behavior.

In the meantime, decisions about what kind of teaching behavior is most effective must be made, and this is the topic of the next chapter.

Chapter Twelve

RESEARCH ON TEACHING EFFECTIVENESS BASED ON ANALYZING VERBAL INTERACTION IN THE CLASSROOM

DECIDING WHAT IS RELEVANT

Suppose you are reading this book because you think it may help you to become a more effective teacher. For those who have this goal, it may help to think of this book as consisting of three parts. First, concepts and techniques for analyzing verbal communication in the classroom are introduced and discussed in Chapters 1 through 10. Second, the possibility that a teacher will become more responsive to pupil ideas and feelings as a result of analyzing his own classroom communication is presented in Chapter 11 and some supportive evidence is discussed. The third part of this book consists of the present chapter. Here we are confronted with the problem of deciding whether becoming more responsive to pupils while teaching does or does not improve the quality of classroom instruction. Most of the research reviewed in this chapter is an attempt to determine whether such changes are or are not improvements. Since researchers do not always agree on the criteria for judging improvements, the paragraphs which follow attempt to specify what is meant by "more effective teaching."

Knowledge about teaching effectiveness consists of relationships between what a teacher does while teaching and the effect of these actions on the growth and development of his pupils. Presumably an effective teacher interacts skillfully with pupils so that they learn more and like learning better compared with ineffective teachers. From this point of view, teaching effectiveness is concerned with those aspects of teaching over which the teacher has direct control and current options. Space and equipment are available, but *how* can they best be organized? Instructional materials are at hand, but *how* are the pupils to use them? Pupils are given, but *how* does a teacher interact with them? Those who study teacher-pupil interaction usually assume that no matter how these options are exercised, the result will shape verbal interaction in the classroom. Therefore, an analysis of communication ought to distinguish more effective from less effective teaching.

As you read the material in this chapter, it would be wise to approach all sections with an alert and active skepticism. Like all research, the results reported may be proven incorrect by subsequent research, in spite of the care that was taken by those who conducted the projects. In order to foster a skeptical attitude, some of the problems of conducting research on teaching effectiveness will be presented first. The review of research then follows. Most of the difficulties and problems of conducting this kind of research are not adequately controlled or eliminated in the research reported. It is this realization which leads to skepticism, to an insistence on replicated findings, and to conservative speculations about possible applications.

DIFFICULTIES IN CONDUCTING RESEARCH ON TEACHING EFFECTIVENESS

The difficulties which are listed in this section are very serious and illustrate possible reasons for the slow progress that has been made in the field. The difficulties which are discussed stand out as having the highest priority in terms of my own research experience.

MEASURING LEARNING OUTCOMES

How pupils act, think, and feel provide criteria for learning outcomes. To decide whether a change in teaching is or is not an improvement requires an assessment of these criteria. The most common learning outcomes are content achievement, skill performance, and attitudes. As suggested on page 318, pupil independence is an additional outcome which may be well worth investigating.

It must be conceded, at the start, that an assessment of educational outcomes is only a sampling procedure. Indeed, testing consists of making careful observations or asking certain key questions so that the results will permit good guesses about how much was learned in one class compared with another. Clever testing procedures help to reduce error when such guesses are made.

Difficulties in measuring pupil achievement

Error is introduced into a study of teaching effectiveness when an achievement test does not adequately measure the knowledge and skills which the teacher attempted to teach. Difficulties can arise no matter whether the researcher designs his own test or chooses to use a nationally standardized, published test.

Nationally standardized tests of educational development introduce error because they often measure knowledge, skills, or perceptions which the teacher did not necessarily intend to teach. At the elementary levels, such tests typically have sections on language skills, arithmetic, interpretation of maps, and so on. The specific knowledge, skills, and perceptions to be taught during a particular research project were not considered when the test was designed. Obviously experiences outside of the classroom could influence the pupils' performance on such tests. Large errors can develop between average test scores and the assessment of classroom interaction because the two are not logically related. This kind of error, for example, is likely to lead to the theory that brighter kids score higher on a nationally standardized test regardless of what a teacher does while teaching. Or another theory might be that any relationship between achievement scores and classroom interaction merely shows how teaching behavior varies when the average ability of the class varies. Such errors can easily hide what relationships do exist between what is learned and teaching behavior in the classroom.

When the purpose of research is to compare different patterns of teaching, it might be wise to select learning objectives that are unrelated, or as unrelated as possible, to what can be learned by watching TV, reading at home, attending other classes, and playing after school. Next, these unusual objectives should be used to construct alternative forms of a test covering the facts, skills, relationships, and other more complicated outcomes. Items should be constructed, tried out on a similar population, and item analysis procedures used to improve the test. Some sections of the test can be devoted to problems which require transferring what has been learned in one context to another in such a way that self-direction in using logical thinking is required. However, this skill in transfer must be based on what is taught in order to minimize the effects of the more generalized skills of problem-solving.

The alternative of constructing a special test rather than choosing a nationally published test is a better solution when the "handmade" tests are of high quality. Unfortunately, a poorly constructed test can introduce as much error or even more than a nationally standardized test.

Another problem in evaluating learning outcomes centers on how much the classroom teacher should know about the test. The test should match the teaching objectives and the teacher must understand these objectives in great detail, but does this mean that the teacher should see the pre- and posttests that will be used to assess the learning outcomes? Assuming that a field study purposely involves teachers with a wide variety of talent, the less effective teachers may teach for the test, that is, for the particular outcomes which the test samples, ignoring the other possible objectives. Perhaps the best solution is not to show the test to the teachers, but to provide each teacher with a careful outline of all objectives. Contamination from the pretest is nevertheless always possible for the inquisitive and persistent teacher and an adequate countermove is costly because it usually requires a larger sample of classes assigned to additional treatments.

Difficulties in measuring attitudes and independence

Pupil attitudes toward a teacher and toward schoolwork are usually measured less effectively than is achievement. The most obvious difficulties arise when these attitudes develop from experiences over which a classroom teacher has no control. The attitudes of most pupils are greatly influenced by earlier experiences with parents, other teachers, peer relatiohips, and so on.

How can a test be designed which filters out nonclassroom forces and assesses perceptions which are products of experience during the instructional periods that are a part of the study? Some suggestions can be found in the development of pupil ratings during microteaching episodes. First, pupil perceptions of the teaching are measured immediately after the teaching period. Second, pupils are given up to 4 hours of training in the use of the rating forms. Third, items in such forms refer to teaching behavior and the immediate reactions to such behavior. Fourth, a part of pupil training might include some kind of feedback in which trends in the average group rating, one teaching period compared with another, can be discussed in terms of validity. That is, the pupils could discuss what a lower score means and whether this was what they intended to indicate. Fifth, the use of average ratings would more likely reflect the opinions of the entire pupil group.

Pupil independence and self-direction are even greater unknowns than either pupil achievement or pupil attitudes. One approach is to make inferences about independence and self-direction from interaction analysis data. The inability of the FIAC system to discriminate between various kinds of pupil statements has been a barrier to progress in this area. Subscripting and multiple coding should be helpful. A variation of interaction analysis coding might involve systematic observer ratings of overt pupil behavior based on time sampling procedures. Finally, paper and pencil tests administered to pupils might help. Cognitive independence measures might be inferred from cleverly designed tests of achievement and problem-solving. Emotional independence may require the development of standardized stimulus situations in which pupil responses are assessed in terms of behavior. Until more progress is made, this type of educational assessment seems to be beyond our reach.

EXPERIMENTAL CONTROLS

The purpose of experimental controls, in this field of research, is to determine with some precision just how teaching behavior affects learning outcomes. One method is to measure as many aspects of the total classroom situation as possible and then analyze the data in one comprehensive multivariate analysis. Used correctly, a multivariate analysis is an efficient and powerful statistical approach in which specific hypotheses about teaching behavior can be tested. A design which attempts to keep all factors constant except one or two variables is too narrow although three or four variables, in a tight design, may be very productive.

A research approach can include too many variables when the total number of tests or observations becomes so numerous that special care and attention to each is sacrificed. It can contain too few variables when factors which could affect the results are not taken into consideration. Hypothesis hunting computer programs, which test all possible relationships among variables, can be easily misused. They have their greatest value in early exploratory studies, but they are misleading when statistically significant relationships "appear" which have no theoretical relationship to teaching behavior, when they maximize relationships through error variance, and when they lead to *post hoc* inferences.

The serious student of control in this area of research should read Campbell and Stanley (21) in order to consider various kinds of research designs which are possible.

The variables listed below should be carefully controlled in most studies of teaching effectiveness.

Class ability

The single best predictor of an educational outcome consists of various measures of the same variable before the study takes place. Since bright pupils learn more and dull pupils learn less, a class with an above average achievement score before a study is most likely to be in the same position at the end of the study. For example, in our Minnesota and Michigan studies involving eighth grade math ($N = 16$), seventh grade combined English and social studies core ($N = 15$), and sixth grade self-contained classrooms ($N = 30$), Coats (25, p. 89) showed that between class average preachievement scores correlated with postachievement scores consistently above 0.92. When I.Q. was also used in a multiple regression, the correlations were above 0.96, which is unusually high.

By themselves, these high correlations overestimate the relative influence of ability on unadjusted final achivement scores compared with other predictor variables. In the Coats study, a stepwise linear regression program was used to select and then add the next "most useful" predictor in order to maximize an association with final unadjusted achievement for 60 classes in the eighth, seventh, and sixth grades. A sense of the relative contributions of different predictors can be obtained by inspecting Fig. 12–1.

Line A shows that the prediction of unadjusted final achievement starts at 0.92 and rises in the next step to 0.96 and then gradually rises to 0.97. The contribution of preachievement is shown by line B which drops to 0.61 from 0.92, when the second variable is added, and then gradually falls to 0.56. Line C shows the contribution of the second variable, I.Q., which starts at 0.40, drops 0.36, and then gradually climbs, to 0.41. The third variable (i/i + d, tendency of the teacher to be indirect) starts out at 0.08 and climbs finally to 0.16 with the

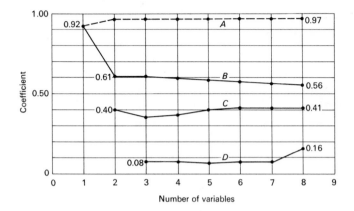

Fig. 12–1.   Partial Regression Coefficients: 60 Classes: Achievement [after Coats (25)].

addition of the eighth variable. Variables four through eight need not concern us here.

The purpose of Fig. 12–1 is to show that class ability, as measured by a pretest of achievement and by tests of I.Q., is significantly associated with unadjusted posttest scores of average achievement between classes. In addition, the relative contribution of a factor like pupil ability can be compared with a factor like indirectness of teaching behavior in terms of relative contribution. It is *definitively inappropriate** to infer from Fig. 12–1 that we can expect to predict pupil achievement with the degree of accuracy that is suggested by a correlation of 0.97. Nevertheless, it is our best predictor.

Initial class ability is very difficult to control in field studies of teaching effectiveness. Besides the difficulties of designing and developing the test itself, mentioned earlier, two additional problems demand a solution. First, how is a measure of gain based on pre- and posttest scores to be calculated? Soar (93, p. 80) observes:

The use of measures of change, while in theory a straightforward way of studying the effect of classroom process on pupils, in practice turns out to have a number of very real difficulties. The principal one is that change measures are much less reliable than the measures of status from which they are derived. . . . [Much] of what determines the status of a person at the time a test is administered will be common to another test administered a year later. When the difference between these two measures is taken,

---

*The issue here is the amount of error variance which inflates a multiple correlation coefficient that is the product of a linear multiple regression equation which, in turn, is the product of the computer program described in the text.

the stable element is removed from both, and the remainder, the measure of change, is then much less reliable.

No system of regression analysis or method of calculating gain scores is without error, and anyone interested in a careful consideration of the statistical problems might start by reading *Problems in Measuring Change* edited by C. W. Harris (50). The ideal experimental design, which is usually beyond the reach of the researcher, would involve the random assignment of pupils to classes from strata based on ability. Under these conditions, statistical procedures used to control the chance differences of initial ability classes are much more effective.

The second problem is less well known and is concerned with the effects of differences in ability on teaching behavior. No matter how measures of learning are adjusted for initial ability, it is reasonable to suppose (Turner, 102) that the ability of the pupils does influence classroom interaction and therefore is associated with teaching behavior. Brighter pupils probably initiate more ideas (Category 9) and the teacher then has more opportunities to engage in level two interaction patterns. If true, then these patterns would be associated with higher gain scores for learning regardless of teacher influence. The presumption that a higher proportion of level two patterns promotes more learning, or that by increasing this proportion pupils will learn more, are both inferences that could be based on secondary associations. Only "true experiments" like those proposed by Campbell and Stanley (21) can sort out these difficulties. Resolving the issue of whether opportunities for level two interaction are created by pupils or depend on the teacher's initiative or both will take many more research projects than are currently published. Theoretically, interaction variables might be adjusted statistically in terms of pupil ability, but this is no more than speculation.

The thrust of this discussion becomes clearer when a specific design for a teaching effectiveness study is considered. Suppose teachers with different patterns of teaching behavior are identified and assigned to two treatments. Each teacher is given a 2-week unit of study to teach. Preachievement and postachievement tests are administered. Comparisons of subject matter achievement and changes in pupil attitude are made between the two treatments, each representing two different teaching patterns and each treatment relatively homogeneous with regard to its teaching pattern. The factor of initial ability and I.Q. among pupils could bias the outcome in spite of a covariance regression analysis of achievement scores. The regression analysis can take into account the variance of the pretest that is associated with the posttest, but the interaction analysis data may still be systematically biased due to the differences in ability between the pupils in the two treatments. Classroom interaction feeds upon itself and a string of events influences what follows. Although a teacher has more power than the pupils to alter a particular trend in communication, the exchange is *interactive*. Pupils present the teacher with alternatives to which he can respond or take the initiative to alter. The weaknesses in this design are twofold: first, the adjustment of the final scores according to the prelearning scores is not without its bias; and second, the effect of ability on the interaction remains uncontrolled.

Situational differences

There are factors other than initial ability which can bias educational outcomes. It is helpful when all teachers have access to the same resource materials. The materials for a unit of study which are specially prepared for a research project, including enough resource materials for the entire class, at least insures that each class has a common starting point. Factors of classroom space, the administration policies of the building principal, the school atmosphere, and similar factors also influence educational outcomes. When different teaching methods are being investigated or when specific patterns of teaching behavior are being compared, it is usually possible to design the study so that these factors do not bias a fair test of the hypotheses. However, these adjustments tend only to equalize treatments. Other features of the data remain nonrepresentative and make comparisons between projects hazardous.

PATTERNS OF TEACHING BEHAVIOR

In a field study involving two contrasting patterns of teaching, such as the one described earlier, the comparisons are based on natural situations. Besides soliciting the cooperation of the teachers, the most difficult problem is to ensure the similarity of teaching within a treatment and to make sure that there are fundamental differences between treatments. Unless the within-group similarities are reasonably consistent and involve identifiable teaching patterns, the intended comparisons may be too weak to permit a fair test of possible differences in the educational outcomes.

Contrasts made in a natural setting can be made sharper by training the teachers, providing the same instructional materials, controlling the teaching strategies, and arranging the situation so that the same tests of educational outcomes can be administered in all classes. Lack of care and thoroughness in making these interventions weakens the test of hypothesis about teaching behavior.

Inconsistency in teaching behavior

It is almost axiomatic that no matter how much care is exercised in purifying a research design, unwanted variations of teaching patterns erode the within-group similarities and between-groups contrast. The spontaneity of classroom interaction may cause these variations, or lack of skill on the part of the teacher might lead to inadvertent contamination of the intended teaching behavior. Even a youngster having a bad day can force a teacher away from a teaching strategy. In research of this type it is most desirable to code the interaction and thereby provide evidence about the consistency between what happened and what the design required. About the only safeguards against these difficulties are to train the teachers, to have several teacher-classroom units in each comparison group, and to observe the same class on several occasions.

Theories and hypotheses

Theories and hypotheses about teaching effectiveness grow out of *how* one thinks about the problem. In turn, this thinking determines what data are collected and the kinds of comparisons that are planned. In general, the more comprehensive a theory, the more abstract are the concepts which make up the theory. Although it is not always true, highly abstract concepts in comprehensive generalizations are less useful for guiding teaching behavior. For example, many generalizations about I.Q. are rather comprehensive: thus, "pupils with high I.Q.s learn more and learn more quickly" presumably applies to all learning situations both inside and outside of the classroom. The concepts "higher I.Q." and "learn more" or "learns quickly" are very general. The utility of this generalization is low. It may influence the expectations of a teacher, but has little to say about the decisions that are involved in controlling teaching behavior.

A generalization that "the reinforcement of certain behaviors increases their likelihood of occurrence" is equally abstract and general, but is slightly more relevant to classroom teaching because it has consequences for how a teacher might act. This kind of conceptualizing starts a researcher, as well as a teacher, toward the study of reinforcement and how it can be provided in the classroom. The things that a teacher does to provide reinforcement are what Brodbeck would call the "coordinating definitions" (20, p. 70) of reinforcement. Exploring these alternatives becomes a research problem in its own right. A concept like reinforcement is so abstract and general, however, that subsequent investigations of it can lead to radically different activities. On the one hand, a researcher might become interested in programmed instruction and, on the other hand, in ways to use Categories 2 and 3 in class discussions. In either case, an extended period of research is required to find out how reinforcement can be used most effectively. Thus, before a comprehensive generalization can be applied, more research that goes beyond what was originally carried out may be required to test the generalization under classroom conditions. This subsequent research may very well produce conclusions that place radical limitations on the original generalization or even alter its meaning.

Later on in this chapter, a very abstract and comprehensive generalization is discussed to the effect that "indirect teaching (above average i/d ratio) is associated with more learning and direct teaching with less learning." The futility of this generalization lies in its low utility because it will take considerable research to show just how the relationship works in a practical situation. The subsequent research may alter the initial generalization. It would be a cruel paradox if the only variables which researchers could measure were features of learning over which a teacher has no control and equally sad if research variables were conceptualized in ways that were unrelated to classroom conditions.

SAMPLING PROBLEMS

When a small group of teacher-class units are selected so that they represent a larger population, the teaching behavior in the sample is descriptive of the population within the limits of sampling error. The logic in extending a conclusion so that it becomes a generalization about a larger population is based on a defensible sampling procedure, one that permits an estimate of the sampling error. This process of extending conclusions so that they become logical generalizations is very difficult in research on teaching effectiveness, for a number of reasons which are now discussed.

Sampling and target populations

The more heterogeneous the target population, the more any commonality within it is likely to be described in comprehensive and abstract concepts. Thus, a generalization which might be established about all teaching may be of the type "brighter pupils learn more than duller pupils, regardless of teaching behavior," and the evidence for this generalization might prove to be statistically significant. Suppose, on the other hand, that a target population consists of classrooms in which pupils are approximately equal in ability, the same age, and all studying the same instructional materials. Then a possible generalization might be "pupils learn more with teaching strategy A than they do with B," and this generalization may also be true even though it apparently contradicts the first generalization mentioned. The reason both can be true lies in the relationships between the concepts investigated, the way the target population is defined, and the nature of the research design.

Teaching effectiveness is by definition concerned with what teachers do that affects educational outcomes. In order to investigate teaching behavior with techniques such as coding verbal communication, sample sizes have necessarily been small, too small to provide a logical basis for extending conclusions so as to generalize about a target population. The target populations, in turn, are difficult to identify in any meaningful way. You may notice that when research projects are reported in the next section, about all that can be said about most experimental samples is how they were chosen. The consumer of these research findings is left in the uneasy position of knowing that certain target populations are designated and then sampled, but how these populations and samples correspond to the total educational enterprise is not at all clear. What does it mean, for example, to report that the classrooms studied represent the range of teaching behavior to be found in one school district, at a particular grade level, in a suburban community? Such a parent population is of no consequence because it does not facilitate making generalizations.

Sometime in the future it may be possible to discuss a universe of communication events. For this to occur, research workers would have to cooperate by collecting and processing their data so that the results from different projects can be compared. For example, the proposals already made about collapsing subscripted category systems to a basic set of categories would be a great help in constructing a universe of communication events within the limitations of the basic system. A data bank of this sort would permit any researcher to specify in considerable detail the similarities and differences of his sample of communication events and a logically related "universe" in the data bank. Such a system would permit a researcher to know how representative his sample was, regardless of how it was selected.

Representative teaching behavior

Once the teacher-classroom units are selected for a project, it has been my experience that at least 10 and sometimes 50 percent of teachers refuse to permit classroom observation. This variation depends a great deal on the skill used in approaching teachers. But in any case, substituting a teacher who is willing to cooperate for another who does not, usually makes the sample less representative in the sense of sampling procedures.

Another problem arises when an observer enters the classroom. Samph (83) has conducted a study among 10 teachers at different grade levels in one elementary school in which he compared classroom interaction for the same teachers under four conditions: (a) no observation scheduled, no observer appears; (b) no observation scheduled, observer appears; (c) observation scheduled, no observer appears; and (d) observation scheduled, observer appears. Using microphones installed in the classroom with the teachers' permission, tape recordings were made without the teachers knowing exactly when a recording was made. All recordings were then coded using the FIAC system. Although the study will have to be replicated before too much confidence can be placed in the conclusions, this study showed that the teachers tended to become more responsive toward the pupils when an observer was present in the classroom (83, p. 69). The incidence of Categories 3 and 4 becomes higher. It would appear that a teacher does make adjustments in his behavior when he is being observed.

This problem of nonrepresentative behavior cannot be solved easily. Teachers who are forced to participate in research projects may be the most likely to alter their normal behavior. Ironically, this could mean that the more rigorous methods of selecting a representative sample are spoiled by biases that the observer's presence causes. It could be that volunteers would provide a more representative sample of teaching behavior because they might be less concerned about adjusting their behavior. There is also the unexplored possibility that teachers could be instructed or somehow conditioned so that the presence of absence of an observer would have a minimum effect.

The consequences of sampling problems

Bias and error are present in all educational research and good research designs can minimize bias and account for error. These problems in research, like those in a marriage, are reduced or brought under control by learning how best to live with them. Techniques of interaction analysis may be used least effectively when the goal is to make generalizations about the teaching behavior that can be found in our classrooms as in a survey. The analysis of classroom communication may contribute much more to the improvement of education when careful comparisons are made between different teaching strategies and behavior patterns in terms of educational outcomes as in an experiment.

SOME SUGGESTIONS

This section contains some suggestions for improving research on teaching effectiveness. The assumption is made that the purpose of research is to study teaching behavior and the effects of this behavior on the pupils' attitudes and subject matter achievement.

Selecting and working with teachers

Suppose a project requires teachers to perform certain teaching patterns under practical, classroom conditions specified by a research design.

1) The most important requirement of the study is that the particular teaching patterns to be investigated do indeed vary and do so in ways that are consistent with the research design. For example, if two ways of using teacher questions are required, verify the performance differences before starting to analyze the outcome data. Teachers may have to be trained in order to create the between-treatment differences. Teachers with special skills may have to be selected. Regardless of how representative a sample may be, it does no good to investigate different ways of asking questions if all questions are asked in the same way or if the variations in asking questions are contrary to the research design. When "representativeness" in a sample

is sacrificed, the conclusions do not represent general practice. In this case, extending conclusions to broader generalizations will occur through replication of the study, if it is to occur at all. The first step, then, is to train teachers to perform teaching patterns in ways that match the research design or to locate teachers who do this in their natural style of teaching.

2) It will help if the teachers can be instructed to maintain consistent teaching behavior when an observer or voice recording team is in the room. Here consistency should not be confused with rigidity. The within-treatment variation should be small, but the contrast between treatments should be large. This takes practice, usually, and teachers will want to know as much about the project as possible without biasing the research design.

3) One advantage of voice and/or video recording is that it can be kept for subsequent additional analysis. For example, a different set of categories can be used to provide more information about sequence or some other feature of interaction. The problems of calculating coding reliability are much easier to handle with recorded interaction. Live observation has the advantage that the observer-coder has more information on which to base his coding judgments.

4) The conclusions from a particular project can be compared to other projects in two ways. First, it may be necessary to use a subscripted coding system for a particular project. A computer program can be used to collapse the expanded interaction data back to the basic system at relatively low cost. Second, when interaction data are voice and/or video recorded, then another researcher's category system can be applied to the data. This procedure involves the cost of personnel who record in the field in addition to training observers and employing them to code all interaction back in the office. Coding the same interaction with a second system also adds to cost.

5) It may be wise to remember that a properly trained observer may be able to code nuances of interaction which pupils and teachers do not recognize. The more subtle distinctions usually require live classroom interaction instead of recorded interaction or, alternatively, have the trained coders present in the room taking notes when the field recording is made.

6) Besides coding interaction, it may be helpful to obtain the pupils' reactions to interaction patterns by developing a questionnaire or making use of interviews.

7) Perhaps the most ambitious attack on evaluating educational outcomes would be a coordinated effort among many researchers to develop and standardize "evaluative teaching units." Such a unit would contain a teacher's manual which outlined the objectives and provided many more suggestions for learning activities than one teacher could possibly use. The kit would also include a wide range of instructional materials so as to fit any preferred teaching style and in sufficient quantity for a class size of

40 pupils. Standardized instructions for the teacher would help to control the class time allocated to the unit. With some imagination, the material itself might cover topics not normally experienced by children of the age in question. Carefully designed tests for the pre- and postassessment of achievement might someday provide normative data. Finally, some basic category system which could be expanded through subscription might be used frequently enough to provide normative expectations. We will never be able to judge more and less effective training programs for preservice and inservice education or study relationships between teaching behavior and learning outcomes until the educational outcomes can be effectively assessed.

SOME RESEARCH RESULTS ON TEACHING EFFECTIVENESS

This section contains a summary of research evidence that makes use of highly selected references. Heavy emphasis is given to my own research primarily because the strengths and weaknesses of each project are more familiar to me. The work of other researchers is considered subsequently. The primary criterion for citing any research conclusion is that the evidence refers to relationships between interaction analysis variables and some learning outcome such as adjusted achievement or positive attitudes of the pupils.

PROJECTS SUPERVISED OR DIRECTED BY THE AUTHOR

There are seven projects which were designed by the author to compare interaction analysis variables with some educational outcome such as measures of pupil attitudes and pupil achievement. These projects are listed in Table 12–1.

The procedure

The procedure followed in each project was essentially the same, except for number 7.

1) An inventory assessing positive pupil attitudes was administered to a sample of classrooms. This sample was chosen so as to be representative of a larger population of similar classrooms in a given geographical area.
2) Average scores on the inventory were calculated for each class. The classes located at the extremes of the resulting distribution of scores were selected for observation, except for projects 5 and 6 which also included classrooms selected from the middle of the distribution. The purpose of selecting extreme classrooms was to increase the range of interaction patterns in the study. However, average attitude scores are far from perfectly correlated with

TABLE 12–1
Projects Completed by the Author

Project Number	Reference Number	Year Data Collected	Location	Number of Classes		Grade Level and Subject	Outcome Variable
				Observed	In Sample		
1	(39)	1955–1956	Minnesota	9	34	7th grade, 2 hour English–social studies core	Attitude
2	(39)	1957	New Zealand	10	33	Standard four, self-contained	Attitude
3 *	(39)	1959–1960	Minnesota	16	38	8th grade, 1 hour mathematics	Attitude and achievement
4 *	(39)	1959–1960	Minnesota	15	37	7th grade, 2 hour English–social studies core	Attitude and achievement
5 *	(42)	1964–1965	Michigan	30	101	6th grade, self-contained	Attitude and achievement
6 *	(42)	1965–1966	Michigan	16	72	4th grade, self-contained	Attitude and achievement
7 *	(42)	1966–1967	Michigan	16	00	2nd grade, self-contained	Attitude and achivement

*Supported, in part, by a research contract with the U.S. Office of Education, Bureau of Research, The Department of Health, Education and Welfare.

with interaction patterns, so at best this procedure * only increased the odds that there would be wider variation among classrooms with respect to inter-action patterns.

3) The classes so isolated were then observed and the classroom interaction coded by trained observers. Except for projects 1 and 2, an assessment was made of content achievement before and after the observations. Final achievement scores could then be adjusted according to initial achievement by a regression technique.

The procedure was similar in project 7 except that at the second grade no pupil attitude inventory could be administered in order to select classes for observation. Teachers were merely selected with the hope that classroom inter-action would vary, one class compared with the next, and that such variation might then be found to be related to either attitude or achievement. At the end of observation, a simplified five-item attitude scale was administered.

In every project, classroom observation occurred only when the teacher gave permission. In this sense, all teachers were volunteers. In every project except 7, one or two teachers initially selected refused to be observed and an-other teacher was substituted.

The general hypotheses in these studies were based on the material already presented in Chapter 10. They can be summarized by saying that teacher in-directness and flexibility would be positively related to average class measures of positive pupil attitudes and final achievement adjusted for initial ability. In the case of projects 3 and 4, additional hypotheses were made about shifting from indirect to more direct patterns of teacher influence as the pupils' percep-tions of the learning goals became clearer, and the results were discussed in Chapter 10.

Predicting outcome criteria

The results of projects 1, 2, 3, and 4 have been reported elsewhere (39). The sum-marization of projects 1 and 2 was reported as follows.

---

*This step in the procedure is analogous to creating treatment differences in a true experiment. Any hypotheses about classroom interaction and educational outcomes can be investigated only when variation exists between classes. Usually teachers are trained to be different in the true experi-ment but must be located so as to ensure differences in an experimental field study.

The alternative to selecting the classes to be observed from extreme scores in a distribution of class averages would be to select them so that they were proportionally representative of some population. This choice helps to make the observed classrooms more representative of some population so that the results are then more typical of classroom conditions in the population. However, a fair test of hypotheses which associate interaction variables with outcome variables may be jeopardized, presuming that such an association exists, due to excessive conformity among classrooms with respect to interaction. The choice favoring the greater range provides more information about the possible association; the choice favoring more representativeness provides more information about typical interaction patterns which characterize current teaching practices.

The major purpose of these preliminary studies was to find out if there were any relationships between patterns of teacher influence and the attitudes of pupils toward their teachers and schoolwork. Classes whose scores were high on an attitude inventory were identified as well as classes whose scores were low. The patterns of teacher influence in the contrasting classrooms were quantified by the use of interaction analysis.

The same [results were] *found in Minnesota and New Zealand, some 8,000 miles apart, in spite of differences in teaching style and pupil expectations. The teachers of classes that scored high on liking the teacher, motivation, fair rewards and punishments, lack of anxiety, and independence used more indirect influence,* while the teachers of classes that scored low used less indirect influence. In New Zealand, but not in Minnesota, teachers in classrooms that scored low used more direct influence, yet in both countries teachers in classrooms that scored high used more indirect influence. The greater use of indirect influence meant asking more questions, clarifying and using pupil ideas, and giving praise.*

The interaction data showed that more than one-half of the statements were concerned with subject matter. It is clear that the main business in the classrooms studied was learning subject matter. Yet eight percent more indirect influence and twelve percent less direct influence (in New Zealand) distinguished the teachers of the high-and-low scoring classes. An analysis of interaction matrices showed that these relatively small differences in the influence patterns occurred at strategic moments in classroom communication. For example, there were important differences in the response of the teacher at the moment when pupils stopped talking, especially in the extended use of clarifying pupil ideas, and in shifting back and forth from giving directions to expressing criticism.

One gets the impression that a small amount of indirect influence lubricates the classroom gears of subject matter learning, and even though the total amount of indirect influence is small, its presence or absence [is significantly related to] *the positive or negative attitudes of pupils, respectively. (pp. 64—65)*

The results for projects 5, 6, and 7 appear in terminal contract reports (42) under the author's name. They are presented here in combination with projects 3 and 4 by following the statistical analysis described below. Incidently, subscripted categories were used in the last three projects, but since the same basic 10-category system was used, the data in the subscripted categories have been collapsed in order to make comparisons possible.

The statistical procedure. First, a factor analysis with a vari-max solution was carried out on 27 interaction analysis variables, selected from a 10 × 10 matrix, and calculated separately for each grade level. There were three strong factors and a fourth moderately strong factor at each grade level. The nature of

---

*See page 102 for a definition of "indirect influence."

these factors is suggested by the variables which loaded the highest: Factor I was associated with the teachers' indirectness and directness; Factor II seemed to be associated with subject matter content; Factor III was involved with teacher questions and pupil response talk; and Factor IV concerned teacher directions and criticism. The factor solutions across grades was quite similar except for the second grade level, which was quite different.

Second, eight variables were selected for special analysis because they represented the four strongest factors. To these eight, the variable of praise (column two total) and flexibility (the difference between the highest and the lowest i/d ratios for each teacher) were added. These last two variables were added because of general interest in praise as a teaching function and because of the research staff's interest in theories which took into account the notion of teacher flexibility.

Third, the 10 variables selected in the second step were used as a pool of interaction predictors for "forward, linear, stepwise, multiple regression analysis." This statistical procedure selects variables from the pool and then weights them in order to obtain the highest possible multiple correlation with one of the two outcome variables, either average scores on a pupil attitude inventory or final achievement scores adjusted for initial ability. The analysis is between classes at the same grade level and the results show how the predictor variables are associated with an educational outcome for that particular grade level. The computer program to accomplish this task* starts by selecting the single predictor variable which is most highly correlated with the outcome criterion. It then searches for the second variable which produces the highest multiple correlation when combined with the first. The cycle is repeated, adding additional variables, but the procedure usually stops short of using all 10 variables, since the last few additional variables make such a small difference that they can be ignored.

The results.   The procedure begins with a set of zero-order correlations. The set for adjusted achievement is shown in Table 12–2. Those for positive pupil attitudes are shown in Table 12–3. There are a number of interesting relationships to be found in these two tables. Before they are discussed, further clarification of how achievement and attitude were measured is in order. In the fourth, seventh, and eighth grades, achievement was measured by a carefully constructed test designed to assess the objectives of a 2-week unit which each teacher taught. In the second and sixth grades, portions of a nationally standardized achievement test covering language and number skills were used to form a composite score. The elapsed time between pre- and posttest in these latter two

---

*The author is indebted to Dr. William Coats for early work in this area and to Dr. Larry Gess for most of the analysis reported here.

TABLE 12–2
Correlations Between Adjusted Achievement and Interaction Analyses Variables

Variable Number	Factor	Interaction Variable	Symbol	Grade Level				
				2nd	4th	6th	7th	8th
1	I	Indirectness	i/i + d	−0.073	0.308	0.224	0.481	0.428
2	I	Sustained acceptance	(3–3) cell	−0.450	0.191	0.303	0.395	0.193
3	III	Indirectness	Columns 1, 2, 3, 4	0.045	−0.078	0.260	0.251	0.449
4	III	Questions	Column 4	0.068	−0.188	0.106	−0.055	0.437
5	II	Teacher talk	Columns 1 to 7	0.302	0.083	0.114	0.015	0.451
6	II & IV	Restrictiveness	Columns 6, 7	−0.100	−0.236	−0.042	−0.606	−0.342
7	I & IV	Restrictive feedback	(8−6)+(8+7)+ (9−6)+(9−7) cells	0.175	−0.338	−0.320	−0.498	−0.433
8	IV & I	Negative authority	(6−7)+(7−6) cells	0.053	−0.227	−0.145	−0.620	−0.251
9		Praise	Column 2	0.249	−0.128	0.357	−0.228	0.297
10		Flexibility	(high i/d − low i/d)	−0.073	0.456	0.194	0.374	0.429
Number of classes				15	16	30	15	16

TABLE 12–3

Correlations Between Class Attitude and Interaction Analysis

Variable Number	Factor	Interaction Variable	Symbol	Grade Level				
				2nd	4th	6th	7th	8th
1	I	Indirectness	i/i + d	0.130	0.636	0.486	0.335	0.584
2	I	Sustained acceptance	(3 − 3) cell	0.128	0.516	0.401	0.331	0.311
3	III	Indirectness	Columns 1, 2, 3, 4	0.445	0.339	0.395	0.163	0.512
4	III	Questions	Column 4	0.485	−0.064	0.270	0.002	0.471
5	II	Teacher talk	Columns 1 to 7	0.375	0.098	0.236	0.147	0.610
6	VI & IV	Restrictiveness	Columns 6, 7	−0.090	−0.166	−0.368	−0.431	−0.657
7	IV & I	Restrictive feedback	(8 − 6) + (8 − 7) + (9 − 6) + (9 − 7) cells	0.023	−0.321	−0.287	−0.469	−0.622
8	IV & I	Negative authority	(6 − 7) + (7 − 6) cells	−0.215	−0.219	−0.320	−0.434	−0.589
9		Praise	Column 2	0.076	0.397	0.351	−0.339	0.377
10		Flexibility	high i/d − low i/d	0.120	0.079	0.407	0.132	0.432
Number of classes				15	16	30	15	16

grades was approximately 3 months, during which the teacher taught the usual subjects. The attitude assessment in the second grade must be considered weak due to reading difficulties and the low number of items in the scale.

The second column, called "Factor," in Tables 12—2 and 12—3 refers to the factor number with which a particular interaction variable had its highest association. In the cases of variables 6, 7, and 8, the interaction variable tended to load on two factors almost equally. The higher loading is listed first.

Notice that the two highest correlations for achievement, Table 12—2, occurred in the seventh grade data for variables 6 and 8. For this grade level, the best predictors of achievement are the negative restrictions of the teacher, shown by combining directions with criticism. One may wonder why positive predictors, like variables 1, 2, and 3, are not the highest correlations, especially since 2-hour, combined English-social studies core classes usually emphasize a philosophy of supporting pupil independence and self-direction through group work projects. One must at least entertain the hypothesis that higher correlations for negative predictors are due precisely to this philosophy. Lack of skill in using group work may result in the teacher giving more directions and criticism so that negative variables become more discriminating statistical predictors for less successful teaching even though successful core teaching is based on, and probably due to, the use of interaction patterns represented by the positive variables.

The total proportion of teacher questions, variable 4, is another interesting predictor. The highest correlation occurs in single hour, eighth grade mathematics. Apparently questions play a more important function in this kind of teaching. On the other hand, the total number of teacher questions as a proportion of all talk fails to correlate with achievement gains in the fourth and seventh grade levels. The units taught at these two grade levels were social studies units on New Zealand. When we remember that most questions are narrow and factual, it may be that the correlations for this third variable illustrate *subject matter differences* in current teaching practice rather than grade level differences.

Teacher talk, variable 5, appears to be highly correlated in both the eighth grade mathematics classes and in the second grade self-contained classes. Yet this variable is almost uncorrelated with achievement in the fourth and seventh grade social studies units.

Turning to the correlations with average pupil attitude scores, shown in Table 12—3, the correlations are somewhat higher. There are again differences among the correlations for different grade levels, different subject matter, and achievement compared with attitude. The relative prediction power of positive and negative variables is about the same.

Perhaps these observations are sufficient to show that patterns of verbal interaction have different associations with achievement and attitude measures across grade levels and when different learning activities are considered. In fact, the positive correlations for variable 10, flexibility, would suggest that more effective teachers tend to modify their teaching behavior, one instructional situation compared with the next. If future studies have similar results, then the following generalization would be supported: *a single interaction analysis predictor is not likely to be associated equally well with different outcome variables, different grade levels, and different learning activities.*

To put it bluntly, the extent to which these five projects replicate each other is a matter of degree. Although the same assessments were made of the verbal interaction, the different grade levels and learning outcomes combine to make each study somewhat different and this tends to make a single predictor inappropriate.

If we assume that a single predictor or a fixed set of predictors is not an appropriate analysis of the data from these different studies, then one alternative is to make use of a pool of predictors such as the 10 selected for this analysis. This decision is analogous to saying that there are certain features of verbal interaction, in this case 10 variables, which ought to be related to pupil attitude and achievement. Just how they might be combined to show this relationship is unknown, in advance, so an analytical procedure is chosen which permits the data to establish a regression equation which is unique to each grade level.

Before turning to the results of the analysis, it may be wise to discuss the limitations of multiple regression equations which are formed by this procedure. It is not possible, for example, to interpret the beta weights in the usual fashion. Except for the first variable, subsequent predictor variables may be selected for their suppression effects* so that the beta weight and its algebraic sign do not necessarily represent a relative positive or negative weighting which, in turn, illustrates the association between that particular variable and the outcome criterion.

The multiple correlation coefficients between interaction analysis variables and the two outcome criteria of pupil attitude and adjusted achievement are shown in Table 12–4 at each grade level in the column marked "R." These coefficients show that relatively high associations exist in our samples between the 10 interaction variables and the outcome criteria. Making an inference from these high correlations considered in combination with other material presented earlier involves several steps. First, there is no doubt that the best prediction of pupil achievement and positive pupil attitudes can be made from pretests of the same variables. Second, when final test scores are adjusted in terms of pretest scores, so that differences in initial ability between classes have less influence, then interaction variables are associated with adjusted achievement and pupil attitude scores which consist of class averages.

---

*For a discussion of suppression, see Guilford (48, pp. 403–406) and Pugh (77).

TABLE 12—4

Stepwise, Multiple, Linear Regression Using 10 Interaction Analysis
Variables to Predict Adjusted Achievement and Positive Attitudes

Grade	Outcome Criterion	Order of Predictor Variables Used*	Multiple		Number of	
			R	R'	Steps	Variables
2	Achievement	2†, 9, 5, **1**, 7, **10**, 4, (5)‡	0.814	0.639	8	6
	Attitude	4, 5, 1, 3, **6**, 9, 10, **8**, 7, 2	0.928	0.717	10	10
4	Achievement	10, **4**, 5, **3**, **9**, 2, (5), **8**, (10), 1	0.764	0.553	10	6
	Attitude	1, **6**, 2, **7**, **8**, **4**, 3, 10	0.970	0.935	8	8
6	Achievement	9, **7**, **6**, 4, 3, 10, 5, **8**	0.569	0.257	8	8
	Attitude	1, 9, 5, **7**, 3, 2, 4, **8**	0.558	0.221	8	8
7	Achievement	**8**, **9**, 2, 1, **4**, 3, (1), 10, 1	0.771	0.436	9	7
	Attitude	**7**, 10, **6**, **9**, **8**, 1, (9)	0.590	0.000	7	5
8	Achievement	5, 4, 10, **6**, **8**, 3, **7**, 1	0.840	0.608	8	8
	Attitude	**6**, 5, 4, 9, **7**, 2	0.805	0.643	6	6

*The predictor variables in Table 12—4 are identical to the variable numbers in Tables 12—2 and 12—3.

† All bold face numbers have a negative zero—order correlation.

‡ All parentheses indicate that a predictor variable was removed.

Third, when a pool of 10 variables includes at least two from each of four major interaction analysis factors, relatively high multiple correlation coefficients result.

The major reservation to the foregoing inferences is concerned with the statistical procedure. It can be argued that these coefficients fit only one small sample of classes and that some more conservative estimate of the multiple correlation would be a better prediction of the results if additional samples from the same population of classes were to be studied. One such adjustment of multiple correlation coefficients has been suggested by Wherry.* He has

---

*R. J. Wherry (105) has the following formula for predicting the shrinkage of the coefficient of multiple correlation:

$$R' = \sqrt{1 - (1 - R^2)\left(\frac{N-1}{N-m}\right)},$$

where R' is an unbiased R, N is the number of classes, and m is the number of predictor variables.

TABLE 12–5
Weights Assigned to Predictor Variables

Variable Number*	Achievement	Attitude
1	0.05	0.10
2	0.025	0.025
3	0.075	0.05
4	0.025	0.04
5	0.05	0.025
6	−0.10	−0.05
7	−0.05	−0.05
8	−0.025	−0.025
9	0.05	0.025
10	0.025	0.025
Constant	0.875	0.835

*Variables are identified in Tables 12–2 and 12–3.

developed a formula which we applied to the R coefficients. The results are shown in the R' column of Table 12–4. This is a less than ideal adjustment and our research staff is disposed to think it is too conservative. The adjustment is particularly severe when the coefficient is less than 0.6 and when the number of predictor variables approaches 10. For example, when the R for seventh grade attitude is 0.590, then R' becomes zero. Yet by referring to Table 12–3, six single variables if used alone would produce positive or negative correlations which range from 0.331 to 0.469 absolute. The unanswered question is whether some fortuitous combination of error variance among the predictor variables does or does not inflate the multiple correlation in a single sample, and if it does, how much error is involved. At the present time a thoughtful answer to this problem is not available, especially when class averages are correlated with composite interaction analysis variables.

A fixed pattern of predictors.   Our research staff was curious about the multiple correlation coefficients which would be produced when the same regression equation was applied to all classes, even though we consider such a procedure inappropriate because the learning objectives are not reasonably comparable from grade two through grade eight.

The formula for the regression equation was developed after studying the regression equations of all 10 variables in the stepwise, linear, regression analysis. The formula was based on the proportional weights shown in Table 12–5. These weights were calculated from a formula proposed by a staff

TABLE 12—6

Correlations with 10 Interaction Analysis Variables When Fixed Weights Are Used

Grade Level	2nd	4th	6th	7th	8th
Achievement	−0.051	0.260	0.284	0.513	0.449
Attitude	0.303	0.466	0.483	0.356	0.672

member where only the sixth, seventh, and eighth grade data were available. They are informed guesses by Gess* which were later applied to the two lower grades.

The results of applying a fixed regression equation across five grade levels, one for achievement and another for attitude, are shown in Table 12—6.

Perhaps the most reasonable statement regarding these coefficients is that it is quite remarkable that they are as high as they are. The differences in teaching purposes, the maturity of the pupils, and the nature of the learning activities were quite different across grade levels. In spite of these differences, there is enough commonality in the verbal interaction pool to produce the coefficients reported. A more appropriate use of a fixed regression equation would be to analyze additional samples of classrooms at each grade level, for the same subject matter, and similar learning activities, so that within-grade comparisons could be made.

Lawful variation of teaching behavior

A single predictor of learning outcomes based on some aspect of teaching behavior is a worthwhile activity only in the beginning phases of research on teaching effectiveness. A measure such as the i/d ratio or the i/i + d ratio has some predictive power, but it fails to provide useful information about the planning and sequencing of teaching behavior. The ultimate goal is to explain and predict the consequences of different patterns of interaction, strung together into sequences which can be called *teaching strategies*. In any teaching strategy some kind of variation in teaching behavior is required. This kind of analysis was carried out in our seventh and eighth grade field projects. The results are reported in Chapter 10, pages 327—31. The reader is invited to turn to these pages and read them at this time.

Future research on variation of teaching behavior may have to depend more and more on true experiments rather than field studies. Contrasting teaching strategies will have to be created, practiced, and then maintained during the experiment. The period of learning will have to be long enough so that pupils will have an opportunity to learn skills, master substantive knowledge, and

---

*Dr. Larry Gess was the staff member.

develop attitudes as a direct result of the interaction. The restrictions of field studies are due partly to the lack of variation in teaching behavior which exists in our current classrooms. Variation cannot be studied unless it exists. Unless there is a fairly high flexibility index, there is no point attempting to trace one or another sequence.

Summary of the seven projects

The seven projects which began in 1955 and ended in 1967 have produced fairly consistent results. The main exception among the projects is the second grade. It is difficult to explain the second grade results. One might point to the fairly high multiple correlation coefficients in Table 12–4 and assert only that the outcomes are somehow associated with the pool of 10 predictor variables. Perhaps a more realistic explanation is that the risk of selecting the teachers without using a pupil attitude inventory actually paid off with failure. For example, the highest and lowest i/d ratios in the second grade sample were 0.640 and 0.130, respectively. This is a very narrow range within which associations with i/d ratio are to be investigated. Perhaps the most reasonable inference is that the difficulties of conducting this kind of research at the second grade level were simply underestimated by our research team.

With regard to six out of seven projects, it appears that when classroom interaction patterns indicate that pupils have opportunities to express their ideas, and when these ideas are incorporated into the learning activities, then the pupils seem to learn more and to develop more positive attitudes toward the teacher and the learning activities. Judging from the results of the stepwise, linear regression analysis, one or another aspect of interaction may show the highest association with a learning outcome in a particular sample. The zero-order correlation coefficients for a pool of 10 interaction variables, shown in Tables 12–2 and 12–3, do show fairly consistent results. The generally positive correlations for variables 1, 2, 3, and 10 and the generally negative correlations for variables 6, 7, and 8 provide an explanation for the predictive power of the i/d ratio. This 10-variable pool provides a basis for predicting desirable learning outcomes which appears to work across different grade levels and different teaching objectives in the classrooms studied.

To make the record complete, two projects (32, 33), based on the author's masters and doctors theses and completed at the University of Chicago prior to September 1949, lend tangential support or directly support the results now being summarized. In an M.A. project, the level of thinking revealed by pupil statements was associated significantly with the pupil's present level of achievement in eighth grade mathematics. The more competent the pupil, the more often higher levels of cognitive problem-solving appeared in his statements. The second project was an intensive analysis of the reactions of seven pupils when they were exposed to fairly concentrated direct and indirect teaching patterns. The pupils were taught to move a hidden lever to record their instantaneous positive and negative perceptions of teacher statements. Galvanic skin response and resistance level were recorded to reveal involuntary reactions of the autonomic nervous system to these same statements. The results were consistent with the research so far cited. Directive and restrictive teacher statements, sustained for more than 10 minutes, tended to produce negative perceptions and greater autonomic activity, suggesting a pattern of anxiety which interfered with subject matter learning. More indirect statements produced response patterns which suggested attention to the cognitive task without interference due to excessive anxiety.

Except for the second grade data, these projects have produced fairly consistent results. However, in the long run, the contribution of this kind of research may not be the substantive relationships between interaction and outcomes that have been reported. Instead the successes and failures in learning how to analyze classroom interaction may be of most value. These substantive relationships do suggest that a search for "the single best predictor," like the search for the Holy Grail, may not succeed and may not contribute to our understanding of teaching.

We turn now to the work of other researchers who made use of the FIAC system or developed slight modifications of this system. It is to be deeply regretted that the pressure of time in completing this manuscript precluded reviewing the research results of those who developed their own category systems for analyzing classroom interaction.

THE RESULTS OF OTHER RESEARCHERS WHO ANALYZED INTERACTION ANALYSIS DATA AND CRITERIA OF LEARNING OUTCOMES

Although it is satisfying to obtain some consistent results during an extended program of research, it is even more satisfying when a system of interaction analysis turns out to be useful in the projects of other researchers. Confidence in reports on teaching effectiveness requires replication, and replication, in turn, occurs when qualified researchers are willing to adopt or adapt the same data collecting procedures. Usually our inability to coordinate separate studies of teaching effectiveness curtails progress in understanding teaching. The various procedures for coding verbal and nonverbal communication must ultimately face the test of being understood, accepted, and then applied in different research projects, in different parts of the country, and by different researchers before the results become impressive. This section reports projects which are comparable in terms of having collected interaction analysis data with the FIAC system or closely related categories. The similarities among the category systems provide an opportunity to see if the same associations between interaction and educational outcomes are found.

The first section to follow reviews recent reports on curvilinear relationships between interaction variables and measures of achievement or pupil attitude. The second section is a review of projects reporting simple linear relationships.

Nonlinear relationships between interaction and learning outcomes

It does not seem reasonable to assert that the more a teacher responds to pupil behavior, the more pupils will learn, unless some limits are established for the generalization. For example, there probably is a point at which higher levels of teacher responsiveness begin to erode the efficient learning of problem-solving skills and principles. A different point may exist for other measures of pupil growth such as positive attitudes, creativity, memory tasks, and other kinds of educational outcomes.

In postulating an optimum balance between pupil initiation and teacher initiation in the classroom, there are some assumptions involved. We assume that a certain amount of pupil initiation during class discussion is essential in order to reach those levels of cognitive functioning that require independent thinking and self-direction. Yet there is a certain amount of teacher initiation required to guide such discussions, to make them more efficient, to correct misconceptions, and to create orderly problem-solving. Is there an optimum balance which can be associated with one or another kind of pupil growth?

Dr. Robert Soar has provided the most thoughtful discussion of these problems. As part of his outstanding work on classroom interaction he reanalyzed his data from 54 elementary classrooms to see if optimum levels of teacher and pupil initiation existed for different learning outcomes. He also reanalyzed those variables which were based on more critical and directive aspects of teacher influence. He first presented these ideas at the 1968 meetings of the American Educational Research Association and has since published them (94). Even though the main credit for identifying and conceptualizing these nonlinear (or curvilinear) relationships belongs to Soar, it is an interesting historical fact that in 1966 Coats (25) discovered similar curvilinear relationships which were statistically significant, plotted them in an appendix of his thesis (25, pp. 158–165), and thereby provided some replications of Soar's work. Coats was reanalyzing unadjusted achievement and pupil attitude scores from projects 3, 4, and 5 of Table 12–1.

Curvilinear associations with achievement.   Soar made separate assessments of pupil growth. He measured creativity by using the Torrance's Toy Dog Unusual Uses Test. A second test measured reading skill, but required very little abstract reasoning. A third test of vocabulary did require more abstract reasoning skill. It is quite unusual to make this distinction between a vocabulary test and a reading test, but Soar explains the differences between the tests in enough detail to make the interpretation reasonable. With a total of 54 classes, it was

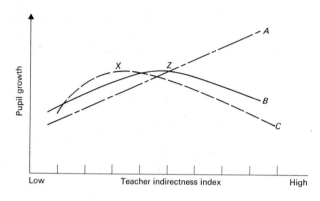

Fig. 12—2.   (After Soar)

possible to have average class scores of pupil growth for each of the three learning outcomes adjusted for initial ability and to associate these with various index scores derived from interaction analysis.

The results of Soar's first analysis is shown in Fig. 12–2, drawn in a way that slightly exaggerates the optimum points. The curve for growth in creativity is almost linear for his sample (see curve A) and no optimum was found. Optimum levels were found for the task requiring more reasoning (curve B), and for the less abstract task (curve C). These results suggest that a task requiring a lower level of thinking has an optimum at point X, which occurs at a lower level of indirectness compared with a task requiring higher level thinking, showing the optimum point at Z. Presumably an optimum point for creativity performance is at some higher level of indirectness than was found in Soar's sample, if it exists at all.

Turning to interaction variables in which the teacher is more direct and critical, Soar found some similar curves which are shown in Fig. 12–3. The most consistent relationship between teacher indirectness and teacher criticism occurs with the task which requires less abstract reasoning, curve C. Apparently this type of pupil growth reaches optima with the least amount of indirectness and a higher level of criticism; see point R in Fig. 12–3 and X in Fig. 12–2. An optimum point for creativity is shown at point Q for curve A in Fig. 12–3. There was no optimum point for teacher criticism found for the higher level reasoning task within the range of Soar's sample (see curve B, Fig. 12–3).

The only statistically significant curvilinear relationships between unadjusted achievement and an interaction variable which were found by Coats existed in the sixth and seventh grade samples involving teacher criticism (25,

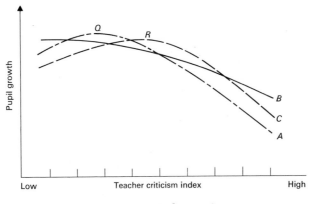

Fig. 12–3.   (After Soar)

pp. 158–161). These are the same variables which are numbered 6, 7, and 8 in Tables 12–2 and 12–3. Samples of these curves are not shown here because they were essentially the same as those which illustrate Soar's work.

There is an aspect of internal validity which exists between the findings of Soar and Coats, on the one hand, and the theoretical formulations in Chapter 10, on the other hand. Note that the pupil growth index which involves memory, a relatively low level cognitive task, can tolerate lower levels of teacher indirectness and higher levels of teacher criticism. Yet higher levels of cognitive reasoning are associated with more indirect and less critical teacher influence patterns. Creativity appears to flourish most with the most indirect patterns. One can infer that as the performance task for pupil growth requires more self-initiative and higher level cognitive functioning, the degree of teacher responsiveness becomes more critical. Such an inference is consistent with the hypotheses proposed in Chapter 10.

These findings help to embellish Rosenshine's (80, p. 4) general conclusion after reviewing nine different studies of criticism:

. . . there is no evidence to support a claim that a teacher should avoid telling a pupil that he is wrong, or should avoid giving him academic directions. However, teachers who use a good deal of criticism appear consistently to have classes which achieve less in most subject areas.

Associations with pupil attitude.   Coats also plotted some curvilinear relationships with pupil attitude, an outcome variable not reported by Soar. The first curve (Fig. 12–4) associates postattitude with sustained acceptance, which is the frequency of the (3–3) cell, and is variable 2 in Tables 12–2 and 12–3. Coats grouped the 16 eighth grade mathematics classes into quartiles, based on

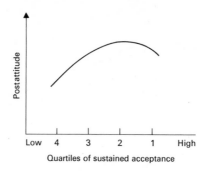

Fig. 12—4.   (Coats, p. 164)

the interaction variable. Notice, in Fig. 12—4,* that in general there is a positive relationship between this aspect of teacher indirectness and between class average scores on postattitude. However, excessive use of sustained acceptance, quartile one, is associated with a reduction in postattitude scores, an interpretation which remained hidden by the analysis used originally by Flanders who first reported these data.

A second curvilinear association with postattitude scores was possible in the Coats analysis because preattitude scores were available. Positive pupil attitudes were first measured in the fall, then again at the end of a 2-week unit of instruction which took place in the spring of the year. This curve is shown in Fig. 12—5 and is the inverse of the curve in Fig. 12—4. Again there is a general positive correlation between pre- and postattitude for the seventh grade combined English and social studies core classes. However, the classes in the lowest quartile on preattitude scored higher on postattitude than did the classes in the third quartile. Although simple regression might account for this, such regression is absent in the case of the first and second quartiles. Even though *post hoc* interpretations are notoriously faulty, looking at this curve brings back memories, now 10 years old, that seem more than mere coincidence. In a class that I visited with a staff observer, one seventh grader who must have been quite perceptive—perhaps even shrewd—said, "Say, what have you guys got on this teacher?" His meaning was quite clear in the conversation, namely, why was this teacher acting so nicely during this 2-week unit compared with the previous 6 months? It is quite possible that some low scoring classes on pupil attitude are the result of neglect and could be improved, because the teacher has the skill. Participation in an experiment, complete with Hawthorne effect, may have been just enough inspiration to motivate a teacher, and in

*The curves in Figs. 12—4 and 12—5 are drawn in with a smoothed, connected line even though a histogram would be more appropriate. This liberty is taken to make them visually more comparable to the Soar curves.

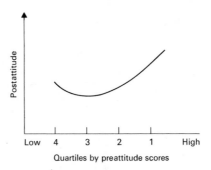

Fig. 12—5.   (Coats, p. 162)

turn the pupils, to work through learning experiences which resulted in more positive attitude perceptions.

Some consequences of curvilinear relationships.   Suppose that further research confirms that many of the relationships between teaching behavior and educational outcomes are curvilinear. This raises some perplexing difficulties in coordinating research in this area and making comparisons between different research studies. Again it is Soar* who seems to understand the problems with the greatest insight. We corresponded with each other to discuss why the results of certain investigations which we had conducted contained certain inconsistencies. To illustrate the point, suppose an interaction variable such as indirectness (i/i + d) is being associated with a learning outcome such as achievement.

Case one.   A linear relationship may exist between these two variables for the lower ranges of teacher indirectness. The curve connecting points A and B in Fig. 12—6 illustrates this association. It may be that any type of learning outcome variable such as memory, simple cognitive processes, creativity, and independence all follow this curve between points A and B. Between these points, the inference would be that the more a teacher is able to use indirect teacher statements, the higher will be any of these learning outcomes.

Case two.   Suppose a sample of classrooms exhibits a relatively narrow, but high level of indirectness. A negative association may be found with a memory performance test such as spelling, illustrated F in Fig. 12—6, by curve. No significant association may be found with a performance variable such as cognitive problem-solving, illustrated by curve E, but a positive relationship may be found with a measure of creativity, illustrated by curve D. Even though the

---

*In a carefully written letter to the author dated May 27, 1968.

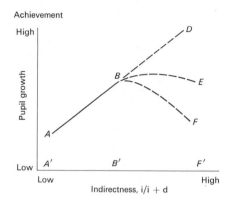

Fig. 12—6. (After Soar)

results for problem-solving and spelling are inconsistent with the results described in case one, the association with creativity scores is consistent.

Discussion. It takes little imagination to anticipate the arguments in the research literature when the results of one study are cited to support or to derogate the findings of another study. Such comparisons can be made only when a researcher provides enough information so that judgments can be made about the following issues.

First, what kind of outcome variable is being used to quantify learning growth? It will be necessary to describe the behavioral characteristics of the performance criteria so that inferences can be made about the level of thinking involved and the relationships between the performance measure and different ways that a teacher might influence such behavior.

Second, what kind of a sample is involved? Are the classes in the sample restricted to a spectrum of teaching behavior that lies between A' and B' in Fig. 12—6? Does the sample cluster around B', and is it very narrow in range? Does the sample fall in between B' and F'? Is it spread all the way from A' to F'? Before these questions can be answered the prerequisite is a standardized set of categories and agreed upon rules for observation. It is the need to answer these questions which has prompted the suggestions in previous sections of this book that data pools be established for a limited number of category systems so that the representativeness of the interaction data can be determined. If necessary, the categories could be subscripted for special problems, but collapsed in order to make comparisons between projects.

Third and finally, just imagine the controversy which could arise if the simple relationships illustrated in Fig. 12—6 grossly underestimated the complexity of the valid functional relationships! A possibility, by the way, that could easily be true. So if we add different valid but curvilinear relationships to the difficulties of sampling, differences in growth measures, differences in teaching purposes, differences in grade level, and the different ways that the use of time can be classified, it is little wonder that some projects appear to have inconsistent results.

Simple linear relationships between interaction and learning outcomes

The projects to be reviewed are listed in chronological order in Table 12–7 according to the date of publication. In each project, interaction analysis data based on the basic 10 categories or a closely related system were analyzed. The designation "experiment" refers to studies in which pupils are assigned to treatments which are then taught by role-playing teachers. In these projects interaction analysis was used to train the teachers and to assess performance in order to prove that the planned treatment differences were created. The designation "field study" refers to making use of existing classrooms and the natural style of a teacher. Interaction analysis was used to identify the direct and indirect classroom in order to form quasi-experimental treatments in a field study design. Some field studies, projects 4, 8, and 9, don't really establish treatments, but make use of a correlation analysis.

For those who like to keep a balance sheet of projects which succeeded and those which failed to find statistically significant relationships between one or more interaction variables and a learning outcome, it may be instructive to point out which studies made use of the same data. Morrison and Samph, in Table 12–7, made use of the sixth grade data listed as project 5 in Table 12–1. Coats, to whom reference was made earlier, used data from projects 3, 4, and 5 in Table 12–1. Furst (45) made use of the typescripts provided by a team headed by Bellack (9). Powell and Weber made use of the same interaction analysis data, but analyzed different outcome variables. Emmer used the baseline interaction analysis data from project 7 in Table 12–1, but collected additional data in order to make his own analysis of changes in the incidence of Categories 3 and 9. Measel also made use of the same second grade data.

Consistency within the 10 basic categories

Perhaps the most obvious questions about a category system are concerned with relationships between category frequencies. Do 5's, 4's, and 8's go together more often than not? Are the 3's and 9's positively correlated? Closely related to these questions are the various attempts to use factor analysis in order to locate variables which seem to be associated. These topics are discussed in this section.

Specific investigations of category relationships.   In a category system which is designed for a particular purpose, one test of the system is to find relationships

TABLE 12–7

Projects by Other Researchers Associating Some Measure of Pupil Learning or Behavior with an Interaction
Analysis Variable Based on the 10-Category System

Project Number	Date Published	Researches and Reference	Grade Level	Design	Criterion Variables and Conditions
1	1957	Filson (30)	7th	Experiment	Independent pupil behavior with ambiguous task. More independent with indirect, $p = 0.01$.
2	1961	Amidon Flanders (3)	7th	Experiment	Adjusted gain in geometry for dependent prone pupils only, $p = 0.01$. For social studies, not significant. (35).
3	1963	Shantz (5)	4th	Experiment	Science principles, assessed separately for high and low ability pupils. For high: immediate recall $p = 0.07$, delayed recall $p = 0.05$. Low ability not significant.
4	1965	LaShier (60)	8th	Field study	Student teachers observed who taught the same unit in biology. Indirect gave higher adjusted achievement, $p = 0.01$.
5	1966	Johns (57)	High school	Field study	More thought-provoking questions asked by pupils in the indirect English classes, $p = 0.01$.
6*	1966	Morrison (69)	6th	Field study	Indirect classes showed higher achievement on arithmetic, language arts, and social studies, $p = 0.01$ for most "internal" and most "external" pupils (top and bottom third).
7	1966	Snider (92)	High school	Field study	Adjusted achievement in high school physics: no significant differences. Significant positive correlation between indirect and positive pupil attitude.

8	1966	Soar (93)	3, 4, 5, 6	Field study	Many different variables. Some results consistent and others inconsistent with indirect and superior pupil growth; relationships shown to be curvilinear.
9	1967	Birkin (12)	About 5th	Field study	Results uncertain, probably no significant results.
10*	1967	Emmer (28)	2nd	Field experiment	Showed that teachers could be trained to use more Category 3 statements, and this resulted in more pupil Category 9 statements.
11	1967	Furst (45)	High school	Field study	Reanalyzed Bellack's data; indirect showed higher achievement in economics, 4 day unit.
12*	1967	Measel (66)	2nd	Field study	No significant differences when testing to see if indirect is associated with higher levels of cognitive pupil statements.
13	1967	Pankratz (73)	High school	Field study	Teachers who were rated "more effective" by composite score on three criteria were significantly more indirect.
14†	1967	Powell (76)	Primary grades	Field study	Pupils exposed to indirect teachers for 3 years in grades 1, 2, and 3 scored significantly higher in arithmetic, but not reading. Fourth grade design contaminated and no significant differences.
15*	1967	Samph (82)	6th	Field study	Analyzed slow learners only for language skills and found higher learning for indirect classes $p = 0.01$.
16†	1968	Weber (104)	Primary grades	Field study	Found that verbal creativity associated with indirect, $p = 0.01$. Figural creativity not significant, but in one case, significantly correlated with direct influence.

*All studies so marked are based on data used by one or more additional studies and therefore cannot be counted as independent replications.
†Powell and Weber used the same interaction analysis data.

among the categories which are logically related to its purpose. The 10-category system is designed to contrast teacher initiation and pupil response versus pupil initiation and teacher response. The logic of this contrast assumes certain positive and negative correlations between events.

Johns (57) investigated one such relationship by seeking to verify that pupils asked more thought-provoking questions, a special case of Category 9, in classrooms in which the interaction was more indirect compared with classrooms which were more direct. His procedure was to administer the Michigan Pupil Attitude Inventory to 18 English classes in grades 10, 11, and 12 and calculate the class averages. In choosing the top and bottom three classes, he assumed that he would locate two groups of three classes each in which indirect versus direct teacher influence would be in contrast. He took this risk because positive correlations between class average scores on the inventory and indirectness have been reported earlier. His risk paid off since his high scoring group had a composite i/d ratio of 4.34 and his low scoring group had an i/d ratio of 0.34. By using subscripts for most of the 10 basic categories, including seven in Categories 8 and 9, for a total of 31 categories, he was able to determine in which contrasting group more thought-provoking questions were asked by the pupils. This kind of pupil verbal behavior is also associated, according to Johns' data, with higher frequencies of thought-provoking statements and questions on the part of the teachers. This latter finding was based on subscripting Categories 4 and 5.

Emmer (28), whose work is also cited with inservice training, chose to investigate the effect of trying to help the 16 teachers in project 7 (Table 12–1) increase the incidence of Category 9, pupil initiated statements. After having established baseline data, Emmer first asked the teachers to try increasing the incidence of Category 9 statements, simply as a request. After this first attempt, 12 of the teachers participated in a discussion of a theory which proposed that type 9 statements depended on the teacher increasing the incidence of Category 3. With this principle, the 12 teachers increased the incidence of Category 9 during a third observation, which was significantly higher than four teachers in a control group who did not have such discussions. One important outcome of Emmer's work is that it demonstrates that a particular change in teaching behavior can alter pupil behavior even when there is a history of previous experience prior to the attempted change.

Consistency of interaction variables.   Cell frequencies in a 10 × 10 matrix have definite patterns which produce logically related factors as a result of factor analysis. For example, Coats (25, pp. 75, 76, and 77) printed a 32 × 32 correlation table of various ratios, column totals, and selected cell frequencies. Some of the expected relationships are illustrated in Table 12–8. These intercorrelations tend to support a negative association between indirect and direct patterns

TABLE 12–8

Intercorrelations of Interaction Events from Sixth, Seventh,
and Eighth Grade Classes

		1	2	3	4	5	6	7
Cells combining 1, 2, 3	1		0.98	0.81	0.05	0.28	−0.59	−0.26
(3–3) cell frequency	2			0.76	0.07	0.28	−0.59	−0.25
Columns 1, 2, 3	3				0.18	0.03	−0.57	−0.09
Column 9	4					−0.49	0.02	−0.03
Column 5 + (4–8) + (8–4)	5						−0.35	−0.56
Columns 6 and 7	6							−0.12
Column 8	7							

of interaction as coded by the basic 10 categories. The low correlations are interesting, but difficult to interpret because the data came from self-contained sixth grade classes, seventh grade English-social studies core, and eighth grade mathematics classes which are quite different educational settings. For example, there are no very strong positive correlations with the incidence of Category 9. The highest negative correlation, −0.49, between the fourth and fifth variables, quite reasonably indicates that pupil initiated talk is negatively associated with teacher lecture combined with a drill pattern. Even with the contributions of Johns and Emmer, we know very little about Category 9 type statements, how such statements can be stimulated, and whether such statements are associated with desirable educational outcomes. Perhaps Category 9 needs to be subdivided because it contains more than one kind of statement.

A comparison between an unpublished factor analysis study by Gess* and factor analyses by Soar (93) helps to illustrate problems of interpretation when interaction variables are correlated and then factor analyzed. In the Gess project the only variables considered were based on the 10 × 10 matrix and a separate factor analysis was made for each grade level. In the Soar project, several factor analyses were completed which made use of more than one kind of interaction data from a combination of four elementary grade levels. With fewer variables Gess selected only four main factors; Soar selected nine. Perhaps a more important difference is that a strong first factor appeared at each grade level in the Gess analysis, which clearly represented indirect and direct patterns of interaction. Soar's first and strongest factor was primarily teacher criticism.

---

*Available at the Offices of Research Service, School of Education, The University of Michigan, attention Prof. N. A. Flanders; to be published sometime in the future.

A more or less pure indirect factor appeared in the Soar analysis only as a relatively weak eighth factor.

These two studies illustrate a difference in point of view. The Gess procedure is more sharply focused on the verbal interchange found in similar classrooms. The Soar procedure included many different variables from different classrooms in the same analysis. It is not surprising to find that the associations between Soar's factor scores and pupil growth scores produce lower correlations, compared with the Gess procedure. Given the differences in statistical procedures, in the transformations of the original data, and in the nature of the data, it is reasonable to expect different results even if the two projects had started with the same classes and observation periods. The more sharply focused approach provides factors which are easier to describe, but take into consideration less of the total situation. When more aspects of the total situation are included, the number of factors increases and each factor, as well as the total factor structure, become more complex.

Summary of consistency.   The field projects of Johns and Emmer and the factor analyses of interaction variables provide evidence of internal consistency within the category system and subscripts of that system. Given the category definitions, we expect teacher initiation to be negatively correlated with teacher response; different acts of teacher initiation to be positively related; acts of teacher response to be positively related; and pupil initiation and response to form complementary relationships with teaching patterns. To the extent that these relationships do exist, they provide evidence of internal consistency among the categories.

Reviewing previously reported projects

The Morrison and Samph studies, to be reviewed in this section, made use of data from projects which are discussed on previous pages. These two projects are not additional independent replications of relationships between interaction and educational outcomes. Instead, they are special analyses of subgroups within a larger, parent project.

Morrison's special analysis of the sixth grade Michigan data.   This thesis project was a part of project 5, Table 12—1. Dr. Morrison was interested in the pupil trait called "internality-externality" and analyzed the data to see if pupils scoring high or low on this trait responded differently to indirect and direct patterns of instruction. Here, only the results related to teaching behavior are reported. Morrison analyzed the data from two-thirds of the pupils in the original sample, since she selected pupils from the top and bottom third based on scores from the internality-externality test. Her results are as follows (69, p. 113).

1. *The students whose ideas were used more often by the teacher made greater achievement gains.*

2. *High praise was accompanied by greater achievement gain scores when Parts of Speech, Punctuation, and Capitalization, Social Study Skills, and Problem Solving (math) were measured; however, there were no significant differences on the Usage, Computation, and Language Study Skills Tests (all of these were sub-tests of adjusted pupil achievement).*

3. *Less teacher criticism was accompanied by greater achievement gain on the tests measuring Punctuation, and Capitalization, Language and Social Study Skills, and Problem Solving, while there were no significant differences on the Usage, Computation, and Parts of Speech Tests.*

Morrison also commented on relationships which were independent of teacher influence patterns. For example, she found significant differences to indicate that pupils with more positive attitudes learned more, received better grades, and scored higher on "internality."

Below average achievers.   Thomas Samph completed an unpublished analysis (82) of the same sixth grade data which interested Morrison. He selected 16 classes from the 30 which were observed in project 5, Table 12—1, such that the I/D ratios were approximately equally spaced across the full range of indirectness. Within these classes, he identified 155 low achievers by selecting pupils who were 2 or more years below their national grade level norm on the achievement pretest. He then attempted to see if indirectness was positively related to adjusted pupil achievement for the total language skill section of the test. He also investigated the relationship with positive pupil attitude. He found that pupils in the more indirect classes made significantly higher gains in achievement and had significantly higher scores on positive pupil attitudes. In a series of subtests, he presented evidence to show that such relationships were not due to the average ability level of the entire class or to the unique contributions of particular teachers.

Summary.   The notion that teacher indirectness has differential effects on different kinds of pupils has not been well supported. Morrison and Samph failed to find such evidence. Anderson (5) showed that female pupils differ from males at the junior high level, by preferring more indirect influence patterns. Flanders (39) found only nonsignificant trends that pupils with higher I.Q. scores could perceive more differences between indirect and direct teachers compared with below average I.Q. pupils. Amidon's experiment with junior high pupils learning geometry, to be discussed in the next section, showed that pupils classified as "dependent prone" made slightly higher gains than the total pupil population when exposed to more indirect teachers; the level of significance for the entire population was 0.05, which shifted to 0.01

when only the scores of dependent prone pupils were analyzed. In two field studies during the year following Amidon's study (projects 3 and 4, Table 12–1), the results failed to reveal differences in the effects of teacher influence for high or low I.Q. and for pupils who scored high or low on dependence proneness. In sum, relationships between indirectness of teaching behavior and pupil achievement or pupil attitudes appear to be fairly uniform when different types of pupils are considered, at least in the research which has been completed.

Associations found in experiments

Using the distinction made earlier in this chapter, an experiment refers to creating contrasting patterns of teaching behavior—known as experimental treatments and then assigning pupils to treatments in ways that control initial ability. More research of this type is needed although it apparently occurs less frequently than field studies.

Dependence-Independence.   Filson (30) created two treatments in which directive teaching behavior was contrasted with indirect when the task required of pupils was relatively ambiguous. The outcome variable was the number of dependent responses made by the pupils. The pupils were asked to make judgments about short selections of music. After an initial attempt, criteria for making judgments like rhythm, melodic line, accent, and musical form were introduced. In one treatment the pupils were told in a directive manner exactly how to apply the criteria. In the other treatment these same criteria were introduced by means of a more indirect pattern of teaching behavior. In subsequent judgments the pupils could ask for assistance from the role-playing teacher, or avoid such requests, which became a measure of dependence on the teacher. The frequency of requests for assistance was significantly higher in the directive treatment, compared with the indirect.

Geometry achievement.   Amidon and Flanders (3) exposed groups of 20 pupils to contrived learning situations in geometry. There were four treatments formed by combining clear and ambiguous goal orientations with direct and indirect patterns of teaching. The differences between clear and ambiguous conditions did not result in statistically significant differences. The differences for all students in geometry achievement were higher for the indirect pattern, barely significant at the 0.05 level, but when the achievement gains of pupils who were above average in a test of "dependent proneness" were considered separately, the same difference was significant at better than the 0.01 level. The pupils were assigned to experimental sessions by stratified random assignment, five above average in I.Q. scores, 10 average, and five below average.

Besides creating experiments in learning geometry, short experimental sessions involving social studies objectives were also carried out (35). There were no significant differences in measures of adjusted subject matter gains between the direct and indirect treatments or between the clear and ambiguous goal manipulation. In both the geometry and social studies experiments, the period for learning was very short, about 45 minutes. In spite of this, learning in geometry was possible to measure, but growth in the social studies test was small and not significantly related to treatment differences.

Fourth grade science. An experiment at Pennsylvania State University was conducted by Schantz (85). She trained a role-playing teacher to provide direct and indirect influence to teach three one-lesson units on static electricity, current electricity, and series and parallel wiring. Sixty-one pupils were selected from the top and bottom quintile according to ability as measured by an I.Q. test and the Iowa Every Pupils Test of achievement. Thus, her experiment had four treatments: (a) high ability—indirect teaching, (b) high ability—direct teaching, (c) low ability—indirect teaching, and (d) low ability—direct teaching. Her results, in terms of adjusted achievement, were barely significant. On the immediate posttest for the high ability—indirect teaching treatment adjusted achievement was higher than it was for the high ability—direct teaching treatment at a chance probability of 0.07. On a delayed posttest, sometime later, the same comparison was significant at slightly less than 0.05 by a t-test. The differences for low ability pupils was not significant and favored the direct teaching method.

The original data from the Schantz experiments were recalculated using analysis of covariance* for both the high and low I.Q. groups, and the differences in pupil growth were found to be significant beyond the 0.05 level. In this analysis, the differential effects of teaching behavior, I.Q., and achievement, originally reported by Schantz, were no longer supported, but the relationship to indirectness was strengthened.

Teacher inservice education. The project on the inservice training of teachers, reported in greater detail in Chapter 11 can also be listed as an experiment in which the role-played indirect and direct patterns of instructor behavior were compared. The differences in instructor behavior and the differences in attitude growth between the two groups have already been explained in some detail. Although there was no real test of achievement, more work activities did occur in the more indirect treatment. Actual change in teaching behavior, which was the primary purpose of the inservice training, was in the expected direction, but not statistically significant when all participants were considered. These results, by themselves, should be considered tentative due to some evidence of contamination between the treatment effects.

---

*The analysis was completed by Dr. Barak Rosenshine, Temple University, and communicated to me by private letter, May 1969.

Summary of experiments.   All of these experiments were conducted relatively early in the history of research on interaction analysis. It takes a great deal of experience to plan, develop, and conduct a treatment experiment successfully. The Filson experiment stands alone and unreplicated as an experiment on dependent behavior. The Amidon and Flanders plus the Schantz experiments were supportive of a positive relationship between indirectness and pupil achievement. The inservice Flanders experiment with adult teachers was also supportive, but suffered some design weaknesses. The Flanders (35) experiments with social studies failed to produce significant results. By way of summary, out of five experiments, there were some statistically significant results, some encouraging trends, and one nonsignificant outcome. In no case were there statistically significant trends in the opposite direction.

These experiments show that role-playing teaching patterns can be produced and, in general, seem to affect learning outcomes. It is unfortunate that more experimental studies have not been carried out. In particular, such studies have an important bearing on the issue of whether bright pupils permit teachers to be more indirect. It would be instructive to design an experiment as follows: in one treatment teachers are trained to be direct or indirect and teach bright and dull pupils; in the other treatment, uninstructed teachers are exposed to bright and dull pupils. Such a comparison would help to resolve issues about cause and effect which so far have not been answered.

Field studies of classroom interaction and educational outcomes

In order to compare more direct teaching behavior with more indirect infield studies, it is necessary to locate classrooms in which the "treatment" differences are present.

Student teachers in eighth grade biology.   LaShier (60) made an independent study of achievement and attitude scores among 10 eighth grade classes taught by student teachers in Texas. The results provided statistically significant confirmation of higher achievement and more positive pupil attitudes in those classes taught by the more indirect teachers. In this case, the I/D ratio (matrix columns 1 + 2 + 3 + 4 divided by 5 + 6 + 7) was used to rank the indirectness.

This replication was carried out with above average care. A special test of achievement was developed for an unusual unit of study. All student teachers were given help in preparing to teach this particular unit. The effects of initial pupil ability were carefully controlled. Attention to observer training was emphasized and reported in detail. What makes the project remarkable is that the principal investigator and those on his thesis committee had no direct contact with previous teams of research at Minnesota, Michigan, or Temple.

LaShier's cumulative matrices for the four most indirect student teachers and the three most direct showed remarkable similarities to the corresponding cumulative matrices reported by Flanders in project 3, Table 12–1. At crucial points such as the frequency of the (3–3) cell, the column 3 total, and the proportion of pupil initiation, a similar configuration can be found.

High school economics.   Furst (45) obtained access to the tape recordings and typescripts from an earlier study reported by Bellack (9). Bellack studied the classroom interaction of 15 teachers and their 345 pupils in seven high schools in the New York metropolitan area. All teachers used the same textbook and agreed to spend 4 days teaching a unit on high school economics. The post-achievement scores, adjusted for initial ability, were accepted as calculated by Bellack. He determined that there were three classes in which achievement levels were higher than could be expected by chance, eight classes in which achievement did not differ from chance, and four classes with achievement lower than could be expected by chance. Furst reached her conclusions by comparing these three subgroups.

Significant differences among these groups included: (a) a ratio of extended indirect teacher influence to extended direct teacher influence, (b) a ratio of indirect teacher influence to teacher direct influence immediately following student talk, and (c) steady state student talk. In essence, the high group differed from both other groups by having more extended indirect influence. By using some of Bellack's categories, the high group also had more variety of substantive-logical processes.

High school physics.   A study of Pankratz (73) is instructive, even though it contains no measurement of pupil growth. He located a physics teacher in each of 32 selected high schools in the Dayton, Ohio area. He attempted to identify the five most effective and the five least effective teachers by making use of three criteria: (a) ratings made by the school principal, (b) the teacher's score on the "Teaching Situations Reaction Test," and (c) the average class score on a pupil inventory which rated the teacher's competence. Having identified the five highest and lowest teachers in terms of competence by these three criteria, he then collected about 6 hours of interaction analysis data in the 10 classrooms. The differences between the five high and the five low groups included (73, p. 86): (a) a ratio of 19.26 to 5.66 in extended indirect influence, (b) a ratio of 8.69 to 10.96 in extended student talk, (c) a ratio of 2.11 to 6.66 in extended silence or confusion, and (d) a ratio of 45.67 to 44.78 in extended direct teacher influence.

The Pankratz study is reviewed here because a measure of pupil attitude was reported. The interaction analysis data were compared to the general notion of teaching effectiveness. While such relationships are not unimportant, the results are less likely to clarify relationships between patterns of verbal interaction and different subject matter learning.

Self-contained elementary classrooms.   Several field studies have been completed in elementary classrooms. In most of these projects nationally standardized tests of pupil growth were used to provide measures of achievement. The short-comings of this kind of test for evaluating teaching have already been discussed.

1) Soar. A 2-year study of grades 3, 4, 5, and 6 was carried out by Soar (93). It was this project which provided the data for the curvilinear relationships already discussed. It has been mentioned that Soar's sample may have been above average in being indirect, that many different kinds of variables were reduced by two successive factor analyses, that the factors as well as the factor structure were complex and not easily interpreted, and that the relationships between the factor scores and measures of pupil growth were relatively inconsistent.

The following results show support as well as lack of support* for a positive relationship between indirectness and measures of pupil growth. Measures of vocabulary and reading were significantly related with a measure of teacher indirectness, $p = 0.01$ and 0.05 respectively (93, pp. 147–148). A variable called "classroom hostility" was compared with pupil growth in vocabulary to show that the greatest gains occurred in the indirect-low hostile classrooms and the least gain was in the direct-high hostile classrooms. This measure of classroom hostility was inconsistent, however, for growth in reading, with indirect-high hostile producing the greatest growth and the direct-high hostile the least growth. Soar's measure of classroom hostility is based on pupil behavior and is not to be confused with teacher criticism. Perhaps the most interesting finding by Soar was greater vocabulary growth over the summer, shown by a test requiring reasoning skills, for the indirect classes. However, summer growth on the reading test was not statistically significant. All first year and summer growth scores on arithmetic and creativity were not significantly related to indirectness. Yet when teacher criticism is isolated through factor analysis, these factor scores are negatively associated with growth in arithmetic over the 2-year period of the study. In most studies which make use of the FIAC system, teacher criticism is negatively correlated with teacher indirectness. In fact, when i/d ratio is used, teacher criticism by definition lowers the ratio.

Soar's results are very complicated and difficult to understand. This is especially apparent when simple linear relationships are investigated. Soar's data provides theoretically consistent results when it was reanalyzed in terms of curvilinear relationships.

2) Powell (76) and Weber (104) published separate studies which were based on the same interaction analysis data. They were able to observe the third and

---

*It was this inconsistency that led Soar to investigate the curvilinear relationship discussed earlier in this chapter.

fourth grade classrooms of 180 pupils in six schools of a suburban school district. While in the third grade, all pupils were completing their third year with the same teacher, having been assigned to this teacher for the first, second, and third grades. All pupils had a different teacher in the fourth grade. Those teachers of the third grade who were above average on a composite score of indirectness were considered to be indirect; those below average were considered to be direct. There were nine teachers involved in the third grade observations and 17 with the fourth grade.

· Powell's measure of educational growth was a separate test for arithmetic, for reading, and a "composite" total score. Weber's measure of educational growth included three tests of verbal creativity and four tests of figural creativity.

At the end of 3 years, Powell found a superiority for pupil growth in the indirect classes most significant for the arithmetic scores (0.01), significant for the composite scores (0.05), and not significant for the reading scores. For the same period Weber found that all three measures of verbal creativity were significantly different, less than 0.01, indicating a superior growth for pupils in the indirect classrooms. None of the four measures of figural creativity showed statistically significant differences between the indirect and direct classrooms.

At the end of the fourth year it was possible to identify pupils who were exposed to one type of teacher for 3 years, and some other kind of teacher for the fourth year. Thus, the pupils could be grouped as having had an indirect to indirect sequence, an indirect to direct sequence, a direct to indirect sequence, and a direct to direct sequence. In analyzing the effects of the fourth year, both researchers used an adjusted fourth year gain score which attempted to eliminate the effects of the first 3 years. Under these circumstances there were no significant results to report in Powell's achievement scores. One significant difference reported by Weber was that the greatest gains in figural creativity occurred for pupils who had experienced the direct to direct sequence.

Field studies which failed to produce significant findings.   There are at least three field studies which failed to support the associations between indirect teaching and gains in pupil growth. None of these studies contradicted earlier results, however, since no statistically significant trends in the opposite direction were found.

1) Snider. Perhaps the most complete field study which failed to reveal significant relationships between classroom interaction and a measure of achievement was the work of Snider (92). He studied a sample of 17 classrooms in which a course called the New York State Regents Physics Course is taught. He administered an attitude inventory, and collected interaction analysis data using the FIAC system. His description of interaction in the high school physics classroom and laboratory was essentially pessimistic, leading him to the conclusion that very little teacher-pupil interaction approached a model of inquiry. Instead it was a typical teacher dominated—pupil response pattern.

Snider's conclusions were not all nonsignificant. He discovered a statistically significant correlation between average class scores on a pupil attitude inventory and the i/i + d ratio which was +0.43 (92, p. 153). This finding showed that there was variability between his classes in terms of teacher indirectness and variability between classes on average attitude scores. Snider may have faced a major difficulty with his tests of achievement in physics. He reports, for example (92, p. 205 and p. 206) that there was very little variation in adjusted achievement between classes. The evidence for lack of variation in adjusted achievement is quite striking. For example, when the classes in his sample are arranged in a rank order on adjusted achievement, a test of differences between the classes above the median versus those below failed to be statistically significant. Such a test is usually very significant when the classes are grouped in this manner. In fact, the top three versus the bottom three classes in achievement produced a barely significant difference at the 0.05 level of chance for the Regents Physics Test. The top two versus the bottom two were barely significant at the same level for the Cooperative Physics Test. Either the extremely bright pupils in these classes scored too high on the pretest measure, or the ceiling of the test was low, or the factor of teacher influence with such pupils in that curriculum was independent of adjusted achievement gain.

2) *Measel.* In a separate analysis of the data from project 7 (Table 12—1), Measel failed to find a significant relationship between indirectness and higher levels of cognitive discourse during class discussions. In this study, higher levels of cognitive discourse were measured by subscripting the FIAC system according to the four levels of thinking which have been described by Taba (99). Measel did find, like Aschner (7), that the pupils tended to respond to the teacher in kind. That is, if the teacher asked a question which was designed to provoke higher levels of thinking, the act of asking increased the odds that the pupil would respond at the higher level. However, both the teacher asking and the pupil responding at a higher level were relatively infrequent events.

One of the difficulties in project 7, and therefore in the Measel study, was the narrow range from the highest to the lowest i/d ratios in the sample. For example, the highest i/d ratio was 0.640 and the lowest was 0.130 (66, p. 70). Thus where Snider had difficulty with variation in his measure of achievement, project 7 had difficulty in variation of teacher influence.

3) *Birkin.* So far, a study of New Zealand data conducted by T. A. Birkin (12) has not been published. Unfortunately, this review is based on a somewhat incomplete mimeographed prepublication copy of a paper delivered in Toronto,

Canada, at the Ontario Institute for Studies in Education. In this paper, only beta weights of multiple regression analysis are reported, and such weights are not reliable figures for interpreting the direction of zero-order correlations. The beta weights reported are not significant (12, p. 20) when various measures of indirectness are associated with measures of reading comprehension in a sample of 34 elementary school classes for children who are approximately 10 years old.

There is some question of whether this study does or does not support the trend of research reported on previous pages. For example, Birkin concludes that "... teacher indirectness is associated with ... classes that are easy going and ready to co-operate ... with the achievement of emotional maturity ... " (12, p. 22). With the information at hand, it can only be said that this unpublished study fails to confirm or disconfirm an association of indirectness with one measure of academic achievement.

Summary of results

Most of the research reviewed made use of the FIAC system or some closely related category system. This means that any conclusions are restricted by the limitations which are inherent in the system. Although these limitations have already been discussed in other chapters, as well as in this chapter, a brief review is in order just before we attempt to present a summary of the research findings.

First, the coding of classroom verbal communication provides a relatively gross description of a small portion of classroom interaction. Most of what takes place is ignored and events are counted in terms of relatively broad categories.

Second, terms such as "teacher indirectness" and the contrast between direct and indirect teaching are even more abstract and more general than the coded events themselves. Such terms are relative, are useful only to compare carefully controlled teaching situations, and easily lead to an oversimplification of complex, interrelated events.

Third, the analysis of pairs of events, such as those delineated in a 10 × 10 matrix, does specify the probability with which pairs of coded events occurred during the observation periods. The utility of such information depends a great deal on the research design, particularly how time periods are to be combined into a single cumulative display, and the relationship of these time periods to the purposes of classroom teaching.

Fourth, without subscripting the categories, the FIAC system is probably most useful for describing the balance between teacher initiative and teacher response and for tracing this balance as it varies with time, instructional purposes, and classroom settings.

These and other restrictions limit any conclusions to be reached by this kind of research. Yet the analysis of classroom interaction appeals to the interest of many different kinds of educators who are most eager and ready to grasp more objective information about what goes on in the classroom. The alacrity with which educators interpret this kind of research evidence in terms of teaching effectiveness, or even more innocently, in terms of an ideal way to teach, is sometimes frightening.

On the other hand, the research results which have been reported in this chapter, as well as in Chapter 11, should not be underestimated. Taken altogether, these research results suggest some first approximations of classroom interaction which beg for more investigation and more refined analysis. Assuming that research on classroom interaction will continue, will increase in precision and skill, and will someday lead to definitive propositions about effective patterns of teaching behavior, the following conclusions are tentatively presented as an early progress report.

Pupil attitudes and content achievement.   After reviewing the research cited in this book as well as the work of researchers who made use of other systems of interaction analysis, Flanders and Simon (43) concluded that:

The percent of teacher statements that make use of ideas and opinions previously expressed by pupils is directly related to average class scores on attitude scales of teacher attractiveness, liking the class, etc., as well as to average achievement scores adjusted for initial ability. (p. 1426)

This statement is bold and perhaps optimistic, but the trend in the research results is clear providing one can accept a relatively loose definition of "making use of pupil ideas." In the context of this book, this statement refers to a small increase in level two and level three patterns of interaction amounting to 5 to 15 percent. Another way to state this conclusion is that by judiciously adapting teaching behavior to the various teaching situations, a small increase in the proportion of time devoted to responding to pupil ideas seems to be associated with an increased pupil growth in both subject matter and positive attitude.

In order to reach this conclusion, the following assumptions are being made. First, statements involving praise, use of pupil ideas, giving directions, and teacher criticism are intercorrelated in known ways so that many different research projects reporting these characteristics of interaction all contribute, in one degree or another, to the above conclusion. Second, the proposed relationship is probably curvilinear and needs to be investigated under a wide variety of conditions in order to be properly interpreted. Third, the conclusion is a first approximation of complex relationships involving the affective and cognitive aspects of teacher-pupil interaction.

Interactive events can be coded, displayed, and analyzed.   Research on interaction analysis involves methodological contributions as well as substantive findings. A part of each project, problems of training observers, developing new category systems, seeking new interaction variables, methods of displaying data, and developing procedures for statistical analysis must be resolved in one way or another. Each increment of progress adds to our general research skill. The ideas presented in this book are products of conducting research on interaction analysis in the classroom.

Effects of pupil ability.   There is considerable evidence among these projects (Schantz, Coats, Soar, etc.) which indicates that the initial ability of pupils will account for variation between classes on measures of pupil growth. A very rough guess is that somewhere between 40 and 60 percent of the variance in predicting achievement or pupil attitude scores is associated with the pretest scores. Whatever effects a pattern of teaching may have on pupil growth, it can easily be hidden by the factor of pupil ability and associated pupil attitudes. Any study of teaching behavior must take into account these differences among the pupils with great care or face the risk of reaching false conclusions. It is difficult to estimate the effect of differences in teaching behavior on the growth and development of pupils, but it must be less than 20 percent in a given year.

One might note in passing that persistent exposure to ineffective teaching over a number of years may produce results which are not reflected by the figures in the preceding paragraph.

Chains, patterns, and strategies.   Although specific variation in teaching behavior during the teaching of a 2-week unit was investigated in only two projects (projects 3 and 4, Table 12—1), it seems reasonable to report a tentative finding that teaching behavior varies with time. In fact, all associations of pupil growth with flexibility of teaching behavior suggest that this kind of variation over time influences educational outcomes. Interactive events form chains which can be identified as patterns. These in turn are strung together to form strategies. This variation with time is seldom investigated. Yet such variation may help to explain why the simple proportional incidence of different events does not always produce consistent results, one project compared with another.

COMMENTS ON UNRESOLVED PROBLEMS

There are a number of unresolved problems on which the research projects reviewed shed little or no light.

CAUSE AND EFFECT DURING CLASSROOM INTERACTION

Does indirect teaching behavior cause more learning and more positive attitudes or do brighter youngsters who can learn more and are more likely to have positive attitudes provide a teacher with the opportunity to be more indirect? The projects reviewed shed very little light on this issue.

Turner (102) was one of the first to raise this question. He suggested that "bright pupils are more likely to produce certain behaviors (longer, more thoughtful responses, more questions to each other . . . which increase the probability that a teacher will appear indirect" (p. 8). Classroom interaction is indeed interactive, and there can be no doubt that there is some validity in Turner's assertion. Below average pupils probably do have fewer ideas and they may be less likely to initiate, as Turner suggests, and this would make it more difficult to maintain an indirect teaching pattern. Perhaps the most appropriate inference is that it takes more skill to maintain an indirect pattern with less able pupils.

An investigation of the relative effects of pupil ability and teacher influence seem likely to provoke a kind of "hen-egg" argument, but it could also provide us with information about the problems which teachers face when confronted with individual differences among pupils and between classes. Teachers will be able to perform more effectively if they know what factors affect classroom interaction and can plan successful strategies for achieving their goals. Meanwhile, below are some related facts:

a) In one experiment (3) randomly assigned pupils who were equal in ability learned more geometry and liked learning better in a more indirect treatment and learned more science (85) in another.
b) In most, but not all, field studies, predominately indirect teaching was found to exist in classrooms which had slightly higher average measures of initial ability. Usually these differences were not statistically significant.
c) A teacher is responsible for the conduct of classroom learning activities and is trained and paid to control these activities.

The quantification of "indirectness"

In the various studies researchers choose different methods of measuring indirectness. Among the more common measures are I/D, i/d, I/I + D, i/i + d, frequency of the (3−3) cell, and the frequency in certain indirect categories. Closely related are measures of directness and teacher criticism which are negatively associated with pupil growth and with the frequency of indirect statements.

It is possible that category systems are not yet well enough established to propose a single way to measure this feature of teaching behavior. Also, the conventions with regard to classifying verbal statements differ, one research team compared with another, and pushing toward a single operational definition may increase error in making comparisons between different studies rather than increasing the precision of our knowledge.

Comparisons between projects

On other pages several suggestions are made about using a common set of basic categories which could form a data bank, but could be subscripted, when necessary, to analyze special problems of interest to the investigator. In Tables 12–1, 12–7, and 11–1, there are 35 different published research reports which made use of the FIAC system or a system that is so closely related that the data could be transformed to the 10 categories. This comparability between research projects extends our knowledge about classroom interaction and about relationships between teaching behavior and its consequences. As this manuscript is being prepared, many other projects making use of the same category system are underway or finished, but unpublished. Two comments seem appropriate. First, a concerted effort to continue this trend should be maintained because this is likely to bring educational researchers closer to classroom problems, and may have lasting effects on the preservice and inservice education of teachers. Second, replications of all research projects should be promoted, not discouraged, either by graduate degree requirements or by funding organizations. It is only when a particular finding has been replicated several times with first-class research skill that we can increase our confidence in its validity.

REFERENCES

1. Adams, R. S., "A sociological approach to classroom research." Paper presented at the Ontario Institute for Studies in Education, Toronto, Ontario, April 1967.
2. Allen, D. W., and Fortune, J. C., "An analysis of microteaching: a new procedure in teacher education. Unpublished manuscript, Stanford University, Feb. 8, 1965.
3. Amidon, E. J., and Flanders, N. A., "The effects of direct and indirect teacher influence on dependent-prone students learning geometry." *Journal of Educational Psychology,* 1961, **52**, 286–291.
4. Amidon, E. J., and Rosenshine, B., "Interaction analysis and micro-teaching in an urban teacher education program: a model for skill development in teaching." Paper presented at the meeting of the American Educational Research Association, Chicago, Illinois, Feb. 1968.
5. Anderson, J. P., "Student perceptions of teacher influence." Unpublished doctoral dissertation, University of Minnesota, 1959.
6. Association for Supervision and Curriculum Development, 1962 Yearbook Committee. *Perceiving, behavior, becoming.* Washington, D.C.: ASCD, 1201 Sixteenth St., N.W., 1962.
7. Aschner, Mary J. M., "The analysis of verbal interaction in the classroom." In A. A. Bellack (Ed.), *Theory and research in teaching.* New York: Bureau of Publications, Teachers College, Columbia University, 1963, pp. 53–78.
8. Bales, R. F., *Interaction process analysis: a method for the study of small groups.* Reading, Mass.: Addison-Wesley, 1950.
9. Bellack, A. A., Kliebard, H. M., Hyman, R. T., and Smith, F. L., Jr., *The language of the classroom.* New York: Teachers College Press, Columbia University, 1966.
10. Benne, K. D., "History of the T-group in the laboratory setting." In L. P. Bradford, J. R. Gibb, and K. D. Benne (Eds.), *T-Group theory and laboratory method.* New York: Wiley and Sons, 1964, pp. 80–135.
11. Biddle, B. J., "Methods and concepts in classroom research." *Review of Educational Research,* 1967, **37**, 337–357.
12. Birkin, T. A., "Toward a model of instruction processes." Unpublished manuscript, School of Education, University of Birmingham, England, 1967.
13. Bloom, B. S. (Ed.), *Taxonomy of educational objectives.* (Cognitive Domain), New York: Longmans, Green, 1956.
14. Bondi, J. C., Jr., "The effects of interaction analysis feedback on the verbal behavior of student teachers." *Educational Leadership,* 1969, **26**, 794–799.

428

15. Borg, W. R., Kallenbach, W., Kelley, Marjorie, and Langer, P., "The minnicourse: rationale and uses in the inservice education of teachers." Paper presented at the meeting of the American Educational Research Association, Chicago, Illinois, Feb. 1968.

16. Borg, W. R., Kallenbach, W., Morris, Merva, and Fribel, A., "The effects of videotape feedback and microteaching in a teacher training model." Berkeley, California: Far West Laboratory for Educational Research and Development, 1968.

17. Borgatta, E. F., and Crowther, Betty, *A workbook for the study of social interaction processes.* Chicago: Rand McNally, 1965.

18. Bowers, N. D., and Soar, R. S., *Studies of human relations in the teaching-learning process.* Vol. V. *Evaluation of laboratory human relations training for classroom teachers.* Final Report, Cooperative Research Project No. 8143, U.S. Office of Education, 1961. Available from R. S. Soar, University of Florida, Gainesville, Florida.

19. Bradford, L. P., Gibb, J. R., and Benne, K. D., *T-group theory and laboratory method.* New York: Wiley and Sons, 1964.

20. Brodbeck, Mae, "Logic and scientific method in research on teaching." In N. L. Gage (Ed.), *Handbook of research on teaching.* Chicago: Rand McNally, 1963, pp. 44–93.

21. Campbell, D. T., and Stanley, J. C., "Experimental and quasi-experimental designs for research on teaching." In N. L. Gage (Ed.), *Handbook of research on teaching.* Chicago: Rand McNally, 1963, pp. 142–170.

22. Campbell, J. P., and Dunnette, M. D., "Effectiveness of T-group experiences in managerial training and development." *Psychological Bulletin,* 1968, **70**, 73–104.

23. Cantor, N., *The teaching-learning process.* New York: Dryden, 1953.

24. Chesler, M. A., and Flanders, Mary, "Resistance to research and research utilization: the death and life of a feedback attempt." *Journal of Applied Behavioral Science,* 1967, **3**, 469–487.

25. Coats, W. D., "Investigations and simulation of the relationships among selected classroom variables." Unpublished doctoral dissertation, The University of Michigan, 1966.

26. Cyphert, F. R., and Spaights, E., *An analysis and projection of research in teacher education, part I: an annotation of recent research in teacher education.* U.S. Office of Education Contract OE-4-10-032. The Ohio State University, School of Education, 1964.

27. Dodl, N. R., "Pupil questioning behavior in the context of classroom interaction." Doctoral dissertation, Stanford University, *Dissertation Abstracts,* 1966, **26**, 642–644.

28. Emmer, E. T., "The effect of teacher use and acceptance of student ideas on student verbal initiation." Unpublished doctoral dissertation, The University of Michigan, 1967.

29. Farson, R. E., "Praise reappraised." *Harvard Business Review,* 1963, **41**, 61–66.

30. Filson, T. N., "Factors influencing the level of dependence in the classroom." Unpublished doctoral dissertation, University of Minnesota, 1957.

31. Finske, Sister M. Joanice, "The effect of feedback through interaction analysis on the development of flexibility in student teachers." Unpublished doctoral dissertation, The University of Michigan, 1967.

32. Flanders, N. A., "Verbalization and learning in the classroom." *Elementary School Journal,* 1948, **49**, 385–392.

33. Flanders, N. A., "Personal-social anxiety as a factor in experimental learning situations." *Journal of Educational Research,* 1951, **45**, 100–110.

34. Flanders, N. A., "Diagnosing and utilizing social structures in classroom learning." In N.S.S.E. 59th Yearbook, Part II, *The Dynamics of Instructional Groups.* Chicago: University of Chicago Press, 1960, pp. 187–217.

35. Flanders, N. A., *Teacher influence, pupil attitudes, and achievement.* Final Report, Cooperative Research Project No. 397, U.S. Office of Education. The University of Minnesota, 1960 (now out of print).

36. Flanders, N. A., *Helping teachers change their behavior.* Final Report, N.D.E.A. Projects 1721012 and 7-32-0560-171.0, U.S. Office of Education. The University of Michigan, School of Education, 1963.

37. Flanders, N. A., "Teacher influence in the classroom." In A. A. Bellack (Ed.), *Theory and research in teaching.* New York: Teachers College, Columbia University, 1963, pp. 37—52.

38. Flanders, N. A., "Some relationships among teacher influence, pupil attitudes, and achievement." In B. J. Biddle and W. J. Ellena (Eds.), *Contemporary research on teacher effectiveness.* New York: Holt, Rinehart, and Winston, 1964, pp. 196—231.

39. Flanders, N. A., *Teacher influence, pupil attitudes, and achievement.* Cooperative Research Monograph No. 12 (OE-25040), U.S. Office of Education. The University of Michigan, School of Education, 1965.

40. Flanders, N. A., "Some relationships among teacher influence, pupil attitudes, and achievement." In E. Amidon and J. Hough (Eds.), *Interaction analysis: theory, research, and application.* Reading, Mass.: Addison-Wesley, 1967, pp. 217—242.

41. Flanders, N. A., "Teacher influence in the classroom." In E. J. Amidon and J. B. Hough (Eds.), *Interaction analysis: theory, research, and application.* Reading, Mass.: Addison-Wesley, 1967, pp. 103—116.

42. Flanders, N. A., et al., "Classroom interaction patterns, pupil attitudes, and achievement in the second, fourth, and sixth grades." Cooperative Research Project No. 5-1055 (OE-4-10-243), U.S. Office of Education. The University of Michigan, School of Education, Dec. 1969.

43. Flanders, N. A., and Simon, Anita, "Teaching effectiveness: a review of research 1960—'66." In R. L. Ebel (Ed.), *Encyclopedia of educational research.* Chicago: Rand McNally, 1970.

44. Furst, Norma, "The effects of training in interaction analysis on the behavior of student teachers in secondary schools." In E. J. Amidon and J. B. Hough (Eds.), *Interaction analysis: theory, research, and application.* Reading, Mass.: Addison-Wesley, 1967, pp. 315—328.

45. Furst, Norma, "The multiple languages of the classroom: a further analysis and a synthesis of meanings communicated in high school teaching." Unpublished doctoral dissertation, Temple University, 1967.

46. Furst, Norma, and Amidon, E. J., "Teacher-pupil interaction patterns in the elementary school." In E. J. Amidon and J. B. Hough (Eds.), *Interaction analysis: theory, research, and applications.* Reading, Mass.: Addison-Wesley, 1967, pp. 167—175.

47. Golloway, C., "Teacher nonverbal communication." *Educational Leadership,* 1966, **24,** 55—63.

48. Guilford, J. P., *Fundamental statistics in psychology and education.* New York: McGraw-Hill, 1956.

49. Hampden-Turner, C. M., "An existential 'learning theory' and the integration of T-group research." *Journal of Applied Behavioral Science,* 1966, **2,** 367—386.

50. Harris, C. W. (Ed.), *Problems in measuring change.* Madison, Wisconsin: University of Wisconsin Press, 1962.

51. Hill, W. M., "The effects on verbal teaching behavior of learning interaction analysis as an in-service education activity." Unpublished doctoral dissertation, The Ohio State University, 1966.

52. Honigman, F. K., *Multidimensional analysis of classroom interaction.* Villanova, Pennsylvania: Villanova University Press, 1967.

53. Hough, J. B., and Amidon, E., "An experiment in pre-service teacher education." Paper presented at the meeting of the American Educational Research Association, Chicago, Illinois, 1964.

54. Hough, J. B., and Ober, R., "The effect of training in interaction analysis on the verbal teaching behavior of pre-service teachers." In E. J. Amidon and J. B. Hough (Eds.), *Interaction analysis: theory, research, and application.* Reading, Mass.: Addison-Wesley, 1967, pp. 329—345.

55. Hughes, Marie M., DeVaney, F. Elena, Fletcher, Ruby J., Miller, G. L., Rowan, Naoma T., and Welling, L., *Development of the means for assessment of the quality of teaching in elementary schools.* University of Utah, School of Education, 1959.

56. Jeffs, G. A., Foss, J., Hollingshead, L., Mills, G., and Reese, D., "The effects of training in interaction analysis on the verbal behavior of teachers." Mimeographed research report, Ed. W. Clark High School, Las Vegas, Nevada, 1968.

57. Johns, J. P., "The relationship between teacher behaviors and the incidence of thought-provoking questions by students in secondary schools." Unpublished doctoral dissertation, The University of Michigan, 1966.

58. Johnson, J. A., *A national survey of student teaching programs*. Final Report, Cooperative Research Project No. 6–8182, U.S. Office of Education. Northern Illinois University, 1968.

59. Kirk, J., "Effects of teaching the Minnesota system of interaction analysis to intermediate grade student teachers." Unpublished doctoral dissertation, Temple University, 1963.

60. LaShier, W. S., "An analysis of certain aspects of the verbal behavior of student teachers of eighth grade students participating in a BSCS laboratory block." Unpublished doctoral dissertation, University of Texas, 1965.

61. Lohman, E., Ober, R., and Hough, J. B., "A study of the effect of pre-service training in interaction analysis on the verbal behavior of student teachers." In E. J. Amidon and J. B. Hough (Eds.), *Interaction analysis: theory, research, and application*. Reading, Mass.: Addison-Wesley, 1967, pp. 346–359.

62. Mager, R. F., *Preparing instructional objectives*. Palo Alto, California: Fearon Publishers, 1962.

63. McClellan, J., "Classroom-teaching research: a philosophical critique." Paper presented at the Ontario Institute for Studies in Education, Toronto, Ontario, April 1967.

64. McLeod, R. J., "Changes in the verbal interaction patterns of secondary science student teachers who have had training in interaction analysis and the relationship of these changes to the verbal interaction of their cooperating teachers." Unpublished doctoral dissertation, Cornell University, 1966.

65. McNaughton, A. H., Wallen, N. E., Ho, S., and Crawford, W. R., "The use of teaching modules to study high level thinking in social studies." In Anita Simon and E. G. Boyer (Eds.), *Mirrors for behavior: an anthology of classroom observation instruments*. Vol. V. 121 S. Broad Street, Philadelphia, Pennsylvania: Research for Better Schools, Inc., 1967.

66. Measel, W. W., "The relationship between teacher influence and levels of thinking of second grade teachers and pupils." Unpublished doctoral dissertation, The University of Michigan, 1967.

67. Medley, D. M., and Mitzel, H. E., "Measuring classroom behavior by systematic observation." In N. L. Gage (Ed.), *Handbook of research on teaching*. Chicago: Rand McNally, 1963, pp. 247–328.

68. Miles, M. B., "The T-group and the classroom." In L. P. Bradford, J. R. Gibb, and K. D. Benne (Eds.), *T-group theory and laboratory method*. New York: Wiley and Sons, 1964, pp. 452–476.

69. Morrison, Betty M., "The reactions of internal and external children to patterns of teaching behavior." Unpublished doctoral dissertation, The University of Michigan, 1966.

70. Morsh, J. E., and Wilder, E. W., "Identifying the effective instructor: a review of quantitative studies, 1900–1952." *Research Bulletin*, October, 1954 (AFPTRC-TR-54-44, Project No. 7714, Task No. 77243). Air Force Personnel and Training Center, Lackland Air Force Base, San Antonio, Texas.

71. Moskowitz, Gertrude, "The attitudes and teaching patterns of cooperating teachers and student teachers trained in interaction analysis." In E. J. Amidon and J. B. Hough (Eds.), *Interaction analysis: theory, research, and application*. Reading, Mass.: Addison-Wesley, 1967, pp. 271–282.

72. Osgood, C. E., Suci, G. J., and Tannebaum, P. H., *The measurement of meaning*. Urbana: University of Illinois Press, 1957.

73. Pankratz, R., "Verbal interaction patterns in the classrooms of selected physics teachers: physics." Unpublished doctoral dissertation, The Ohio State University, 1966.

74. Pankratz, R., "Verbal interaction patterns in the classrooms of selected physics teachers." In E. J. Amidon and J. B. Hough (Eds.), *Interaction analysis: theory, research, and application.* Reading, Mass.: Addison-Wesley, 1967, pp. 189–209.

75. Parakh, J. S., *A study of relationships among teaching behavior, pupil behavior, and pupil characteristics in high school.* Cooperative Research Project No. S-269. U.S. Office of Education. Cornell University, 1965.

76. Powell, E. R., "Teacher behavior and pupil achievement." Paper presented at the meeting of the American Educational Research Association, Chicago, Illinois, Feb. 1968. Based on unpublished doctoral dissertation, Temple University, 1968.

77. Pugh, R. C., "The partitioning of criterion score variance accounted for in multiple correlation." *American Educational Research Journal,* 1968, **5**, 639–646.

78. Rogers, C. R., "The process of the basic encounter group." In J. F. T. Bugental (Ed.), *Challenges of humanistic psychology.* New York: McGraw-Hill, 1967, pp. 261–276.

79. Rosenshine, B., "Objectively measured behavioral predictors of effectiveness in explaining." Paper delivered at the meeting of the American Educational Research Association, Chicago, Illinois, Feb. 1968.

80. Rosenshine, B., "Teaching behaviors related to pupil achievement." Paper presented at the annual meeting of the National Council for the Social Studies, Washington, D.C., 1968. School of Education, Temple University.

81. Roubiczek, P., *Existentialism for and against.* Cambridge, England: Cambridge University Press, 1966.

82. Samph, T., "Teacher's behavior and slow learner's achievement." Term paper for Secondary Education 205, Temple University, 1967. Available from N. A. Flanders, The University of Michigan, or from the author of the paper at Syracuse University, New York.

83. Samph, T., "Observer effects on teacher behavior." Unpublished doctoral dissertation, The University of Michigan, 1968.

84. Sanders, N. M., *Classroom questions: what kinds?* New York: Harper and Row, 1966.

85. Schantz, Betty M. B., "An experimental study comparing the effects of verbal recall by children in direct and indirect teaching methods as a tool of measurement." Unpublished doctoral dissertation, Pennsylvania State University, 1963.

86. Scott, W. A., "Reliability of content analysis. The case of nominal coding." *Public Opinion Quarterly,* 1955, **19**, 321–325.

87. Skinner, B. F., *The technology of teaching.* New York: Appleton-Century-Crofts, 1968.

88. Simon, Anita, and Agazarian, Yvonne, *Sequential analysis of verbal interaction.* 121 S. Broad Street, Philadelphia, Pennsylvania: Research for Better Schools, Inc., 1966.

89. Simon, Anita, and Boyer, E. G. (Eds.), *Mirrors for behavior: an anthology of classroom observation instruments.* Volumes I–VI. 121 S. Broad Street, Philadelphia, Pennsylvania: Research for Better Schools, Inc., 1967.

90. Smith, B. O., and Meux, M. O., "A study of the logic of teaching." In Anita Simon and E. G. Boyer (Eds.), *Mirrors for behavior: an anthology of classroom observation instruments.* Volume IV. 121 S. Broad Street, Philadelphia, Pennsylvania: Research for Better Schools, Inc., 1967.

91. Smith, T. A., "Communications." In *Prospective changes in society by 1980: including some implications for education.* 1362 Lincoln Street, Denver, Colorado: Designing Education for the Future: An eight-State Project, Edgar L. Morphet, Project Director, July 1966, pp. 173–180.

92. Snider, R. M., *A project to study the nature of effective physics teaching.* Cooperative Research Project No. S-280, U.S. Office of Education. Cornell University, 1965.

93. Soar, R. S., *An integrative approach to classroom learning.* Final Report, Public Health Service Grant No. 5-R11 MH 01096 to the University of South Carolina and Grant No. 7-R11 MH 02045 to Temple University. Temple University, 1966. Available from the author, at the University of Florida, Gainesville, Florida.

94. Soar, R. S., "Optimum teacher-pupil interaction for pupil growth." *Educational Leadership*, 1968, **26**, 275–280.
95. Stanford University, Stanford Teacher Education Program. *Microteaching: a description.* Articles written and materials developed by members of the Stanford team, 1967. Available from the Director of the Stanford Teacher Education Program, Stanford University, Palo Alto, California.
96. Stock, Dorothy, and Thelen, H. A., *Emotional dynamics and group culture.* New York: New York University Press, 1958, pp. 192–206.
97. Stock, Dorothy, "A survey of research on T-groups." In L. P. Bradford, J. R. Gibb, and K. D. Benne (Eds.), *T-group theory and laboratory method.* New York: Wiley and Sons, 1964, pp. 395–441.
98. Taba, Hilda, and Hills, J. L., *Teacher handbook for Contra Costa social studies, grades 1–6.* San Francisco: San Francisco State College, 1965, p. 11.
99. Taba, Hilda, Levine, S., and Elzey, F., *Thinking in elementary school children.* Cooperative Research Project No. 1574, U.S. Office of Education, 1964.
100. Thelen, H. A., *Education and the human quest.* New York: Harper Brothers, 1960.
101. Thelen, H. A., "Emotionality and work in groups." In L. White (Ed.), *The state of the social sciences.* Chicago: University of Chicago Press, 1956, pp. 184–200.
102. Turner, R. L., "Pupil influence on teacher behavior." *Classroom Interaction Newsletter*, 1967, **3** (No. 1), 5–8. Available from Anita Simon (Ed.), Research for Better Schools, Inc., Suite 1700/1700 Market St., Philadelphia, Pennsylvania, 19103.
103. Urbach, F., "The study of recurring patterns of teaching." Unpublished doctoral dissertation, University of Nebraska, 1966.
104. Weber, W. A., "Relationships between teacher behavior and pupil creativity in the elementary school." Unpublished doctoral dissertation, Temple University, 1968.
105. Wherry, R. J., "A new formula for predicting the shrinkage of the coefficient of multiple correlation." Annals of Mathematical Statistics, 1931, **2**, 440–457.
106. Withall, J., "The development of a climate index." *Journal of Educational Research*, 1951, **45**, 93–99.
107. Wright, Muriel J., *Teacher-pupil interaction in the mathematics classroom.* Technical Report No. 67–5, Minnesota National Laboratory, Minnesota State Department of Education, May 1967, pp. 1–12.
108. Zahn, R., "The use of interaction analysis in supervising student teachers." Unpublished doctoral dissertation, Temple University, 1965.

Appendix 1

SOURCES OF INSTRUCTIONAL MATERIALS WHICH HELP TO DEVELOP SKILLS FOR ANALYZING CLASSROOM INTERACTION*

This appendix provides a brief description of instructional materials which can be obtained from various centers. Some items on the list are sources of inservice instructional materials for programs designed to improve teaching behavior. Most items are sources of material for studying the 10 basic categories of the FIAC system.

INTERACTION ANALYSIS

(1) *Research for Better Schools, Inc., Suite 1700/1700 Market St., Philadelphia, Pa., 19103.* This is a regional educational laboratory supported by federal funds.

(a) *Classroom Interaction Newsletter.* There have been two issues per year of this mimeographed newsletter starting with Vol. I, No. 1, dated December 1965. A subscription can be obtained by writing to the editor, Dr. Anita Simon, at Research for Better Schools. The articles in the newsletter cover a variety of topics relating to coding systems. Some back issues are still available. This is a source of general information.

(b) Simon, Anita, and Boyer, E. G. (eds.), *Mirrors for Behavior, An Anthology of Classroom Observation Instruments.* Philadelphia, Pennsylvania: Research for Better Schools, Inc. and The Center for the Study of Teaching, Temple University, 1967. This limited edition in six volumes is available at some libraries and most regional laboratories. Write to the publisher for information concerning how to locate the nearest edition.

A second edition of *Mirrors for Behavior* is scheduled for publication late in 1969. The two editions together will describe close to 50 different coding systems.

---

*Compiled July 1969.

(2) *Paul S. Amidon and Associates, 5408 Chicago Ave. South, Minneapolis, Minnesota, 55417.* This is a private firm which produces and distributes a variety of educational materials.

(a) Amidon, E. J., and Flanders, N. A., *The Role of the Teacher in the Classroom.* This is a manual written especially for classroom teachers. It introduces the notion of investigating verbal communication as an approach to the improvement of classroom instruction. Methods of interpreting a matrix are explained. Single copies were priced at $1.50 (in 1969) with reductions for quantity orders.

(b) A variety of other instructional aids can be obtained from Amidon and Associates. These include voice tape recordings with a typescript for practicing coding with the basic 10-category system, video tapes for the same purpose, and programmed materials which introduce increasingly complex teaching skills.

A complete inventory of the materials can be secured from the publisher. Consultant services can also be arranged in the design and conduct of workshops for the inservice training of teachers or administrators.

(3) *Prof. Ned A. Flanders, School of Education, University of Michigan, Ann Arbor, Michigan, 48104. Attn: Reprint secretary, Offices of Research Service.* There are a number of articles, manuals, and instructional materials which are either distributed free—in single copies, or for which the cost equals the approximate printing and postage expenses. No royalties are involved and all receipts are used for research and dissemination purposes. A first step is to write to the reprint secretary requesting a *List of Reference Materials.* Some of the items most frequently requested are listed below.

(a) Flanders, N. A., *Classroom Interaction Analysis, A Manual for Observers.* A cost of $1.00 covers printing and mailing expenses and helps to provide free copies for graduate students and others who cannot requisition materials.

(b) "A training aid for the basic 10 categories: voice tape recording and typescript." This training aid permits practice in coding and in the interpretation of the data. A charge of $3.50 covers the local costs of duplicating the voice tape recordings, mimeographing, and postage.

(c) Flanders, N. A., *Teacher Influence, Pupil Attitudes and Achievement.* This is a complete copy of the Cooperative Research Monograph No. 12 (1965), originally printed by the U.S. Government Printing Office, but which is now out of print at that source. Local printing costs make it necessary to charge $1.00 for this reference.

(d) Assistance in the design of research involving interaction analysis and professional help in the design of inservice training programs can be secured by writing to: Teacher Consultants, Inc., c/o Dr. Dan N. Perkuchin, 221 Williams, Bowling Green, Ohio, 43402. This group was formed by individuals who completed their graduate education at the Offices of Research Service, University of Michigan.

(4) *Northwest Regional Educational Laboratory, Lindsay Building, 701 S. W. Second Ave., Portland, Oregon, 97204.* This is one of the federally supported regional educational laboratories.

Staff members of Northwest have been experimenting with instructional materials necessary to teach interaction analysis to teachers. In January 1969, a tentative draft was completed which outlines an inservice training curriculum for three weekend meetings. The instructional materials include playback recordings, reading materials for the teachers, and a manual for the instructor.

(5) *Teaching Research Division, Oregon State System of Higher Education, Monmouth, Oregon, 97361.* This is a special research agency of the State of Oregon.

Twelker, P. A., and Haines, T. R., *Using Films of Classroom Interaction Situations (FOCIS) for Interaction Analysis Training: A Manual for Teachers.* This material is designed for use by classroom teachers who are interested in analyzing their own classroom interaction.

MICROTEACHING AND MINICOURSES

The possibility that microteaching and short courses on teaching skills can be used by themselves or combined with interaction analysis has been discussed in Chapters 8 and 9. Materials are under development at various centers which would be helpful to those interested in such a program. Below are some sources of information and materials which would help.

(1) *Dean Dwight W. Allen, School of Education, University of Massachusetts, Amherst, Mass., 01002.* Dean Allen did his early work on microteaching at Stanford University and is now developing new and interesting programs for the preparation of teachers. His most recent book on microteaching is cited below. Letters requesting general information about microteaching can be sent to the University of Massachusetts.

Allen, D. W., and Ryan, K., *Microteaching.* Reading, Mass.: Addison-Wesley, 1969.

(2) *Far West Laboratory for Educational Research and Development, 1 Garden Circle, Hotel Claremont, Berkeley, California, 94705.* This is a regional educational laboratory supported by federal funds.

A team under the direction of Dr. Walter Borg has been working on the development of what are called "minicourses." A "package" consists of printed materials for a teacher to read, a sound motion picture or video sound tape giving directions and showing examples of teaching skills, and a series of lessons which form a self-development curriculum. Some 15 or more courses are being designed and developed or have been completed. Some of the materials are sent only to teachers who have access to video equipment which they are expected to use in a microteaching format.

SUGGESTIONS FOR IMPROVING VOICE RECORDINGS IN CLASSROOMS

Voice recordings are very helpful in analyzing classroom interaction. The success of a voice recording is judged by the proportion of intelligible discussion which occurs in a sound tape recording or sound track (the latter is used in magnetic video recording). The goal is to have minimum loss. The fundamental principle in making a good voice recording is *to have the microphone as close as possible to the lips of the speaker.* If this principle is applied, an intelligible recording can be made with a microphone even in a boiler factory, because the record volume can be set low to eliminate much of the extraneous noise.

One difficulty in making suggestions is that the proper placement of the microphones and associated equipment depends on what kind of recording equipment is used. In this section, the discussion begins with the least expensive equipment and then moves on to more elaborate setups. In each subsection, two purposes for making the recording are considered. First, the recording may be made for one person, or a team of two or three persons, with the intention of coding the communication. Second, the recording may be made for audience presentation and will therefore require higher standards of intelligibility.

STANDARD TABLE-SIZE OR MINIATURE MONAURAL TAPE RECORDERS

(1) *Single microphone, monaural recorder.* Ordinary monaural tape recorders with one microphone cost about $40 or more. Usually the microphone is of high impedance and omnidirectional, and has a cord that varies from 6 to 10 feet in length.

Choose the slowest tape speed, which is probably $1\frac{7}{8}$ or $3\frac{1}{4}$ inches per second. Set the microphone on something soft, like a chalkboard eraser, at about table or desk height, and at a location roughly equivalent to the first or second row, directly in front of where the teacher is likely to be located. This usually turns out to be about 12 feet from the teacher. The face of the microphone should be up, toward the ceiling. The pupils who talk softly should be seated near the microphone, the others seated in a fan-shaped, semicircular arrangement, with the microphone at the point of the fan.

The record volume is the most important adjustment and varies from one piece of equipment to another. Set the level so that a single loud voice occasionally peaks into overmodulation. If the recorder has a needle, overmodulation occurs when the needle swings into a red zone. On other recorders a second neon light, or both sides of a single neon light, are used to indicate overmodulation. Read the manual of instructions for the equipment to find out exactly how overmodulation is indicated.

The arrangement described above is barely satisfactory for recording a discussion that is to be coded; it is unsatisfactory for making a recording for audience presentation, because the distance from lips to microphone is too great. Of the various suggestions made in this section, this minimum arrangement will produce the highest loss in intelligibility, because all the noise in the classroom, as well as the verbal communication, is being recorded at the same level. This kind of recording can be used for coding only if the pupils have been trained to be relatively quiet.

(2) *Two microphones, monaural recorder.* The first improvement in the above setup can be made by purchasing a second microphone just like the one which came with the original equipment. Have a radio technician or repairman connect both cords to the same microphone plug. It is also possible to purchase a special plug with two built-in receptacles for the two microphone plugs; this has the advantage that when the second microphone has to be attached you can "do it yourself."

Place one microphone on some kind of cushion on the teacher's desk, about 6 feet from the teacher. Use the full length of the cord by placing the tape recorder as far as possible toward the center of the classroom. Extend the cord of the second microphone away from the teacher as far as possible along the same axis, on the other side of the recorder. Place the second microphone on a cushion. Move all pupils toward the back of the room and cluster them around the second microphone so that there is considerable unoccupied space between the teacher and the class. Set the record volume control a little lower than you would for the previous setup. The main advantage of the distance between the class and the teacher is that everyone tends to talk louder, as one does when addressing someone on the other side of a room. Thus the level of the voice is increased while room noise is decreased slightly in relation to the voices, because a lower setting of the record volume is now possible.

This arrangement produces better recordings than the one-microphone arrangement because the distance from lips to microphone is smaller in relation to the level of the voices.

STANDARD TABLE-SIZE STEREO TAPE RECORDERS

Relatively inexpensive stereo tape recorders are now available at prices starting around $100. The big advantage of a stereo recorder is the dual microphones, the dual record volume controls, and the dual volume controls for playback. Use the same placement as described above for the second microphone for the pupils, and set the record volume control for that microphone at the same level suggested for the two-microphone monaural setup. Now, however, the microphone for the teacher can be placed even closer to his lips by raising the microphone or standing it in a vertical position with the back toward the class. Now the teacher's record level control can be set slightly lower than in the previous setup. This decreases room noise on the teacher's channel, yet permits an adequate record level for the teacher, particularly if the unoccupied space between the teacher and the first row of pupils is maintained.

This arrangement is the first which is practical for making recordings for audience presentation. Any recording made for subsequent audience presentation forces some kind of compromise between two conflicting conditions. First, there is usually a desire to avoid disrupting normal classroom seating arrangements. Second, there is our rule about distance from lips to microphone, which makes the real difference between a good and a poor recording. We often underestimate the need for clean audio recording when an audience is involved. Persons in the audience are totally dependent on being able to understand what is said, since they are usually not acquainted with the pupils, the teacher, or the recording situation. It has been my experience that we also underestimate the adjustment which a teacher and his class can make when they understand that the recording is for audience presentation. A clear recording of reasonably natural interaction usually requires a change in the class formation.

Suppose an earlier recording of minimum quality indicates that a particular teacher and his class can perform some phase of instruction that is of particular interest. A good recording can be made by the following procedure. First, select about 10 pupils who speak clearly and are alert enough to understand the role required of them; send the rest of the class to the library, out to play, or off on a field trip. Second, place the pupils as far away from the teacher as the microphone cords will permit. Seat the 10 pupils so that their lips are as close to the microphone as possible. Set the teacher's microphone right in front of the teacher, as close as possible. Now set the record volume controls at the best setting that can be discovered during the first, warm-up classroom interaction. In other words, approach the problem as you would a theatrical production and subordinate the need for normal classroom conditions to the needs of a good recording.

MULTIPLE MICROPHONES AND FM WIRELESS MICROPHONES

It is now possible to purchase FM wireless microphones for as little as $70 or as much as $600. The less expensive wireless microphones usually make use of a normal, home FM receiver or FM tuner. The output of this receiver is connected to the radio (high-level) input on one channel of a stereo tape recorder. The microphone is worn by the teacher and, on some models, a lightweight yoke permits the microphone to be within 6 inches of the teacher's lips. This arrangement is the only one that permits both the teacher's and the pupils' speech to be adequately recorded when the teacher walks around the room and consults quietly with individual pupils at their seats. Wireless microphones used in this way can produce very close to 100 percent intelligibility on the teacher's channel in spite of room noise.

Some care is necessary in placing the receiver antenna for the FM microphone, which is usually a normal rabbit-ear antenna of the type that can be purchased at any TV store. Locate the best position for the antenna by trial and error, seeking the position that provides a strong signal from the areas which the teacher most often occupies while teaching. The possibility of fadeouts at certain positions in the classroom is a function of the distance between the teacher and the receiver antenna. Sometimes moving the antenna about 6 feet closer or farther away eliminates these fadeouts.

With more elaborate equipment, it may be possible to improve the quality of the recording of the pupils' voices, but much depends on the extent to which the normal classroom seating arrangements can be changed. Two or three low-impedance microphones, mixed and preamplified, will not really improve the recording quality unless these microphones are within 2 feet of the pupil, so that the record volume control can be set lower. Setting the record volume lower is the only way to reduce general room noise.

In our research, we have used very expensive equipment in an effort to obtain good-quality recording of the pupils' talk. After much experimentation I believe that two or three omnidirectional, high-impedance microphones wired in parallel and located in the center of the classroom, picking up room noise along with the pupils' conversation, is about as satisfactory as any other setup so long as the class seating arrangement must be kept normal. This microphone setup feeds one channel of a stereo recorder.

We have made studio-quality recordings in classrooms by the following method. For the teacher, use a good FM wireless microphone feeding one channel of a stereo recorder. Use three microphone stands at the far end of the classroom and let four pupils *stand* close to each microphone. Mix these three microphones and feed them into the second channel. Both the teacher and the pupils tend to speak louder because of the distance. After the teacher's talk, the pupils' talk, and bursts of noise have been properly logged, make a second tape recording from the original. Constantly adjust the two volume controls, one for each channel, while the duplicate is being made, according to the log notes. When the teacher is talking, suppress the room microphone completely. Pick up the room microphone when the log shows that the pupils are about to talk. The duplicated second recording can be of very high quality.

INDEX

ABCDE79876543210

DATE DUE